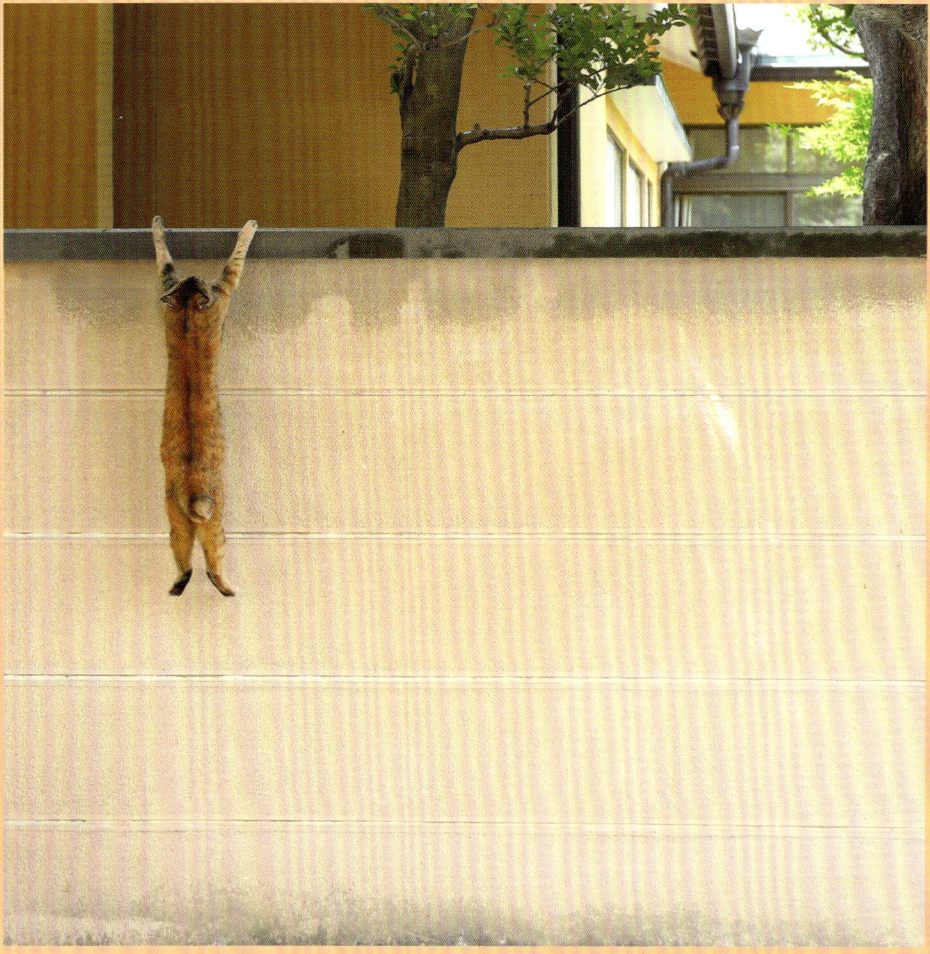

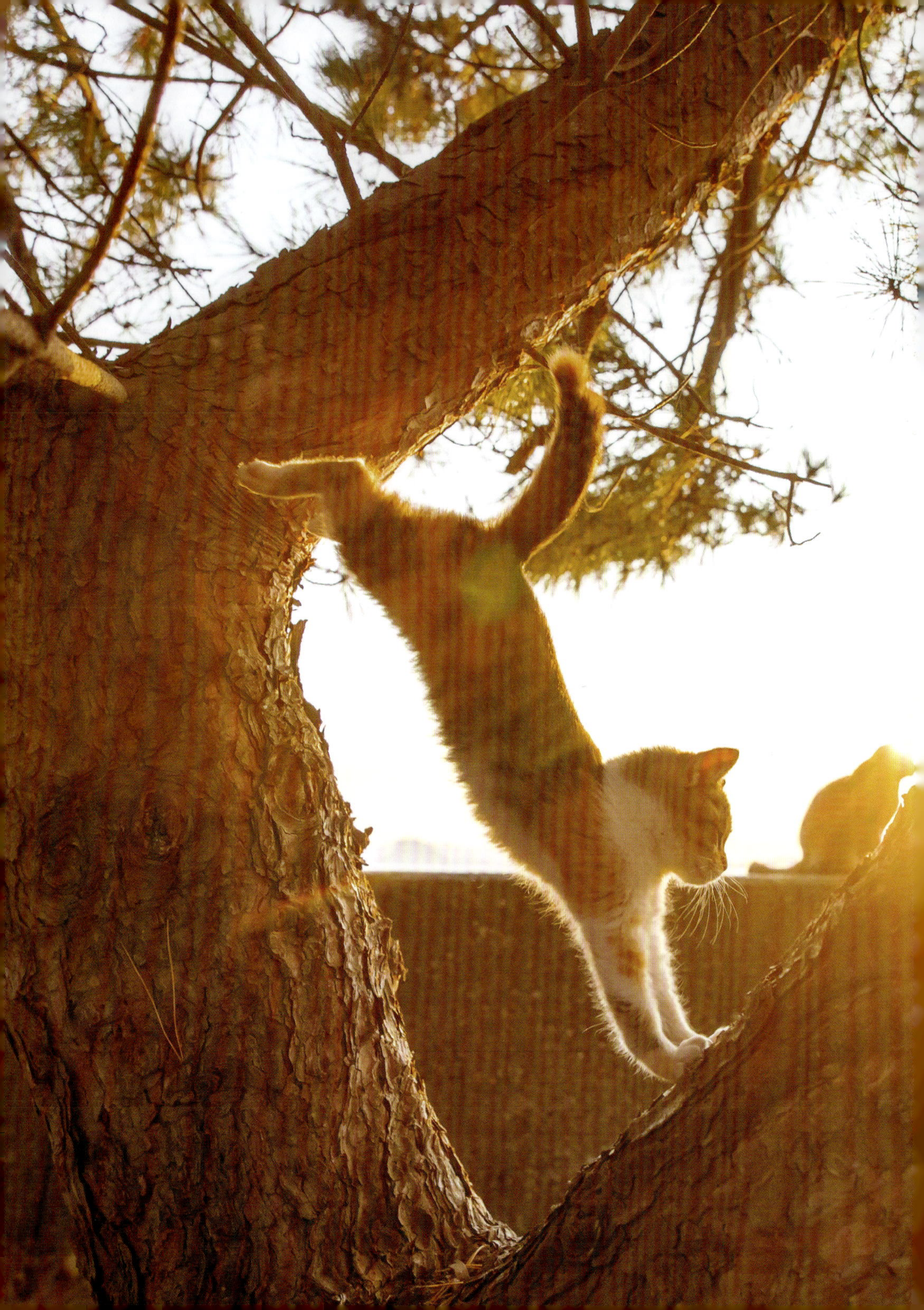

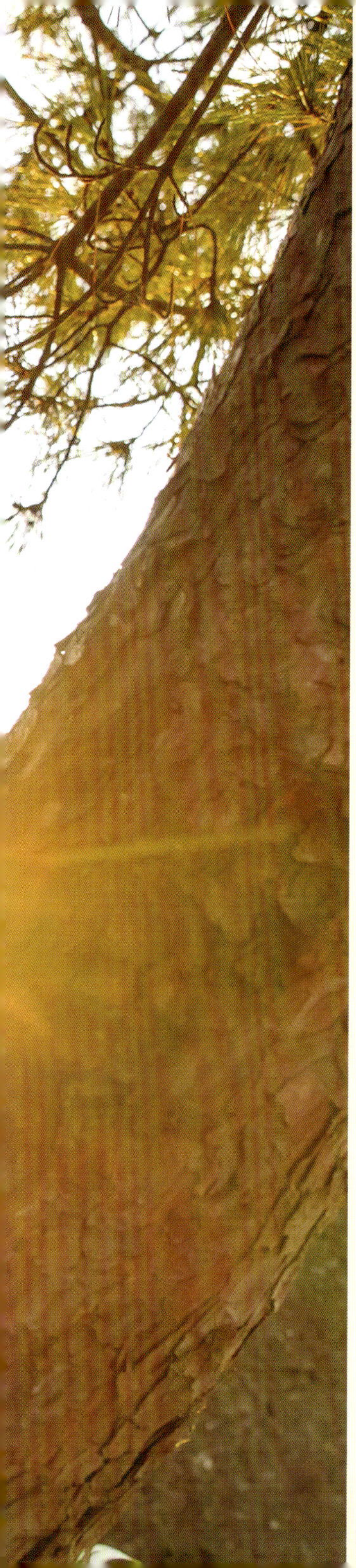

NEKO

CATS OF JAPAN

MASAYUKI OKI

Smith Street Books

On New Year's Eve in 2013, I met a cat called Busanyan-senpai at a park during my work break. The cat had a noble appearance and looked like a mix of an American shorthair and an exotic shorthair. It was sleeping outside in the middle of the path, looking free.

I fell in love with this cat at first sight, and so the next day I brought my camera to work and took a picture of her. That's when my life photographing cats began.

I posted the image on Instagram, and cat lovers from all over the world responded with positive comments.

This feedback inspired me and I began posting photos of cats every day. Back then, it was just a hobby. Then, in 2015, at the age of 37, I quit my job and, with that momentum, became a full-time cat photographer.

There have been some twists and turns along the way, but I'm proud to say I have published 20 photo books of cats in Japan. *Neko* is my first publication overseas and I'm so happy that my dream continues to come true, little by little.

Of course, cats are wonderful and adorable to photograph, but I like to focus on their inner world – the emotions we imagine from their expressions and behaviour, as well as the complex relationships between them, which feel almost human. These are the moments I try to capture.

猫・ネコ

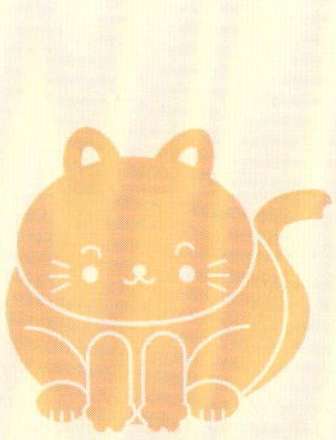

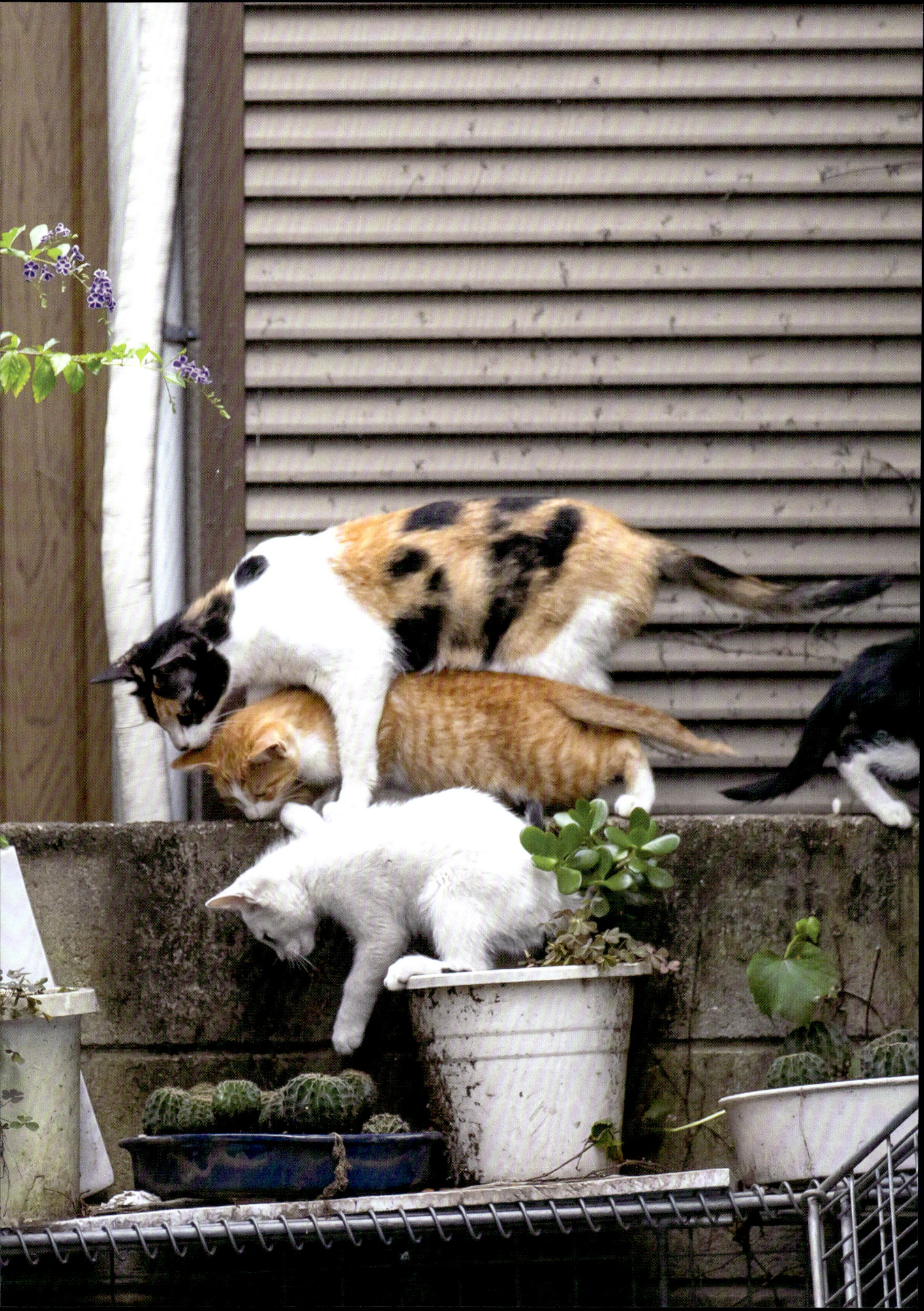

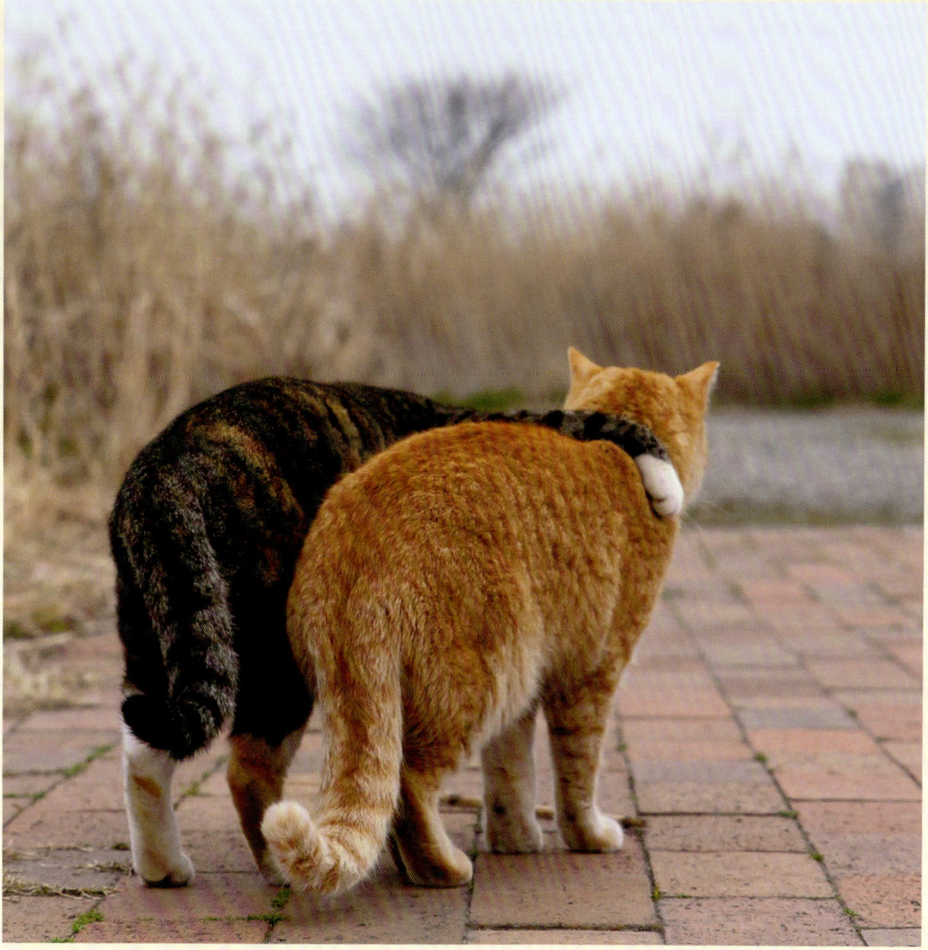

Before I began photographing cats, I assumed outdoor cats were strays with no one to care for them. When I started photographing in the downtown area of Tokyo, I quickly learned that many people feed these cats in the early morning or evening, while others rescue injured cats, take them to the vet and pay for their care. Because of these daily acts of kindness, the cats are rarely nervous of people and they will often open up to me when I meet them for the first time. I believe I'm able to capture such wonderful moments thanks to the many people who collectively care for Japan's cats.

During the ten years I've been photographing cats in Tokyo and other urban areas, their numbers have decreased thanks to Japan's TNR (Trap, Neuter, Release) program, so now I regularly visit Cat Island for about a week at a time. My method is to wait until the cats feel comfortable with my presence, without offering any food or toys. I carry my camera from dawn to dusk and observe their behaviour: this one always leaves its scent on that branch; these cats are friends; these two are fighting; and here are two parents with their kittens …

I watch them for several days until I feel I know their interactions well enough to capture the perfect image. However, because I'm dealing with cats, I often miss the shot and end up wondering what I was doing with my day.

Even so, the feeling I get from seeing cats relaxed in their own environment – watching them sleep, play, greet each other happily and stay healthy – outweighs my disappointment and makes me want to do even better tomorrow.

I've been photographing cats for a long time, yet I still witness amazing moments that I've never encountered before. Cats are fascinating creatures that I never tire of, and I consider myself lucky to be able to do this job. I'll be even happier if this book puts a smile on your face.

Thank you very much,
Masayuki Oki

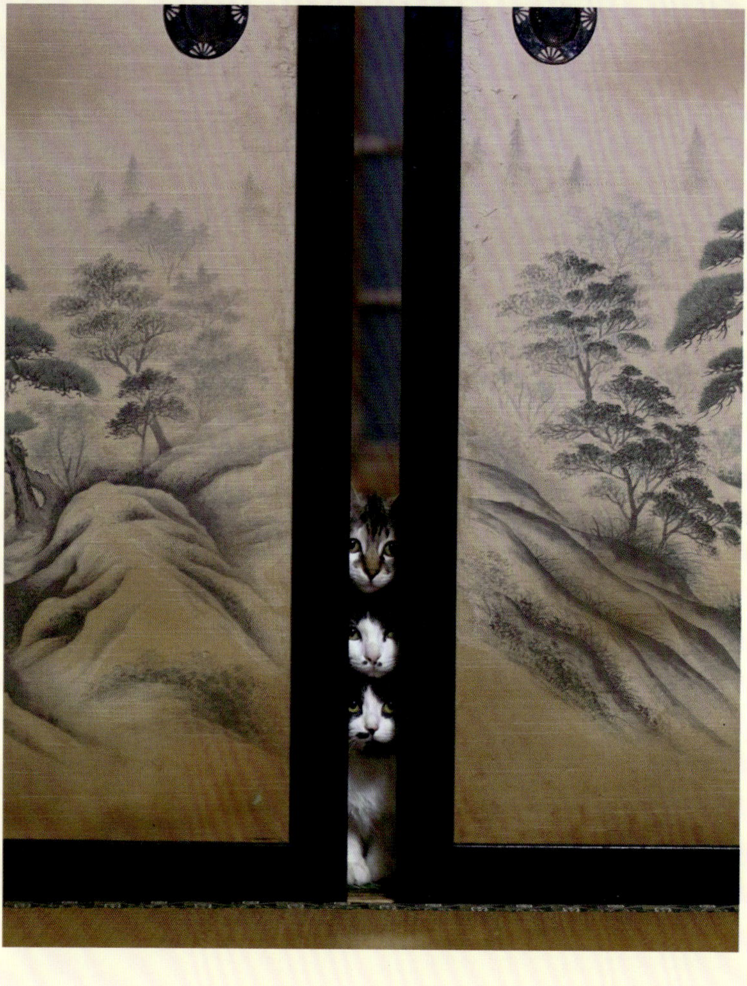

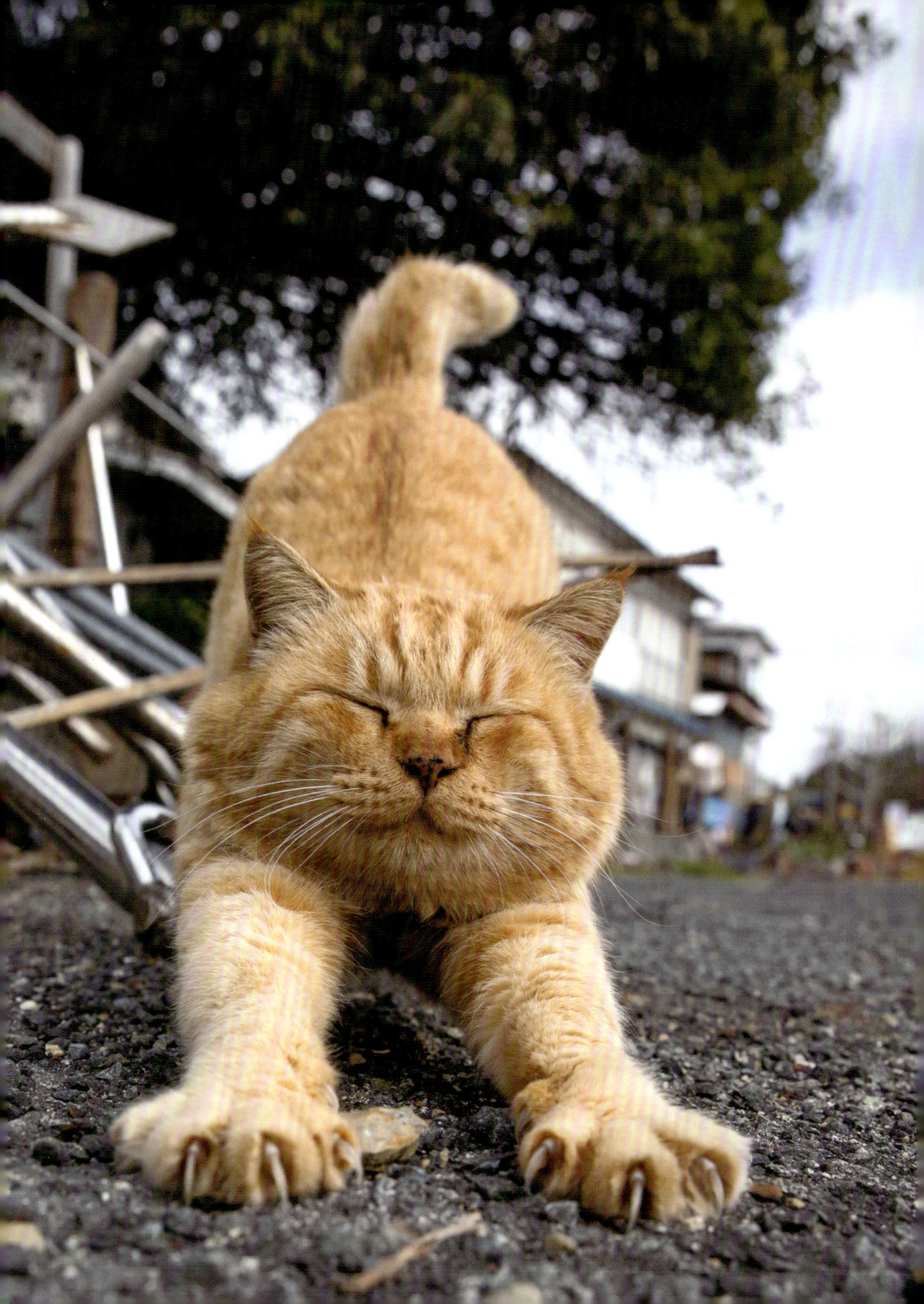

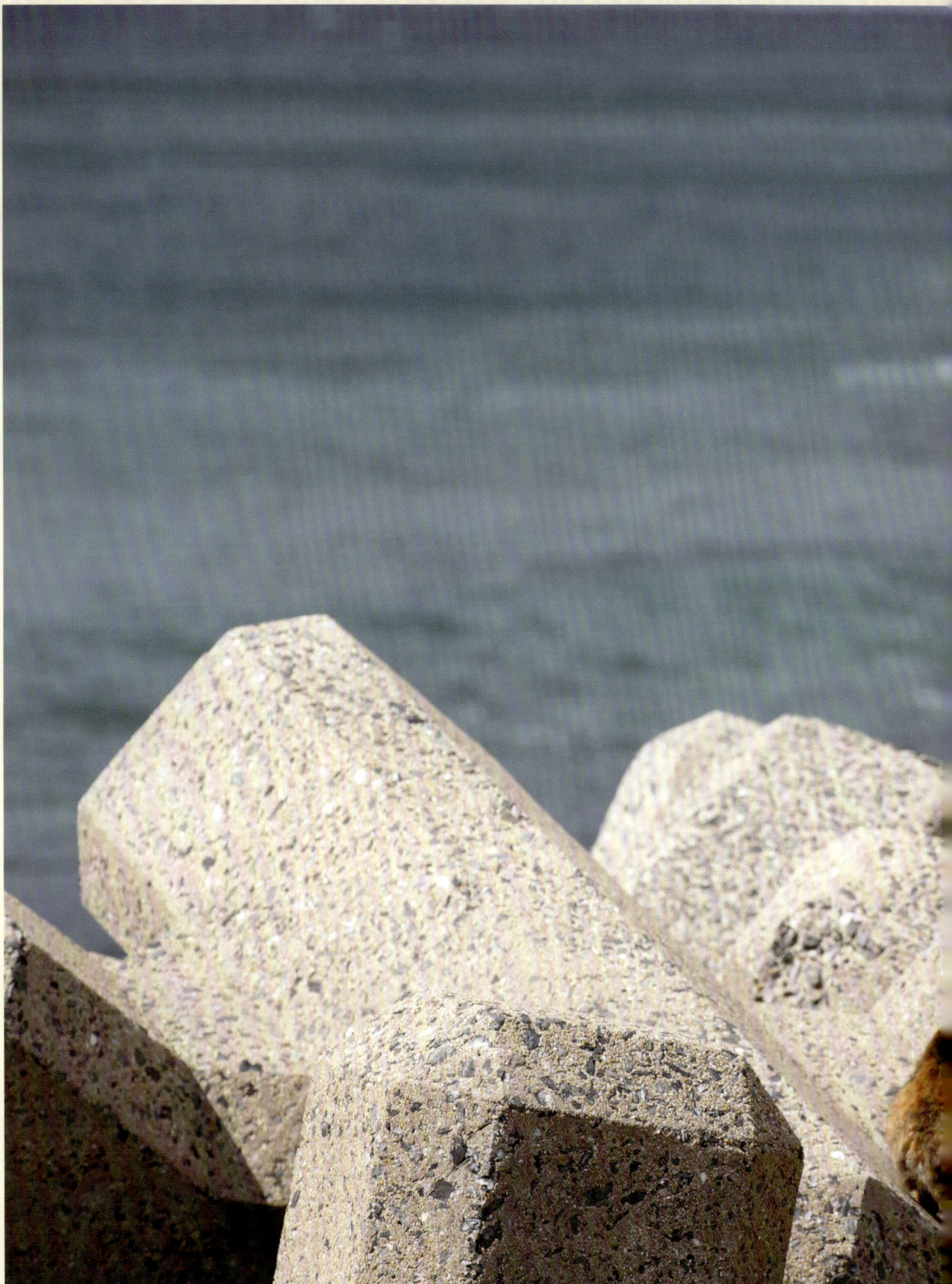

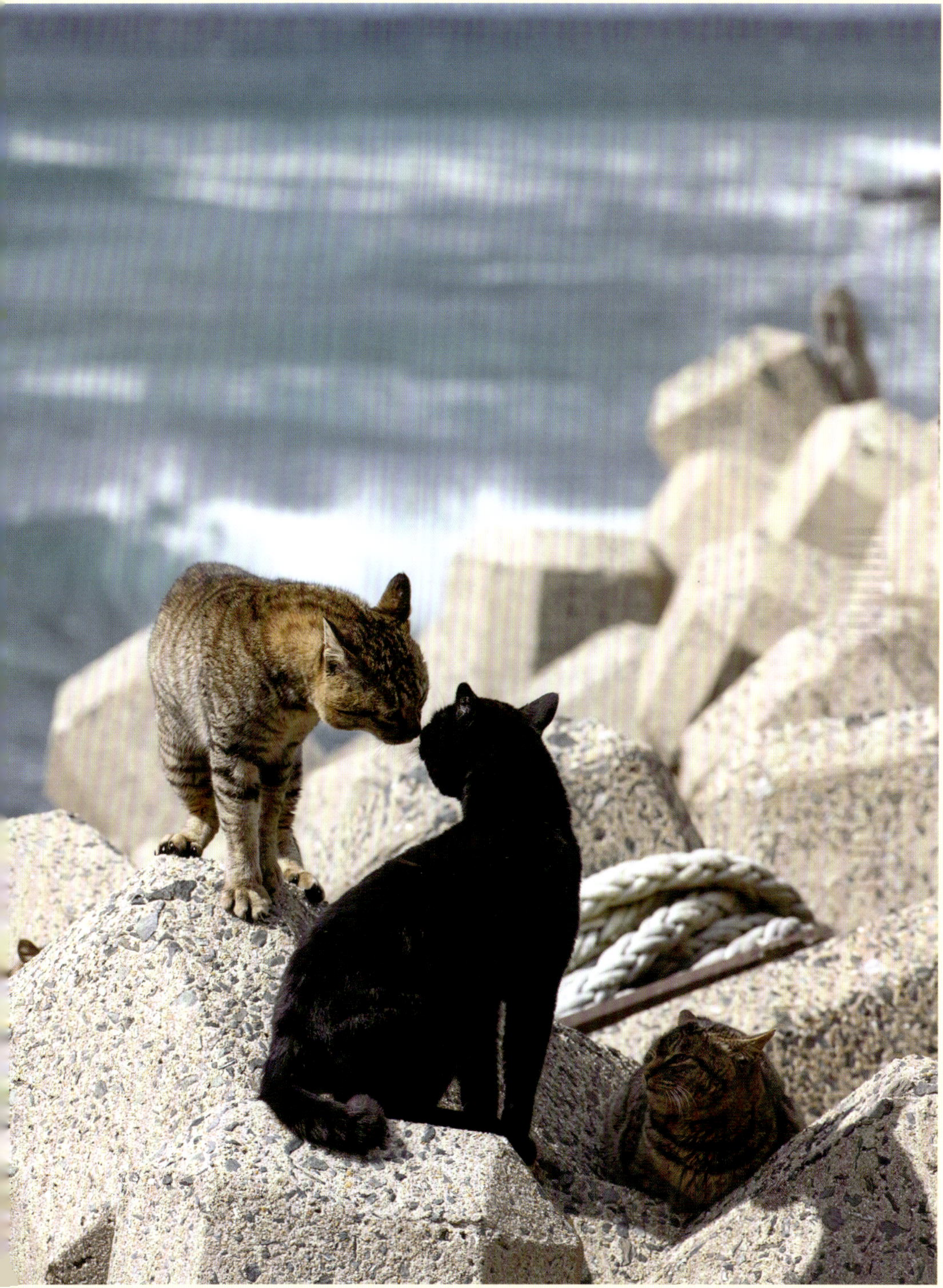

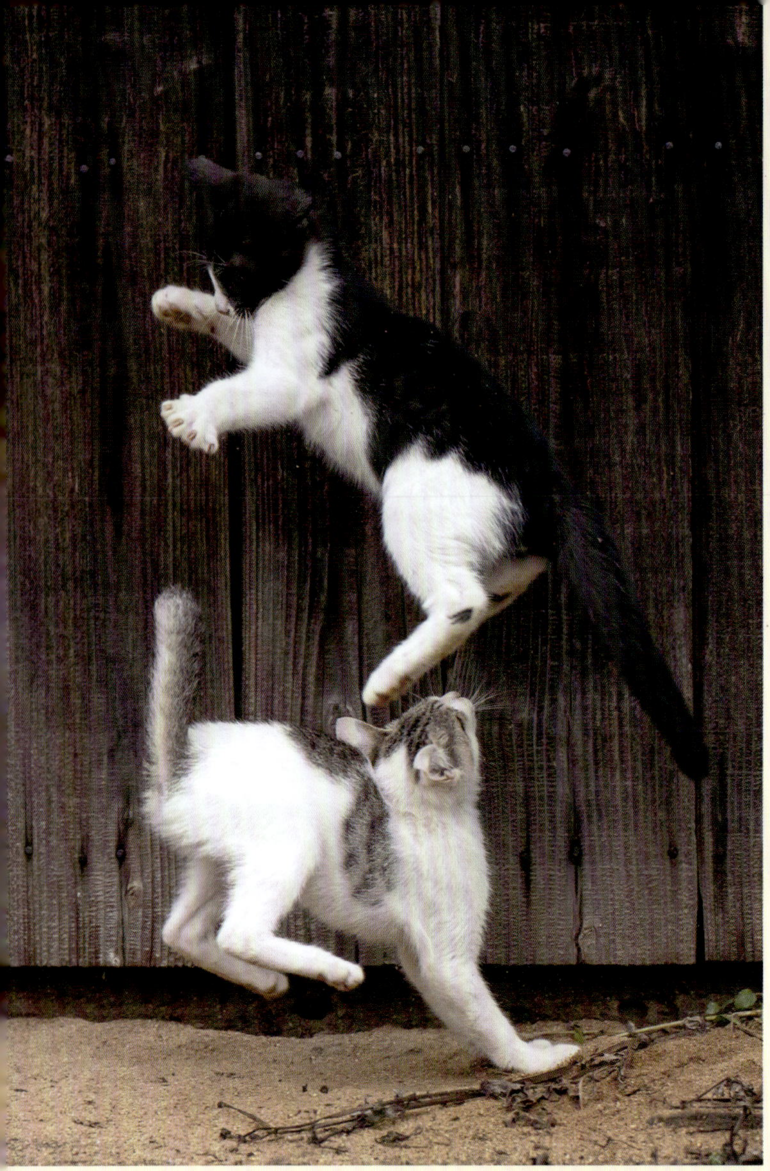

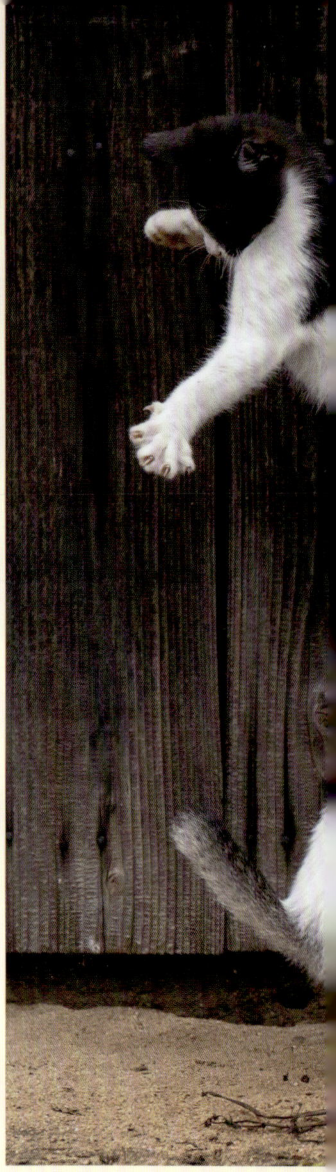

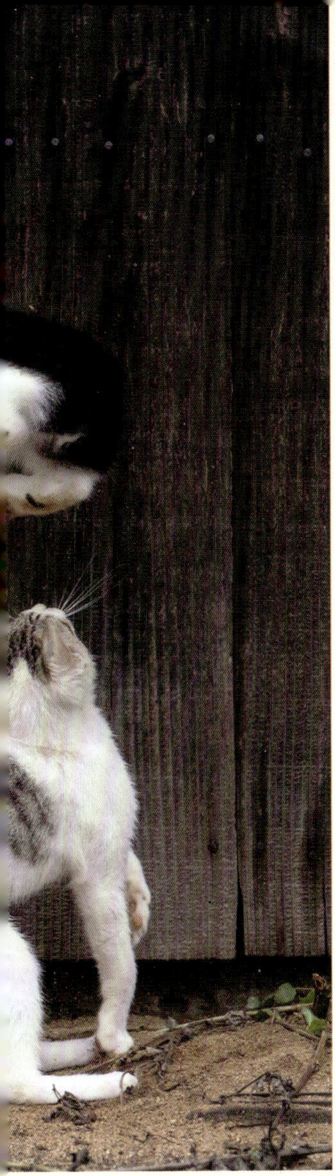

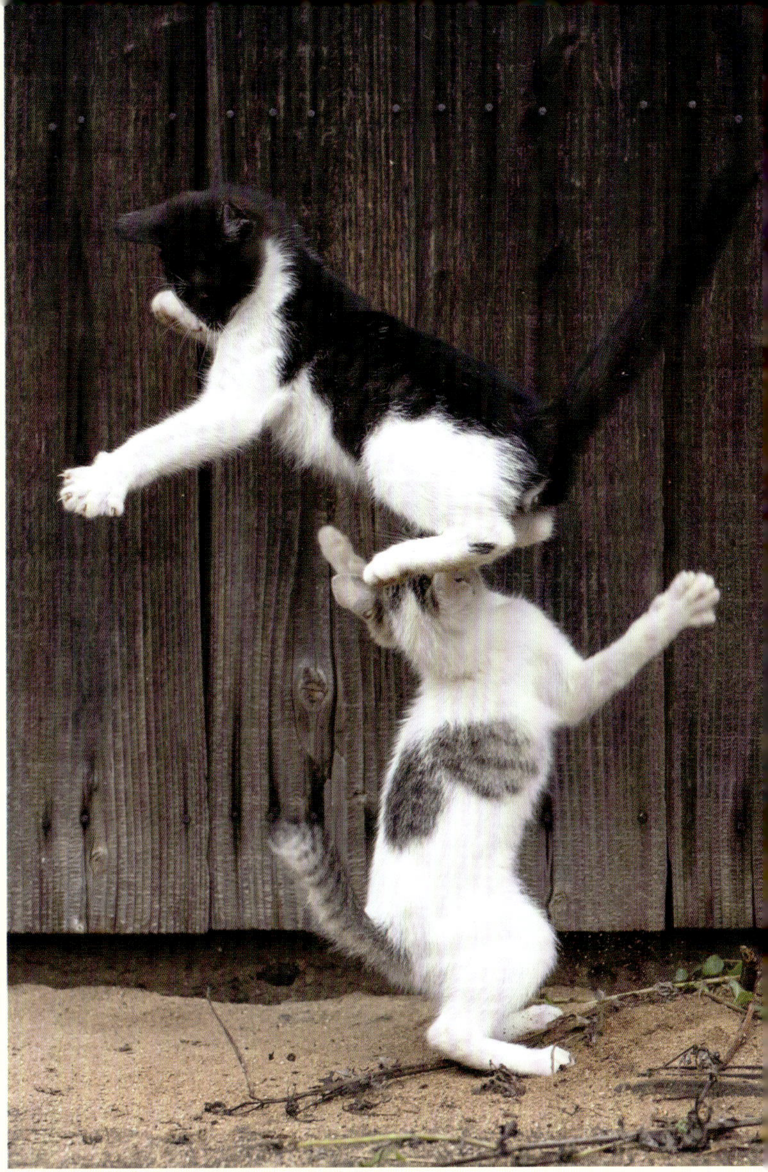

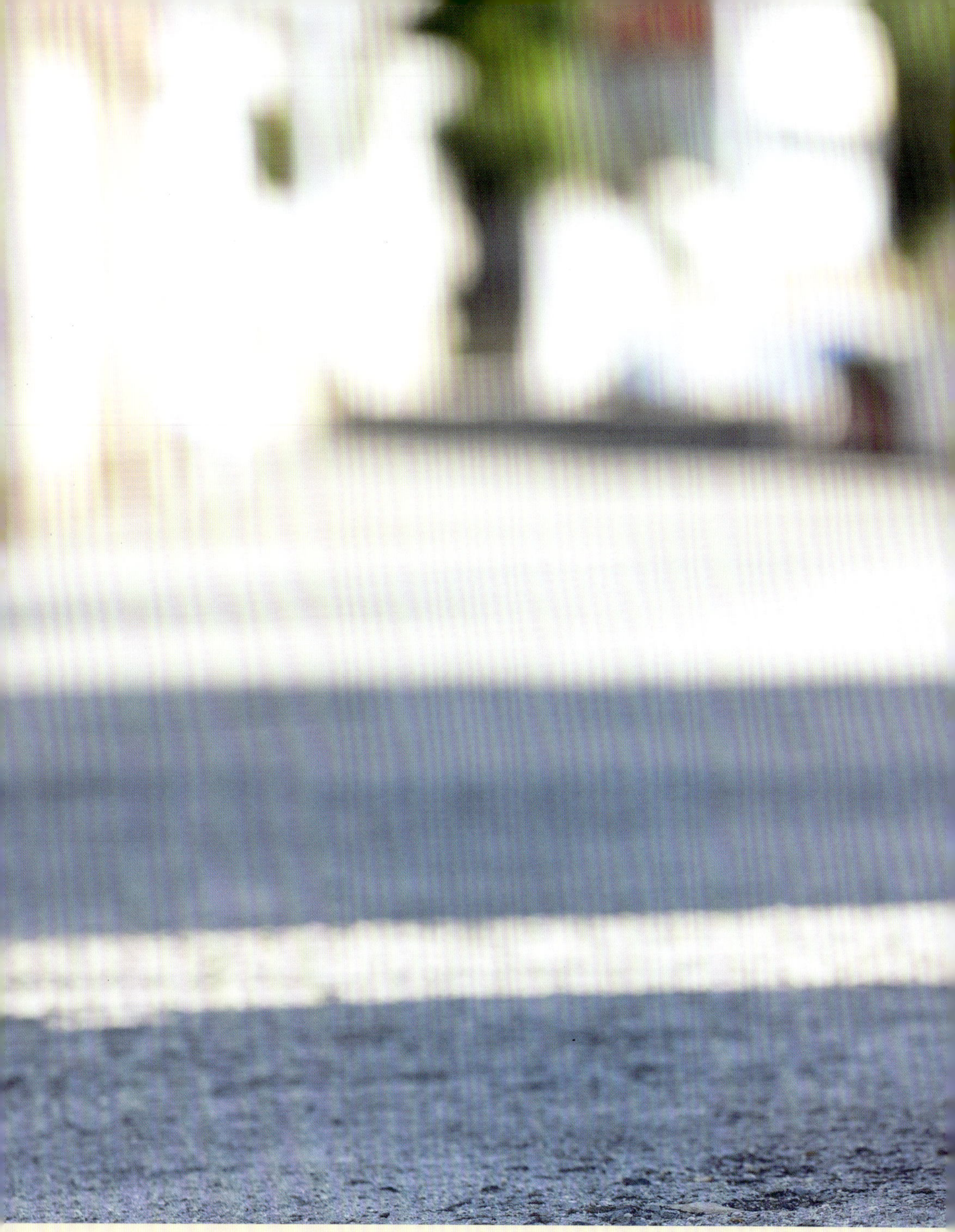

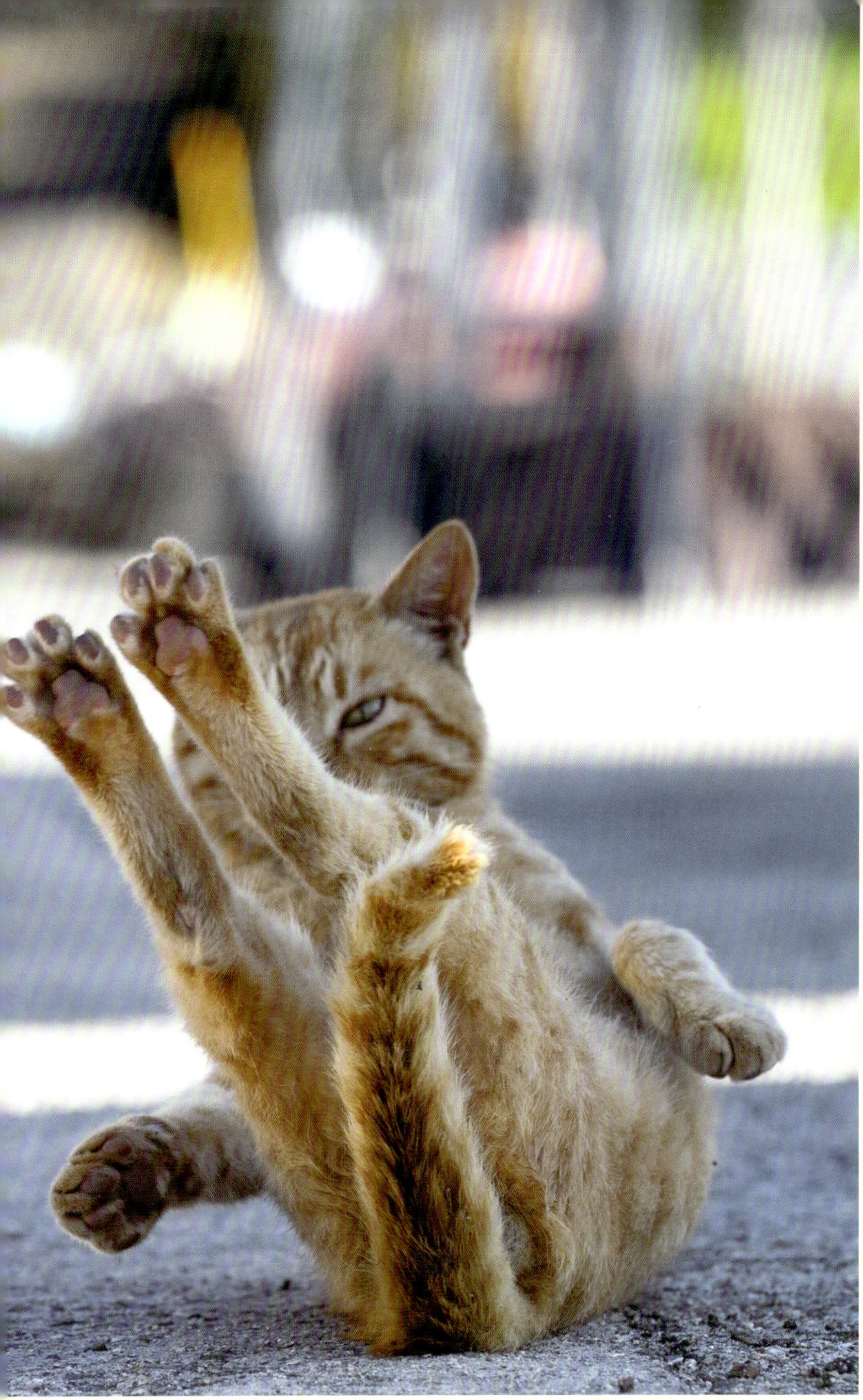

猫・ネコ

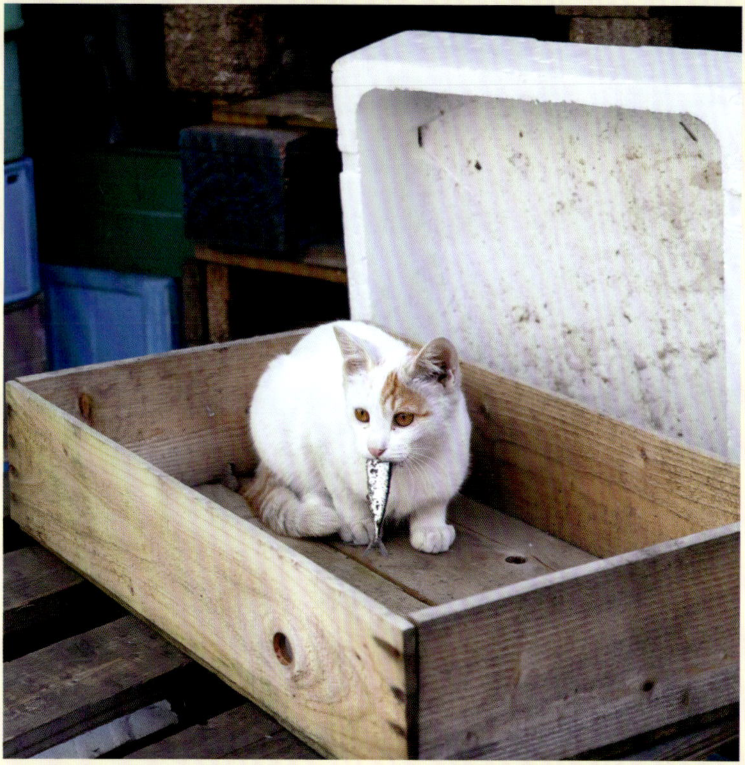

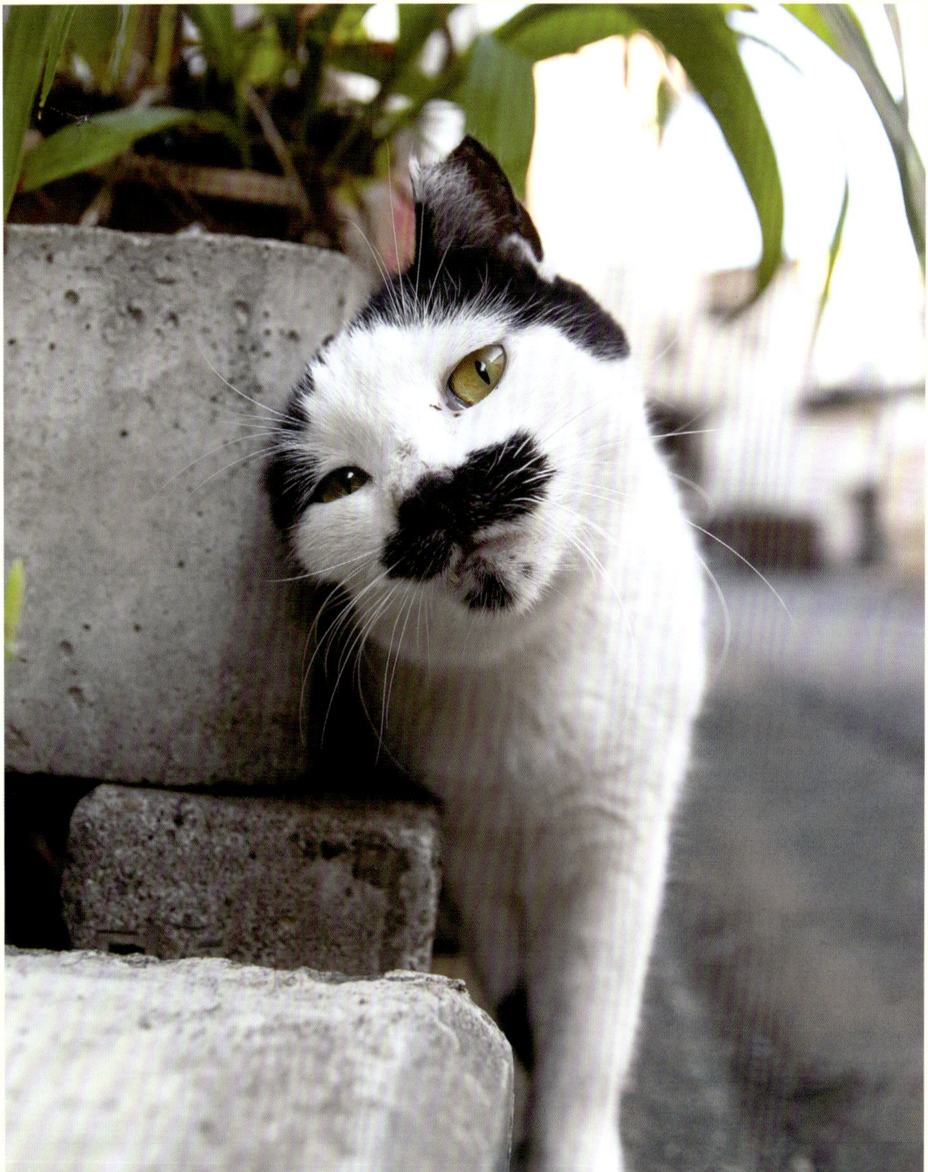

猫・ネコ

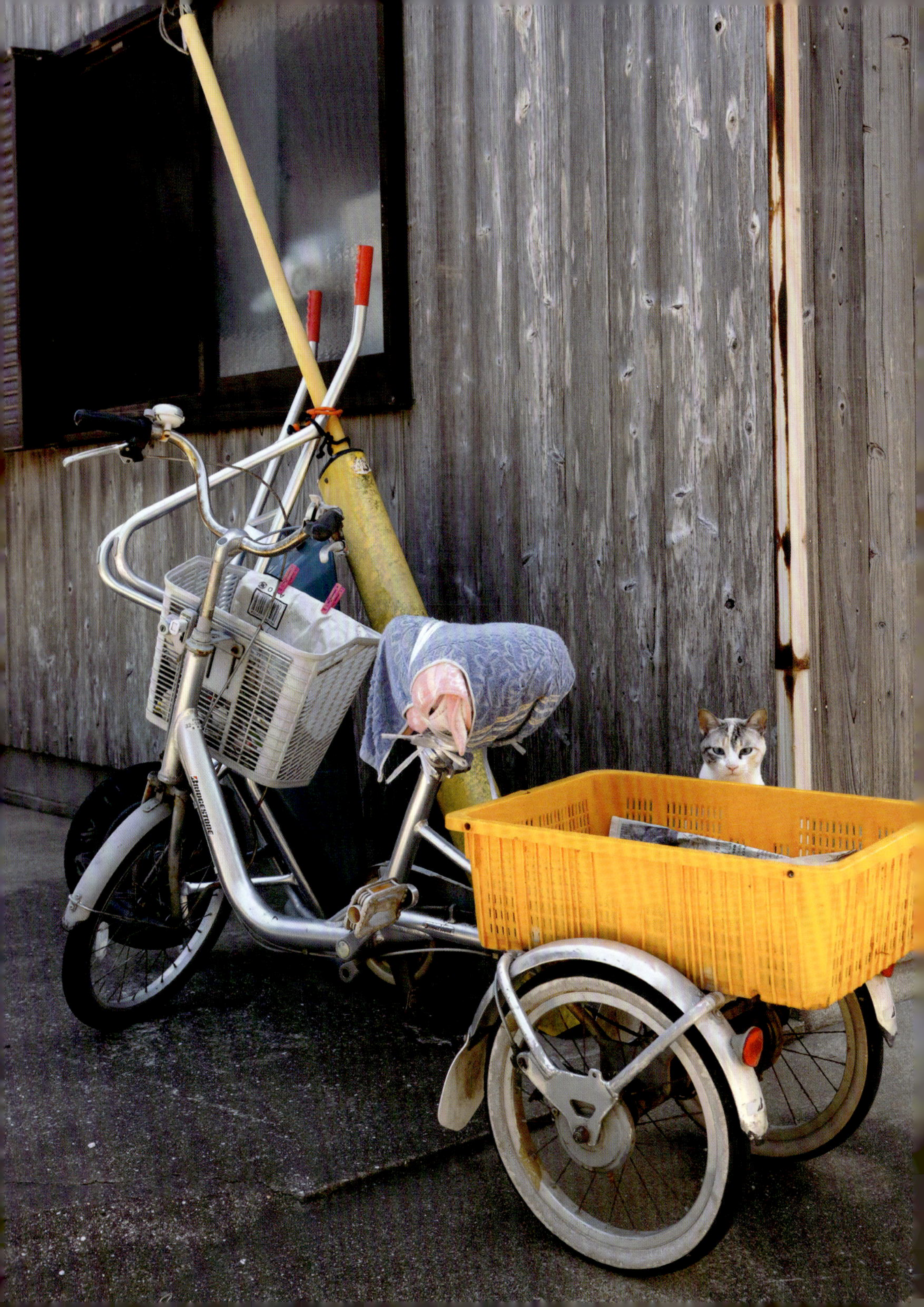

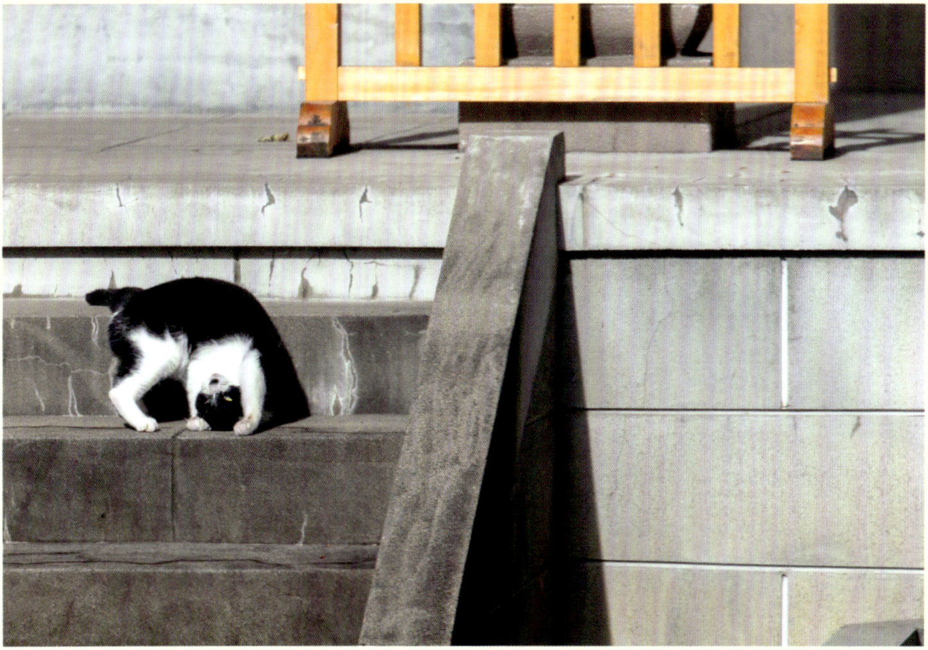

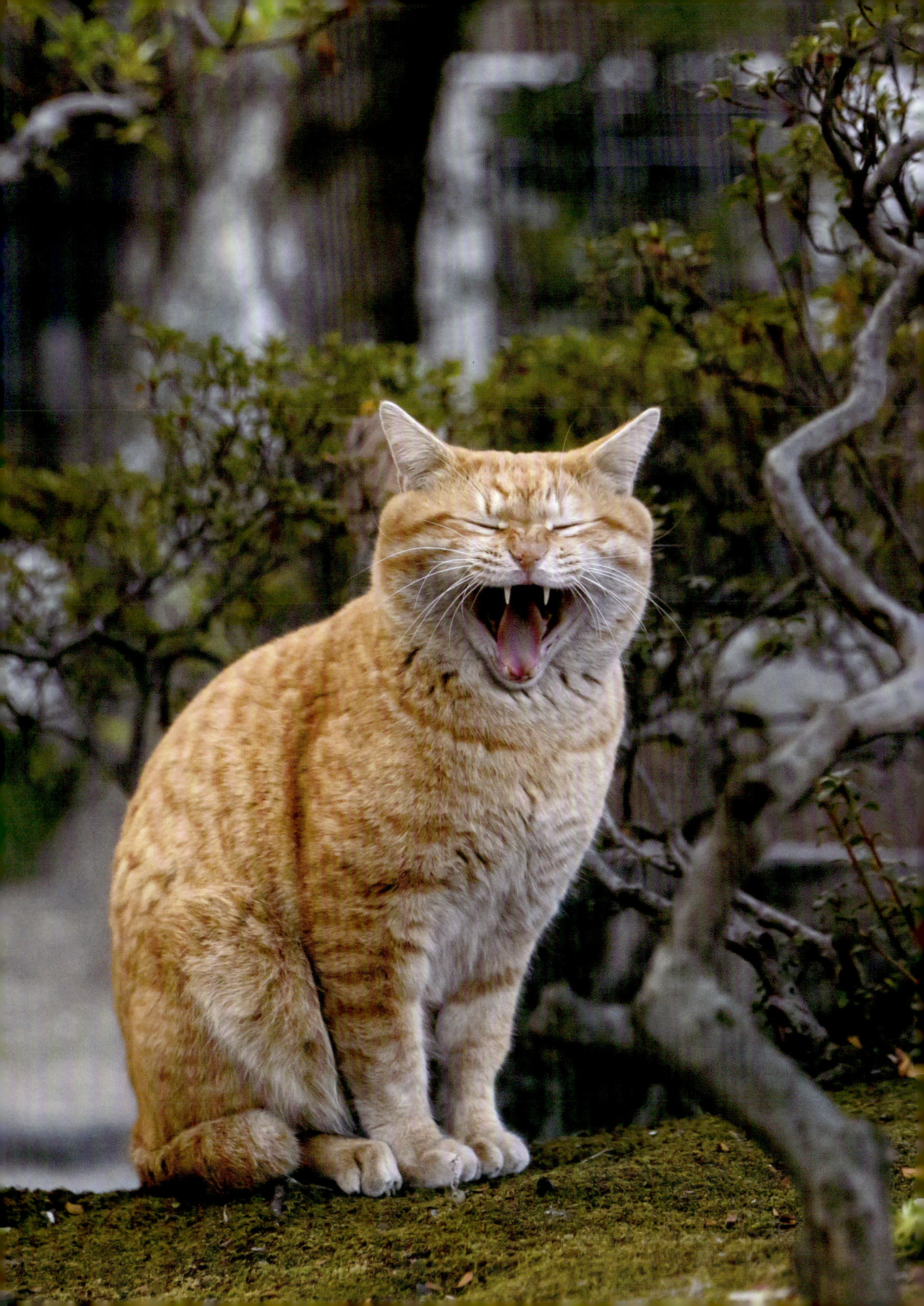

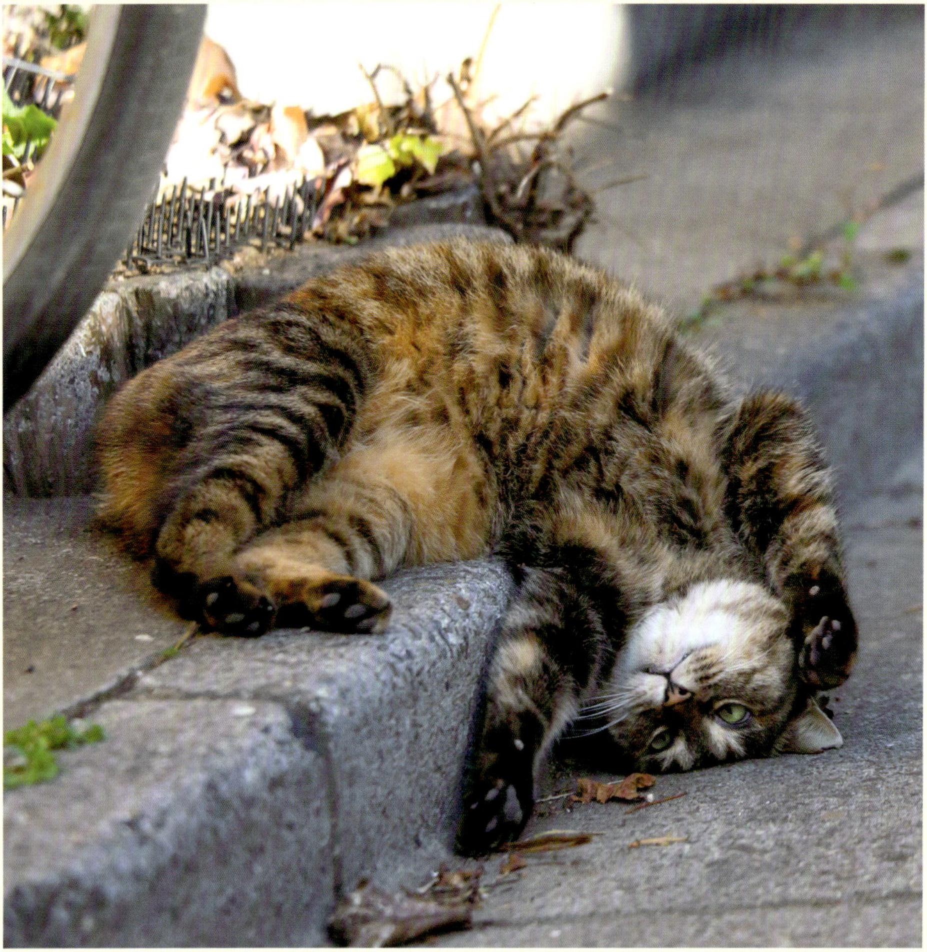

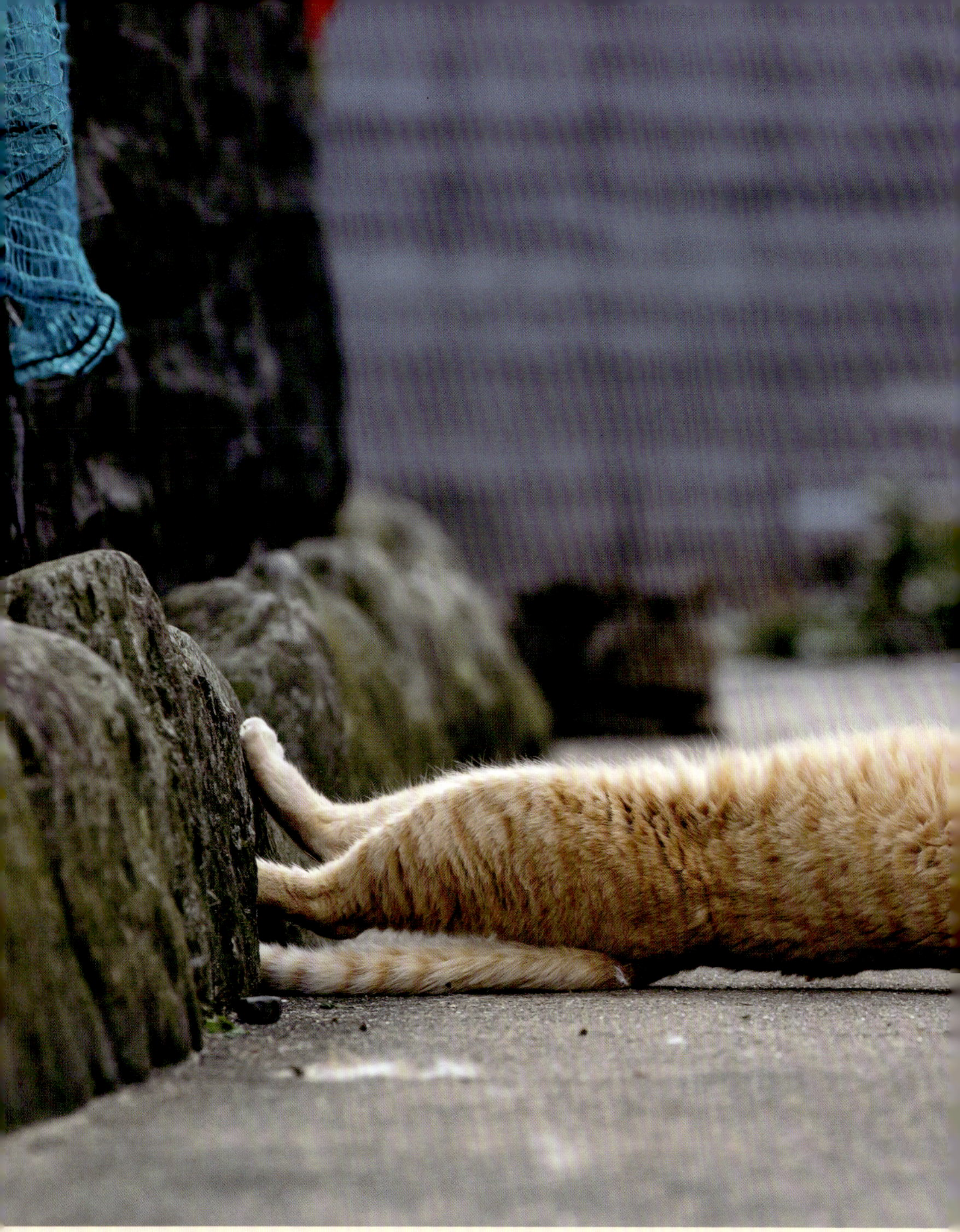

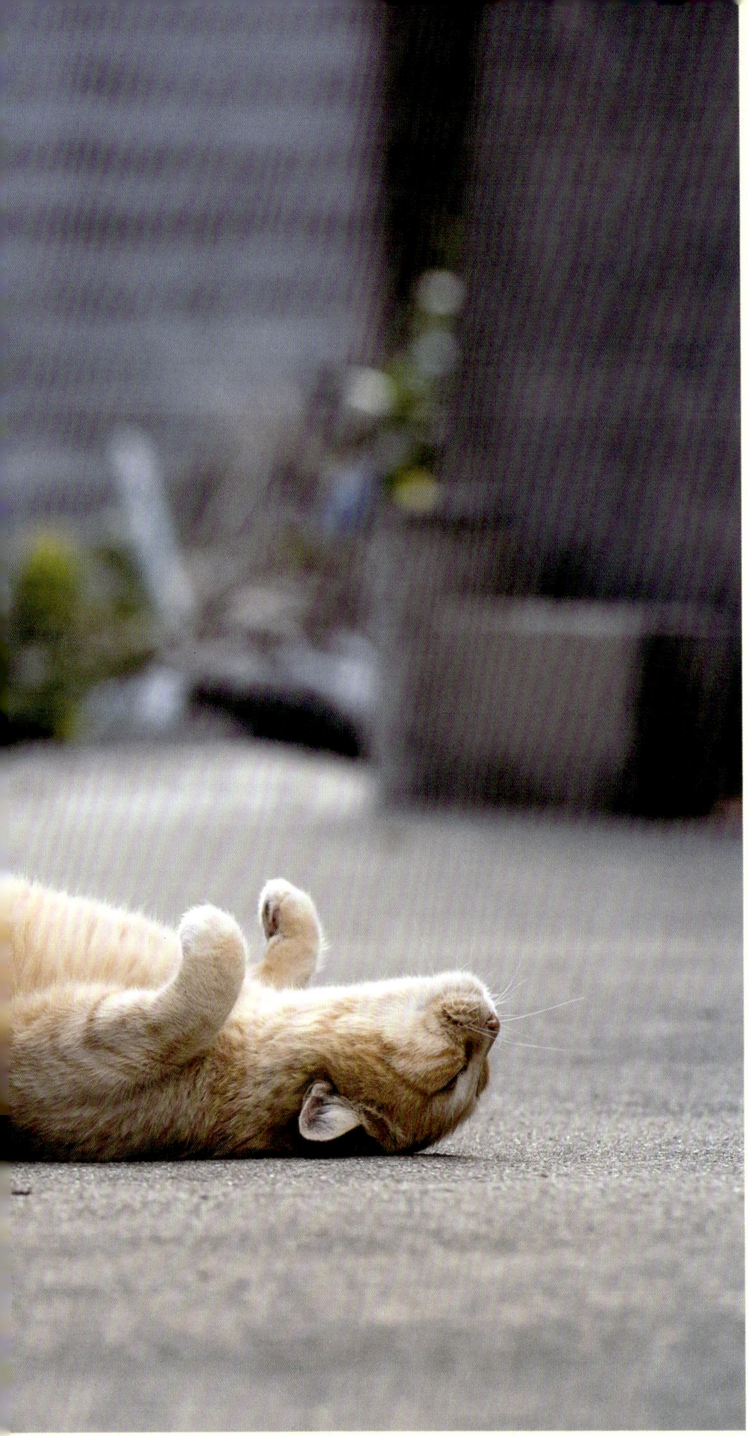

猫・ネコ

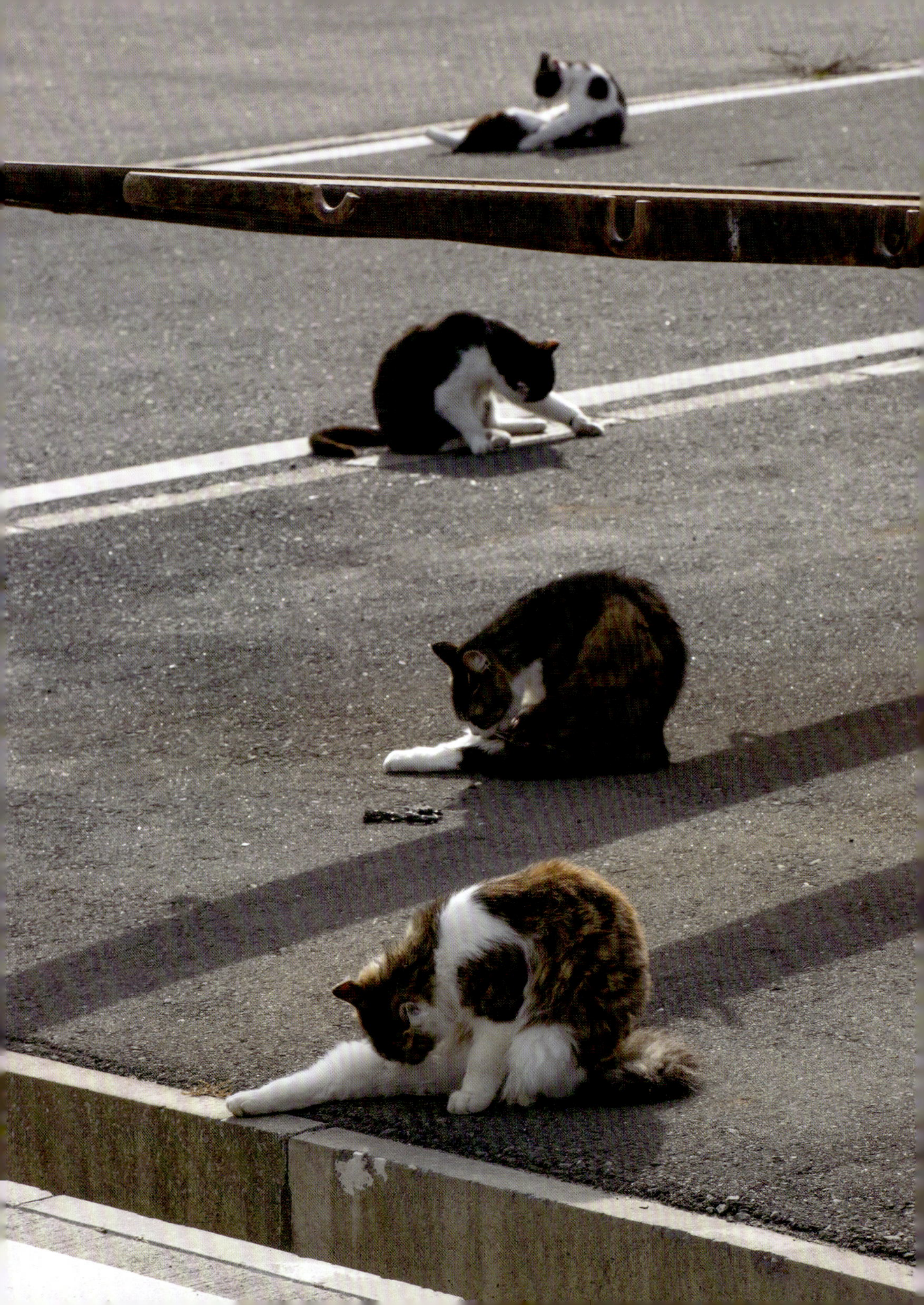

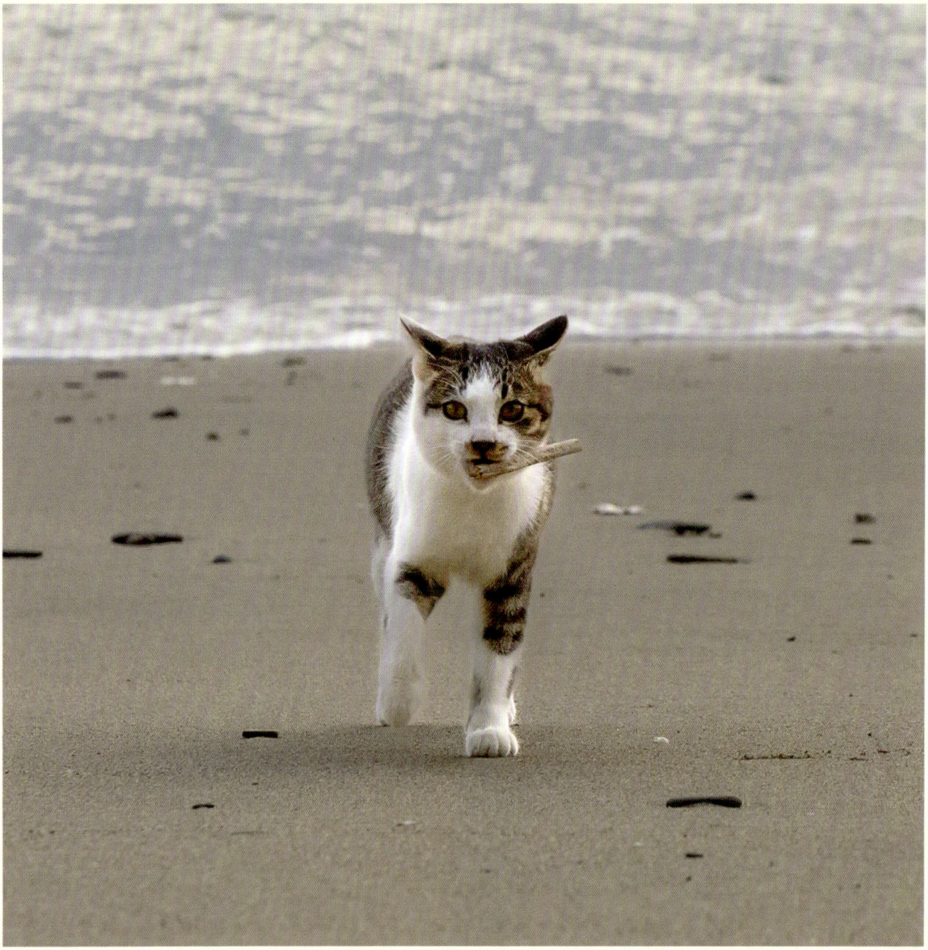

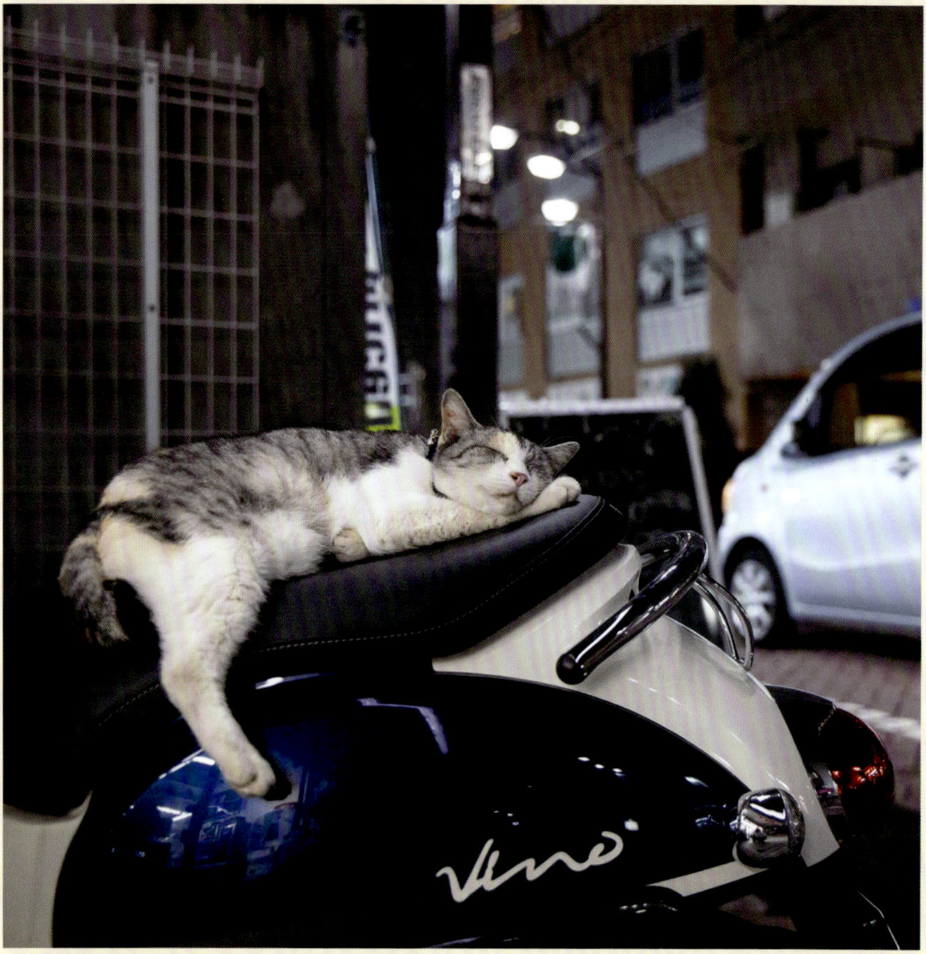

猫・ネコ

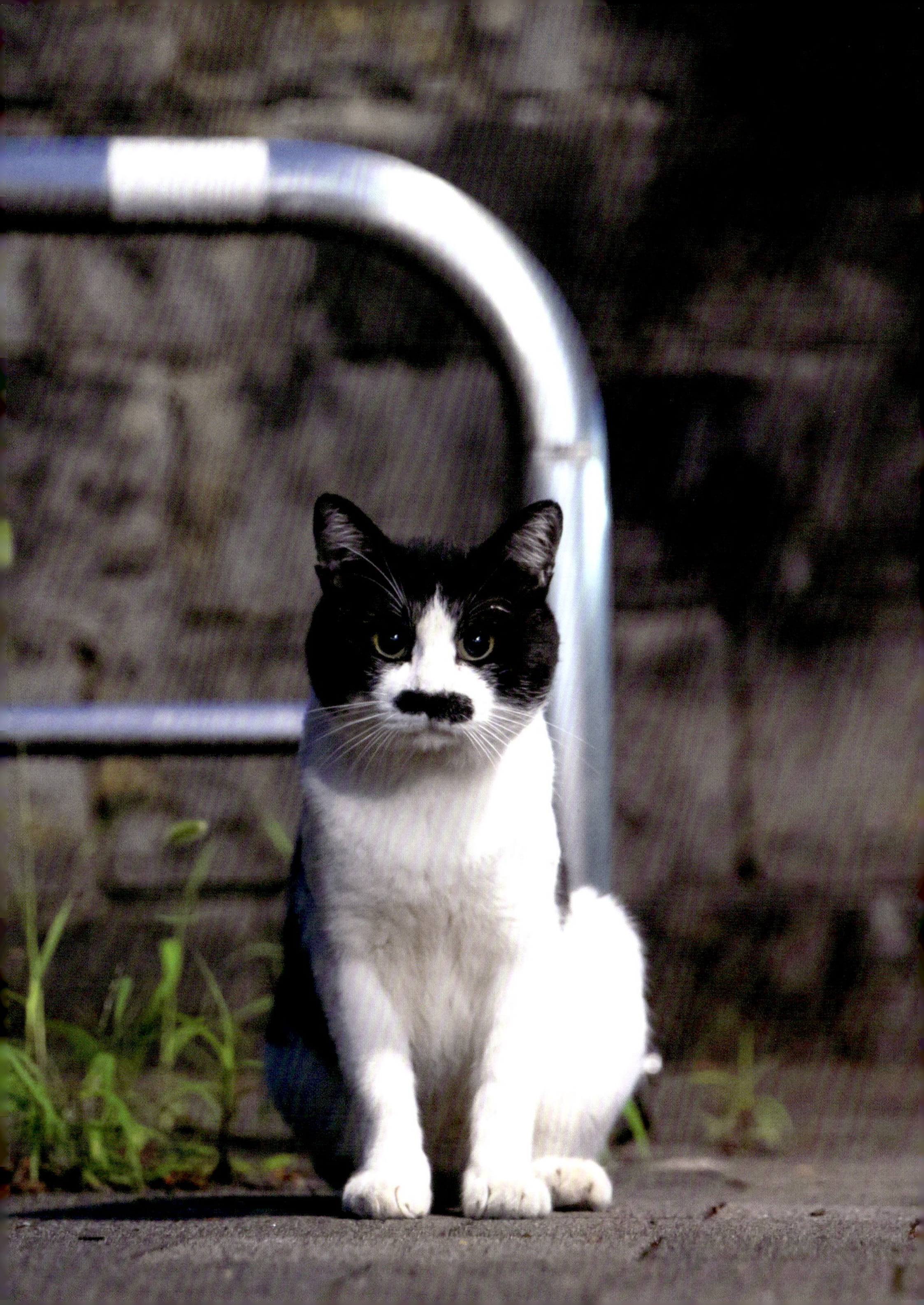

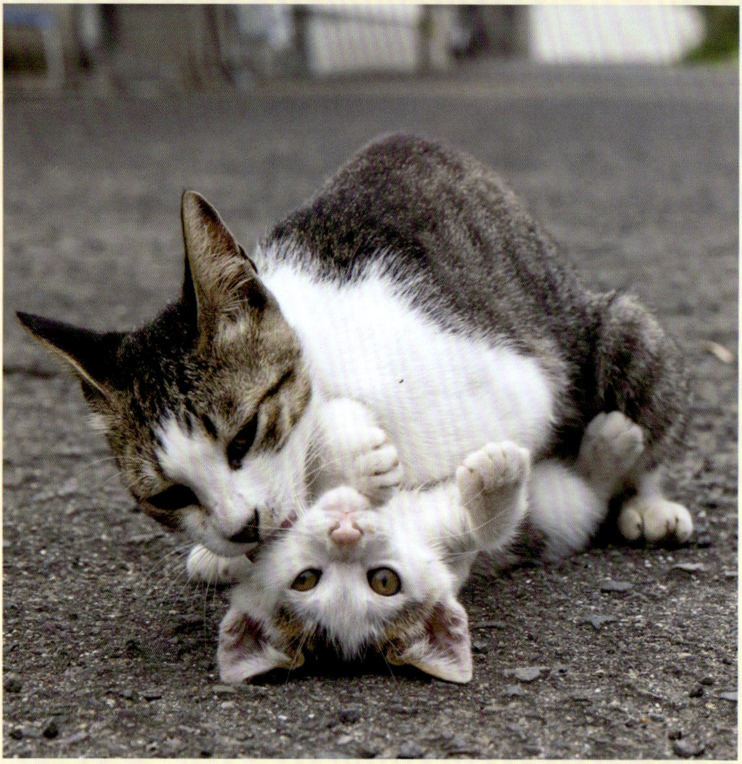

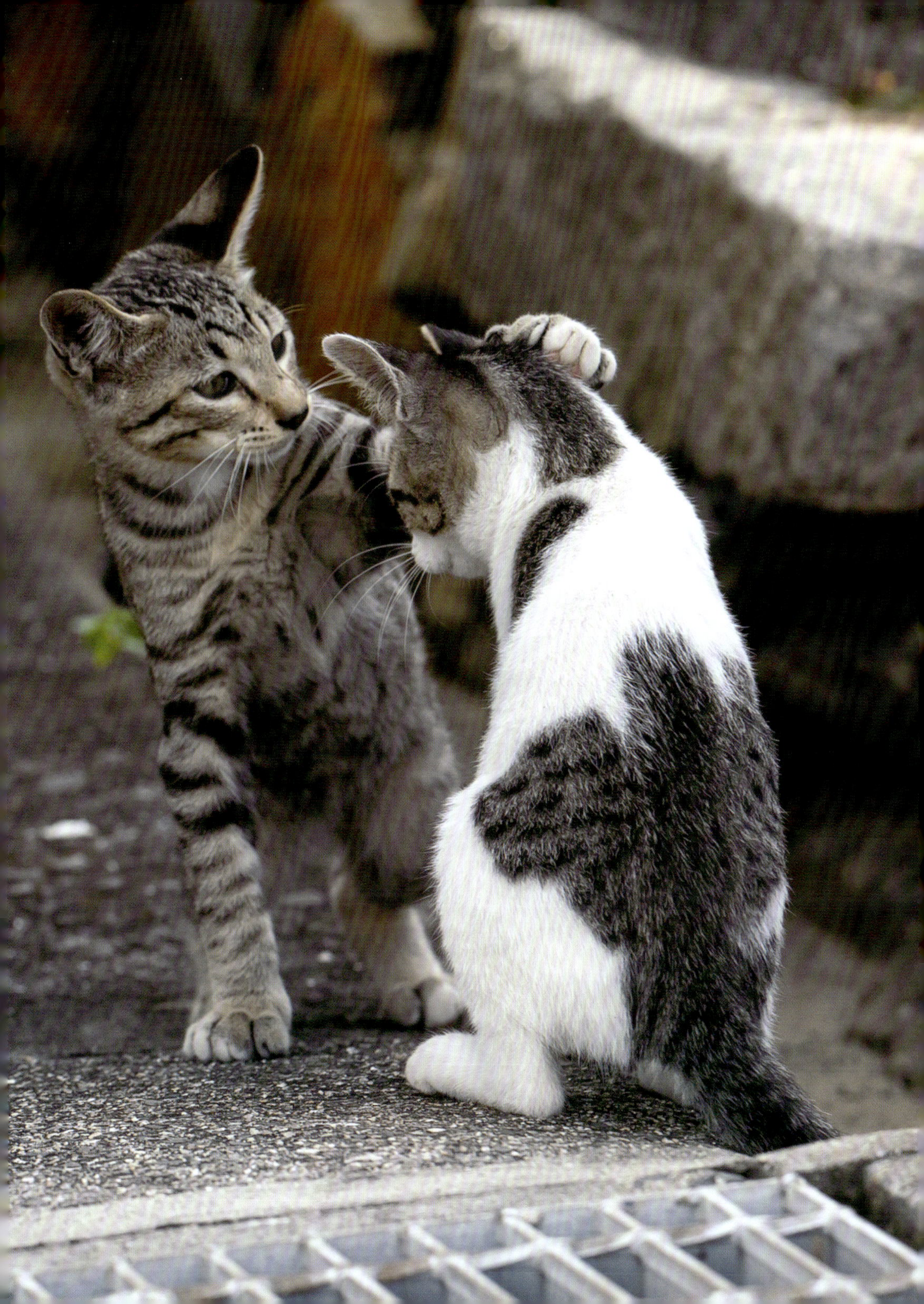

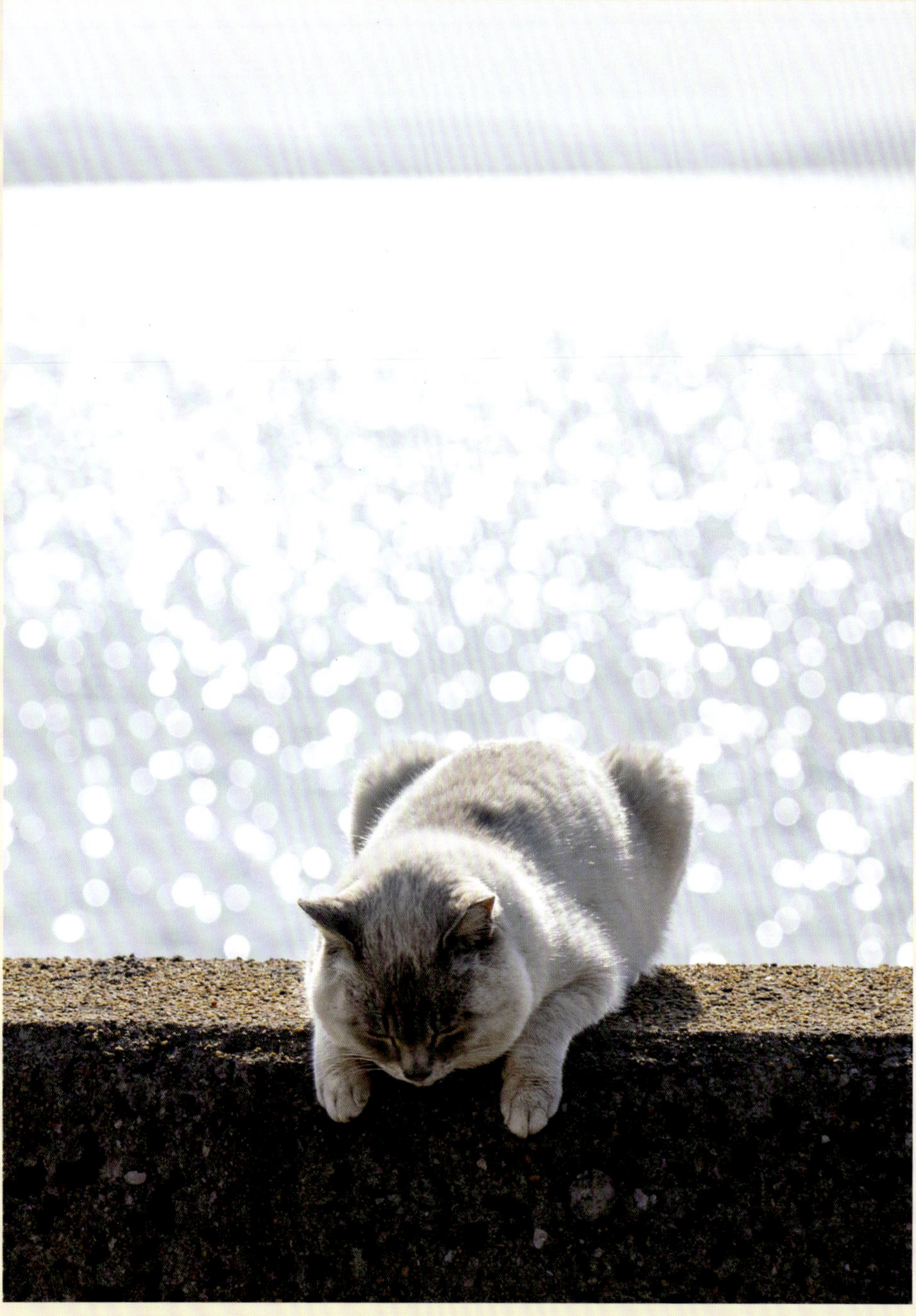

猫・ネコ

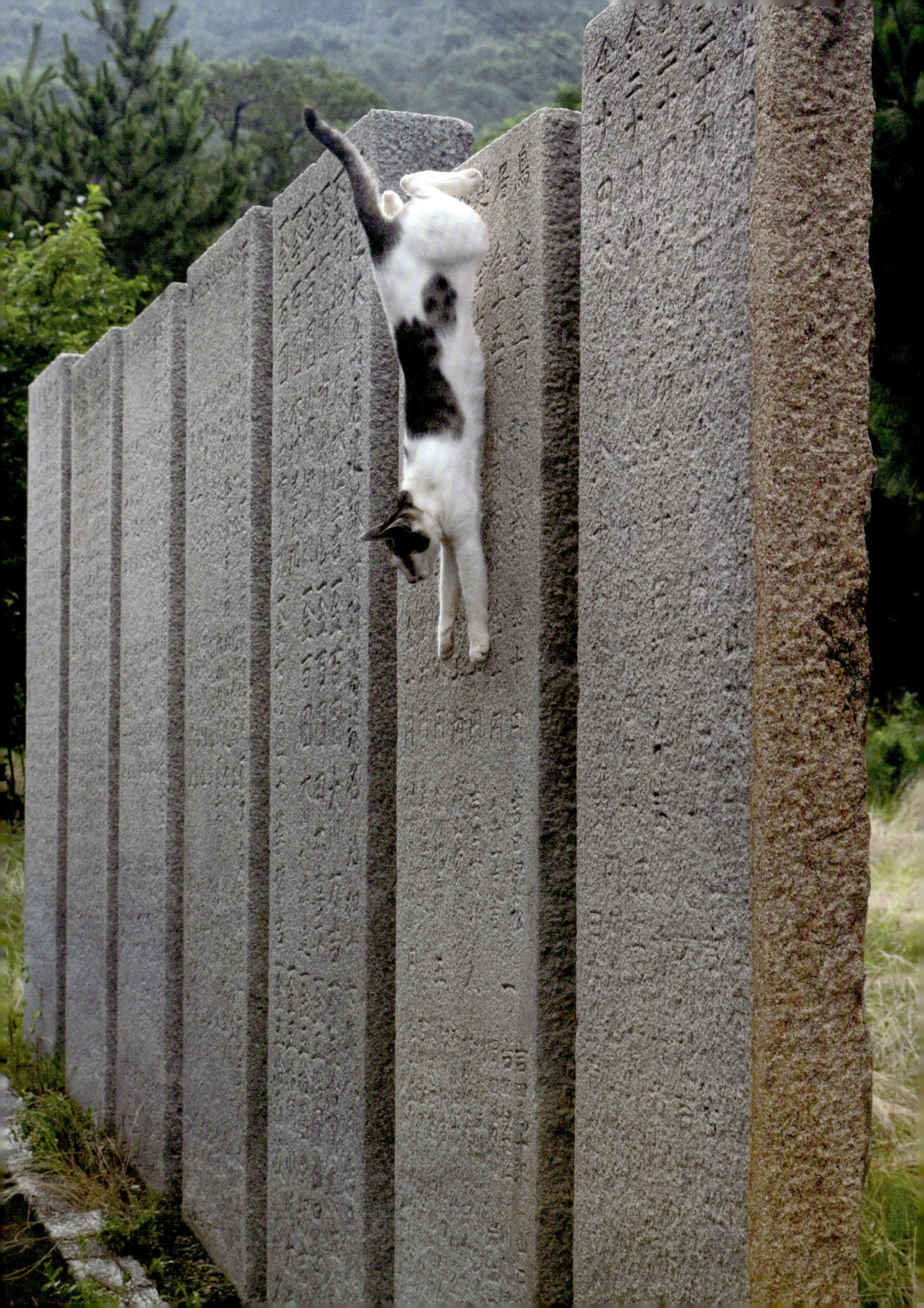

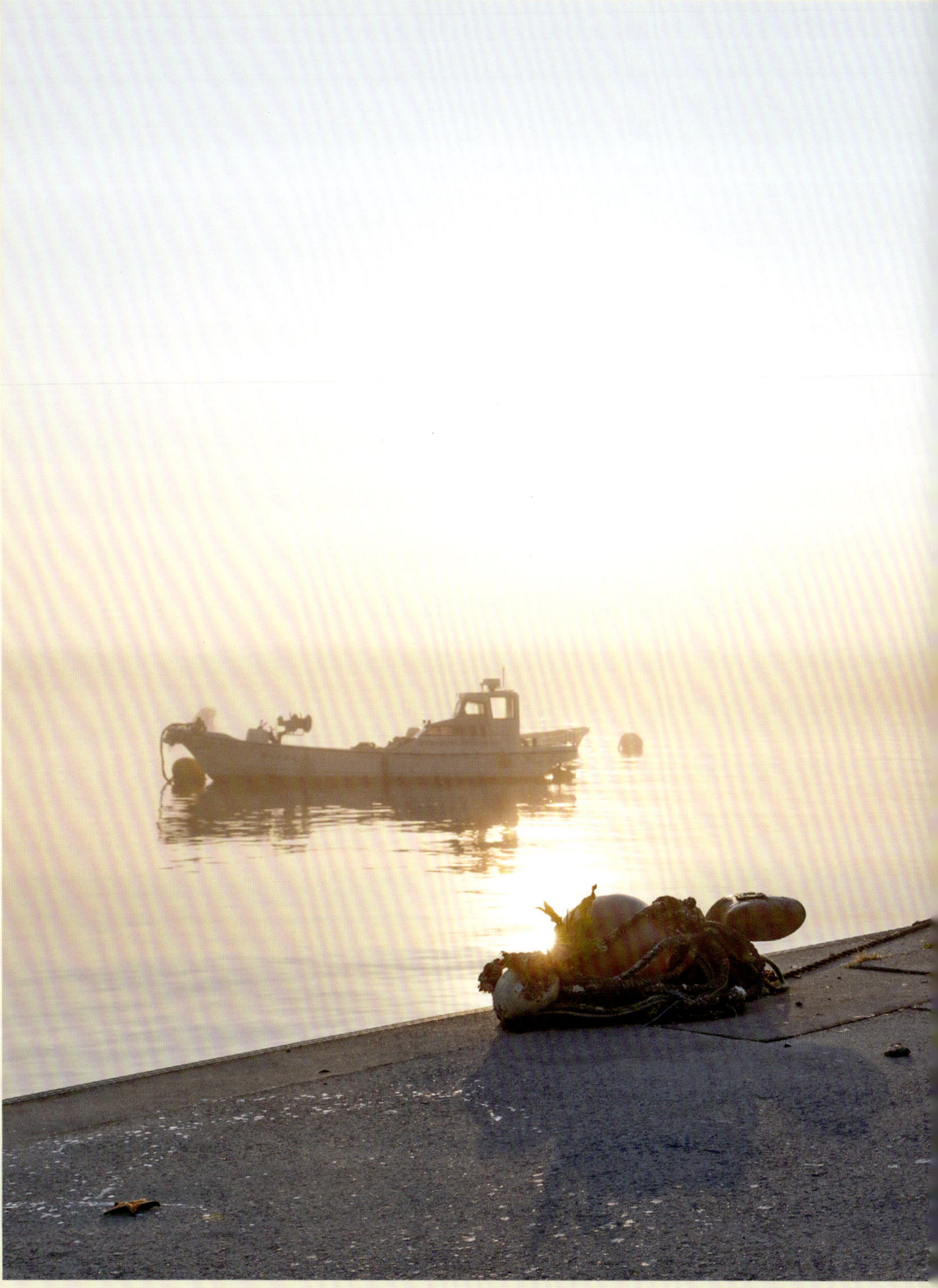

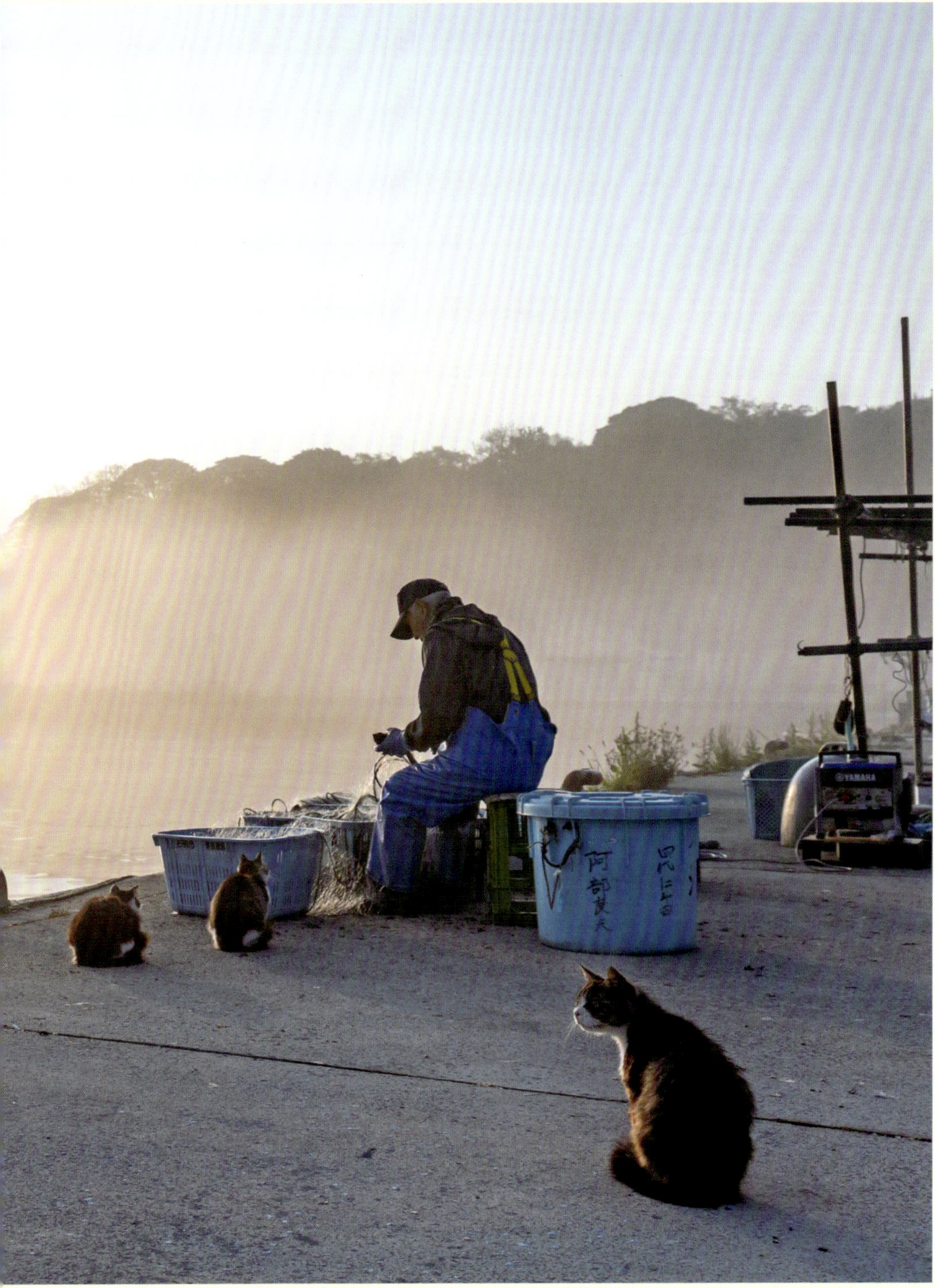
YAMAHA
阿部良夫

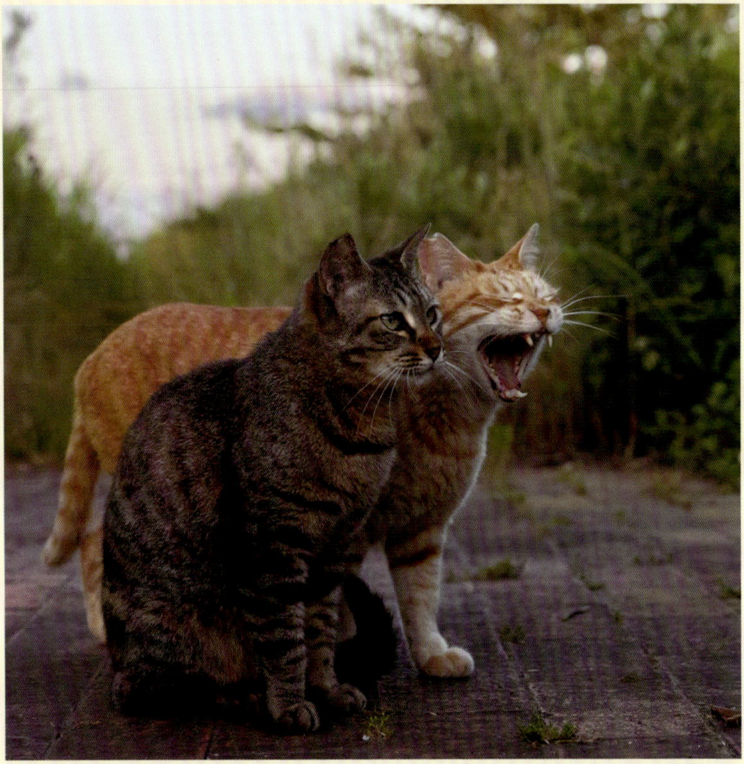

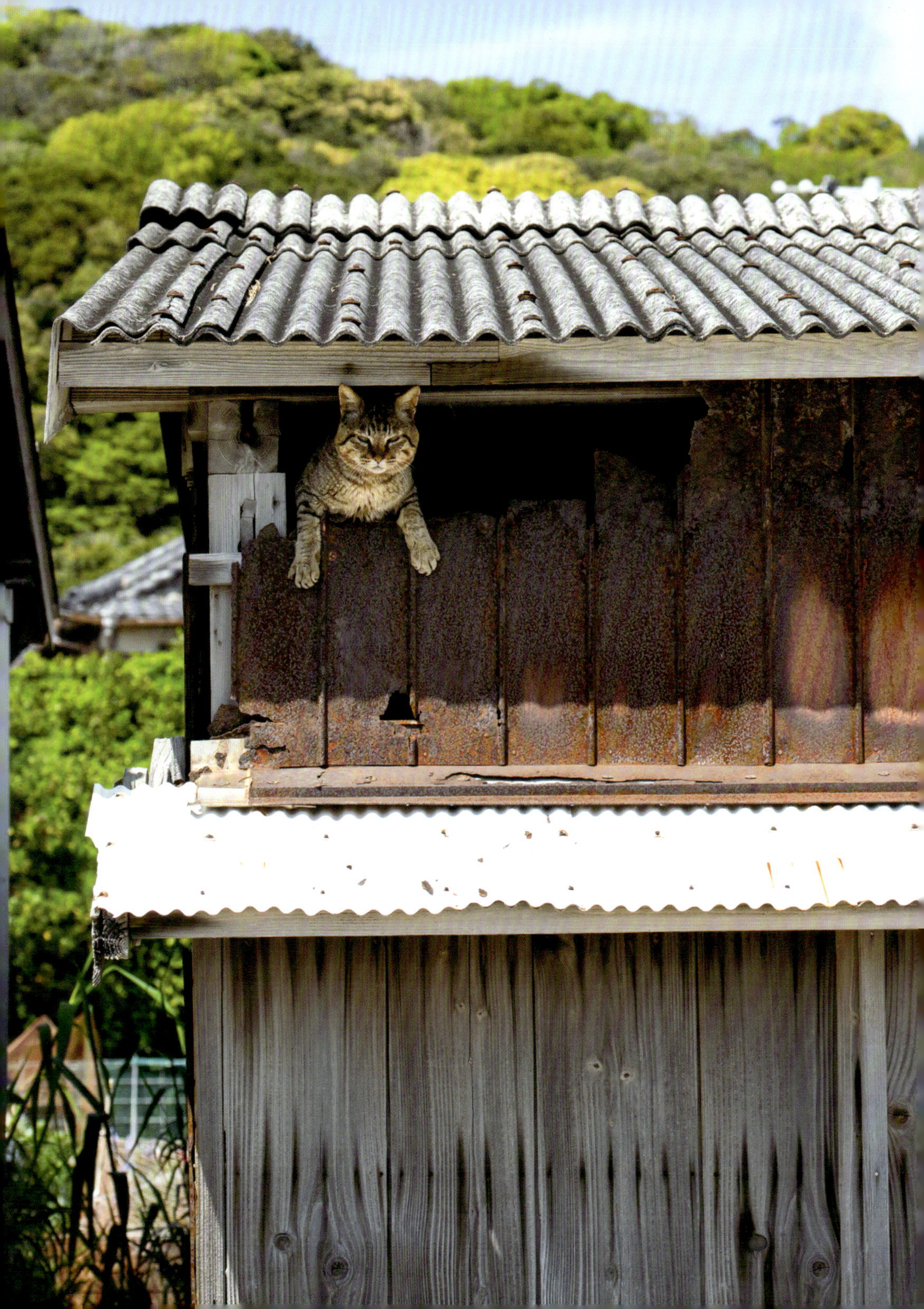

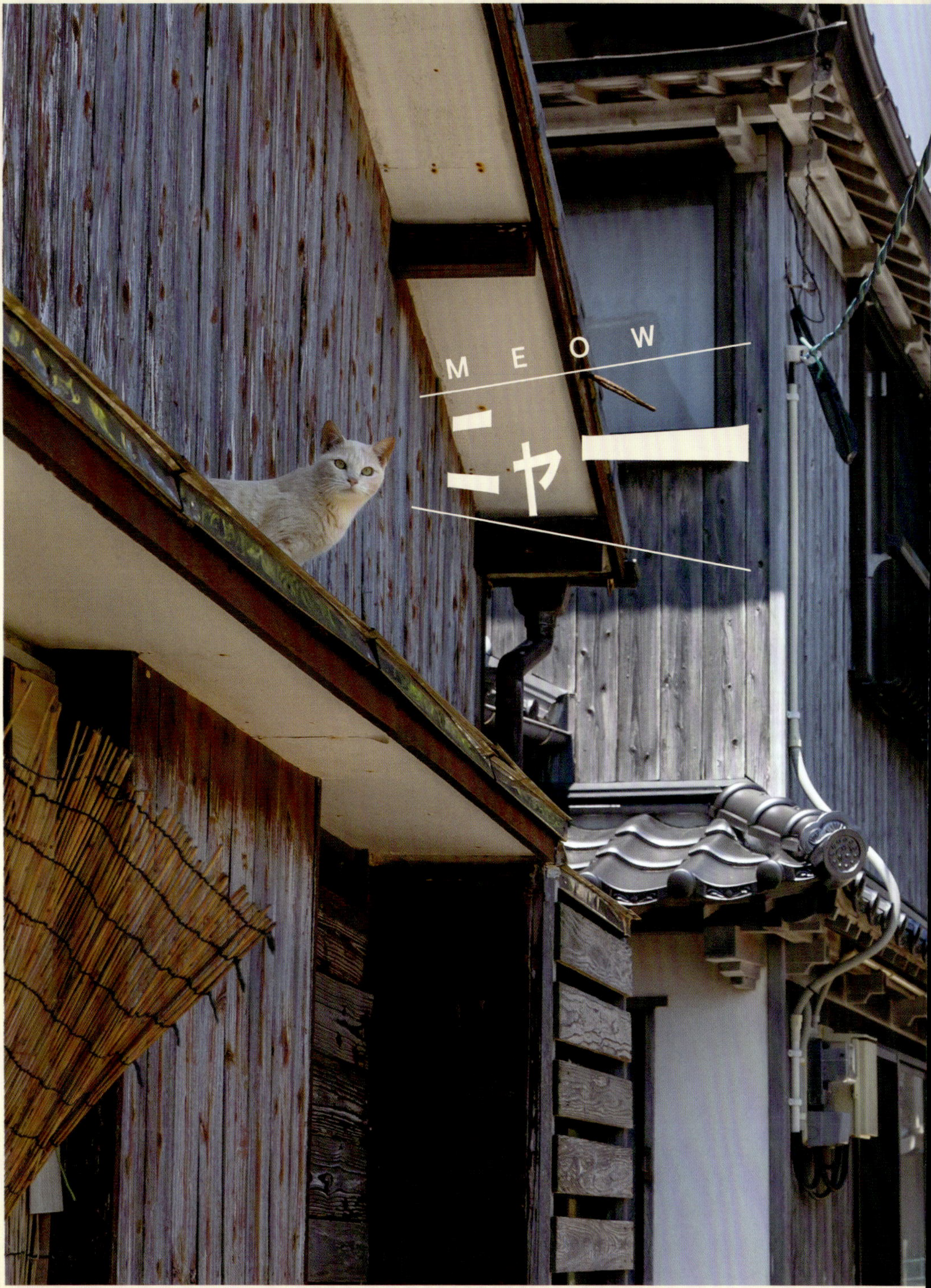
MEOW
ニャー

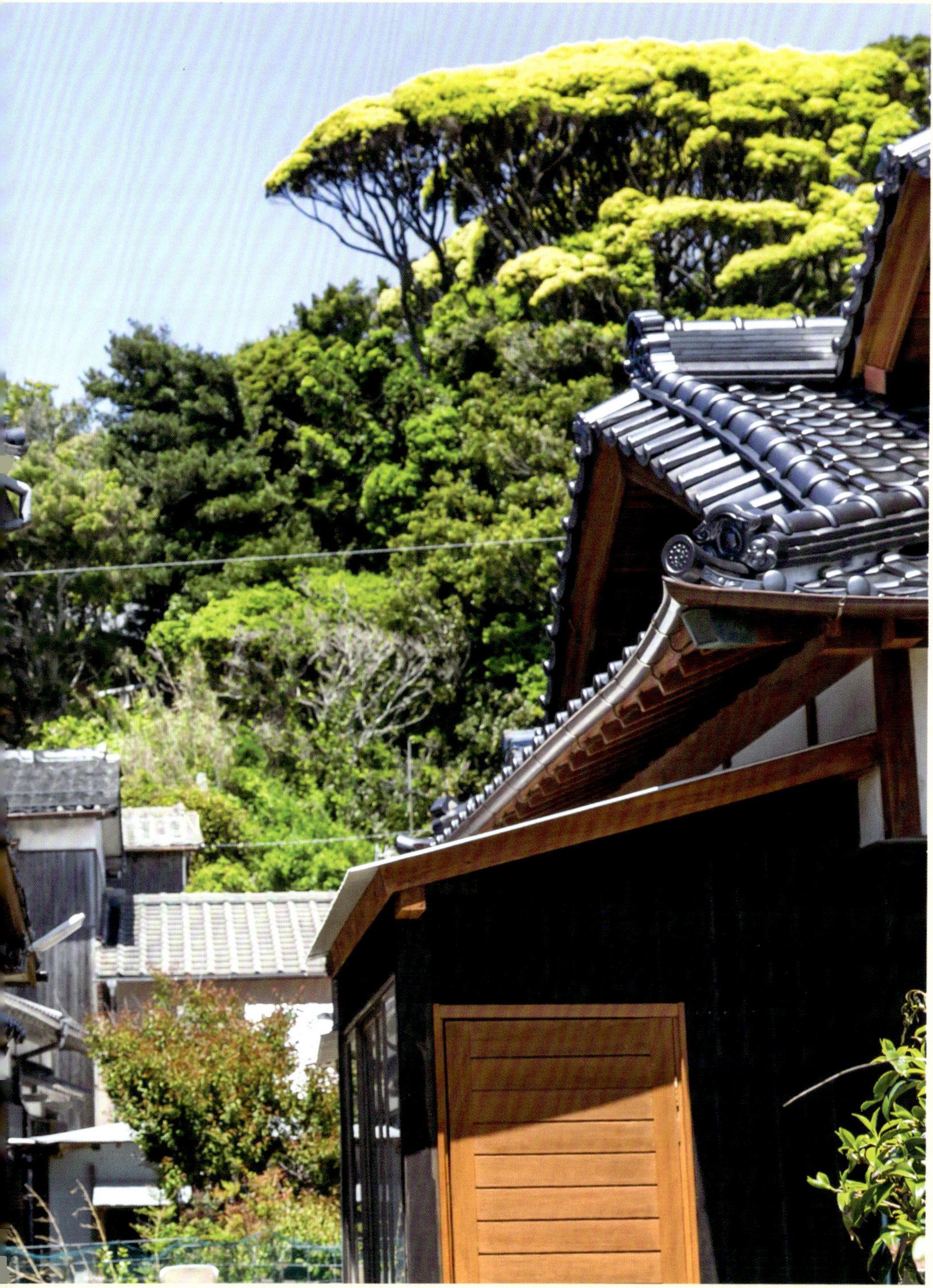

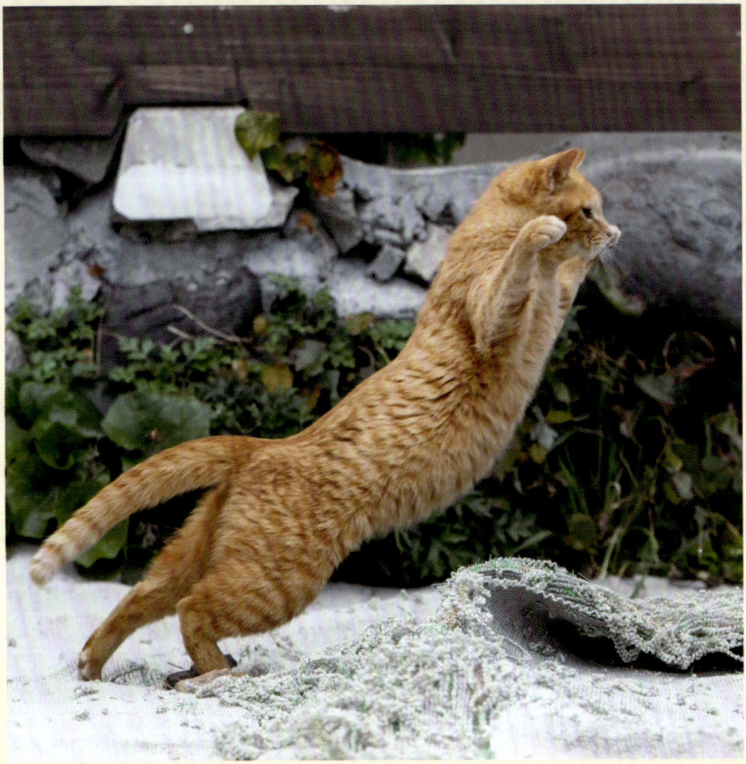

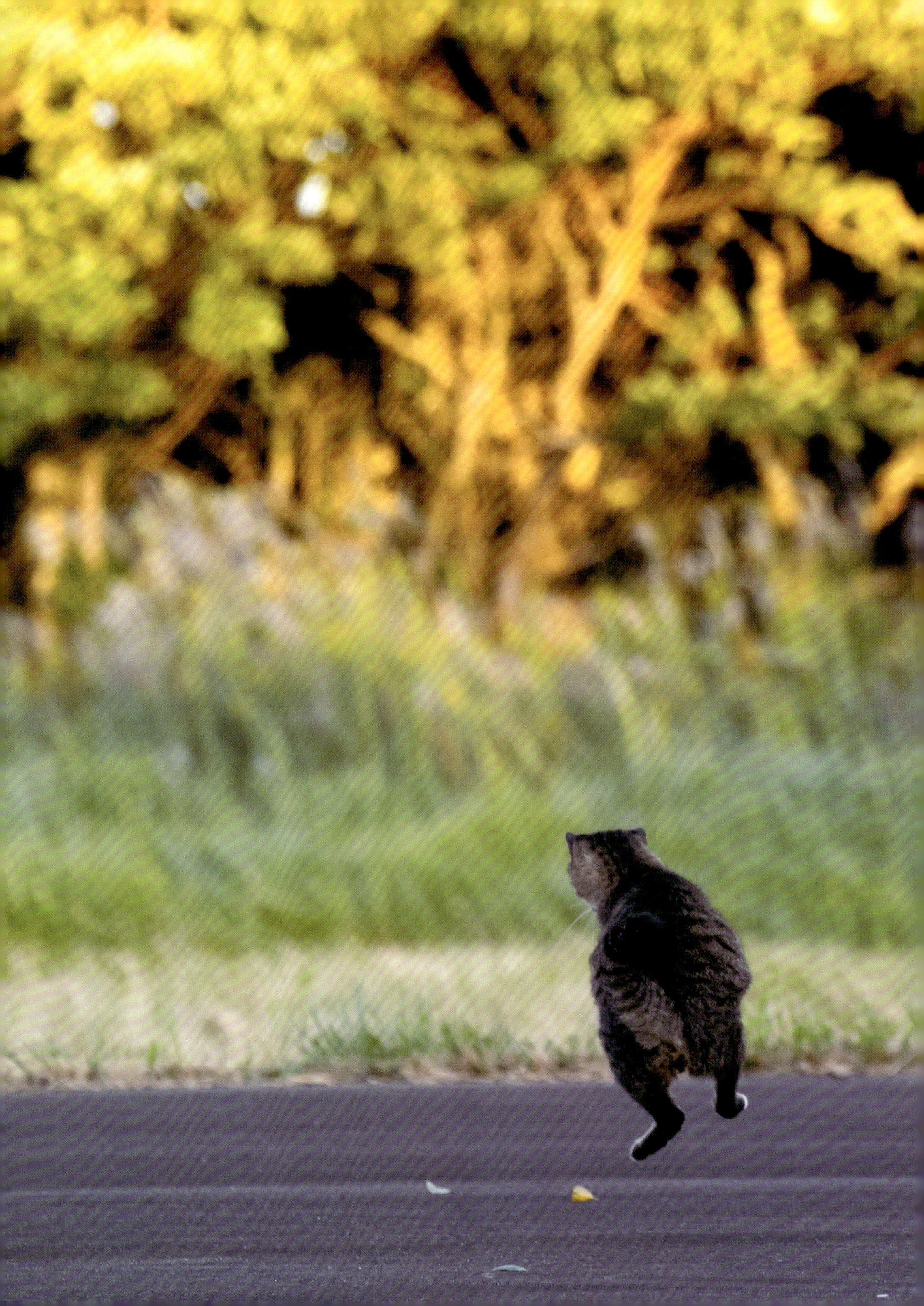

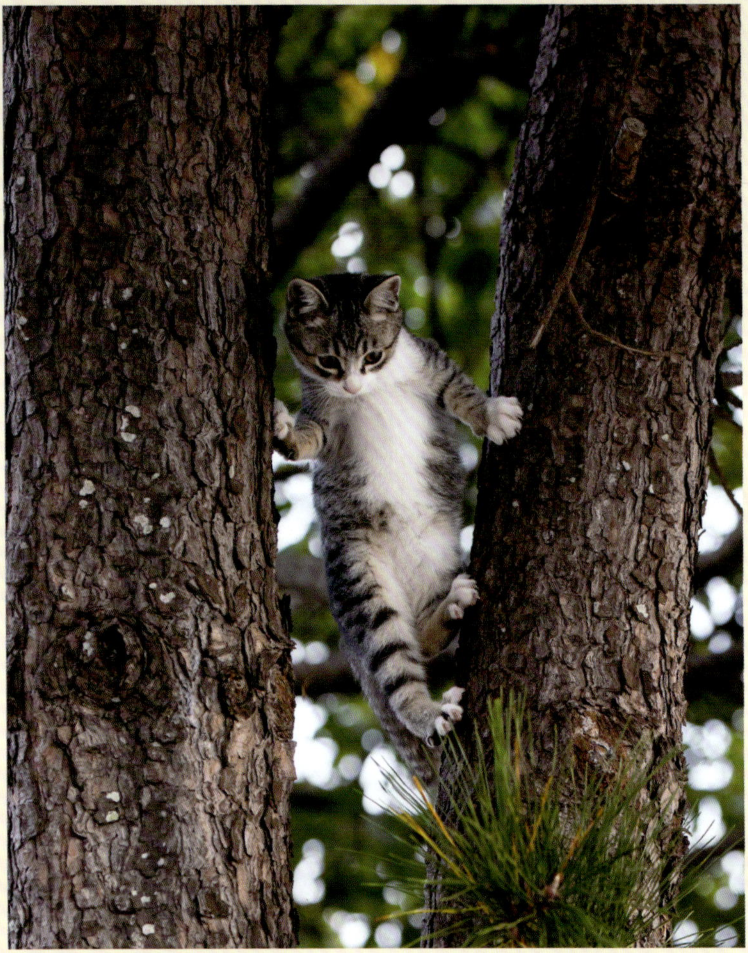

猫・ネコ

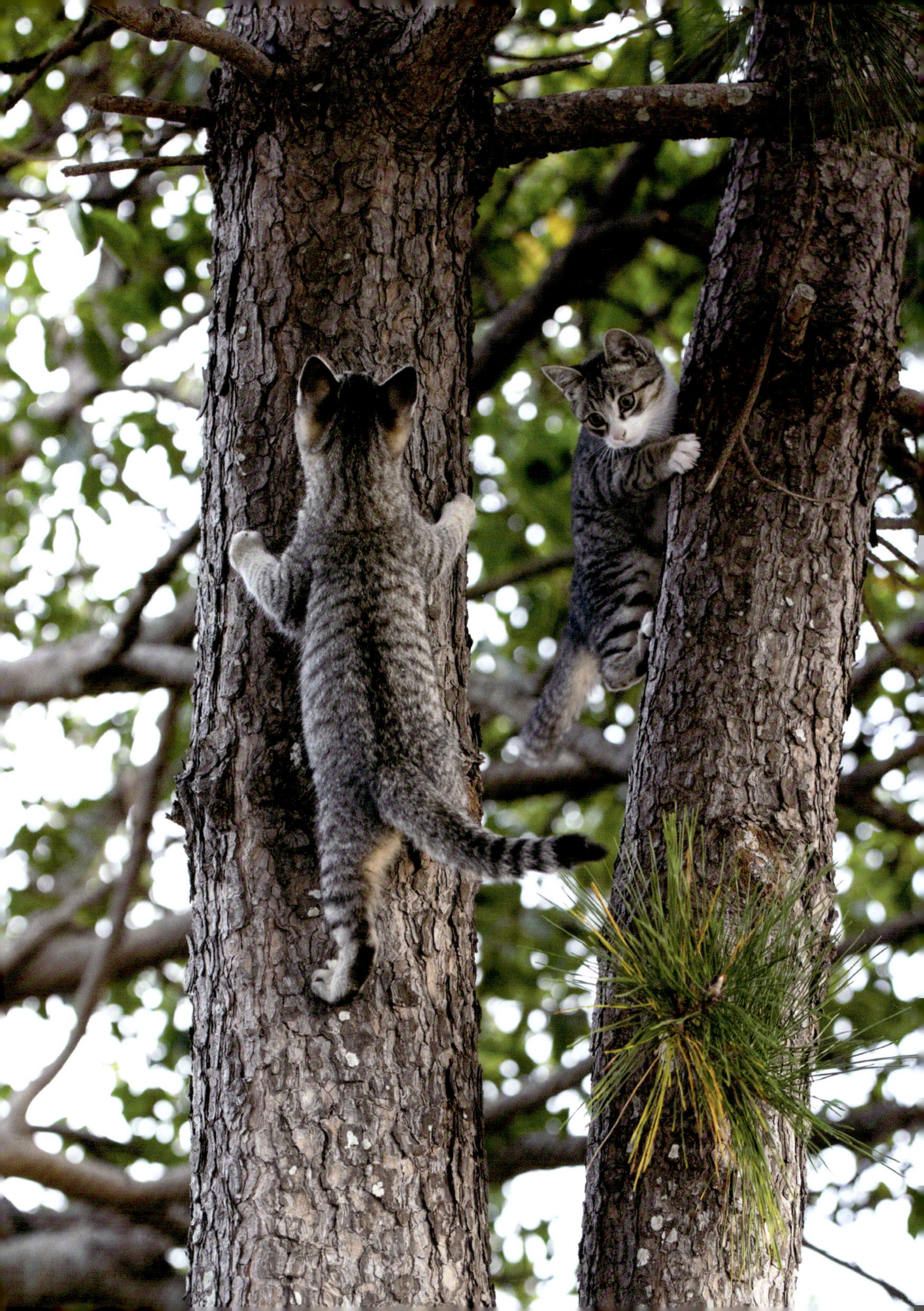

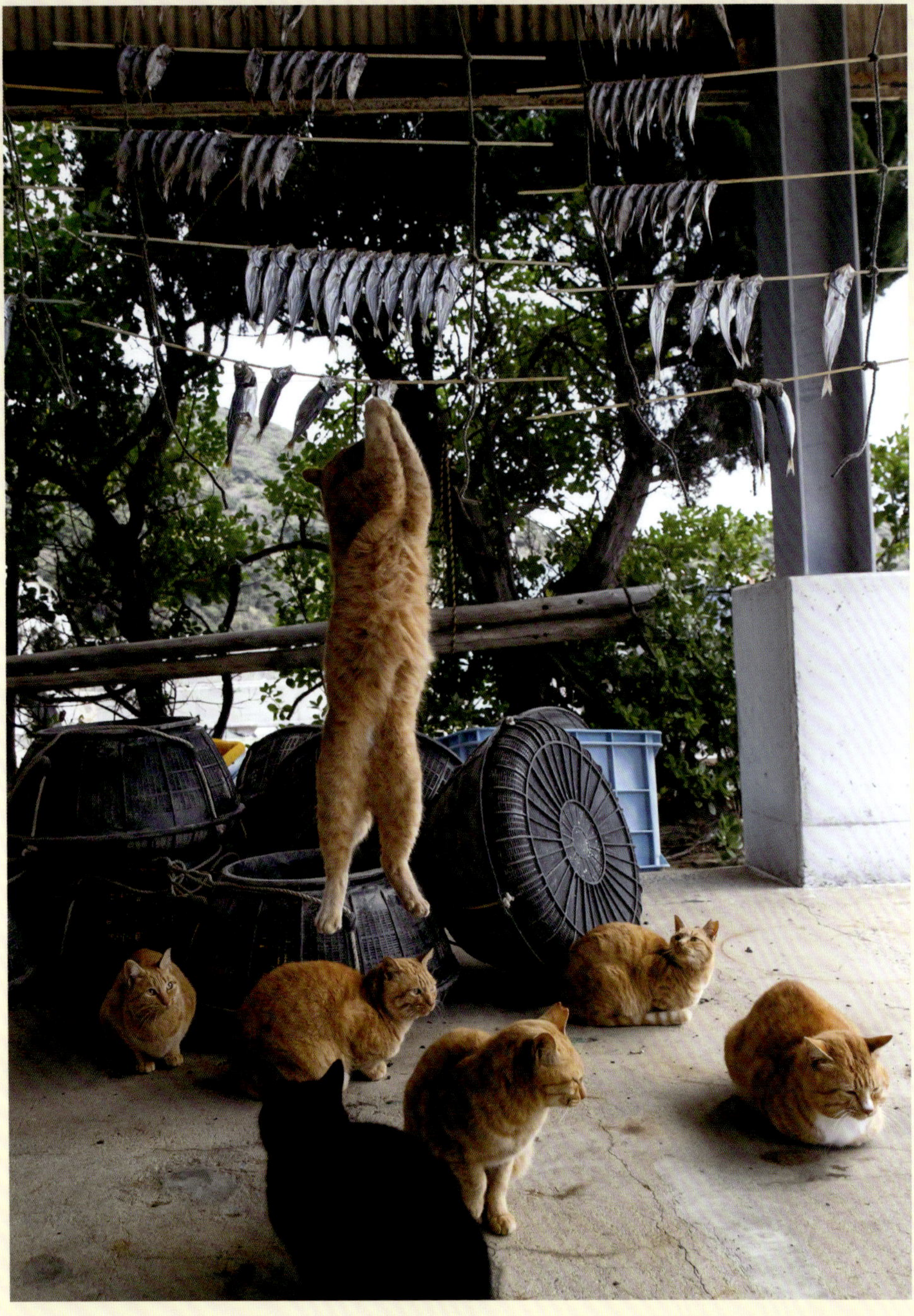

猫・ネコ

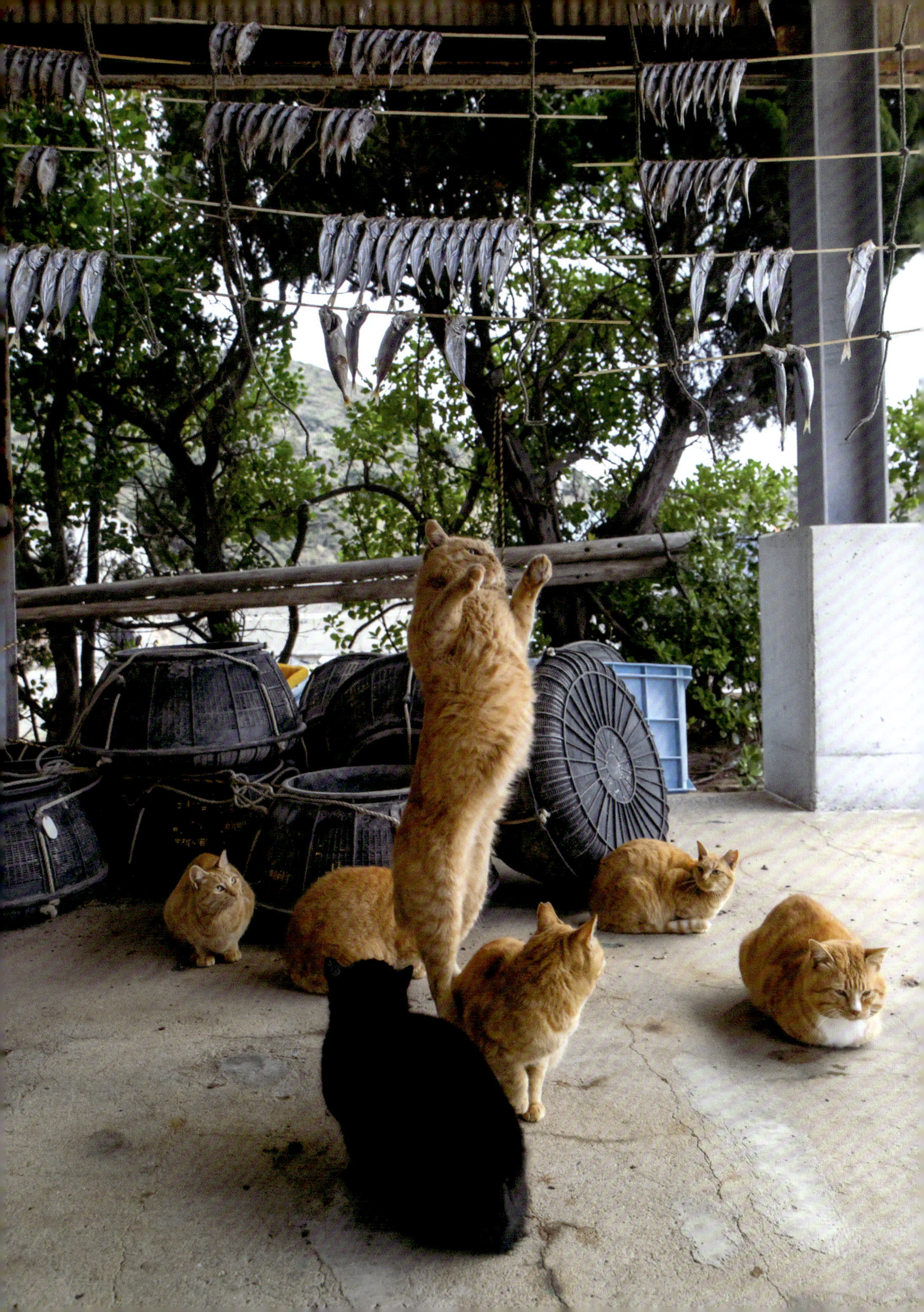

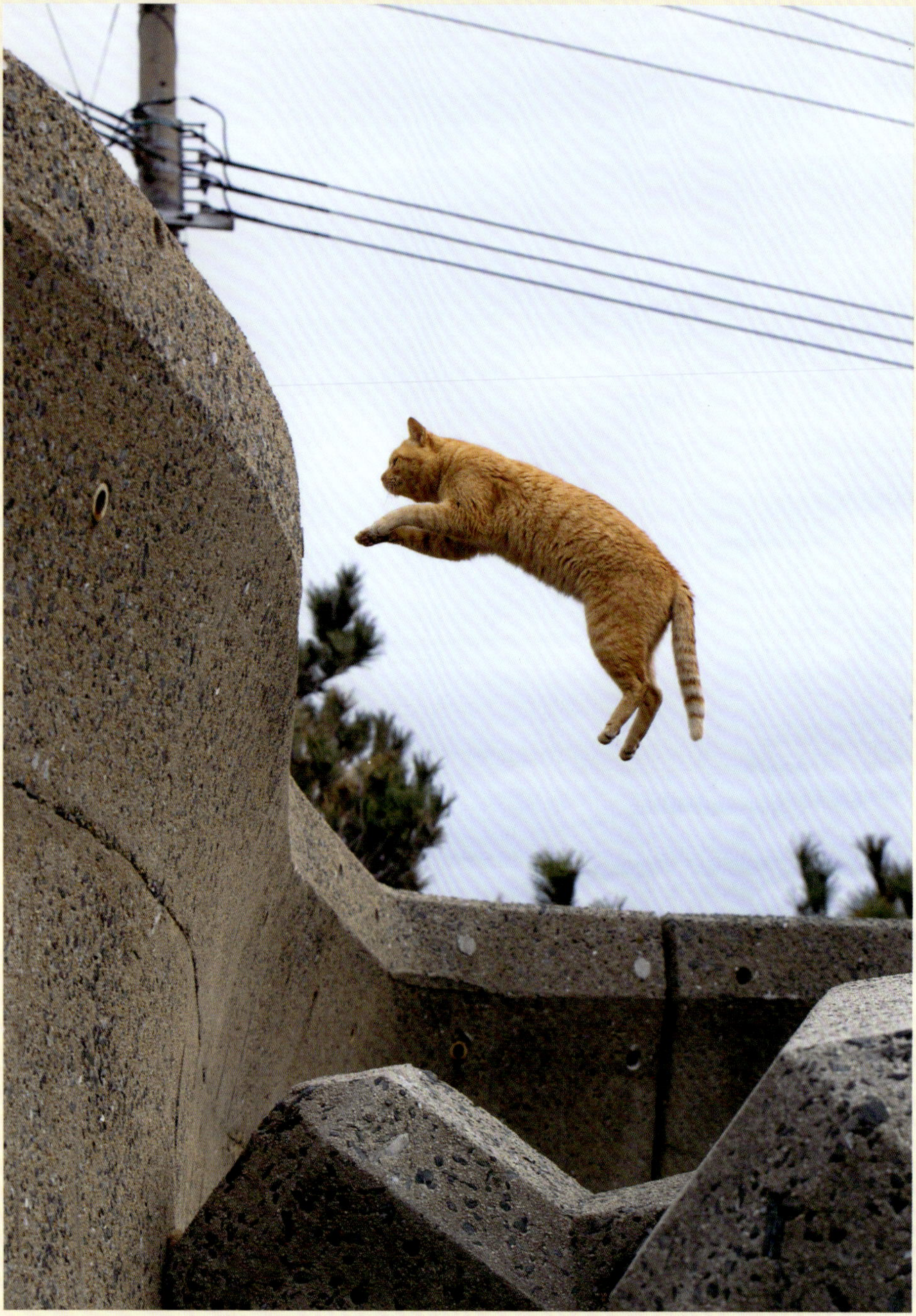

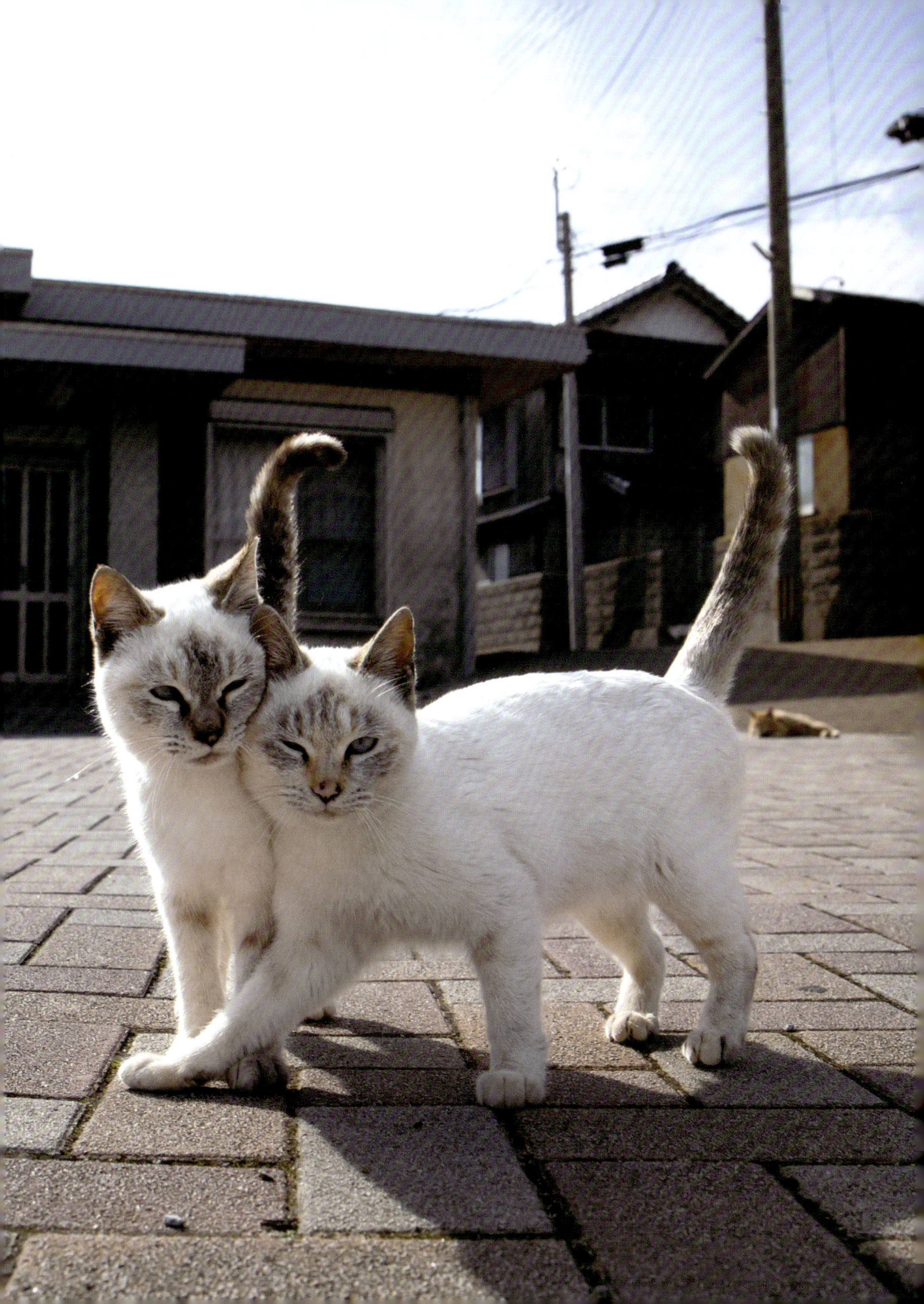

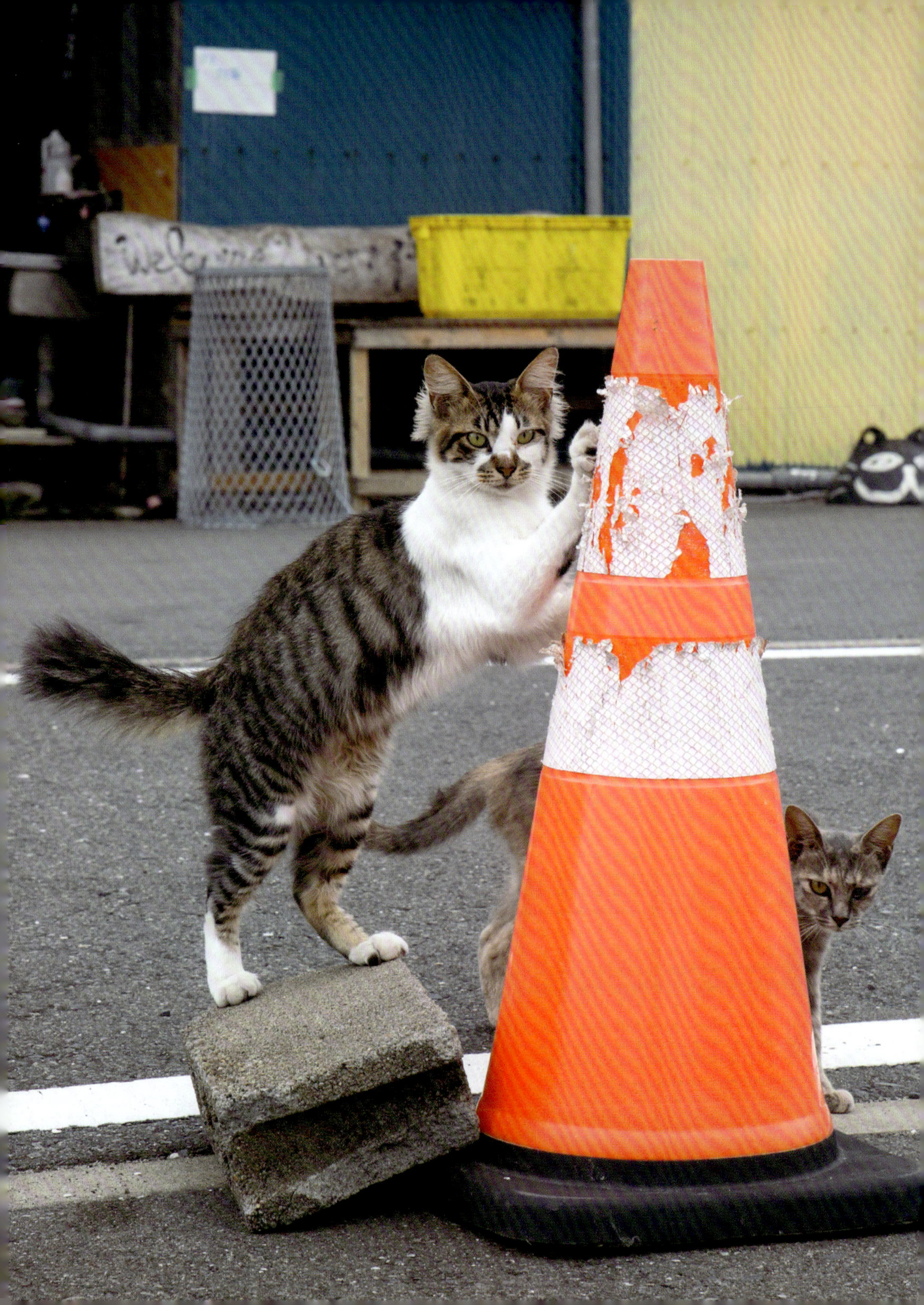

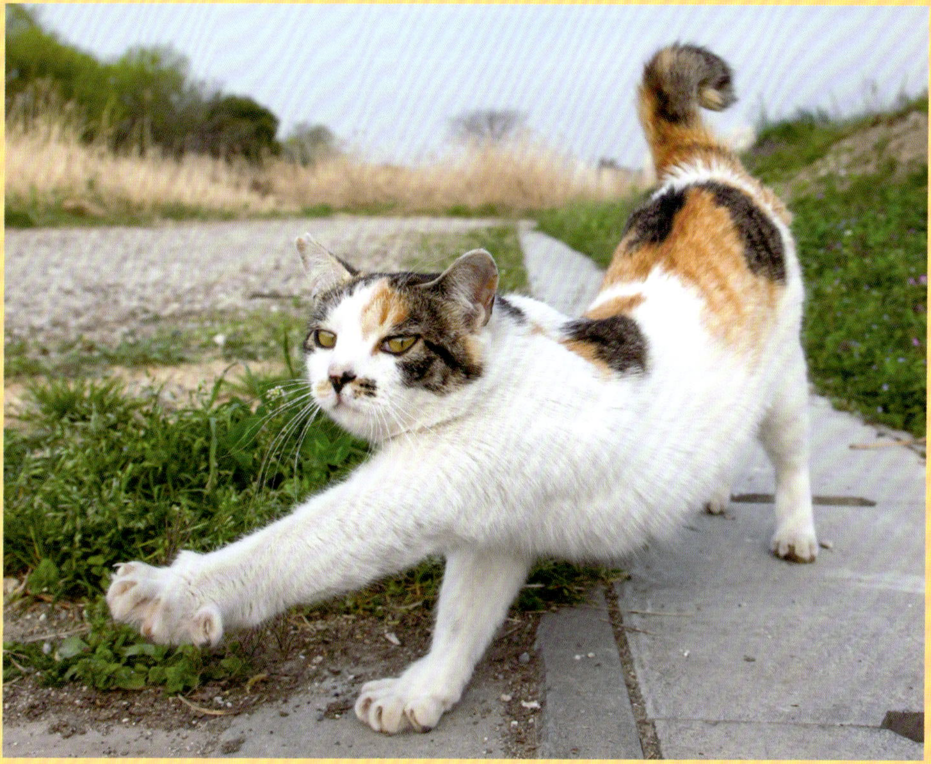

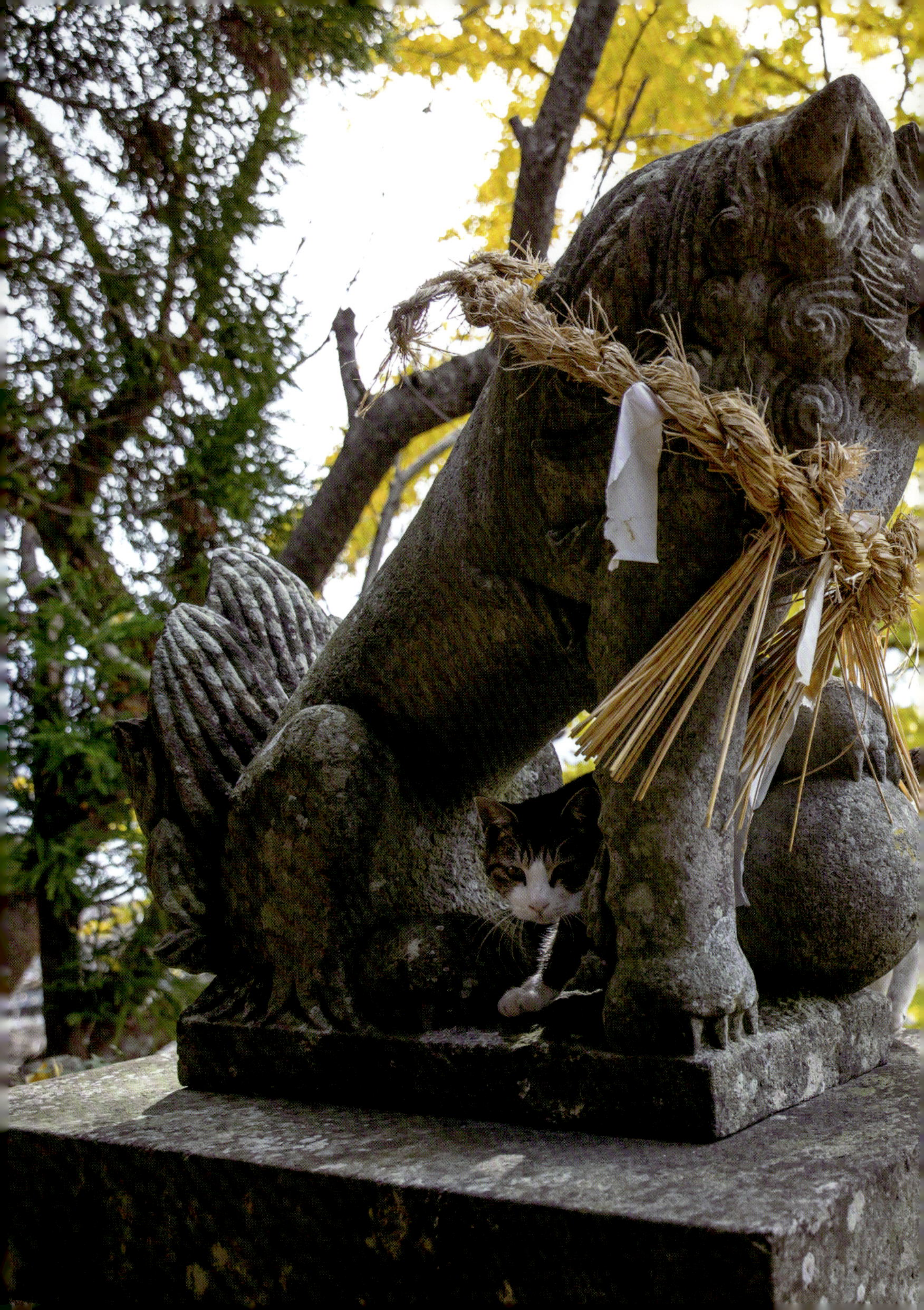

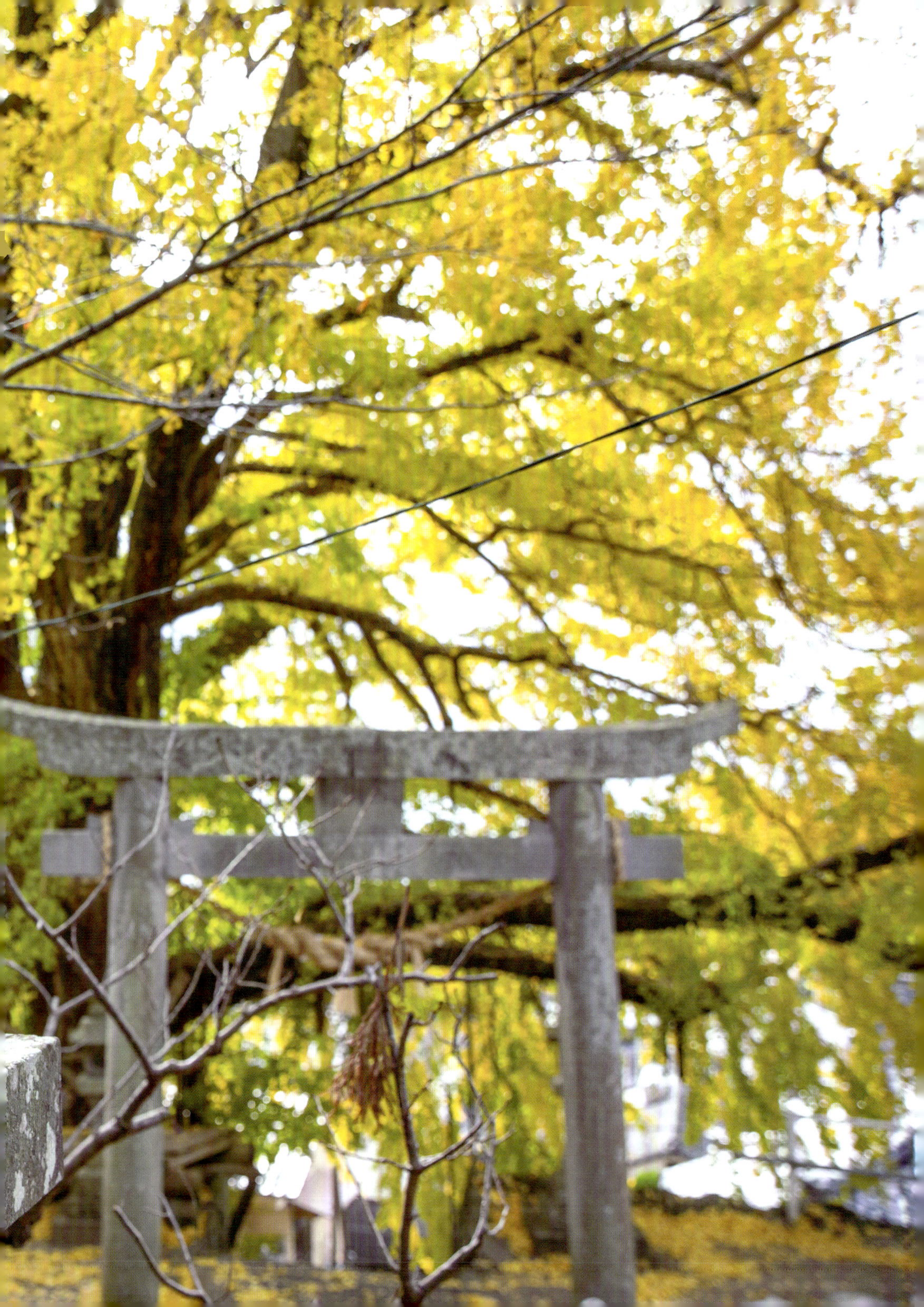

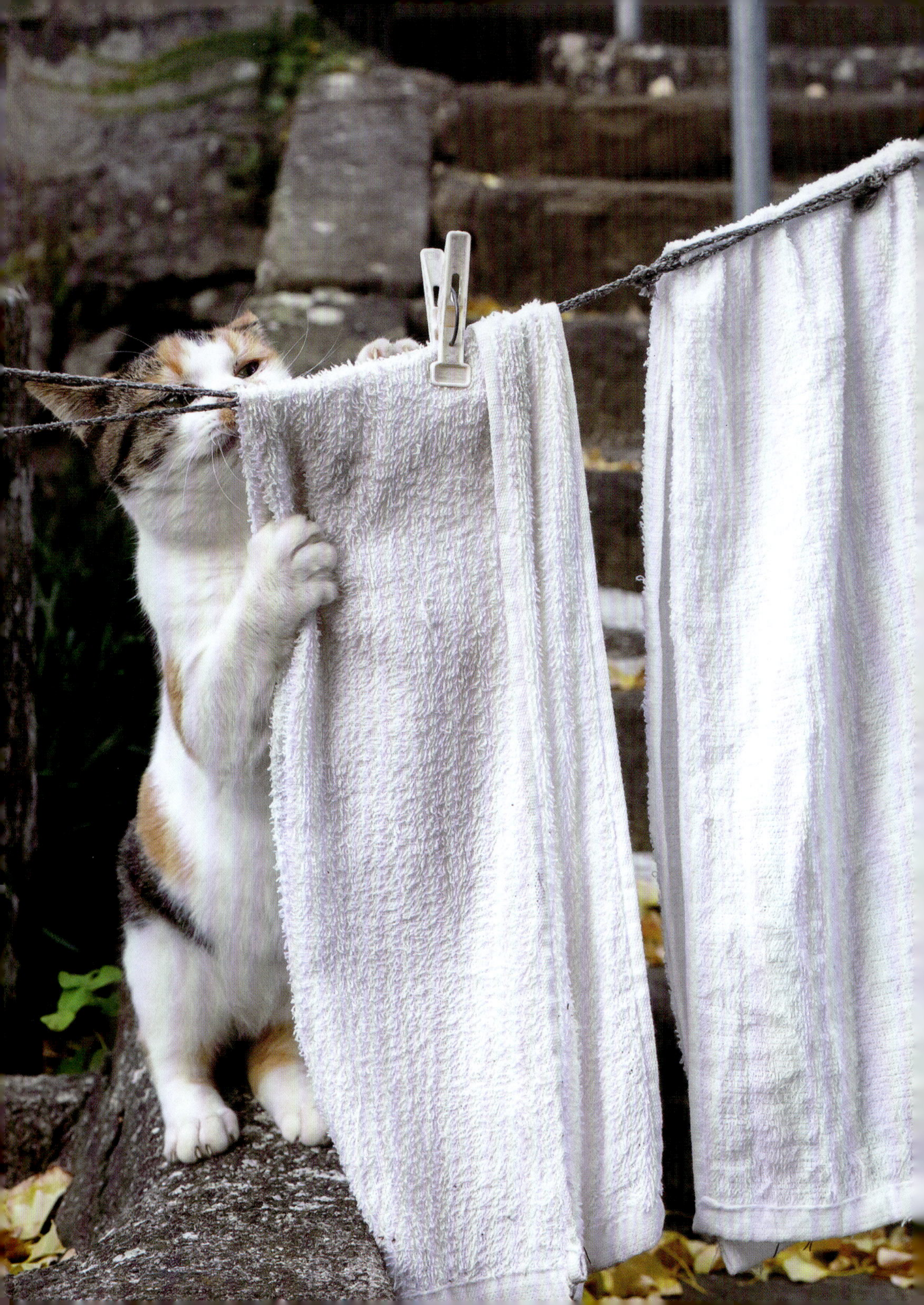

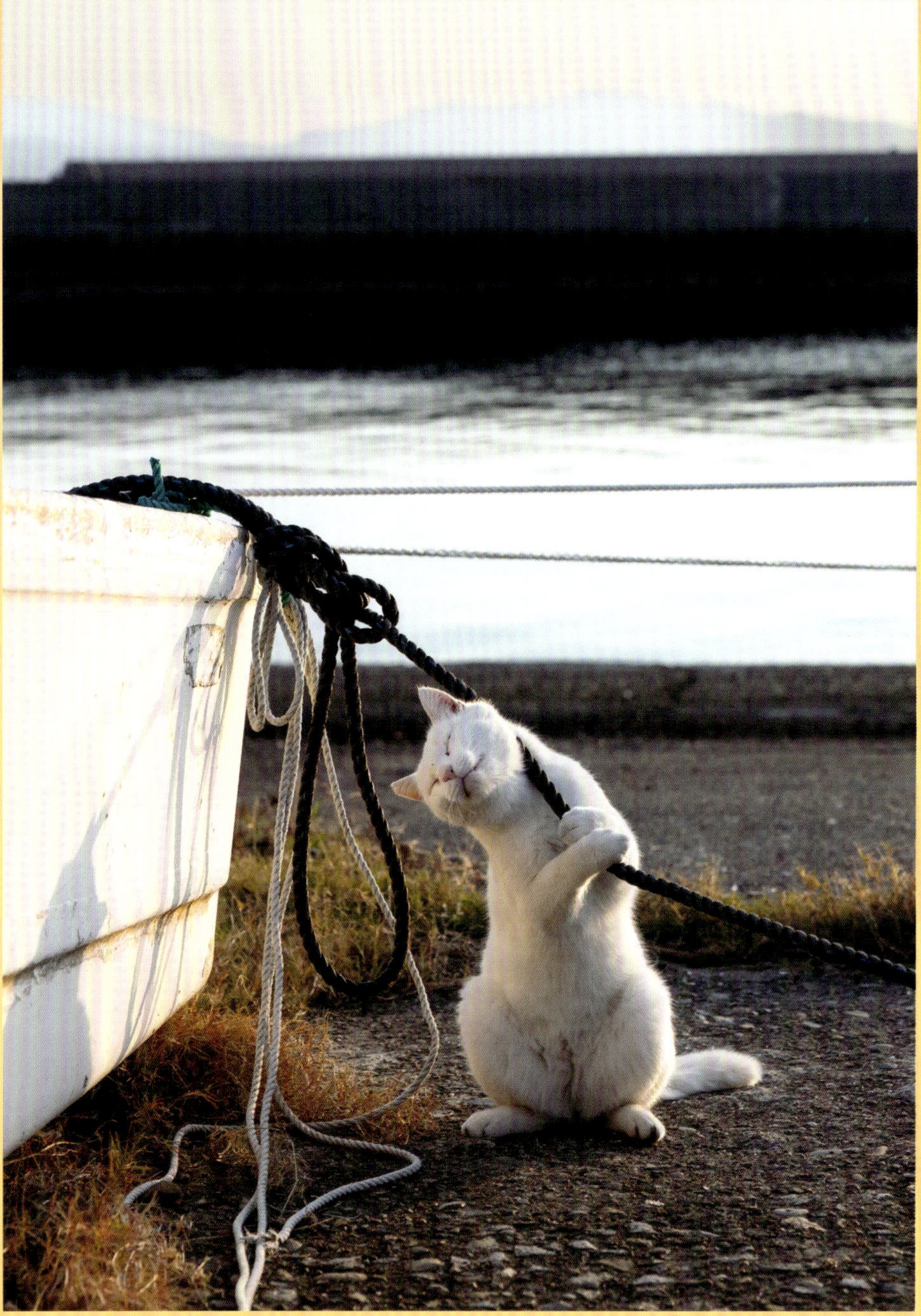

猫・ネコ

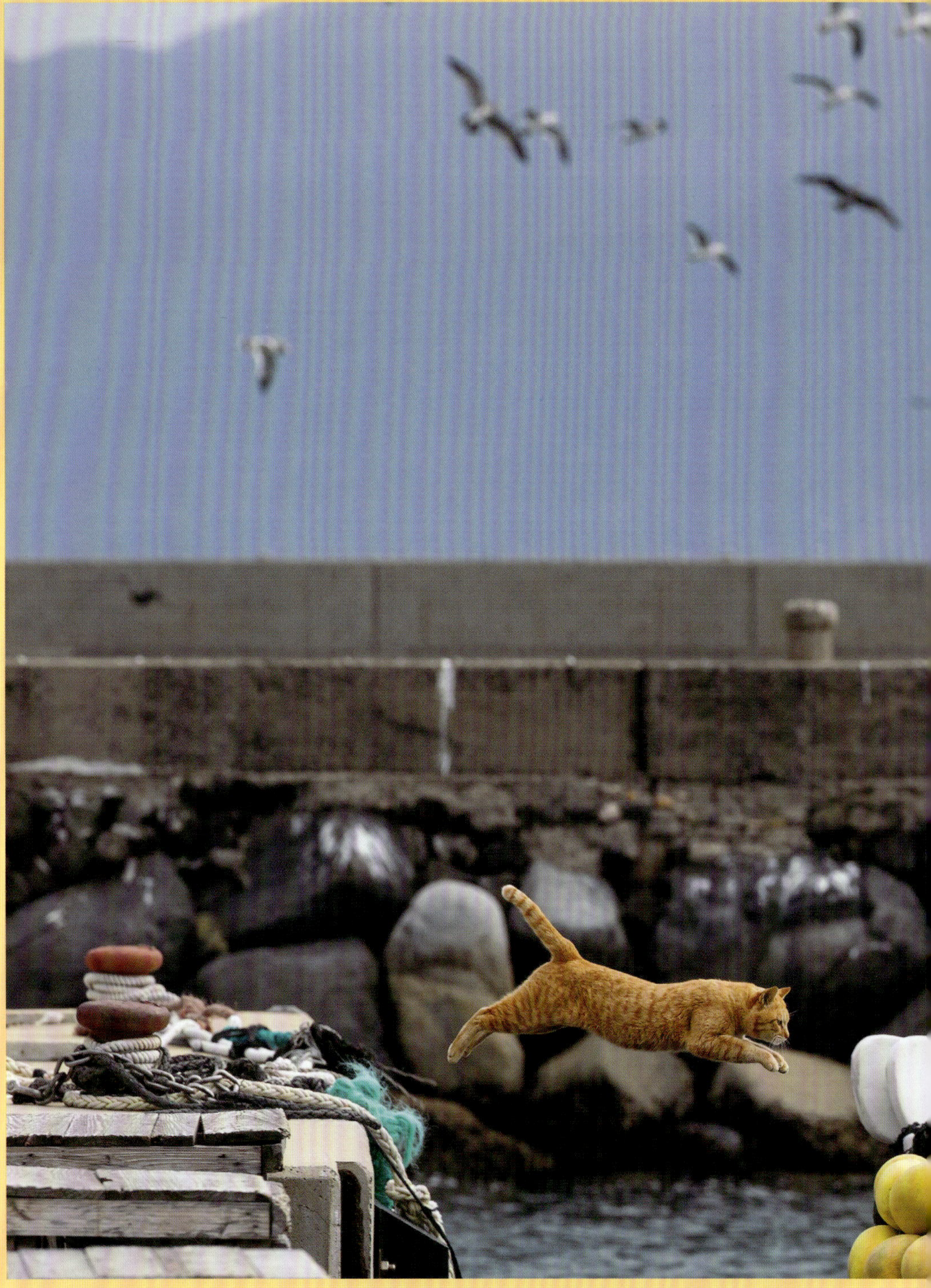

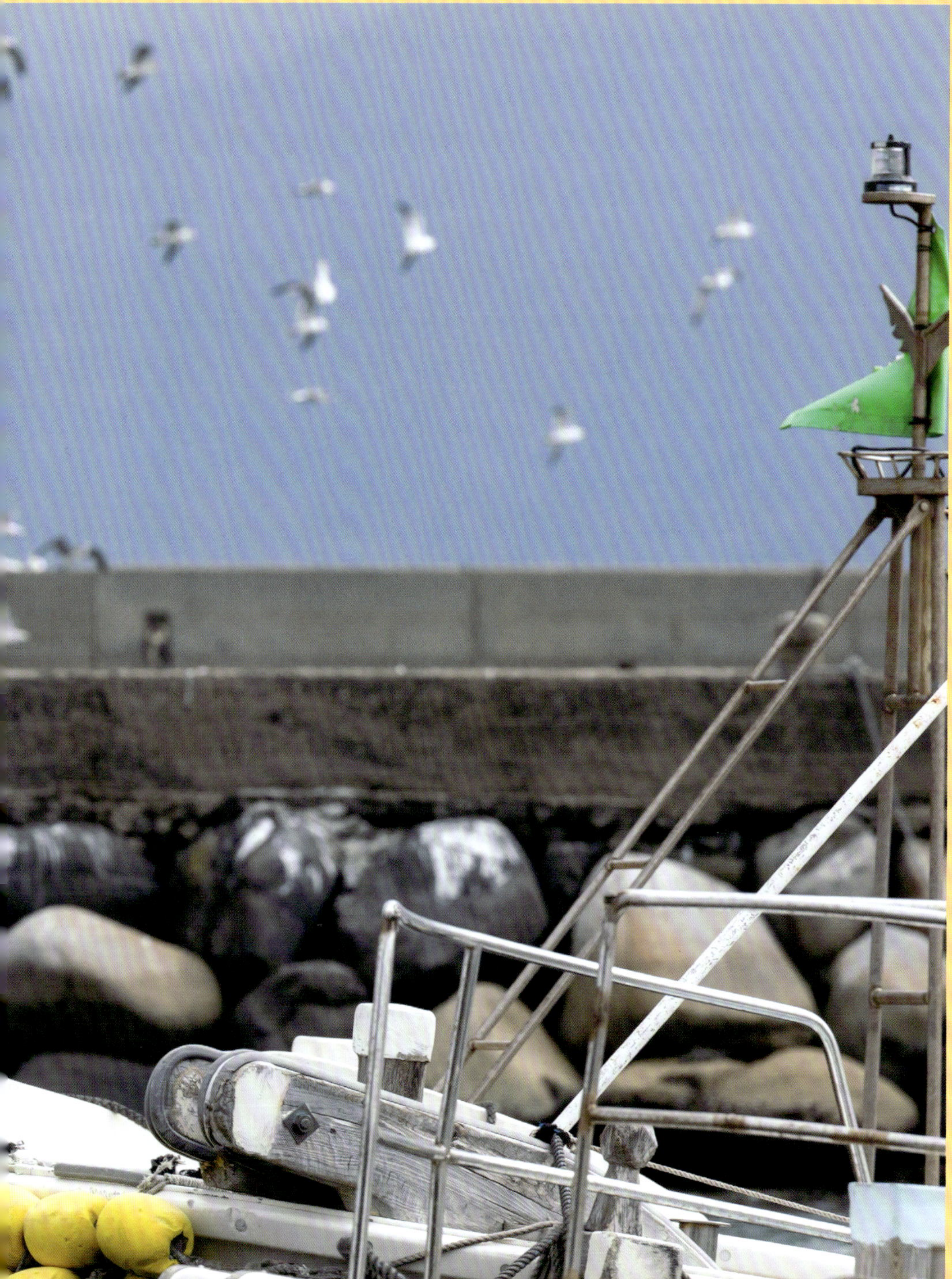

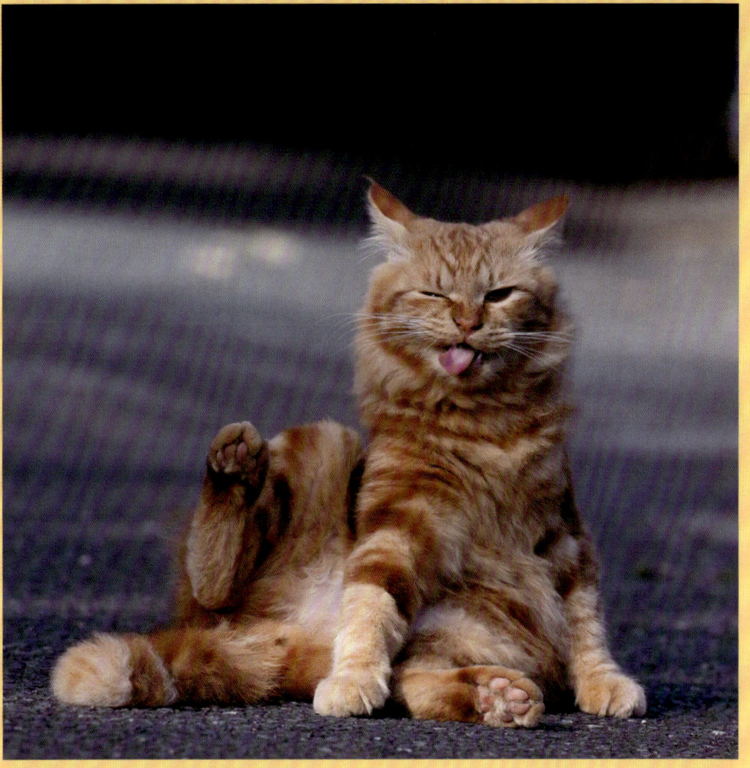

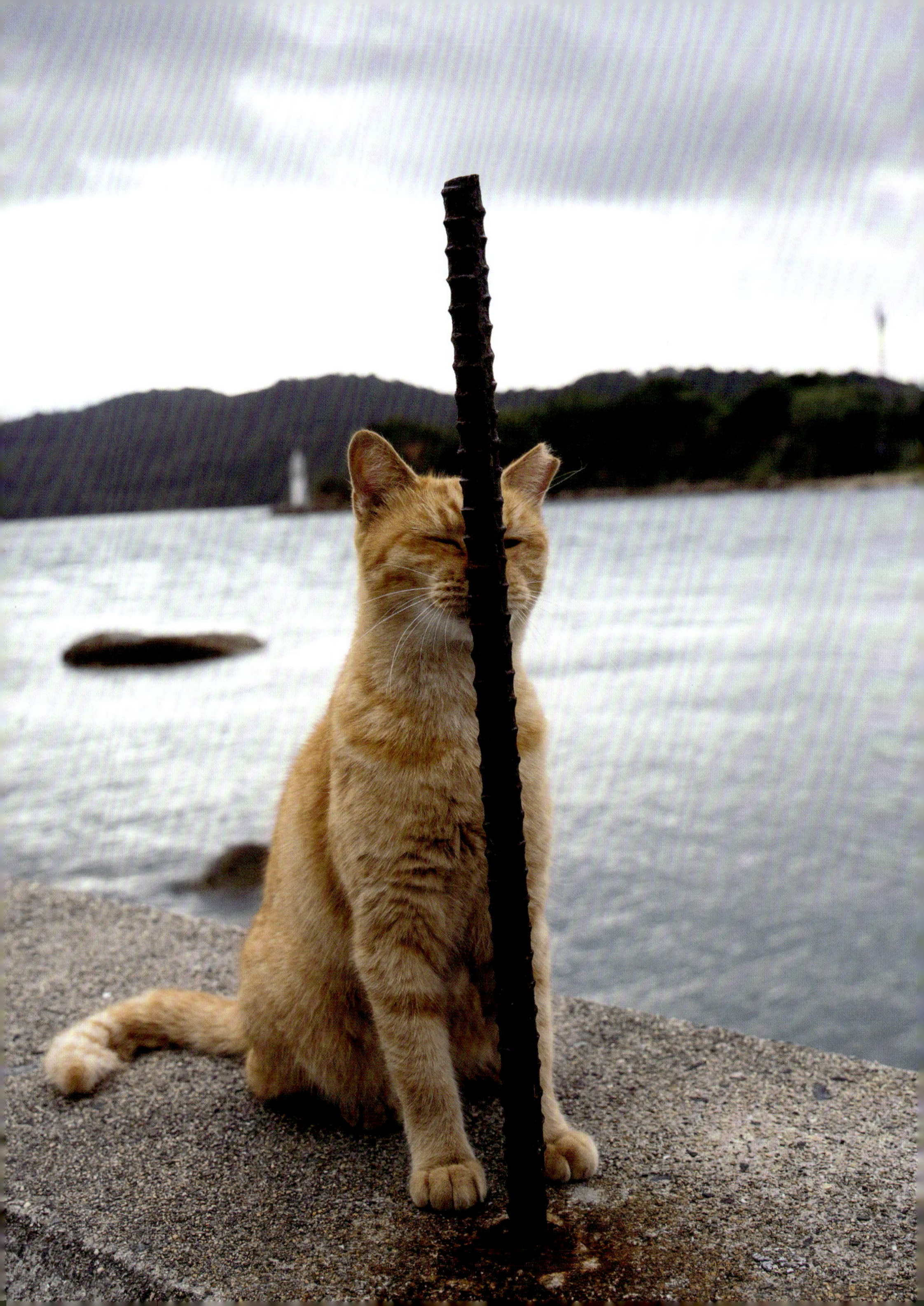

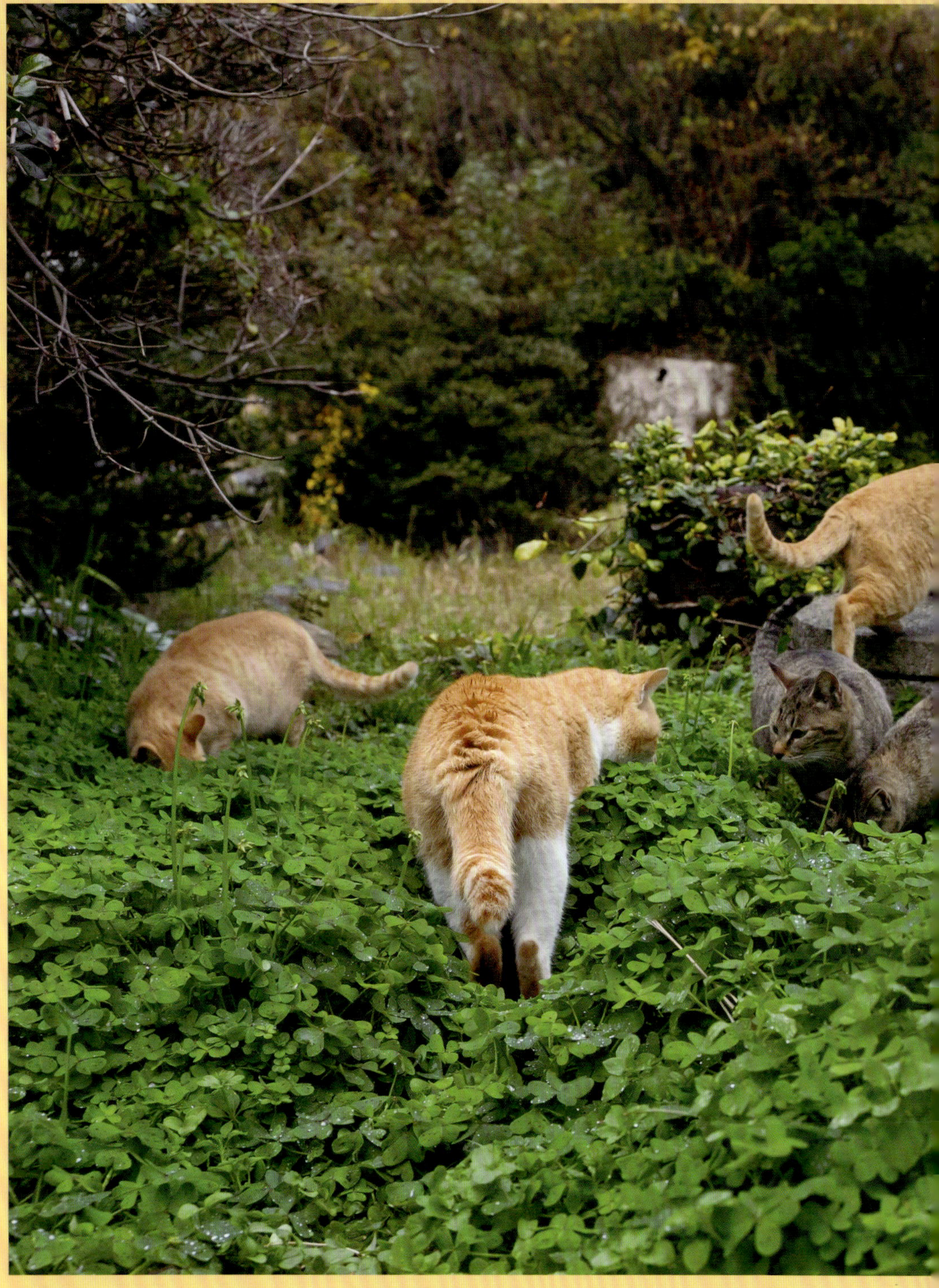

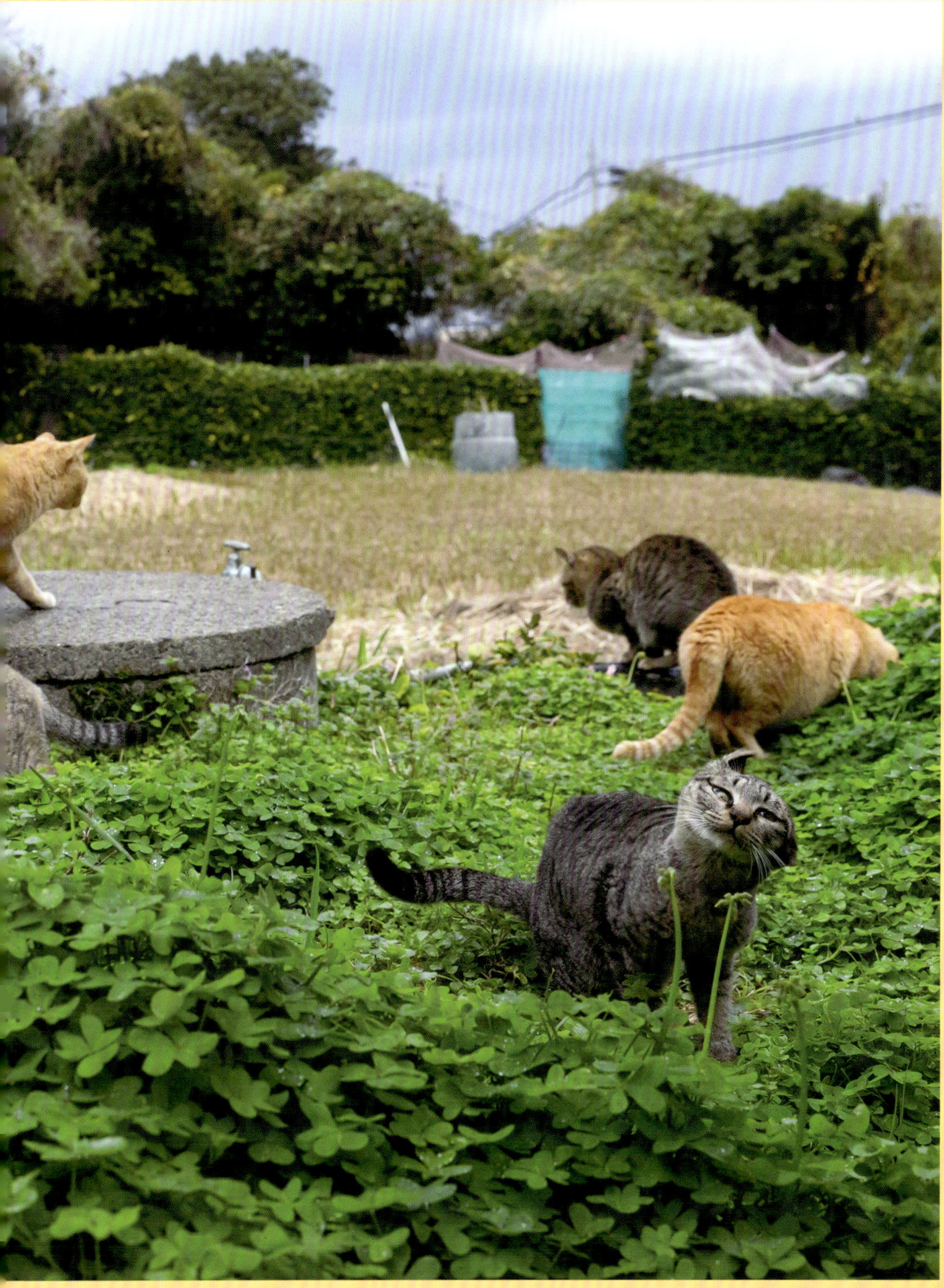

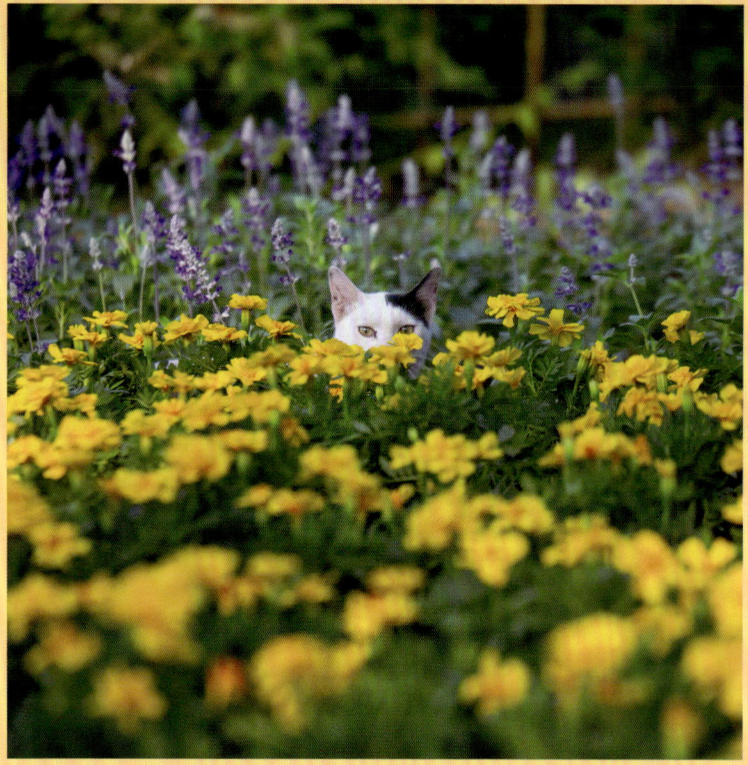

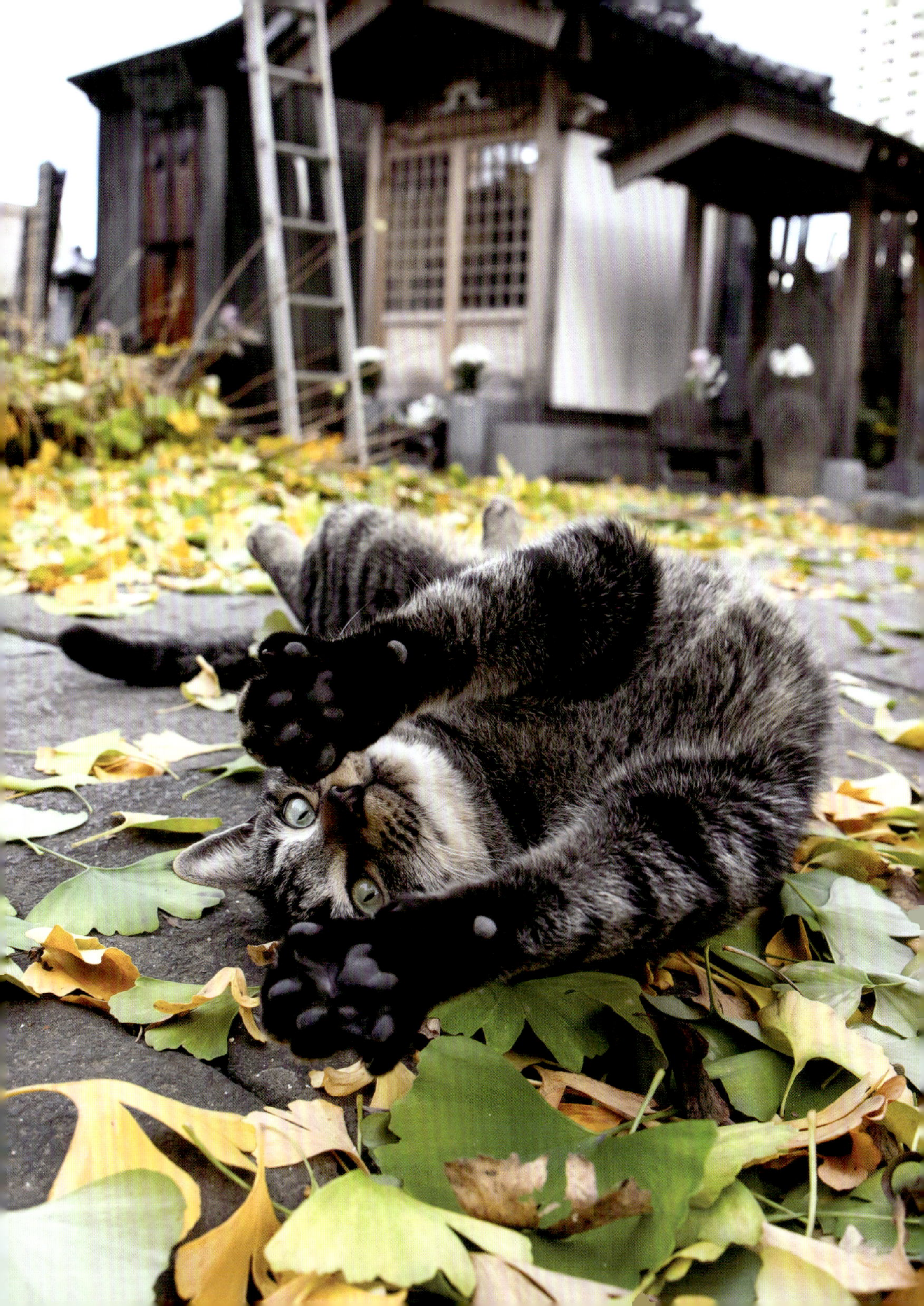

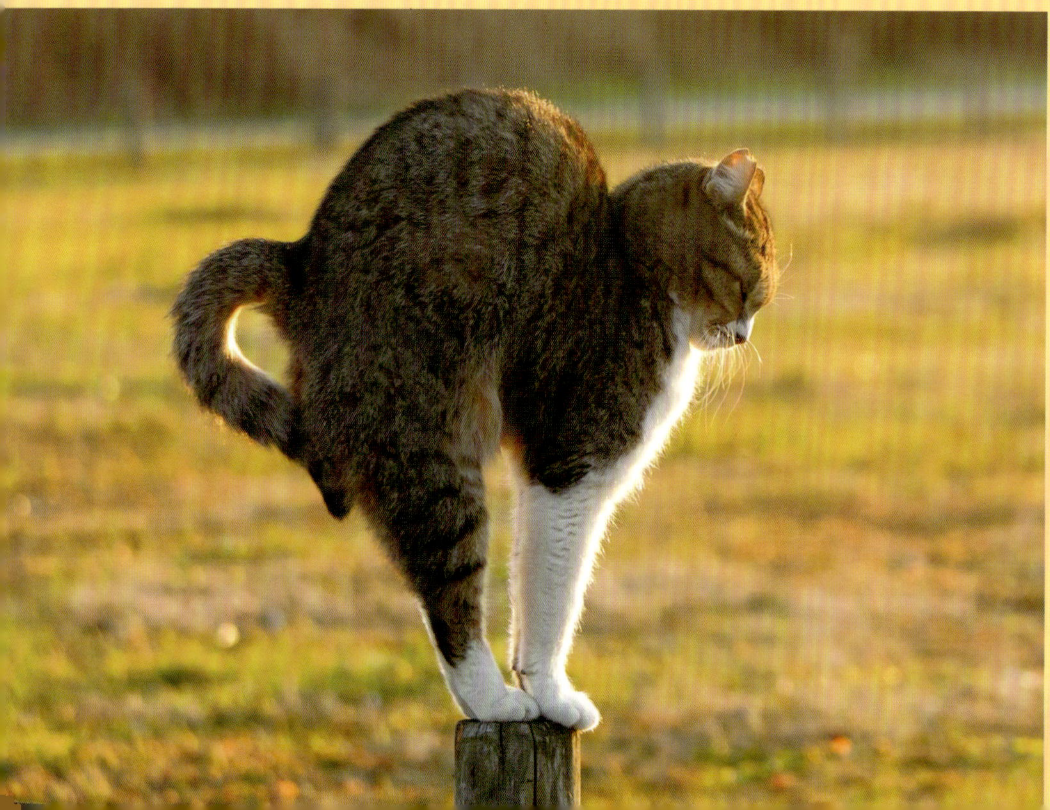

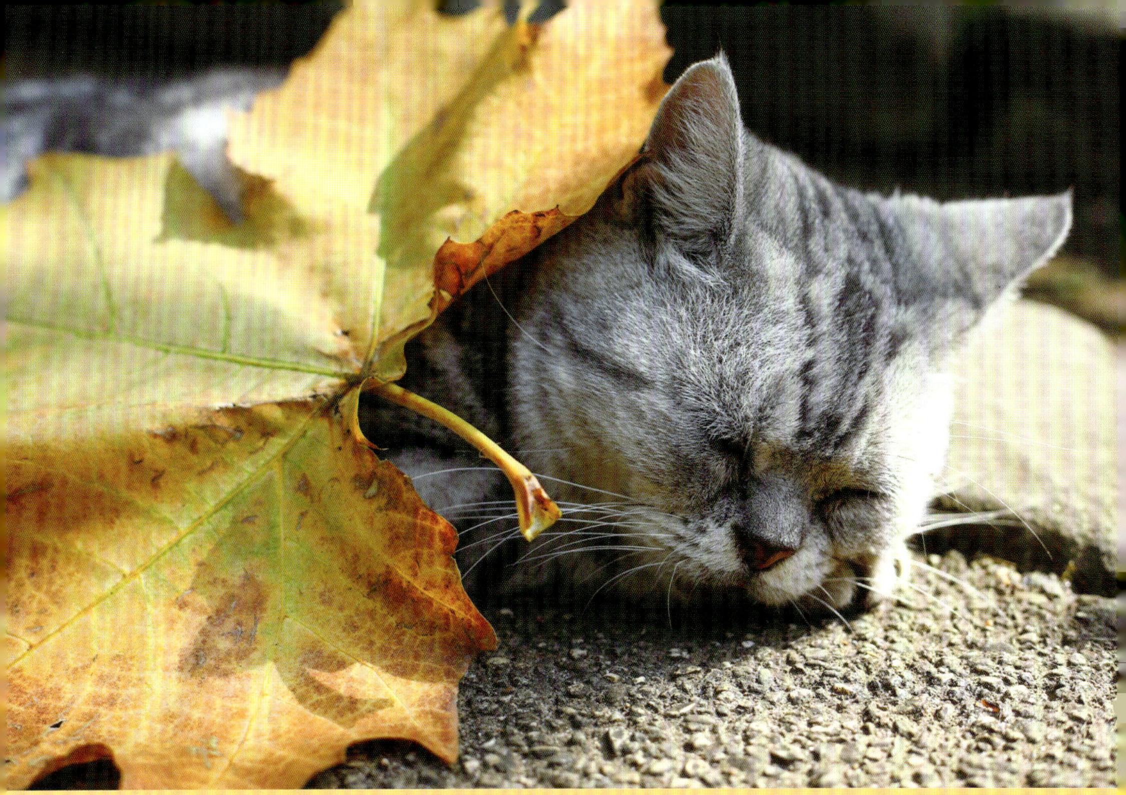

猫・ネコ

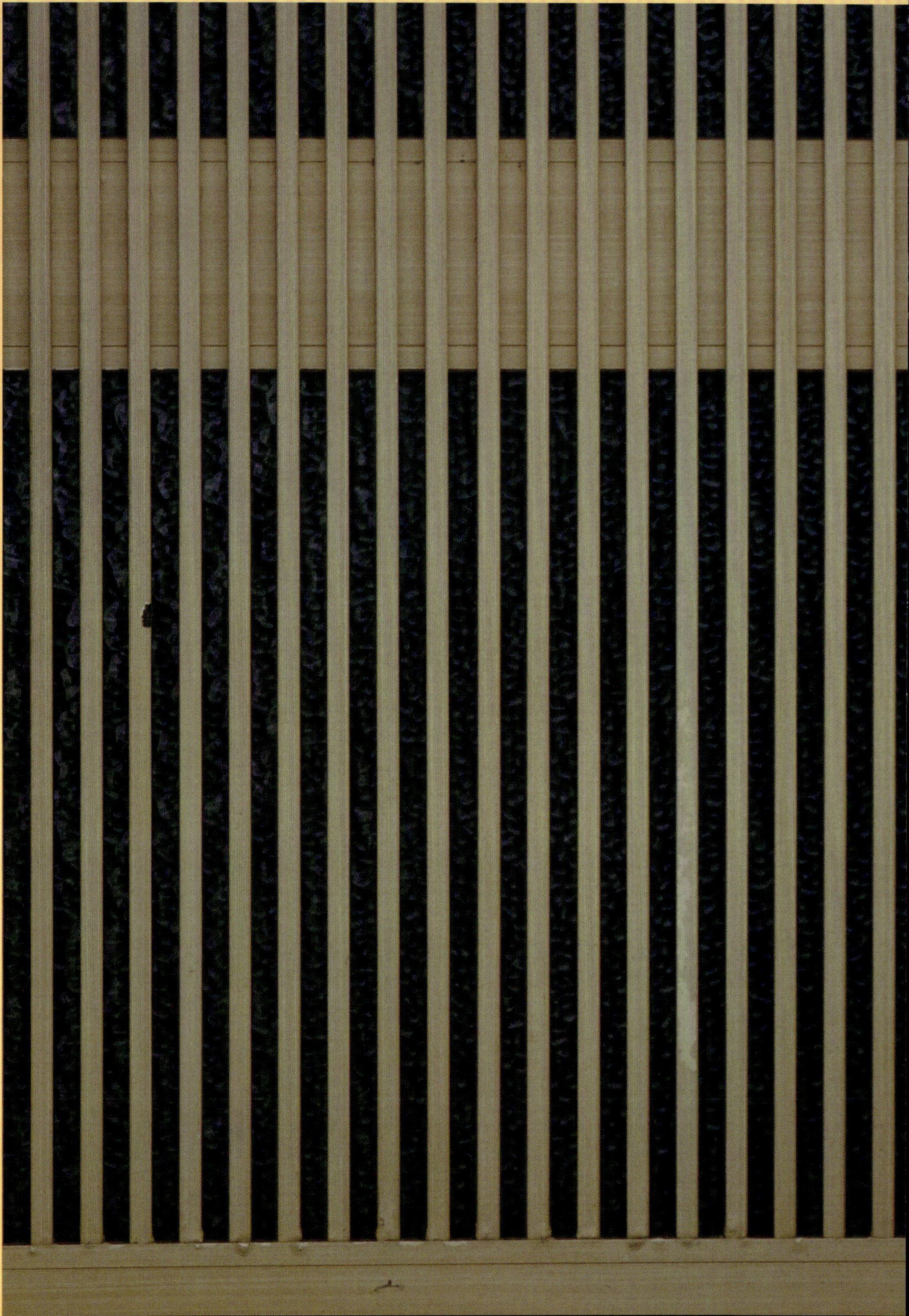

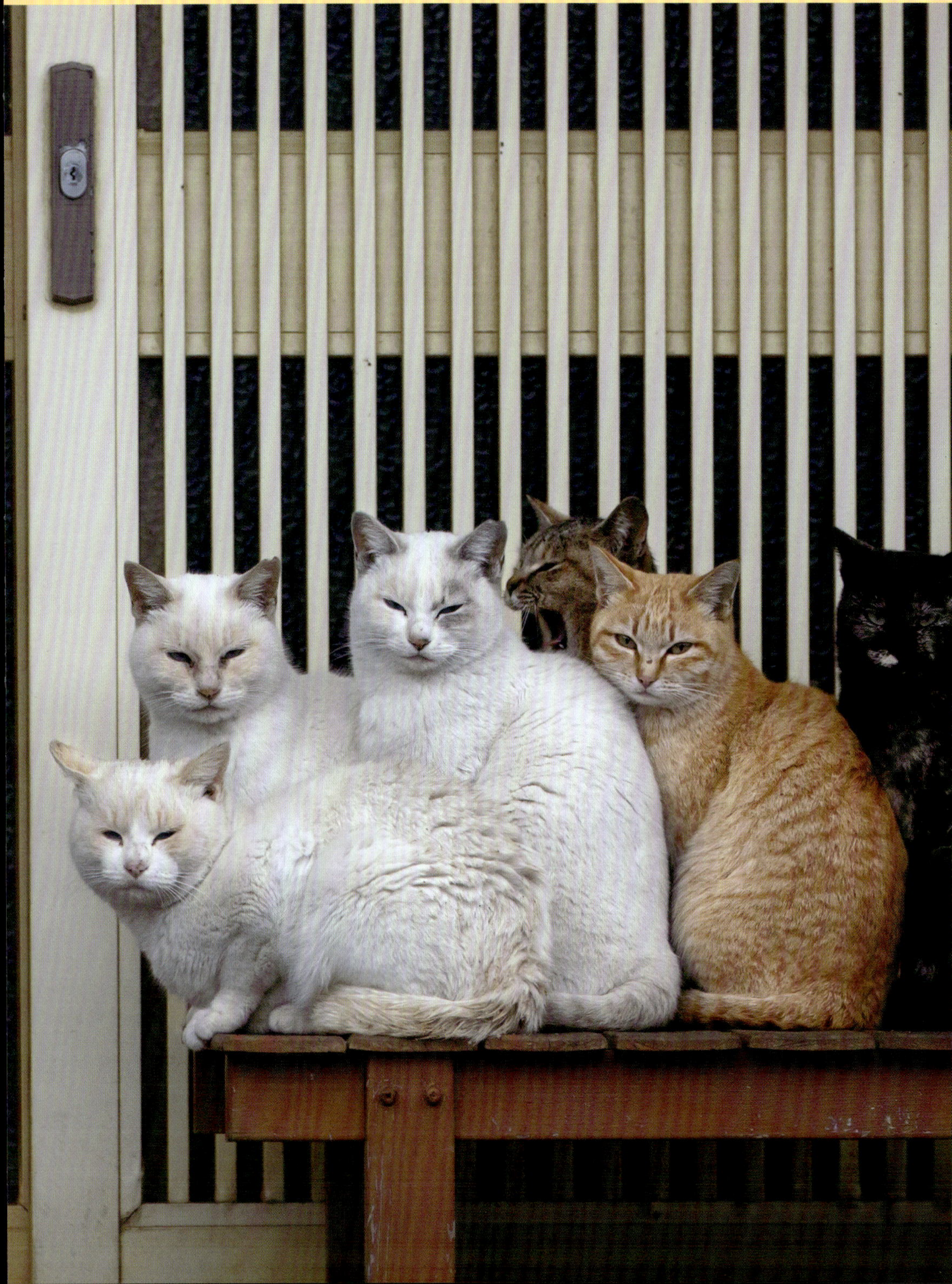

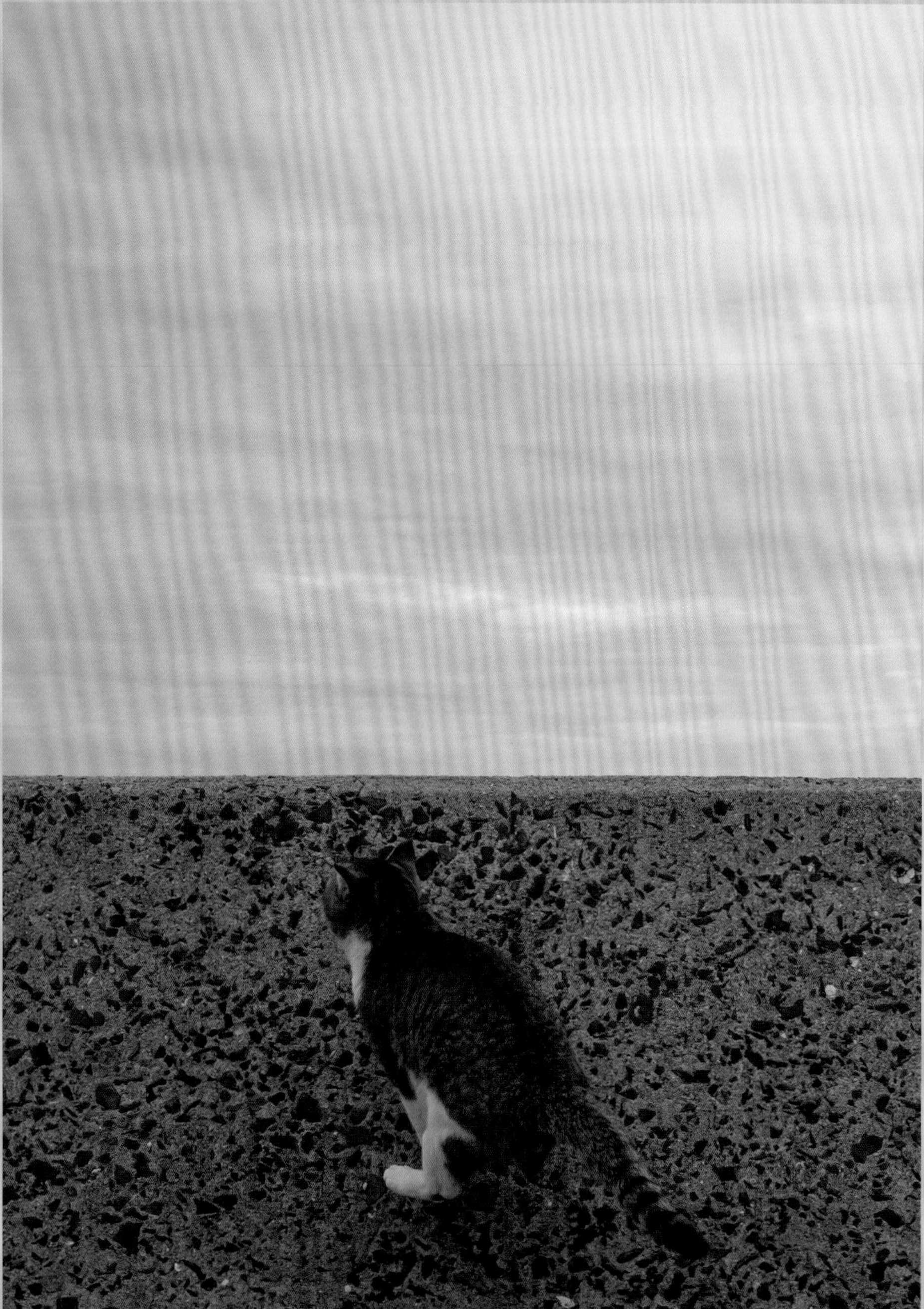

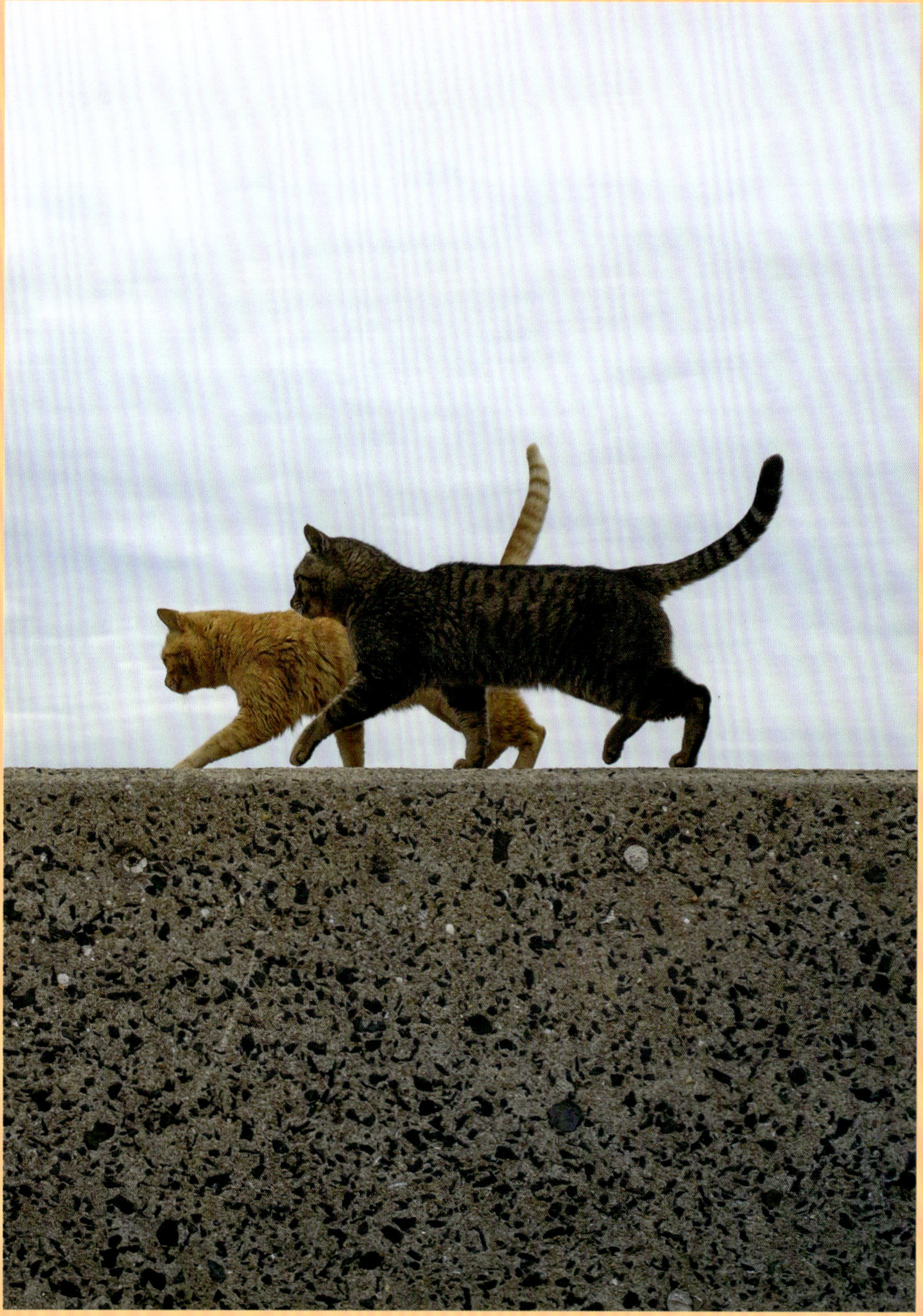

猫・ネコ

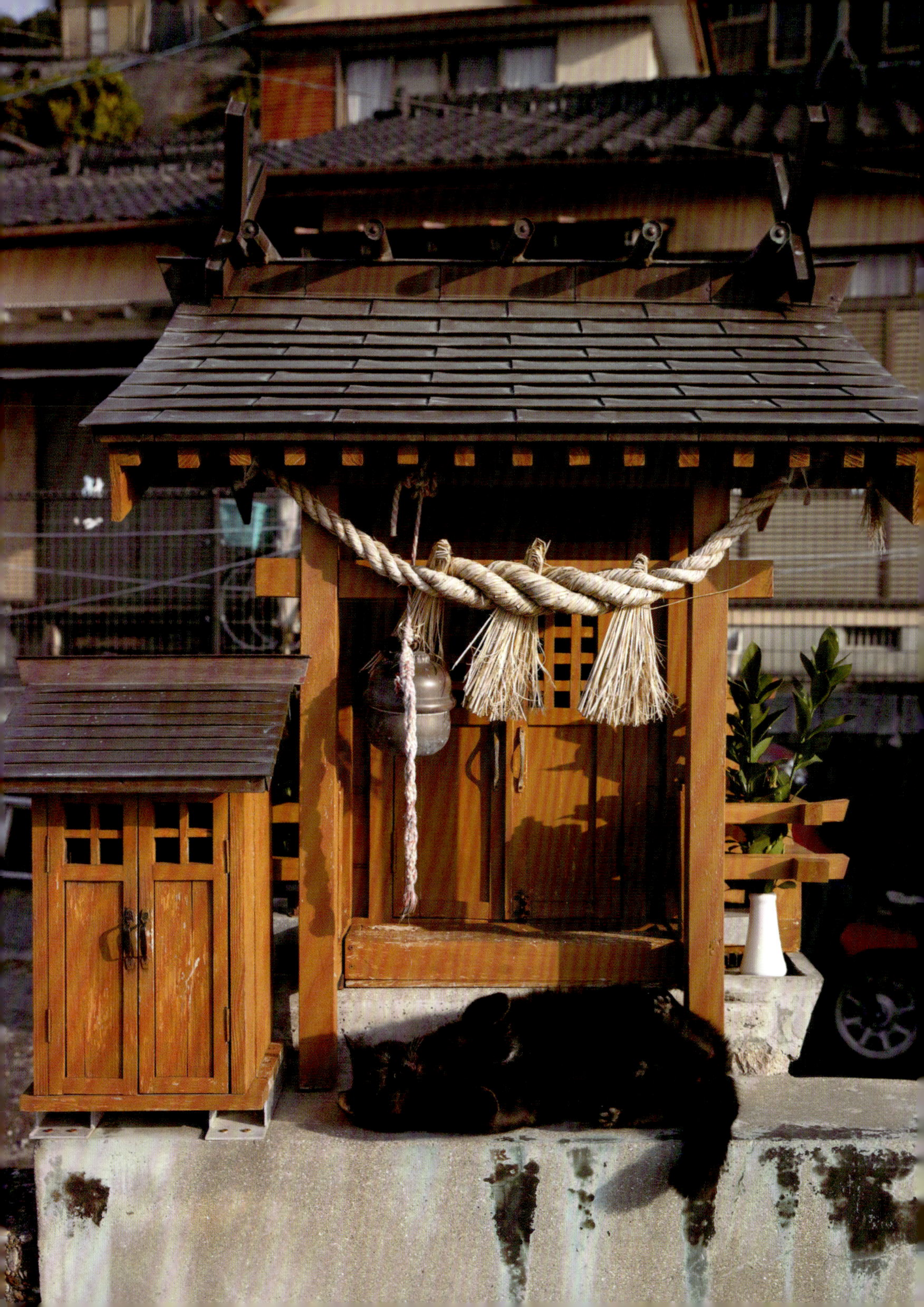

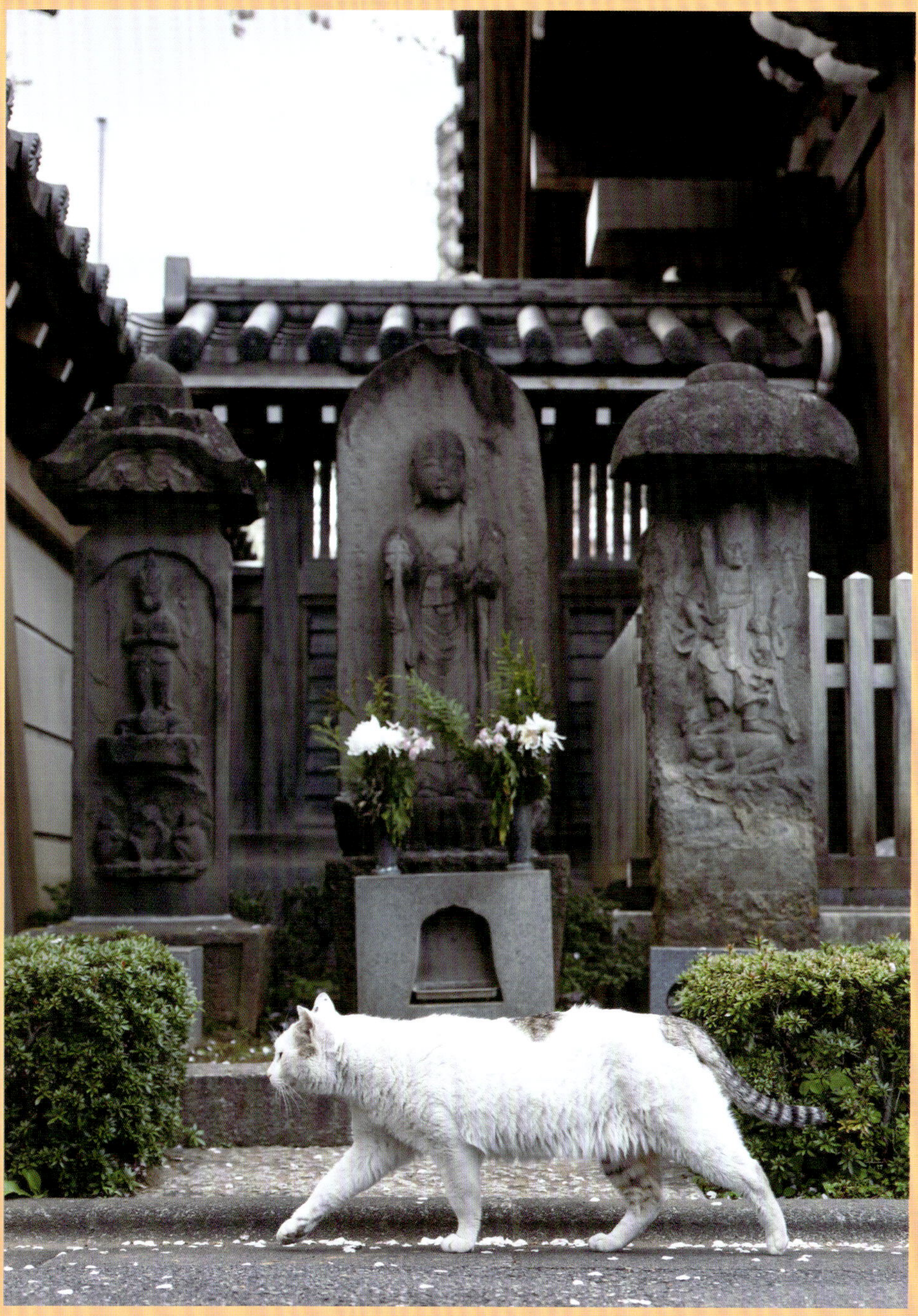

猫・ネコ

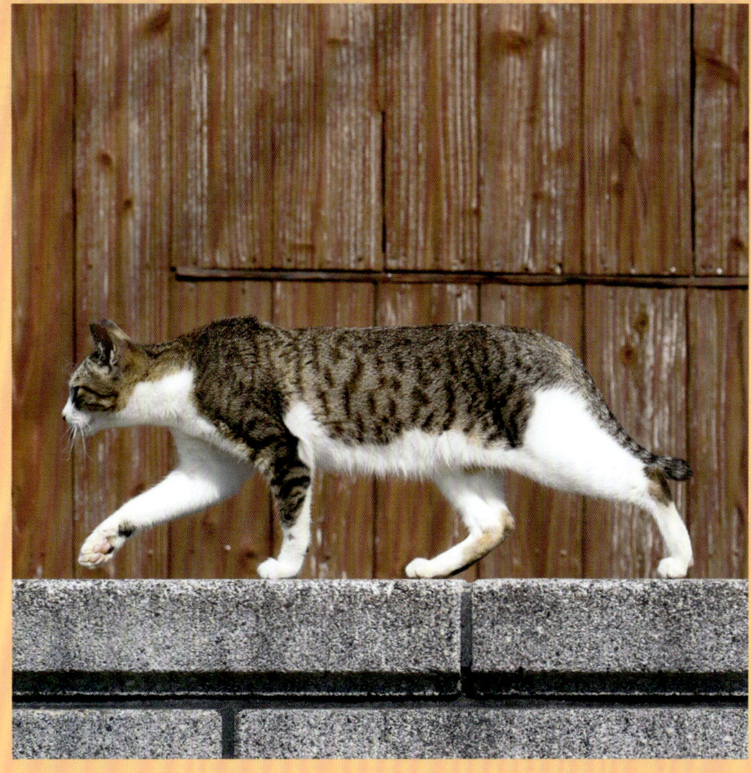

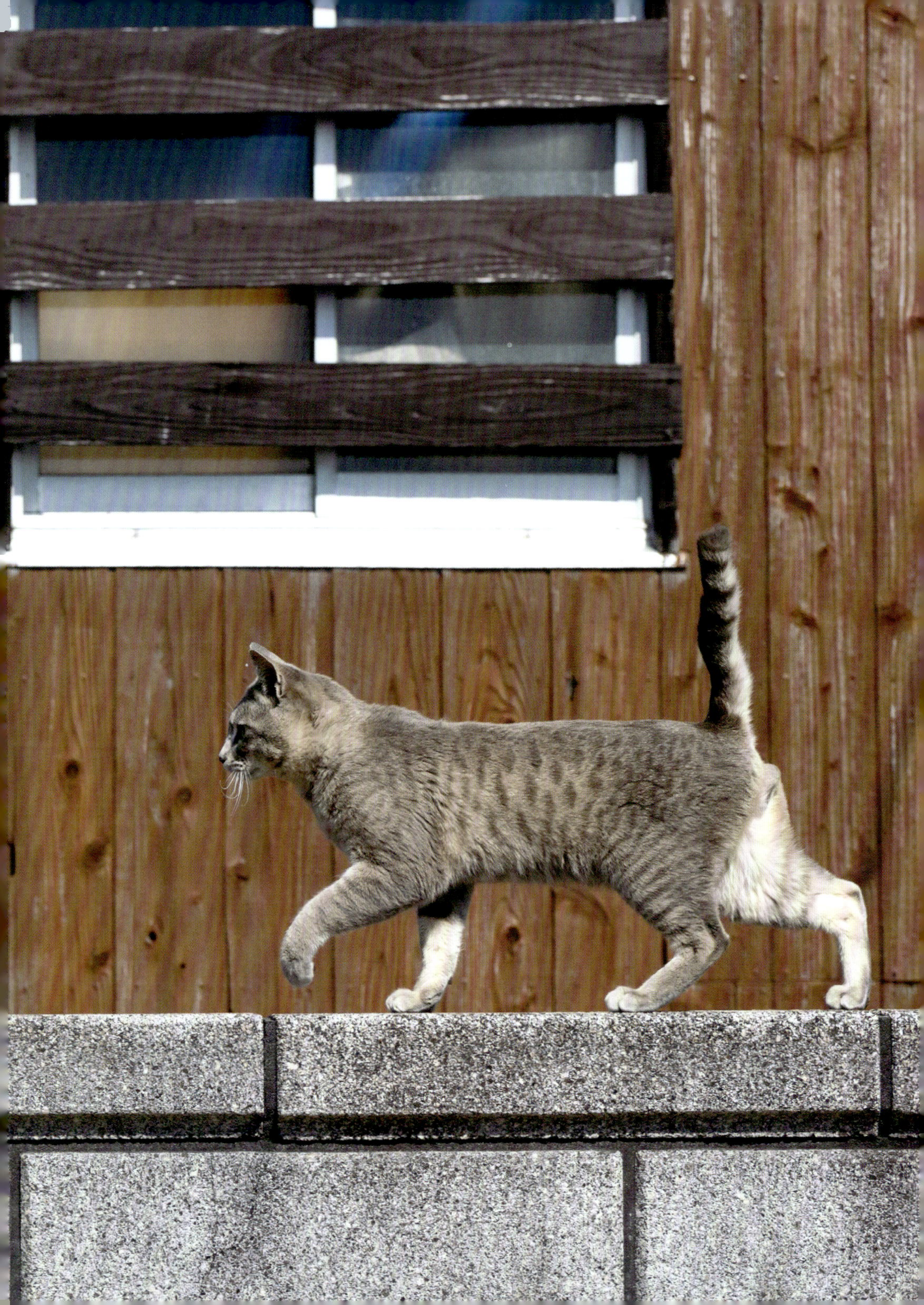

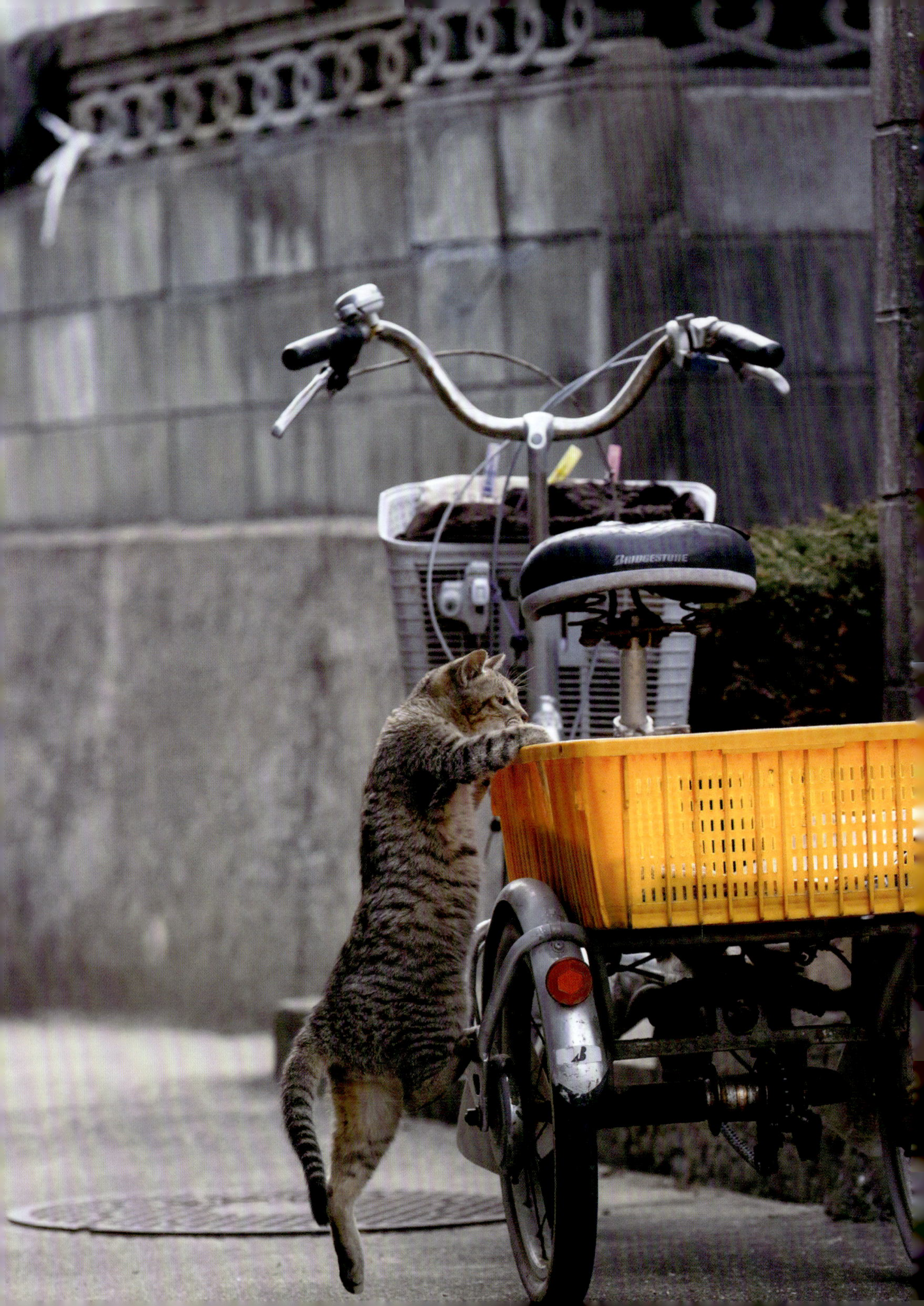
BRIDGESTONE

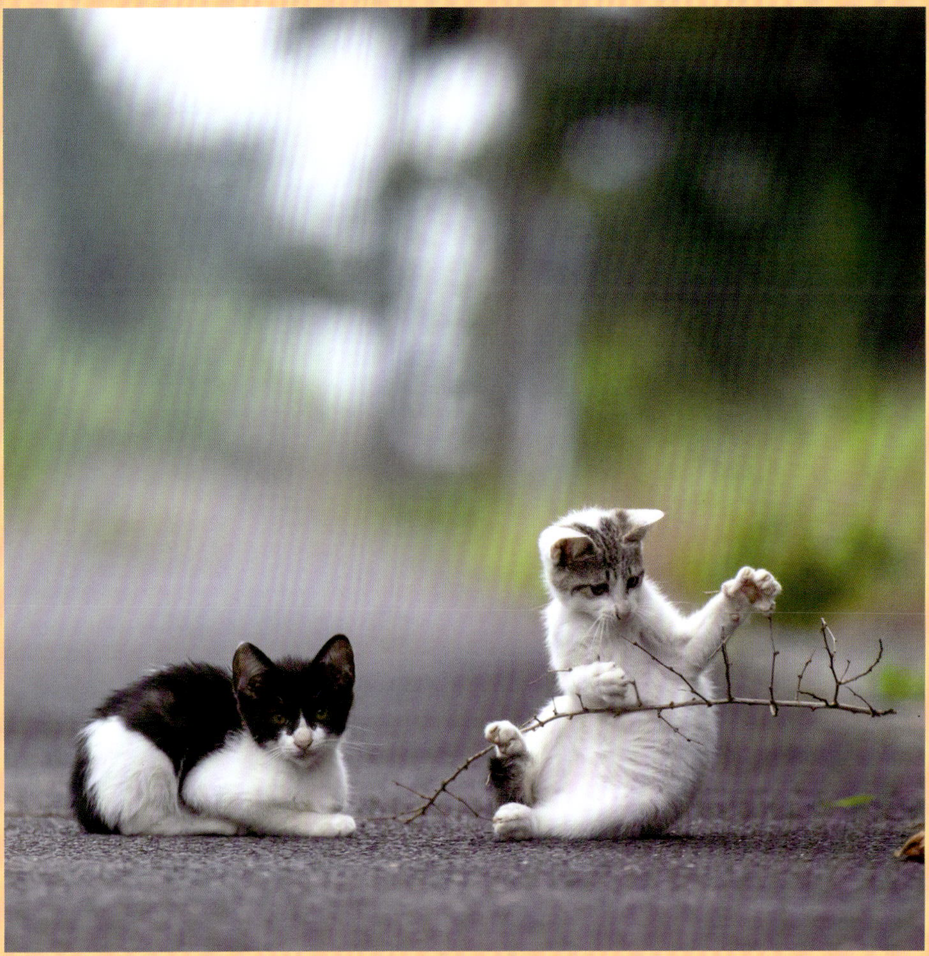

猫・ネコ

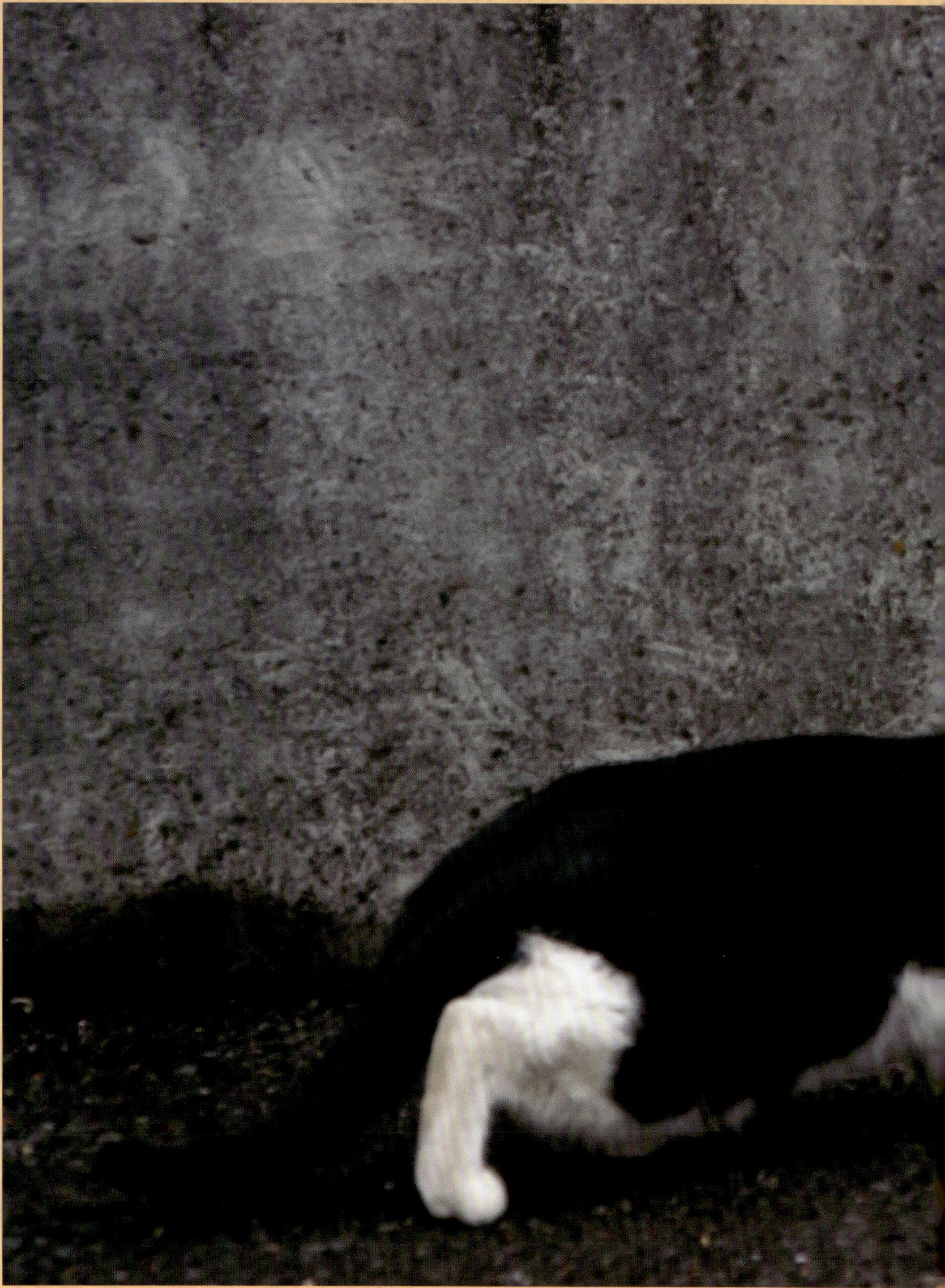

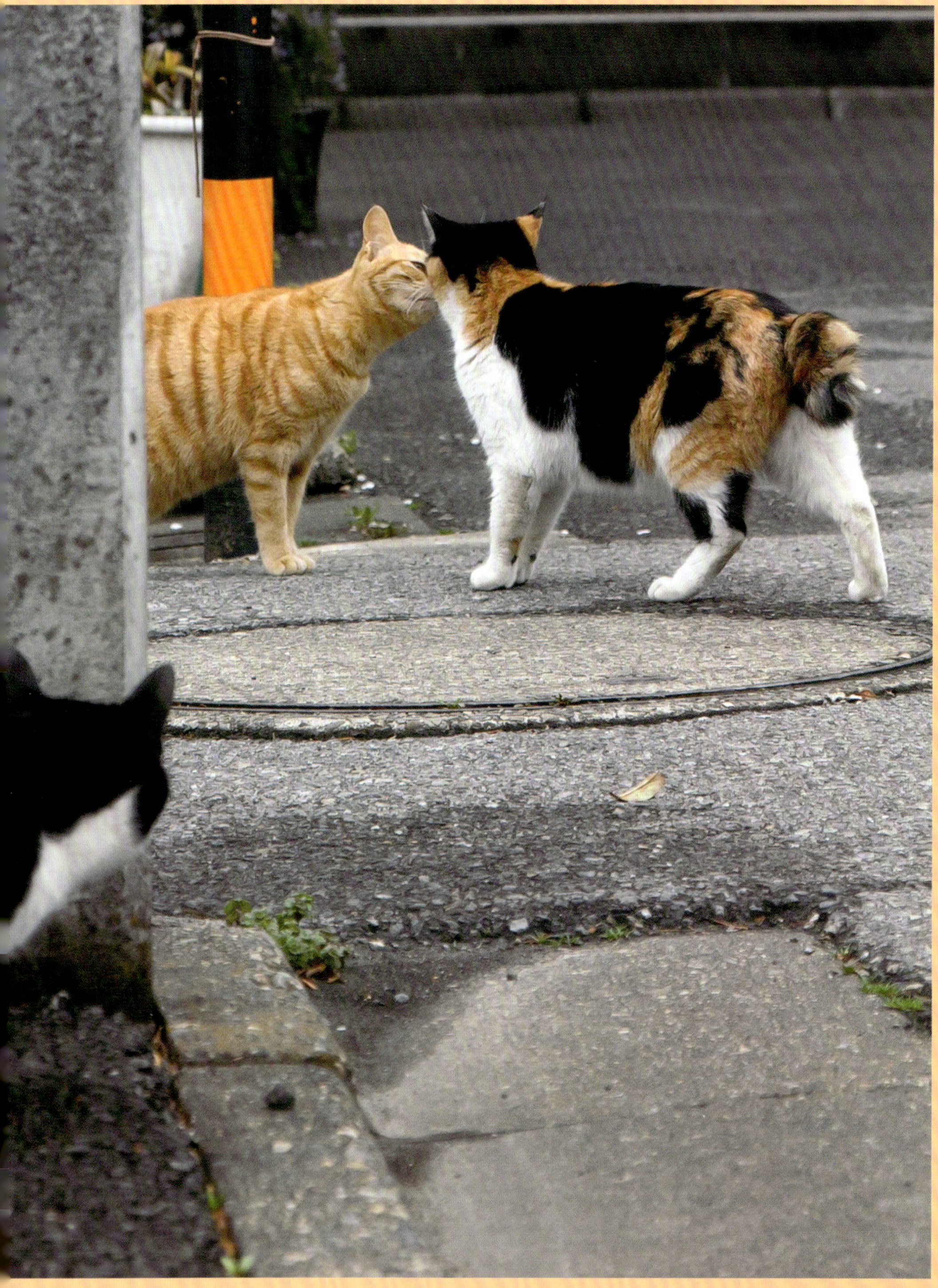

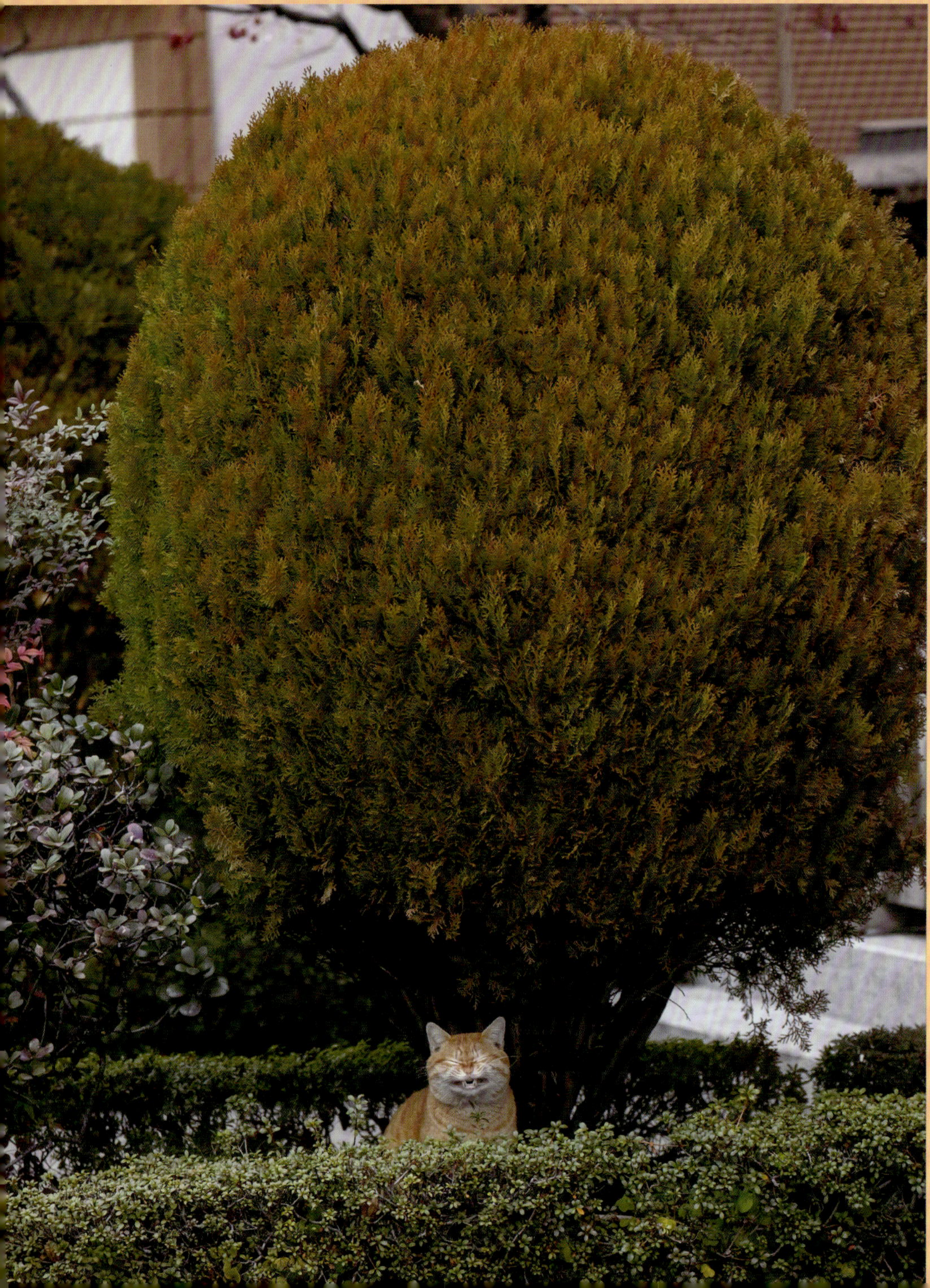

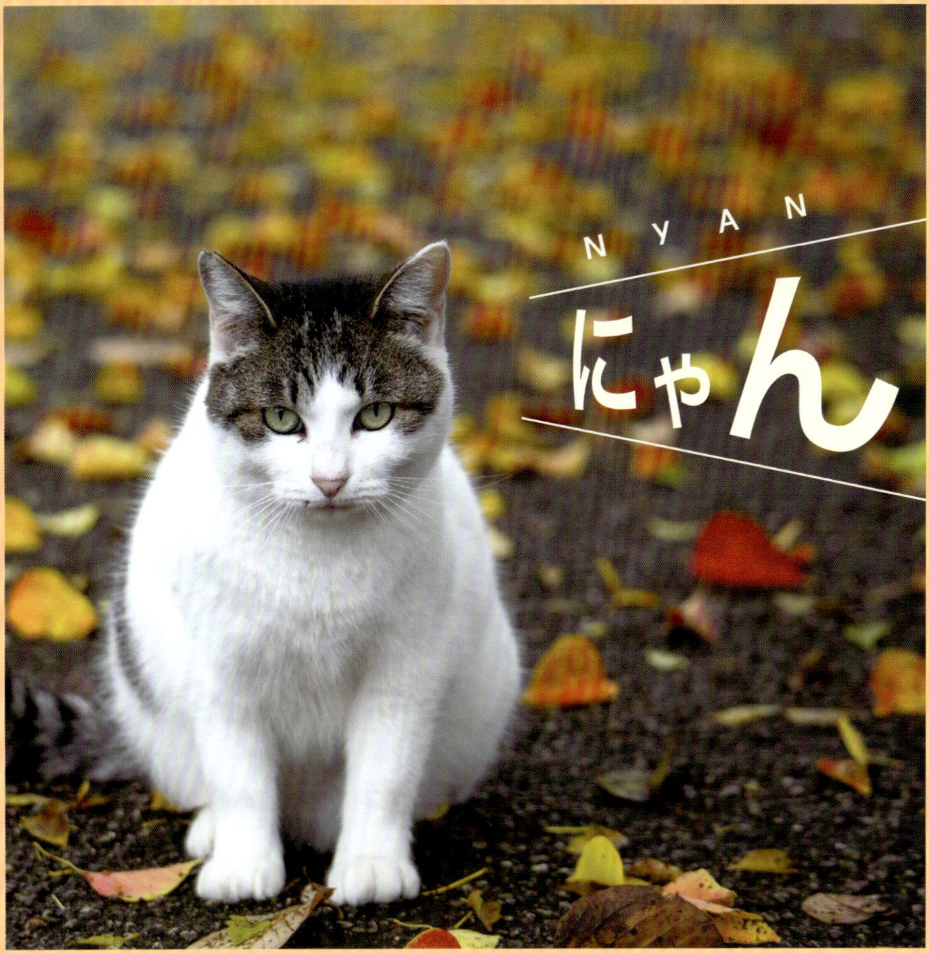

猫・ネコ

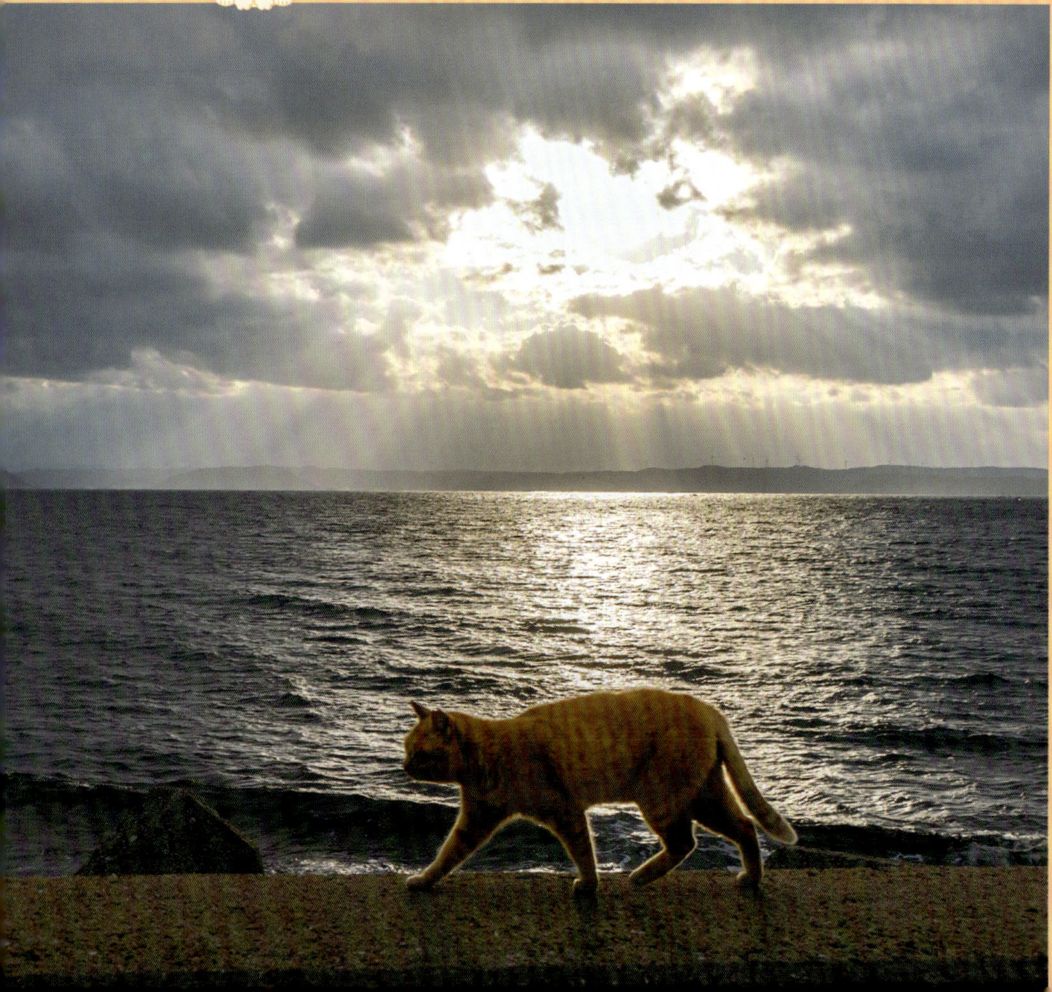

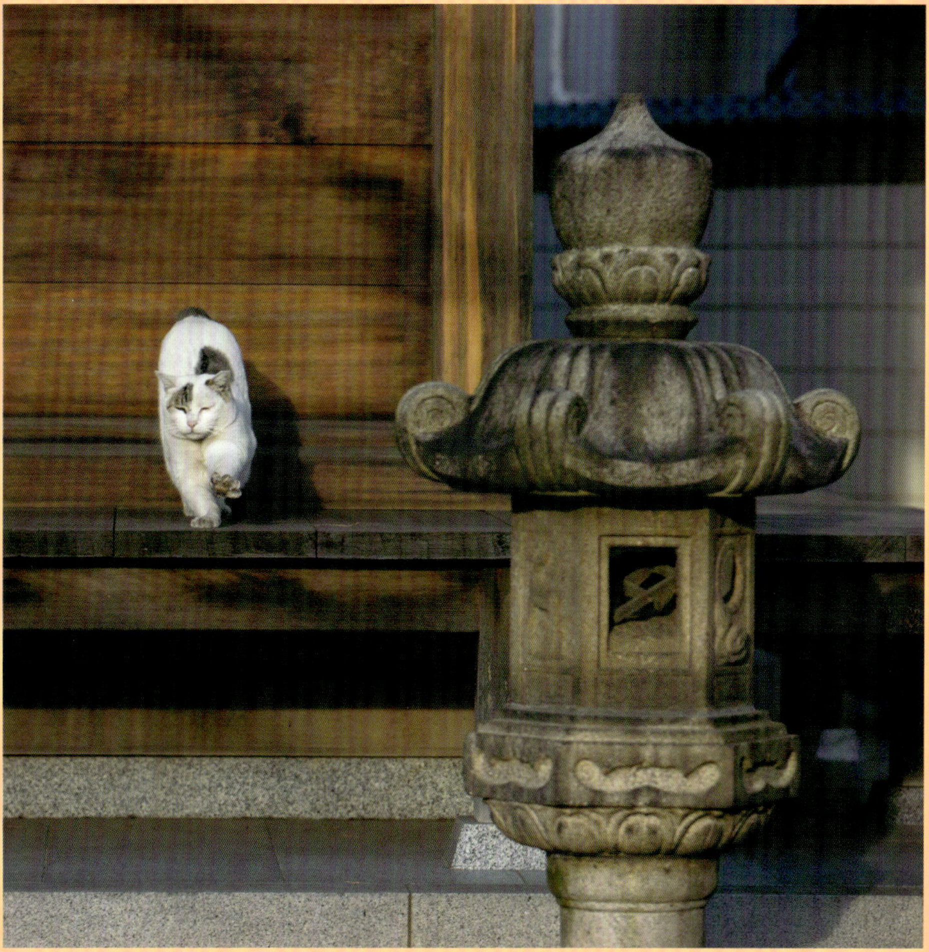

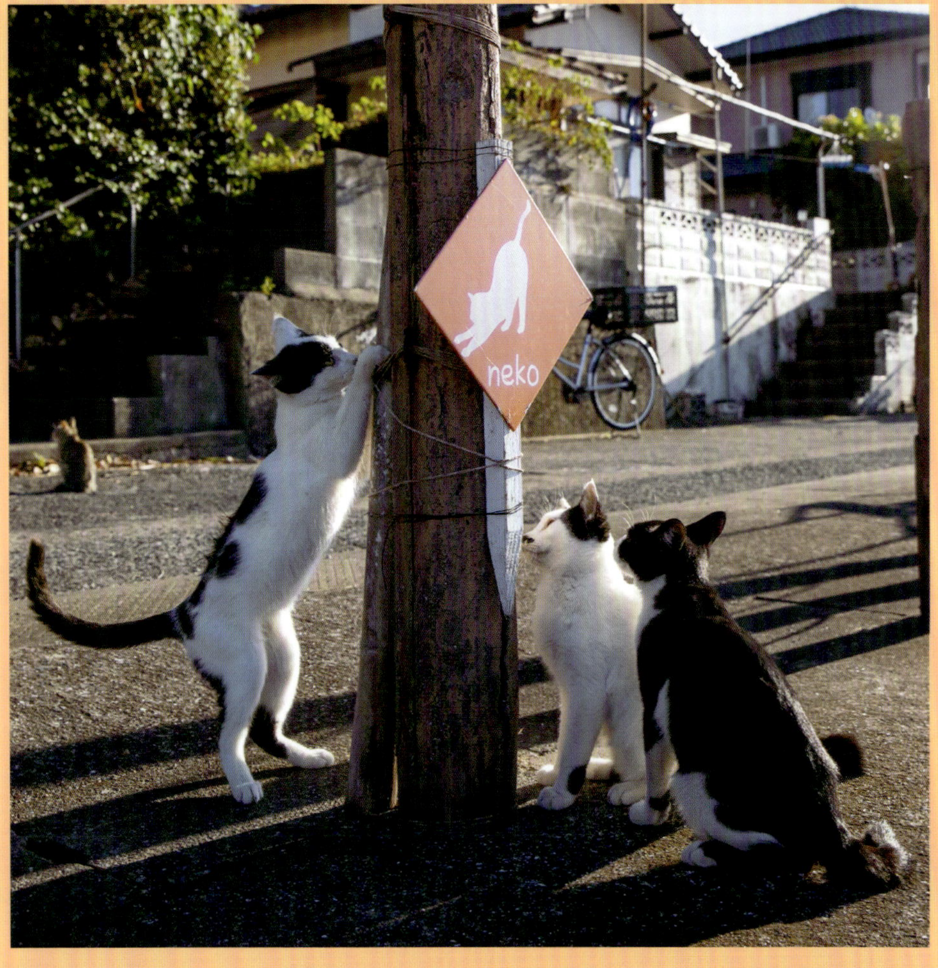

猫・ネコ

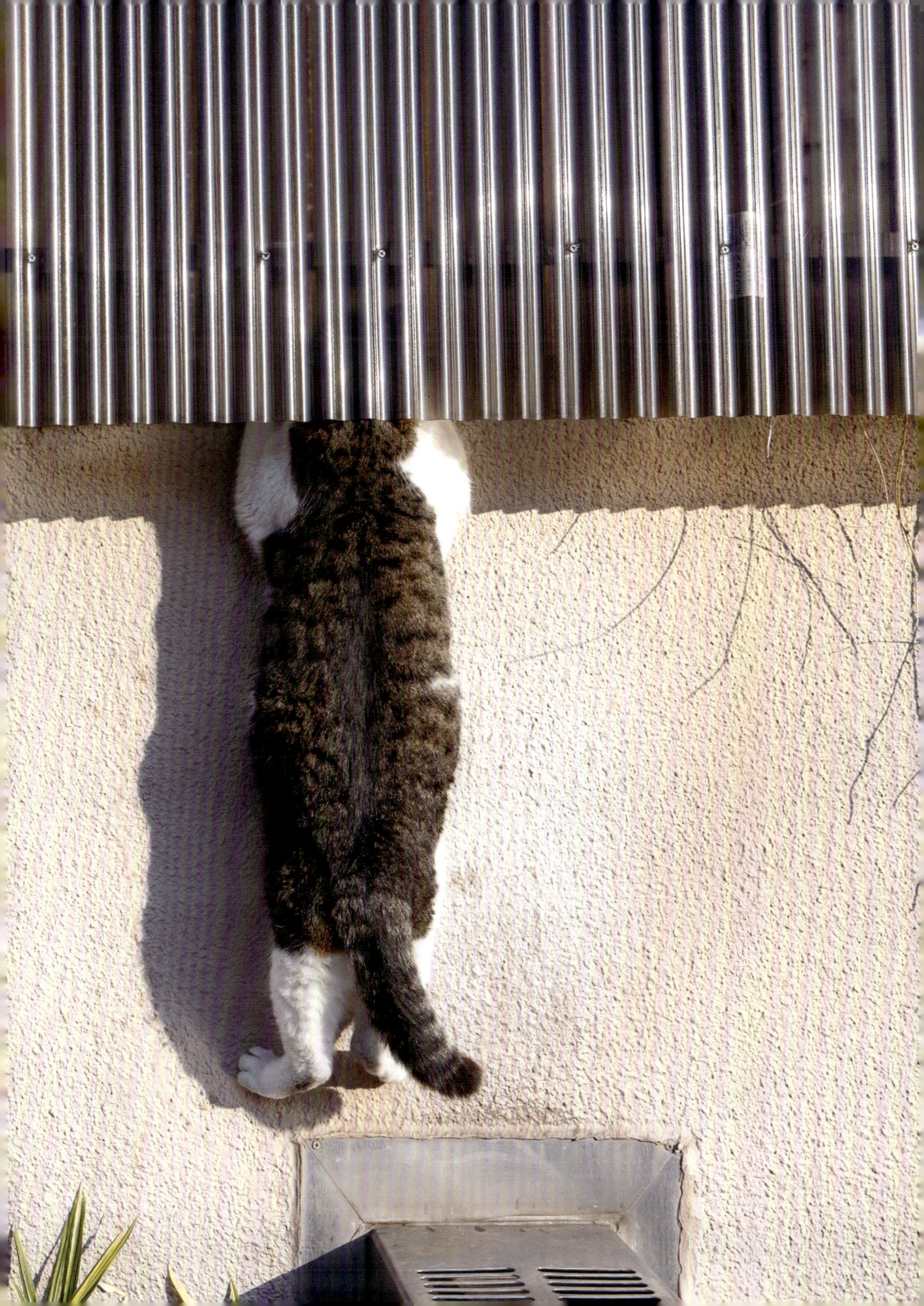

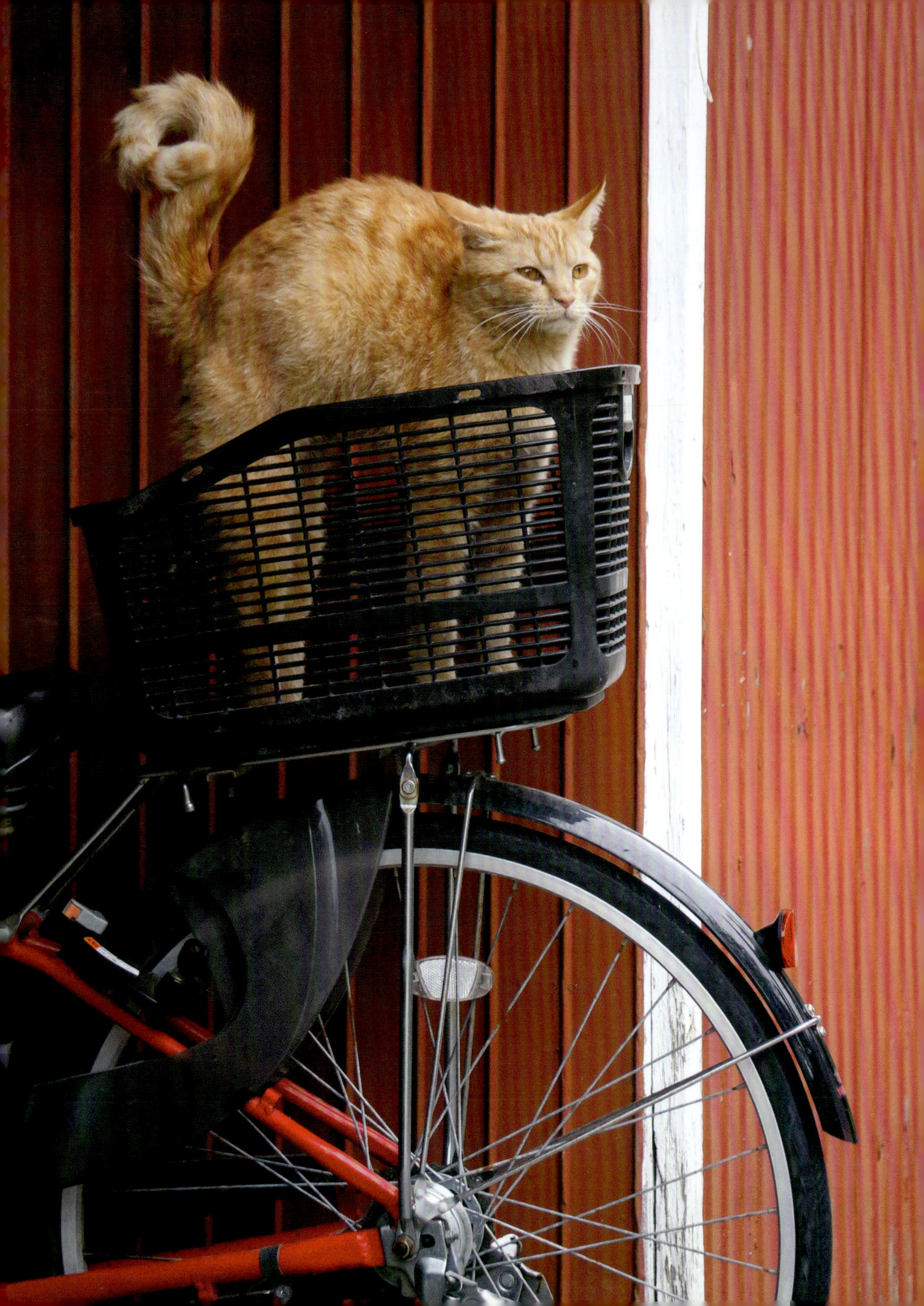

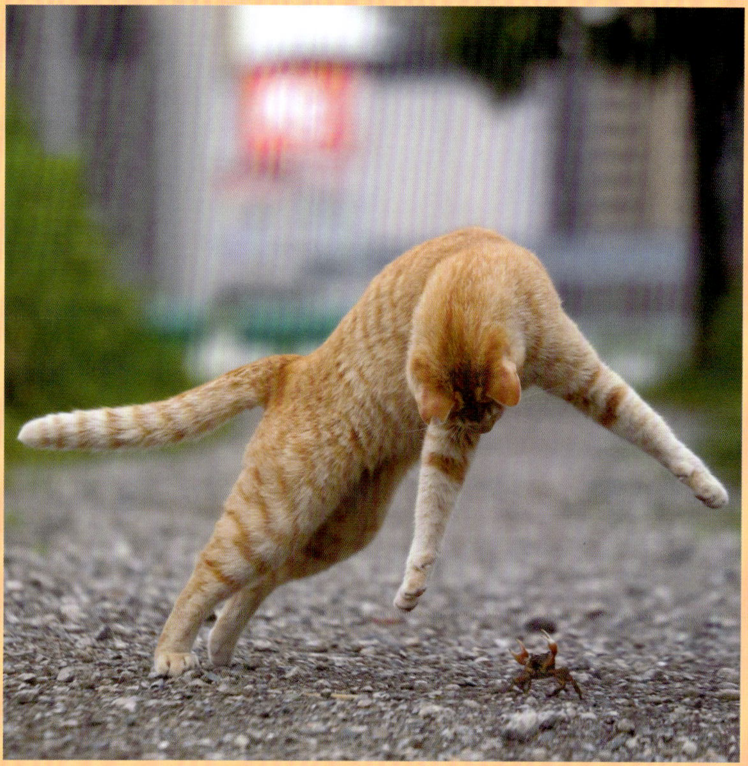

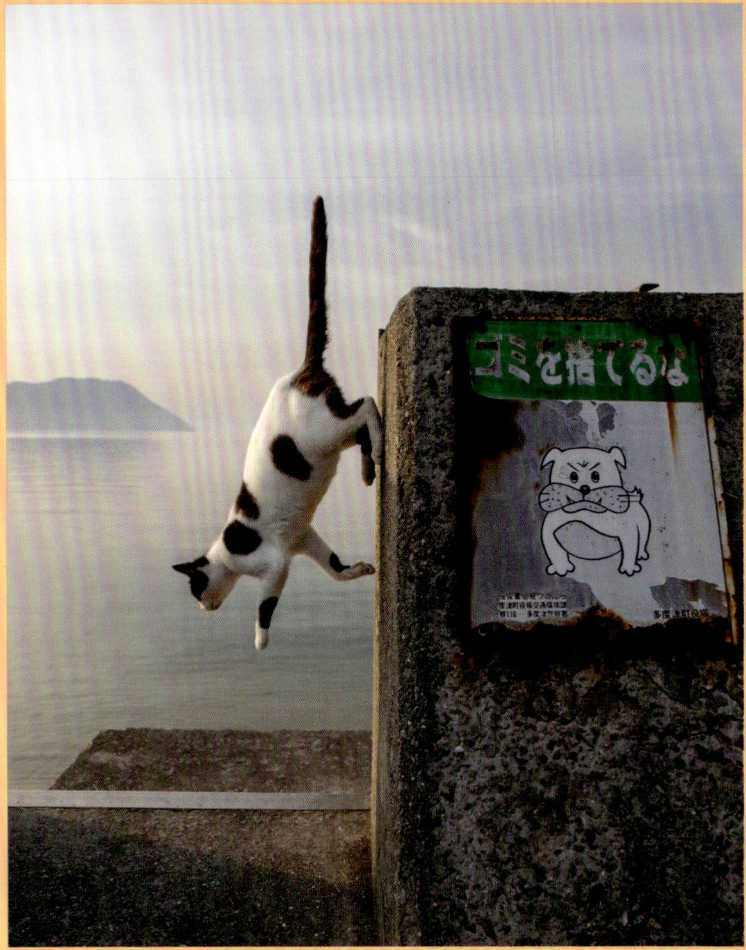
ゴミを捨てるな

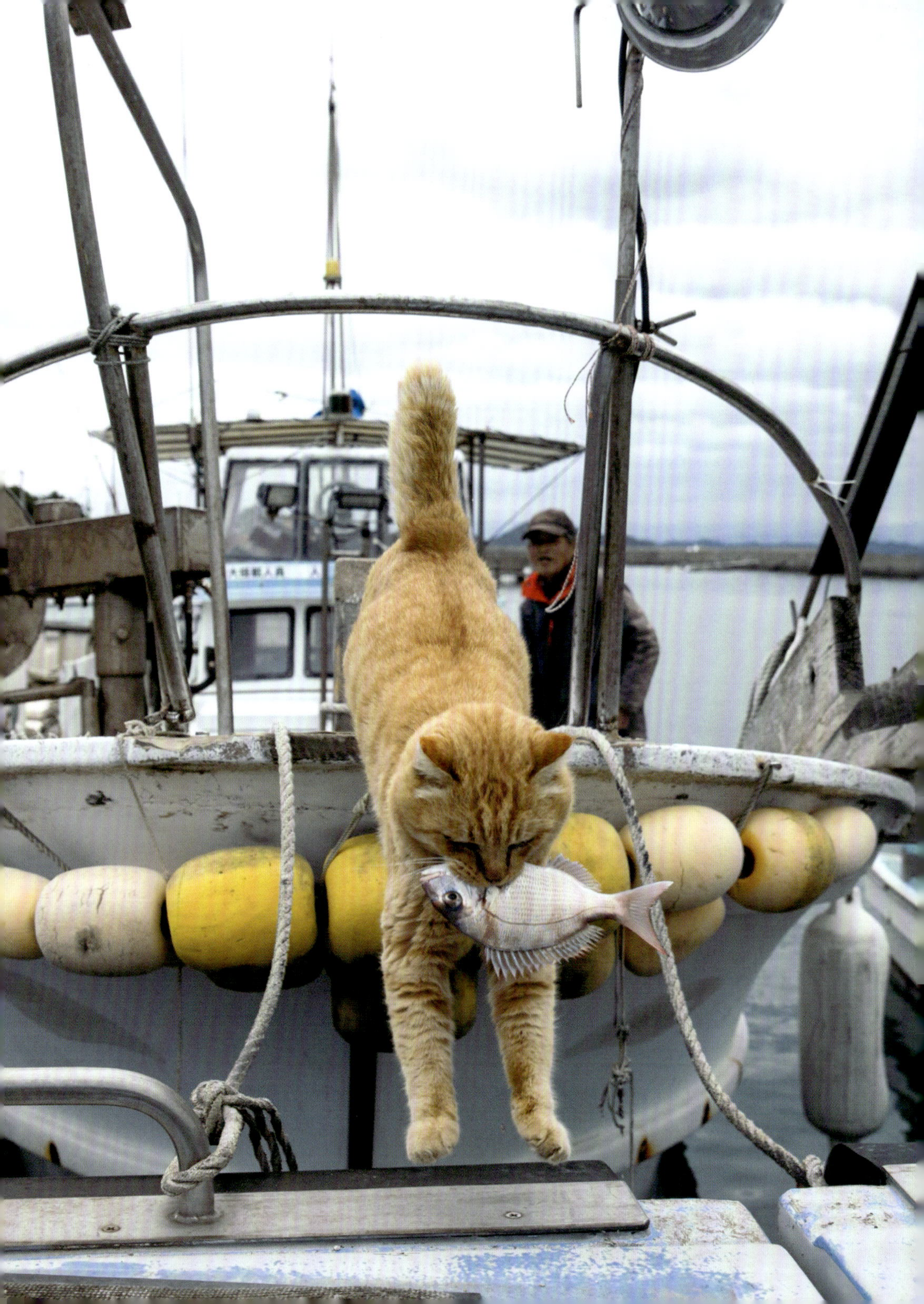

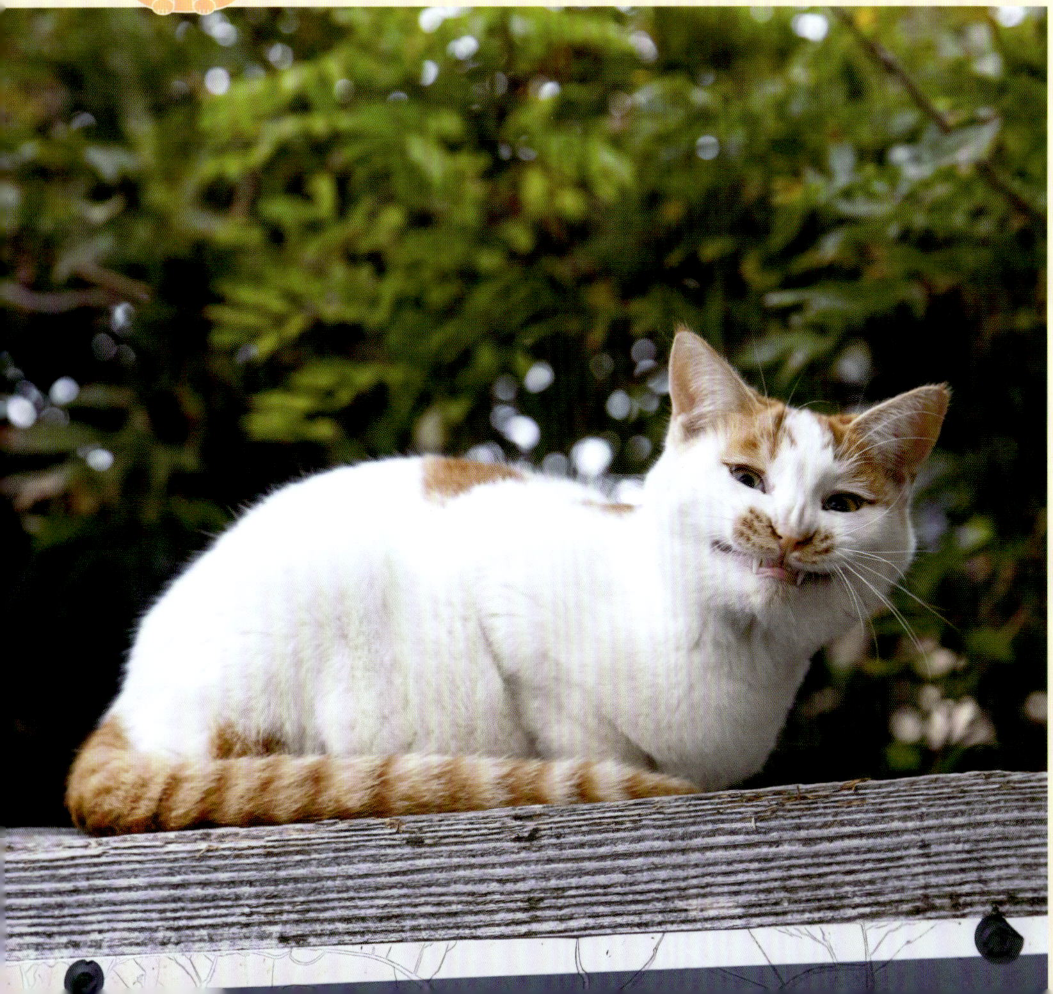

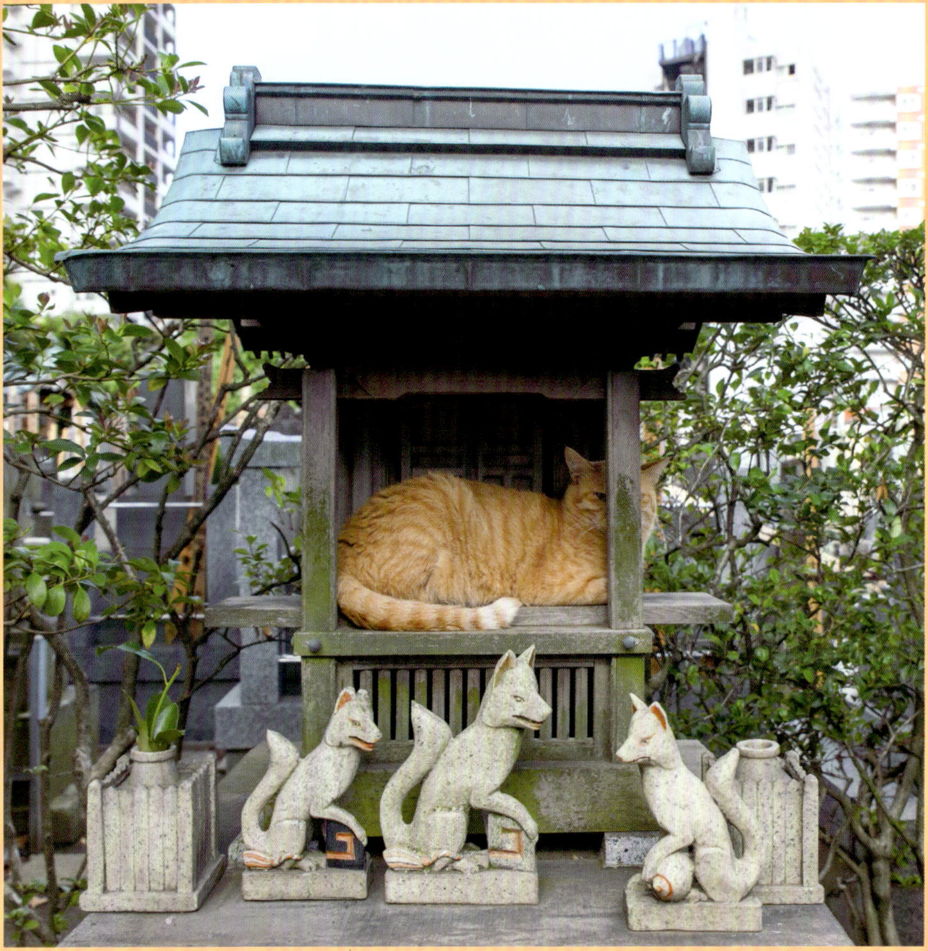

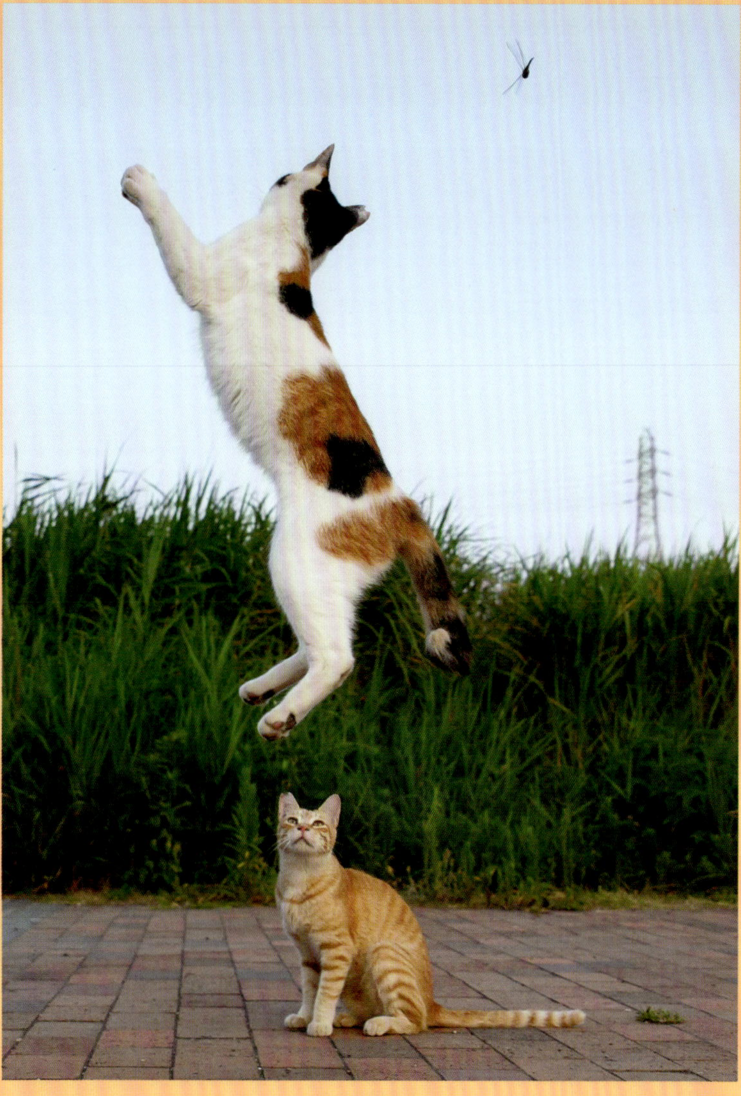

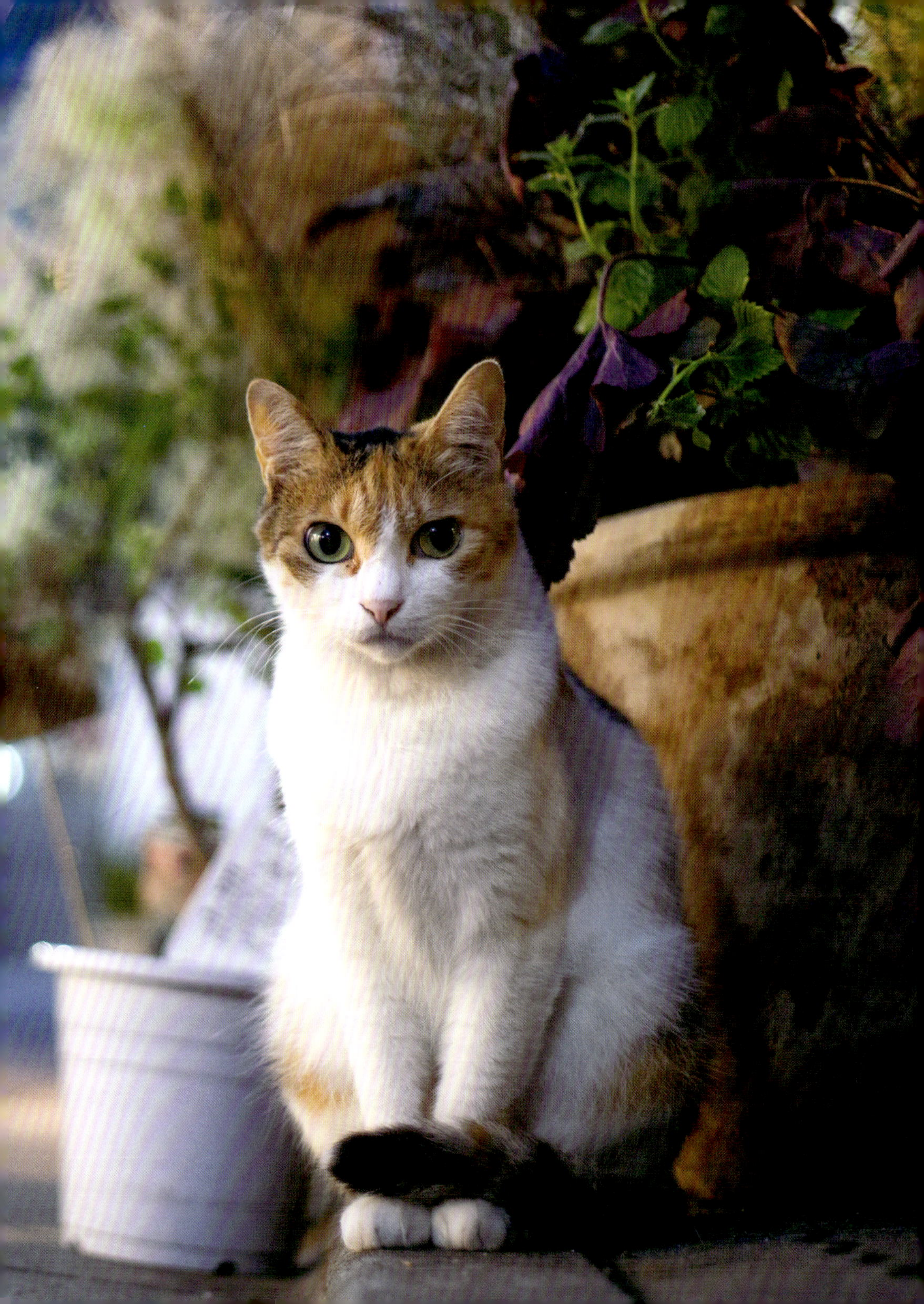

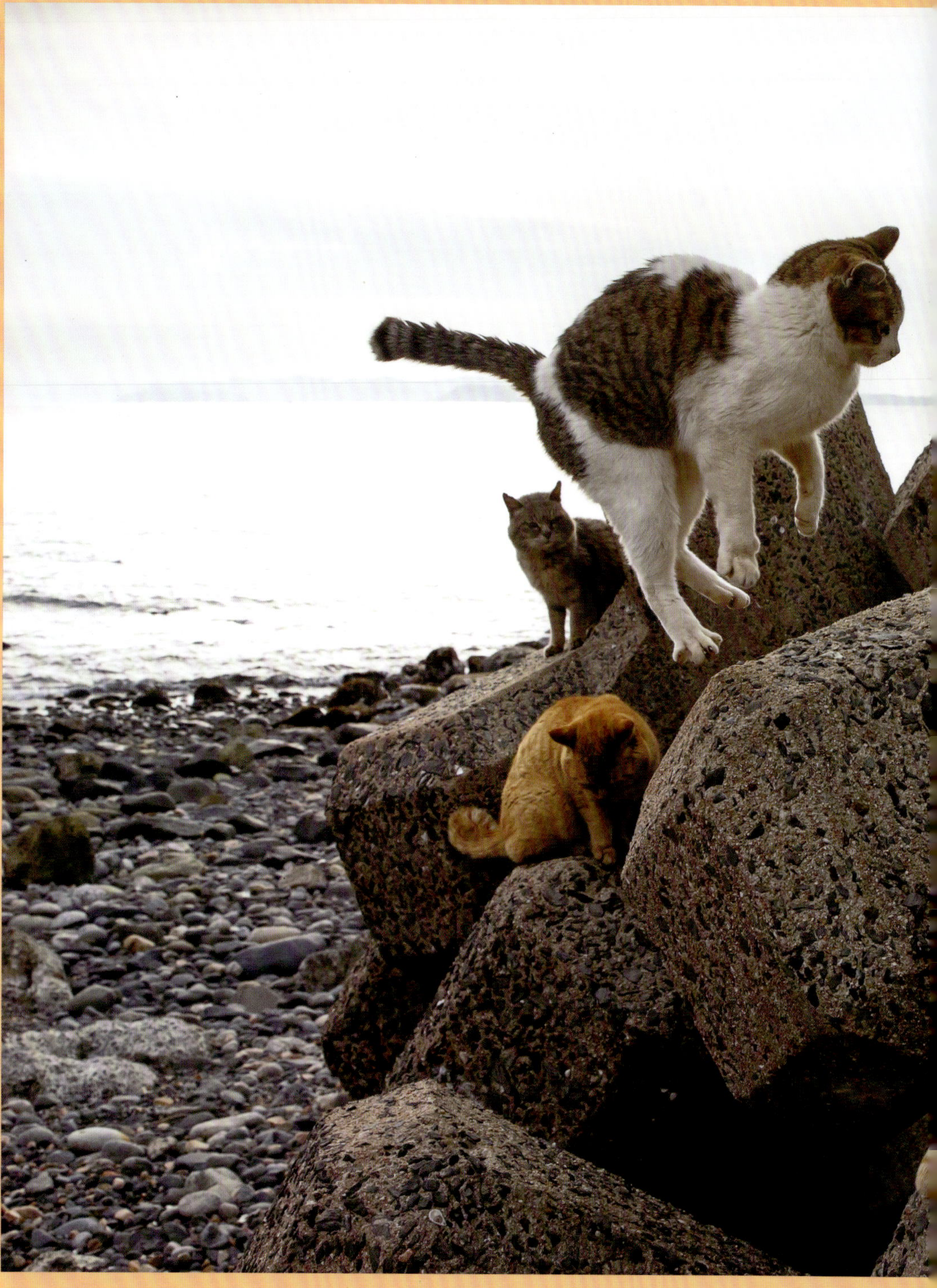

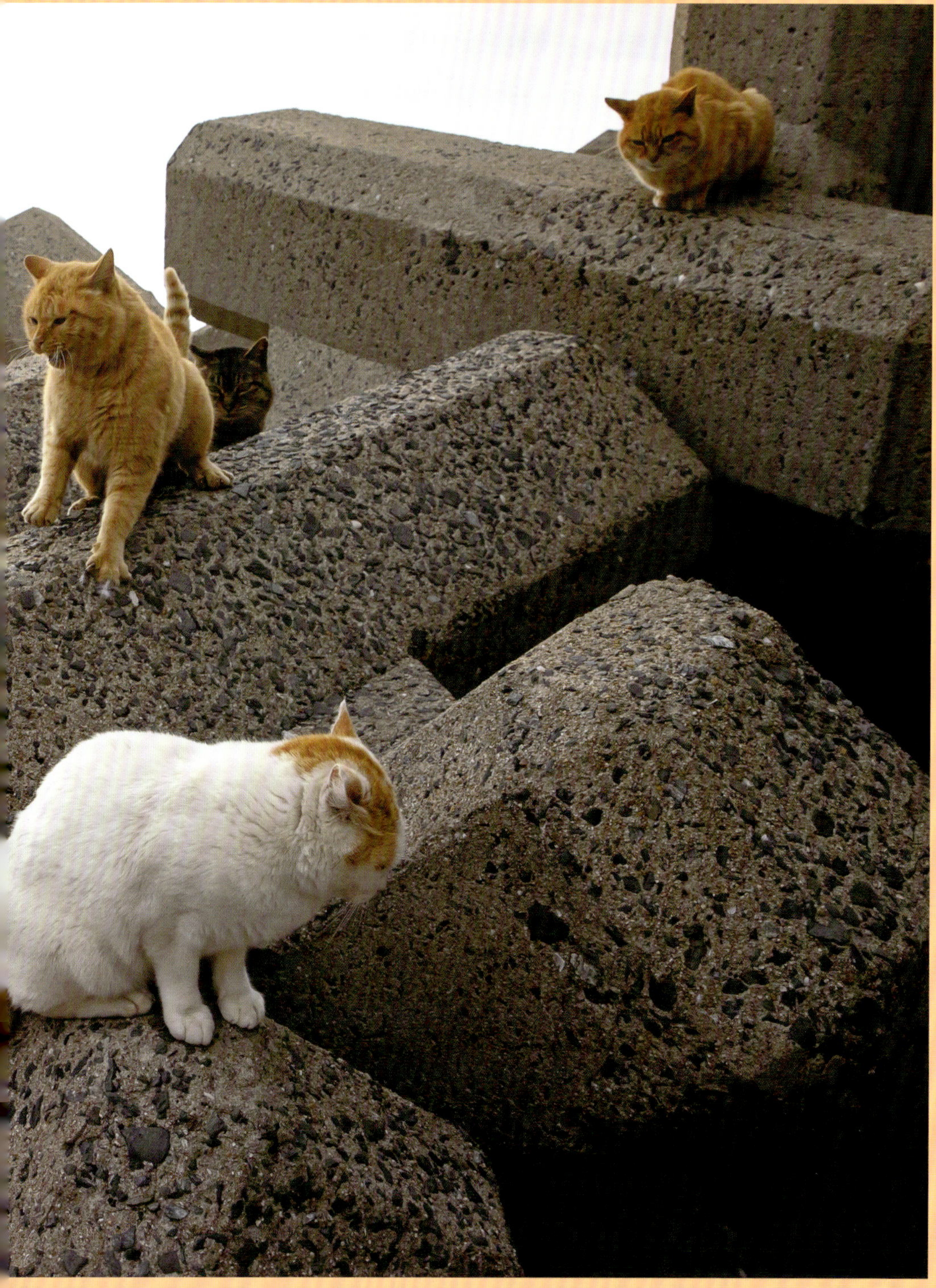

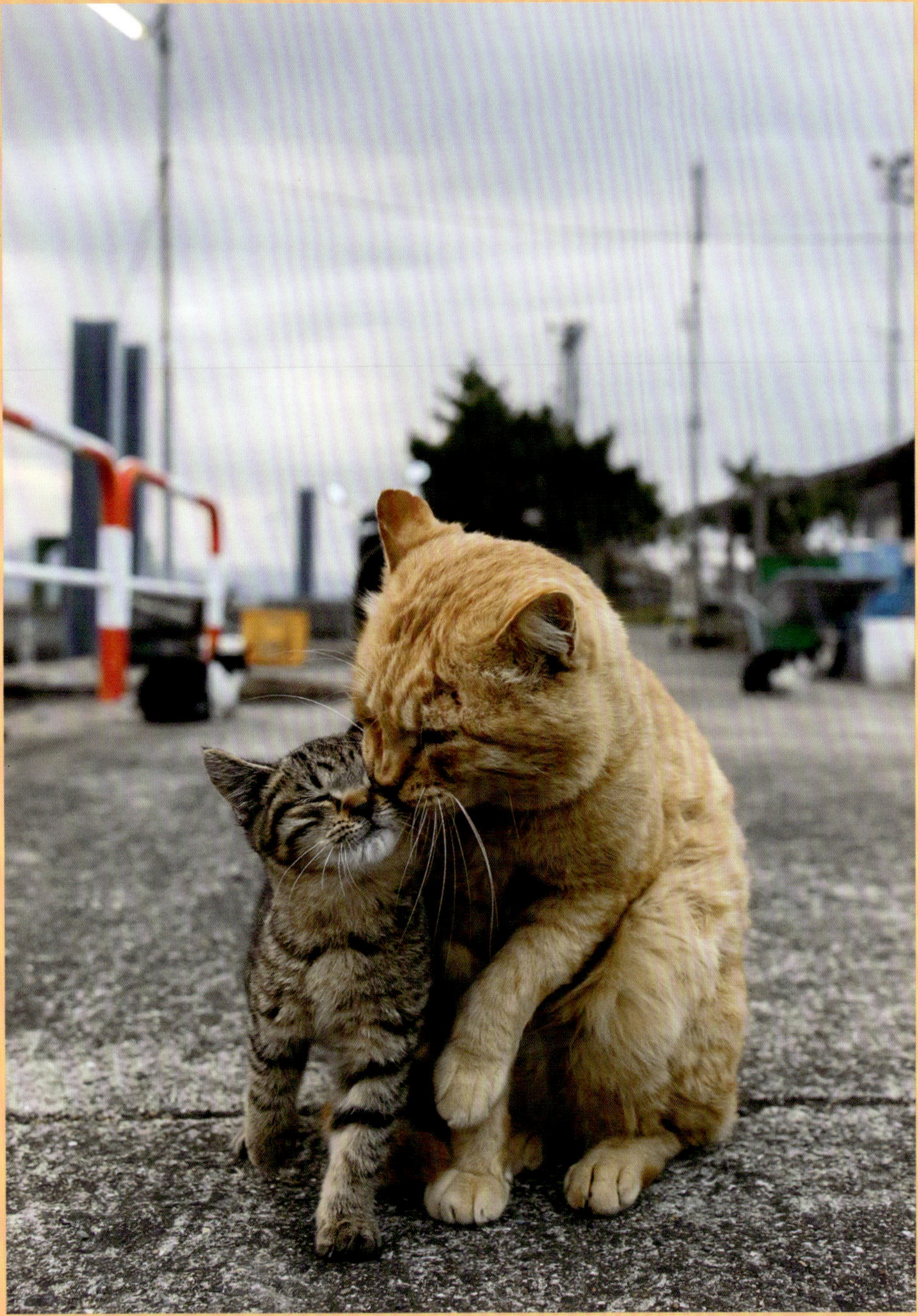

猫・ネコ

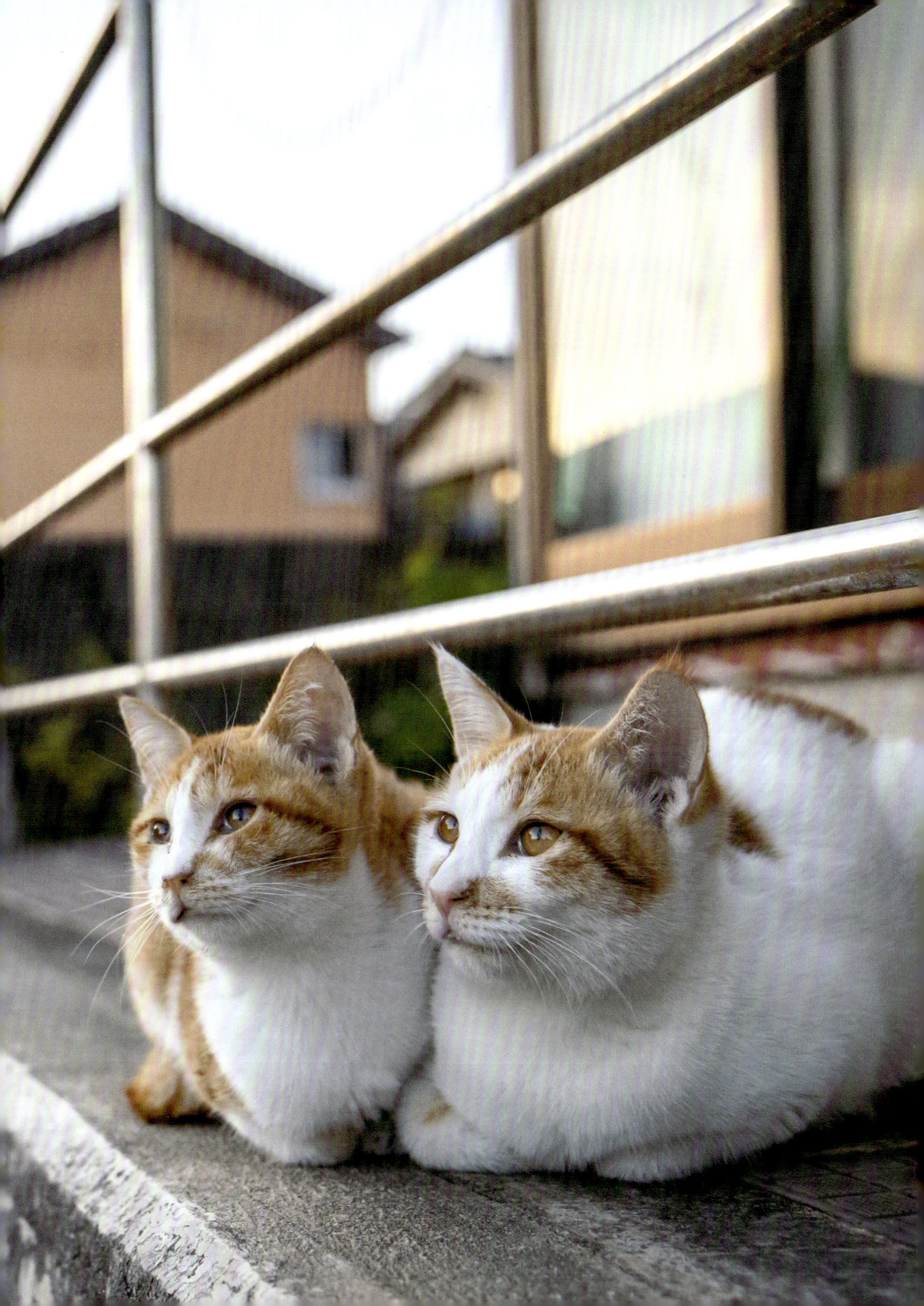

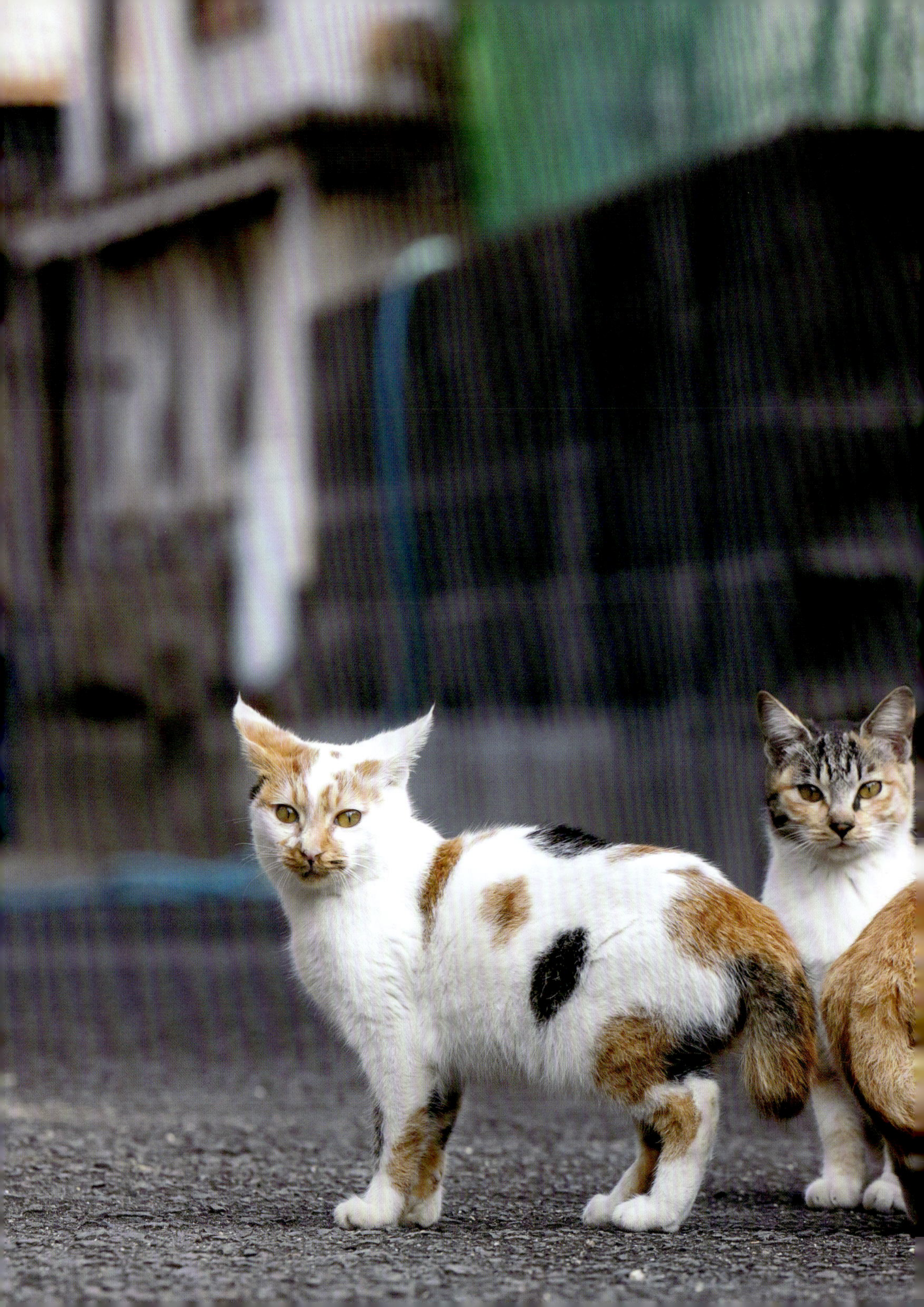

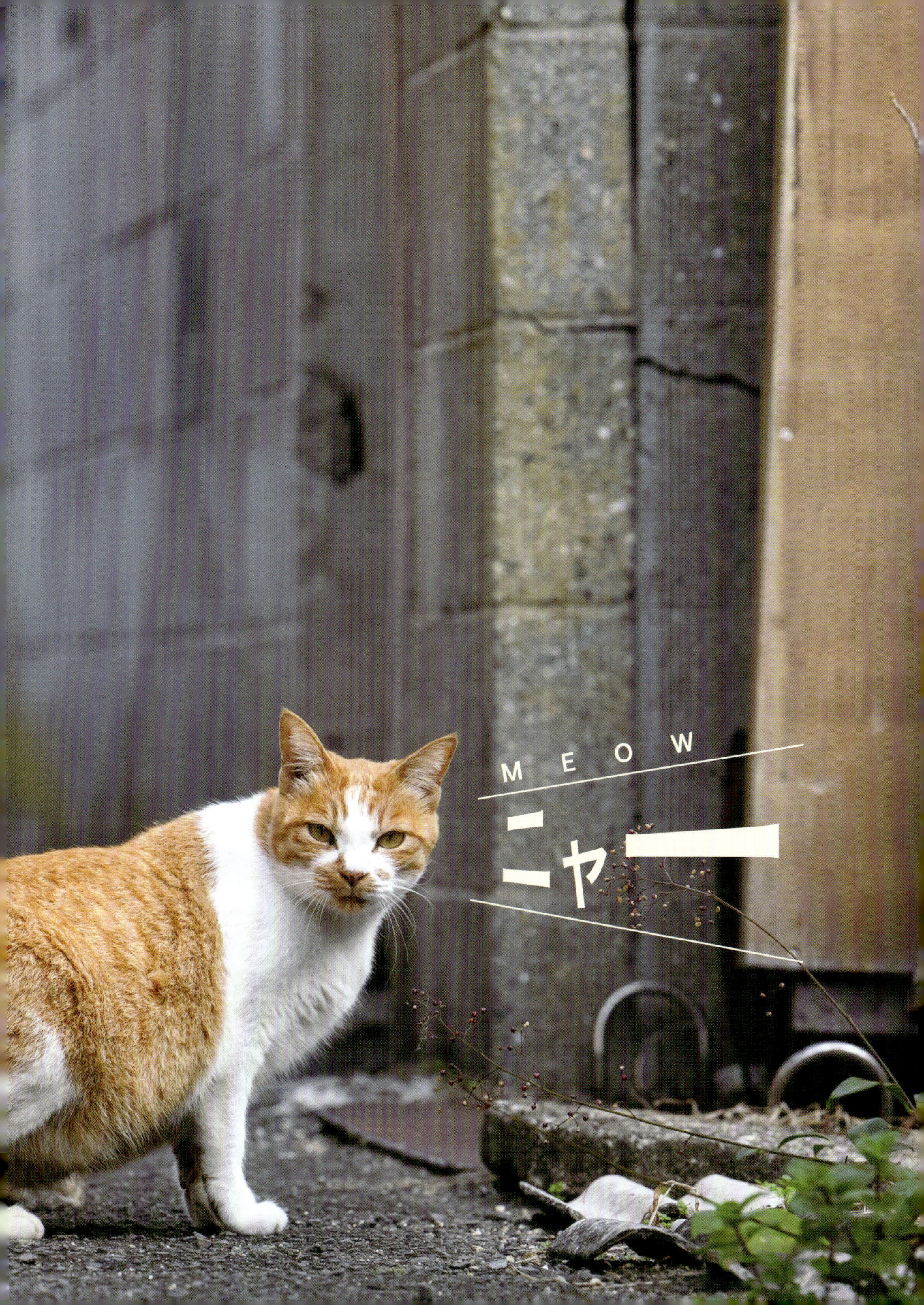
MEOW
ニャー

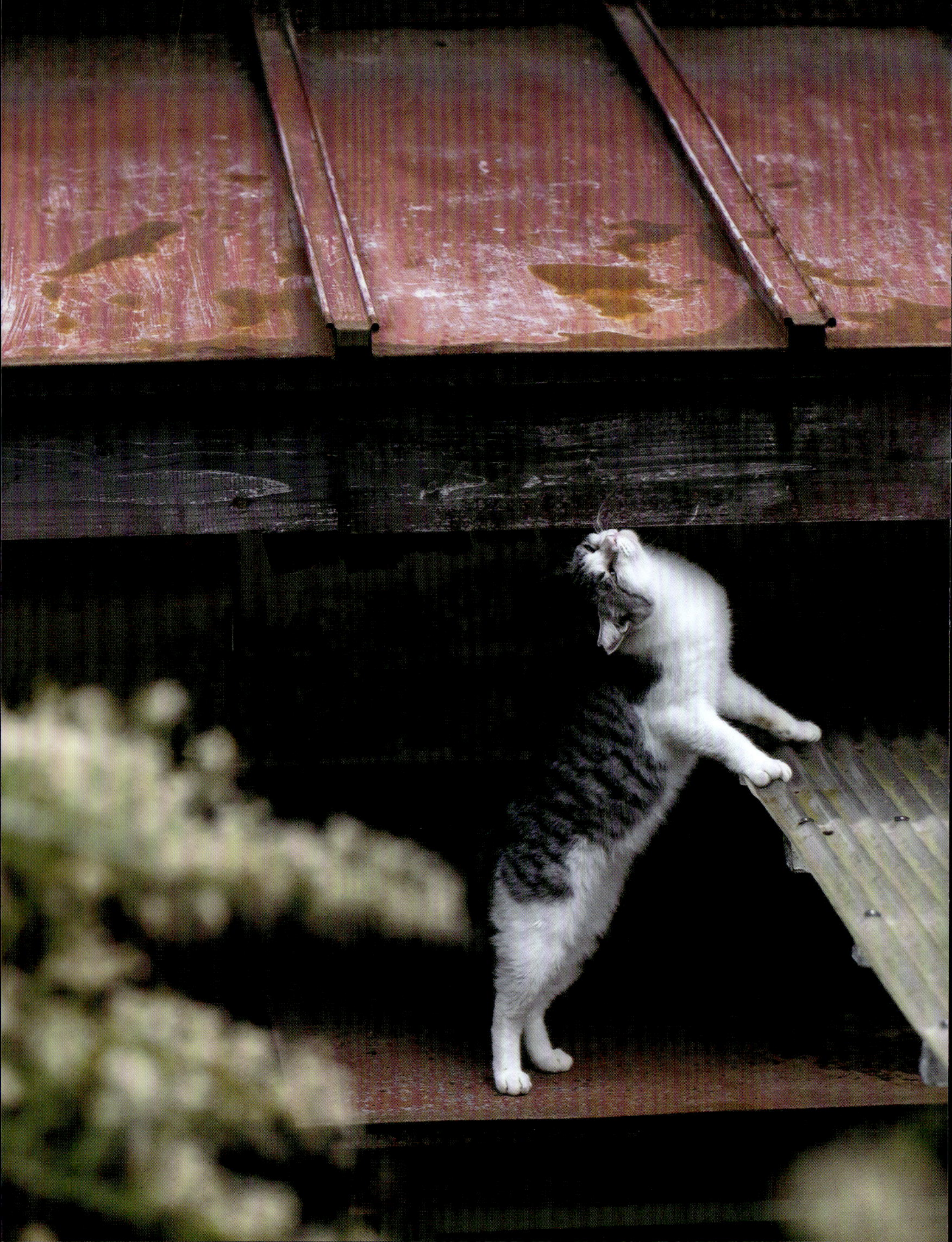

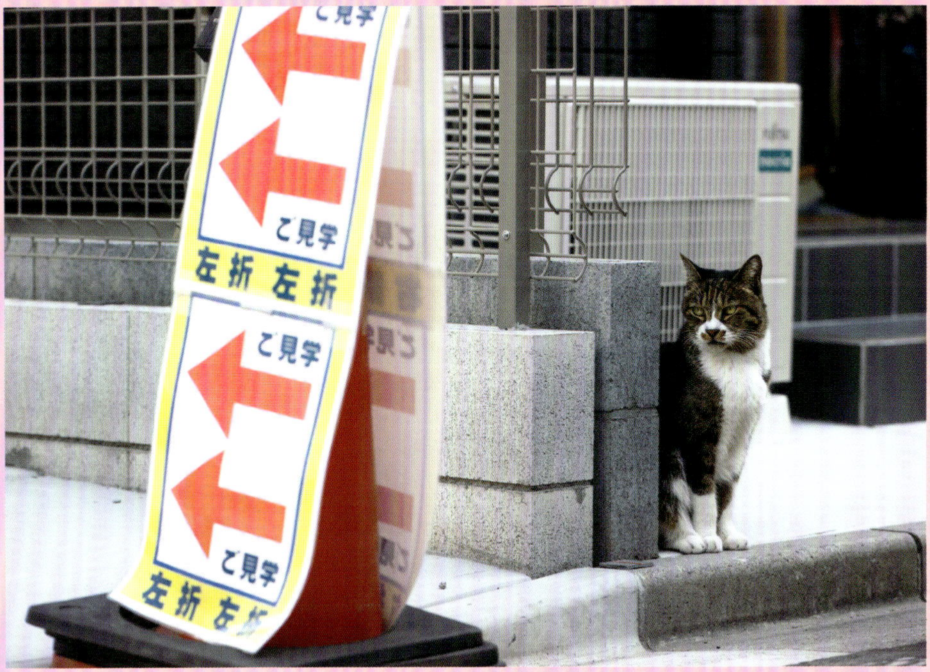

KITTEN

子猫

猫・ネコ

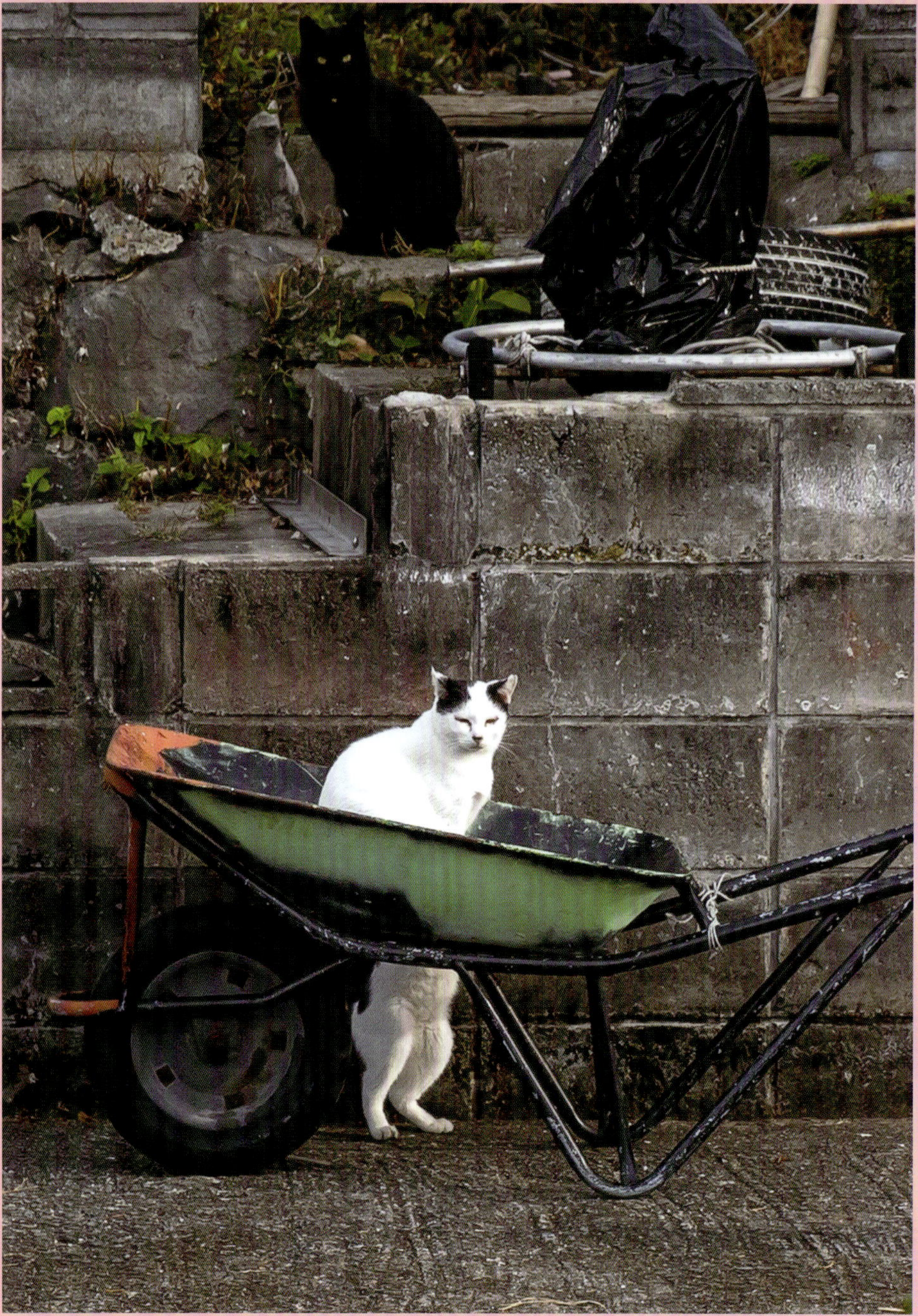

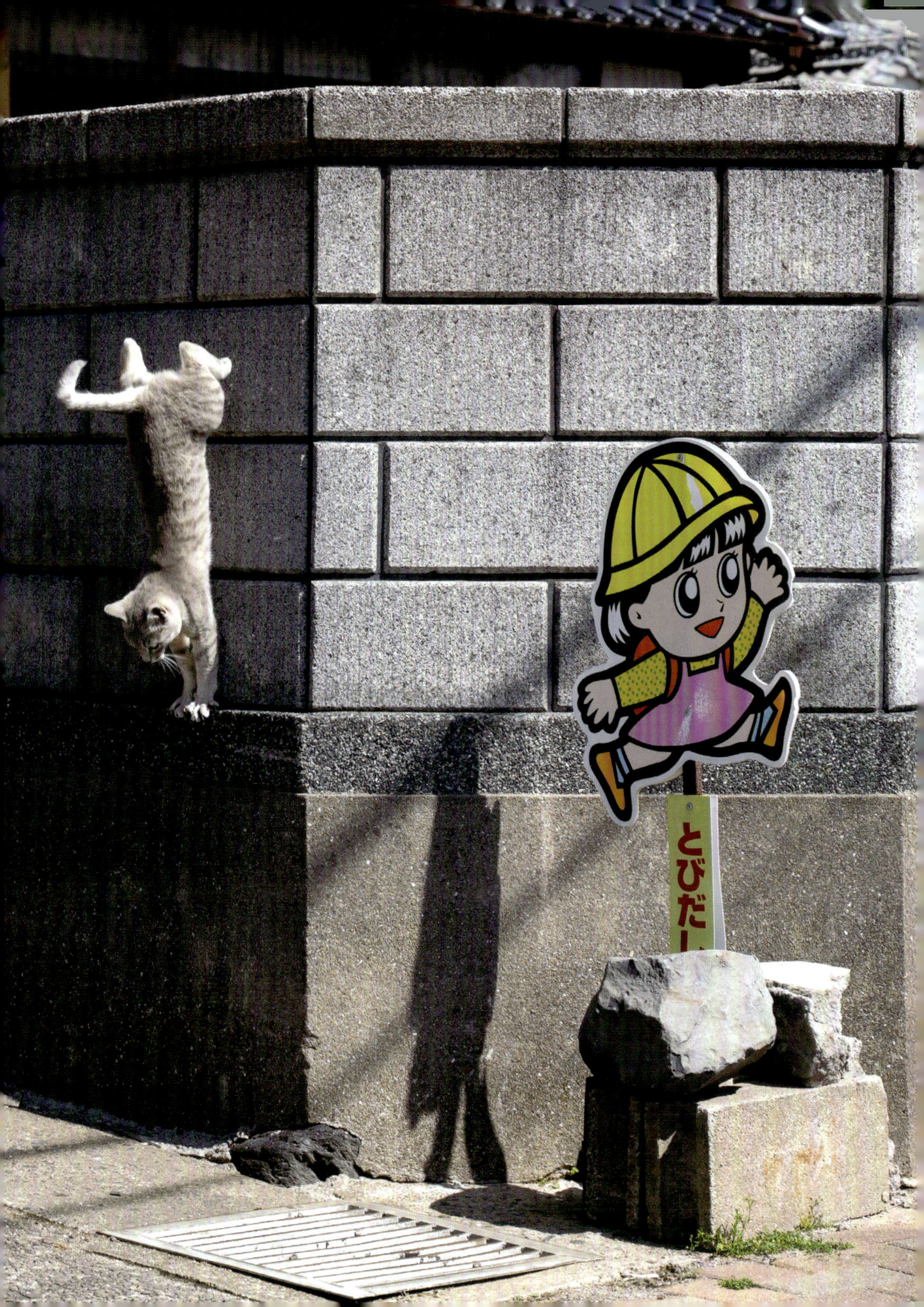
とびだ

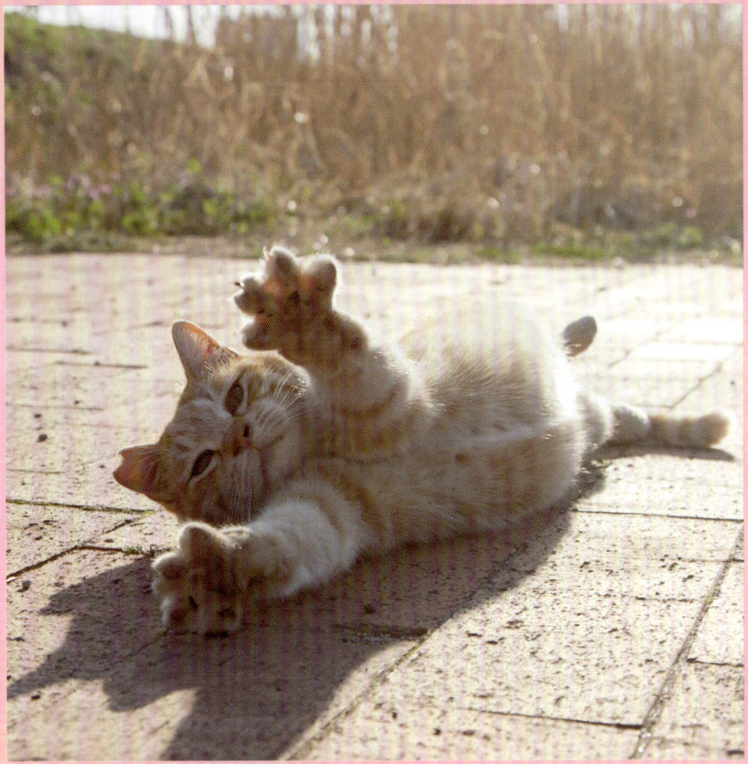

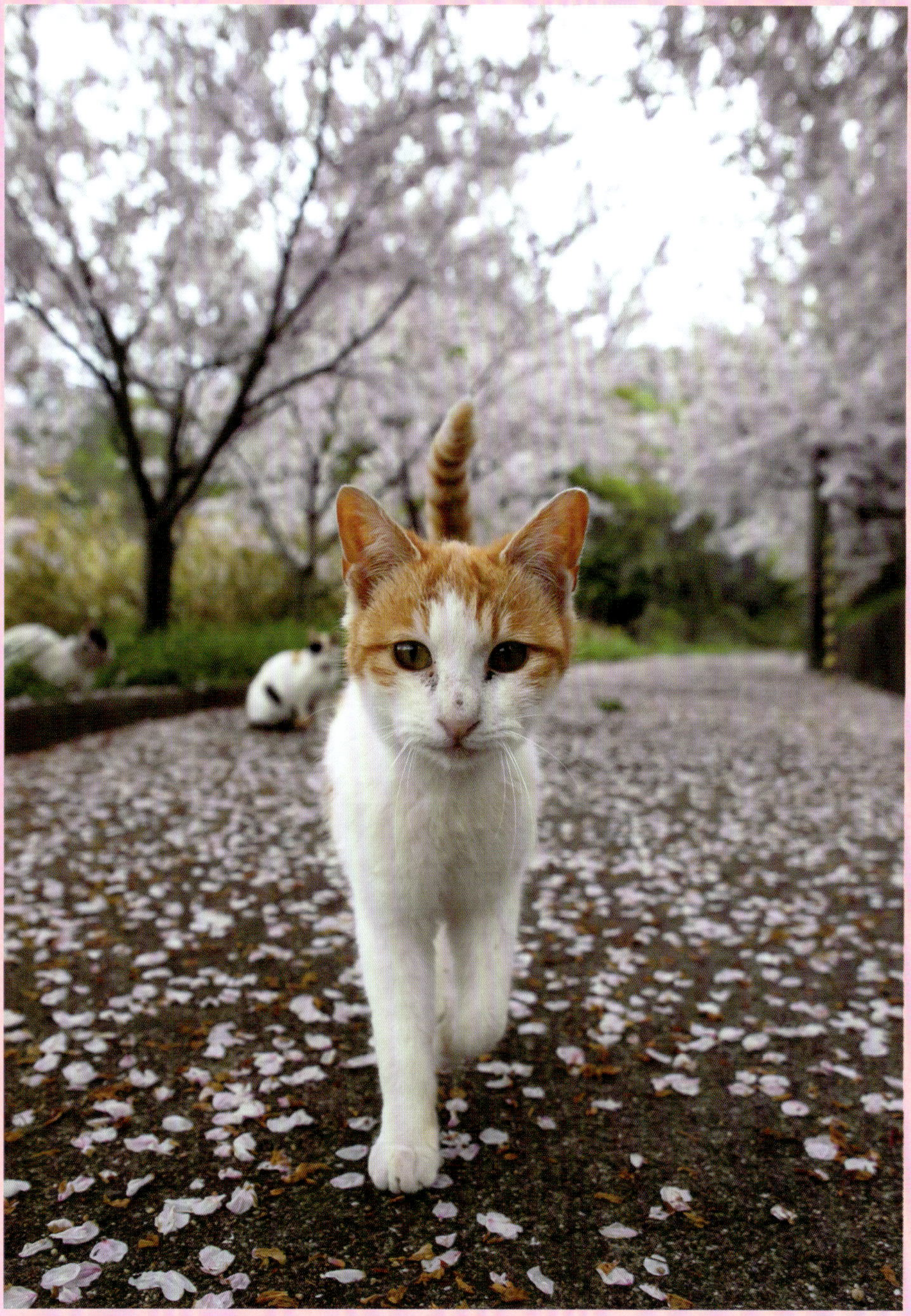

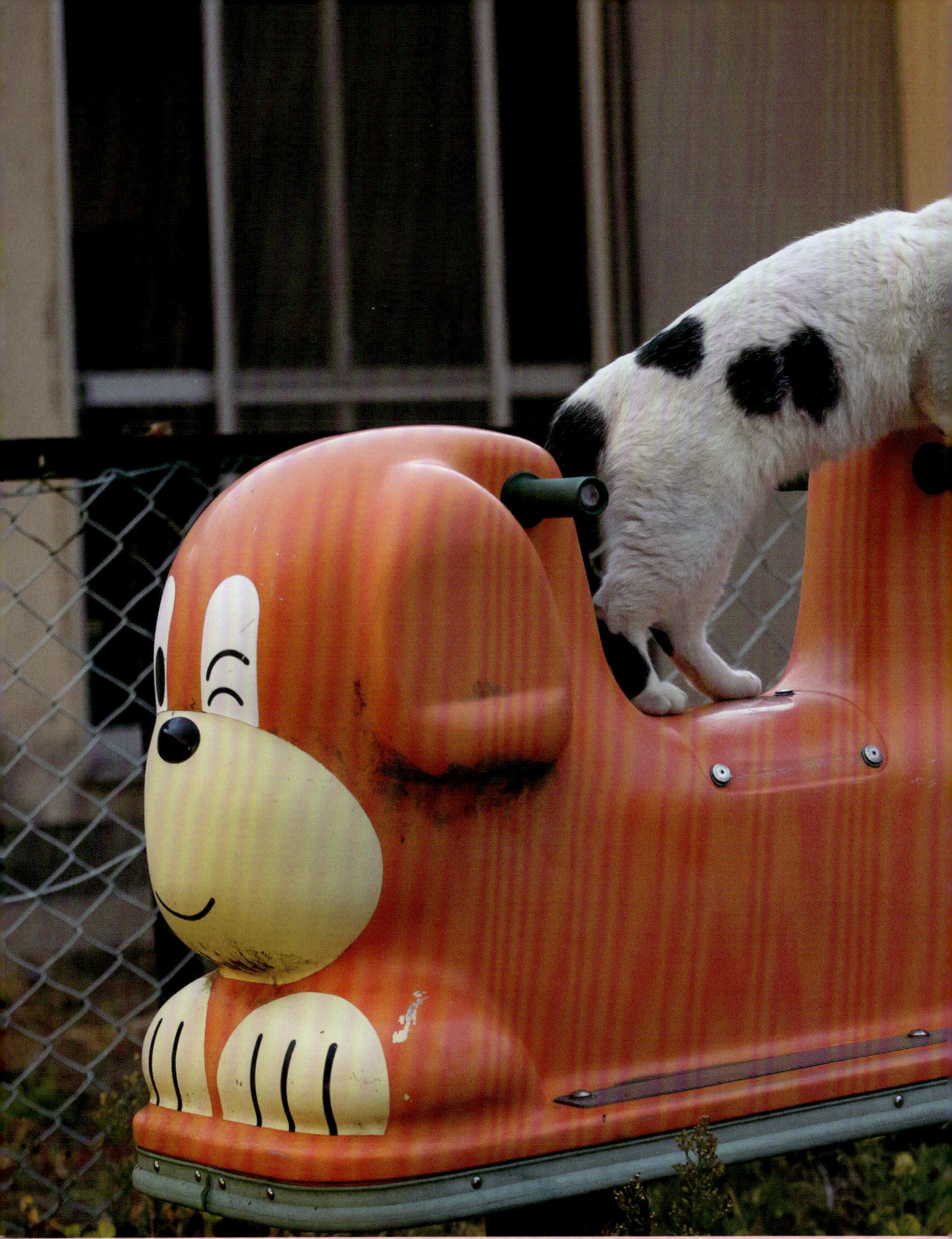

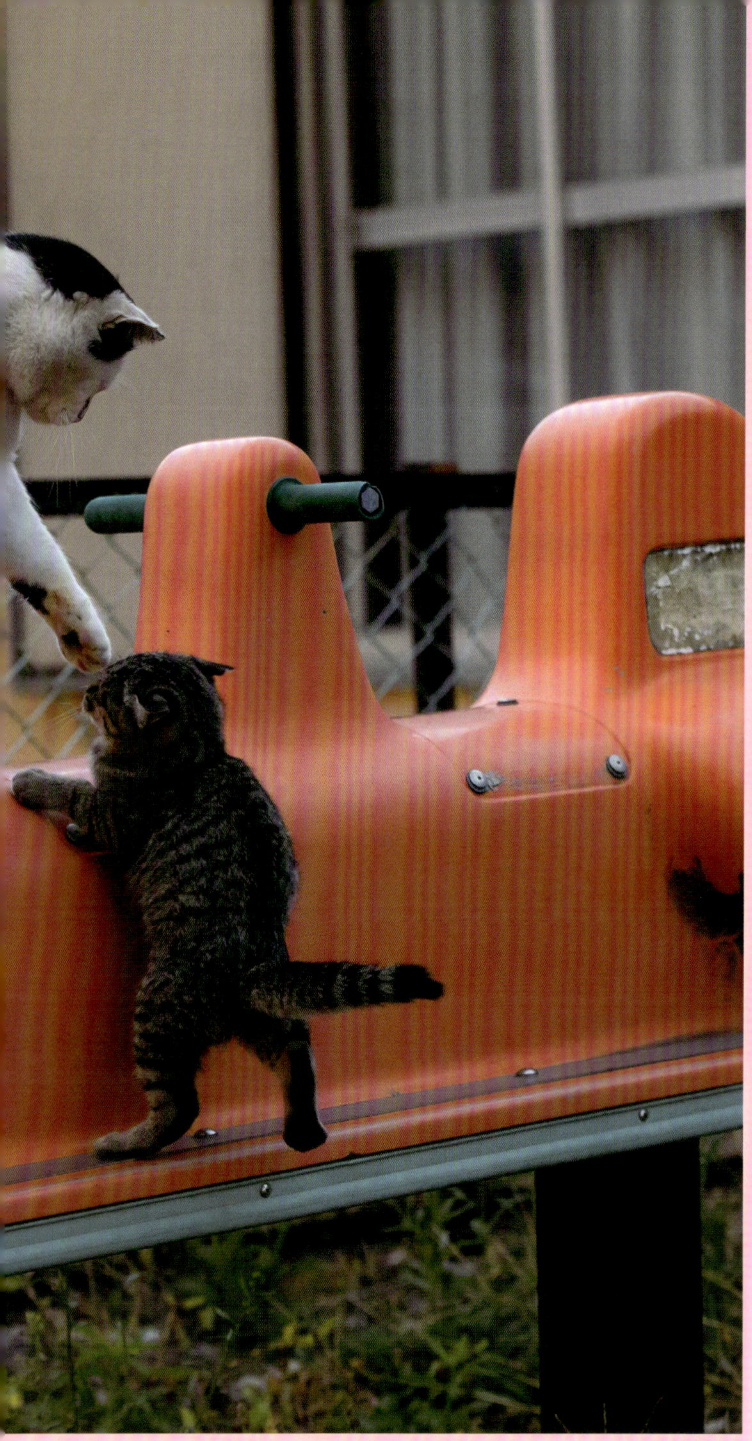

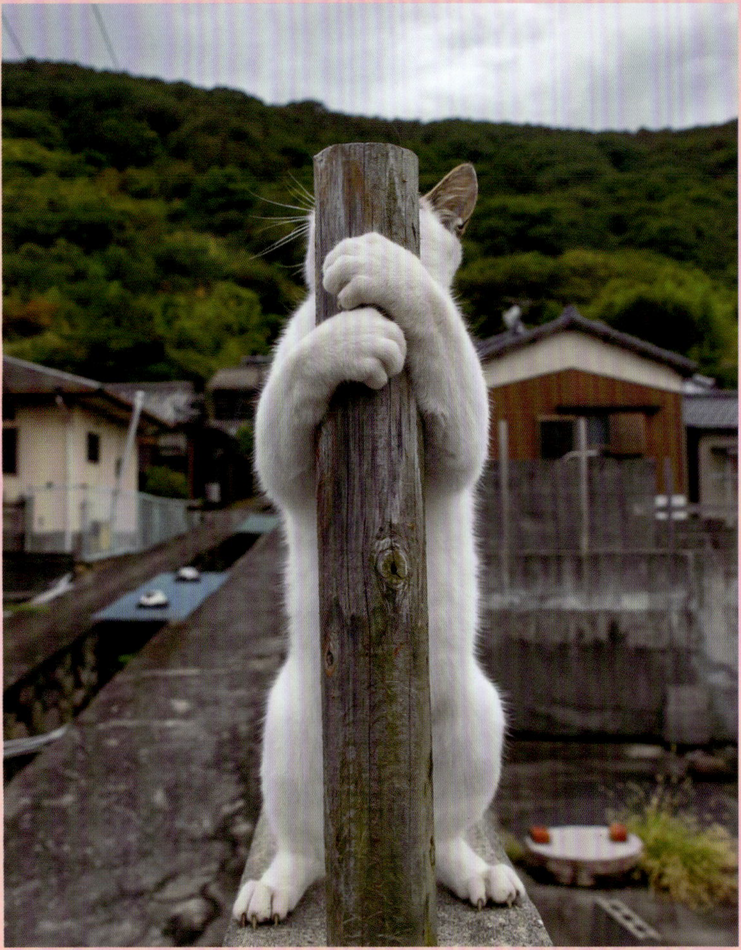

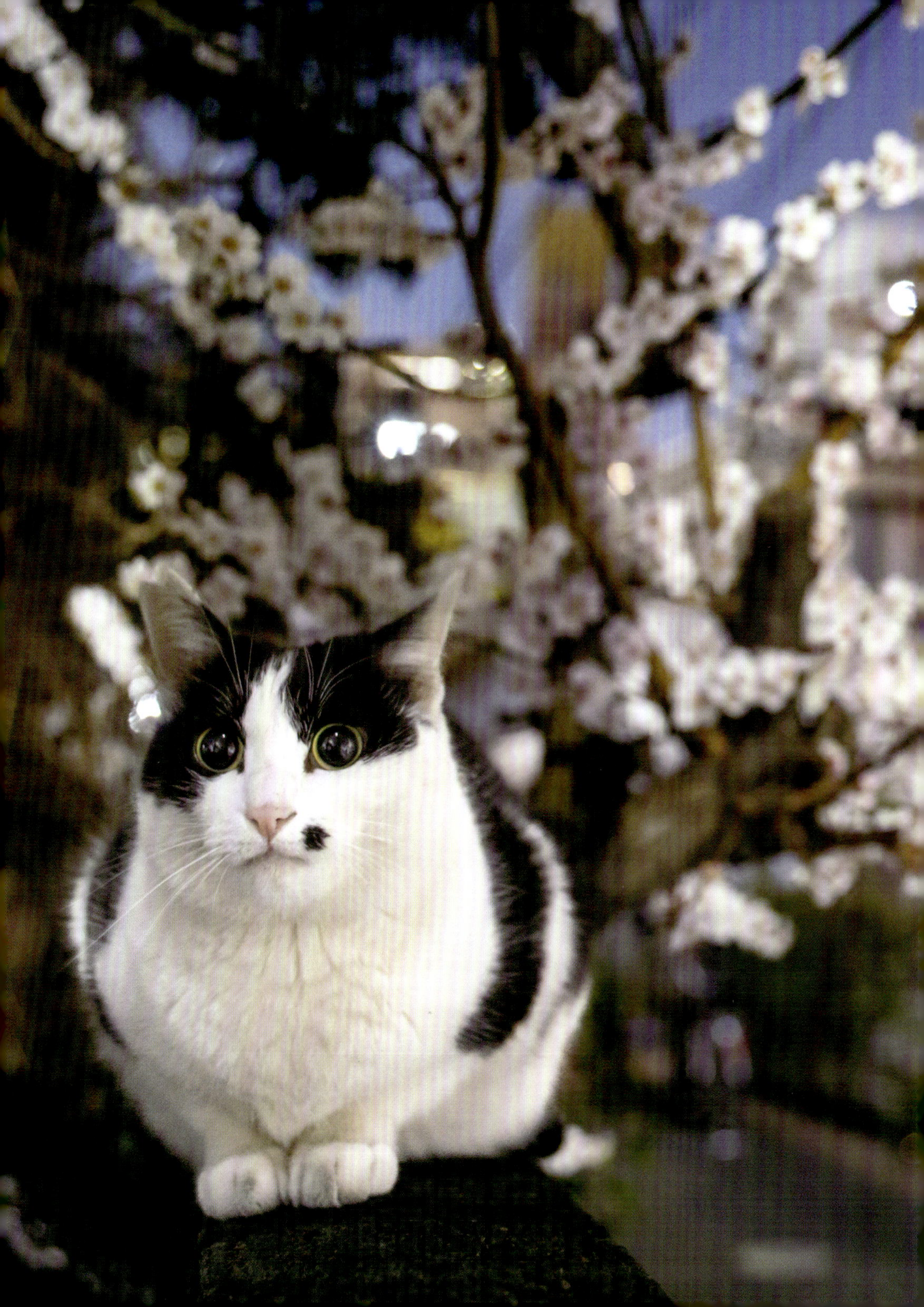

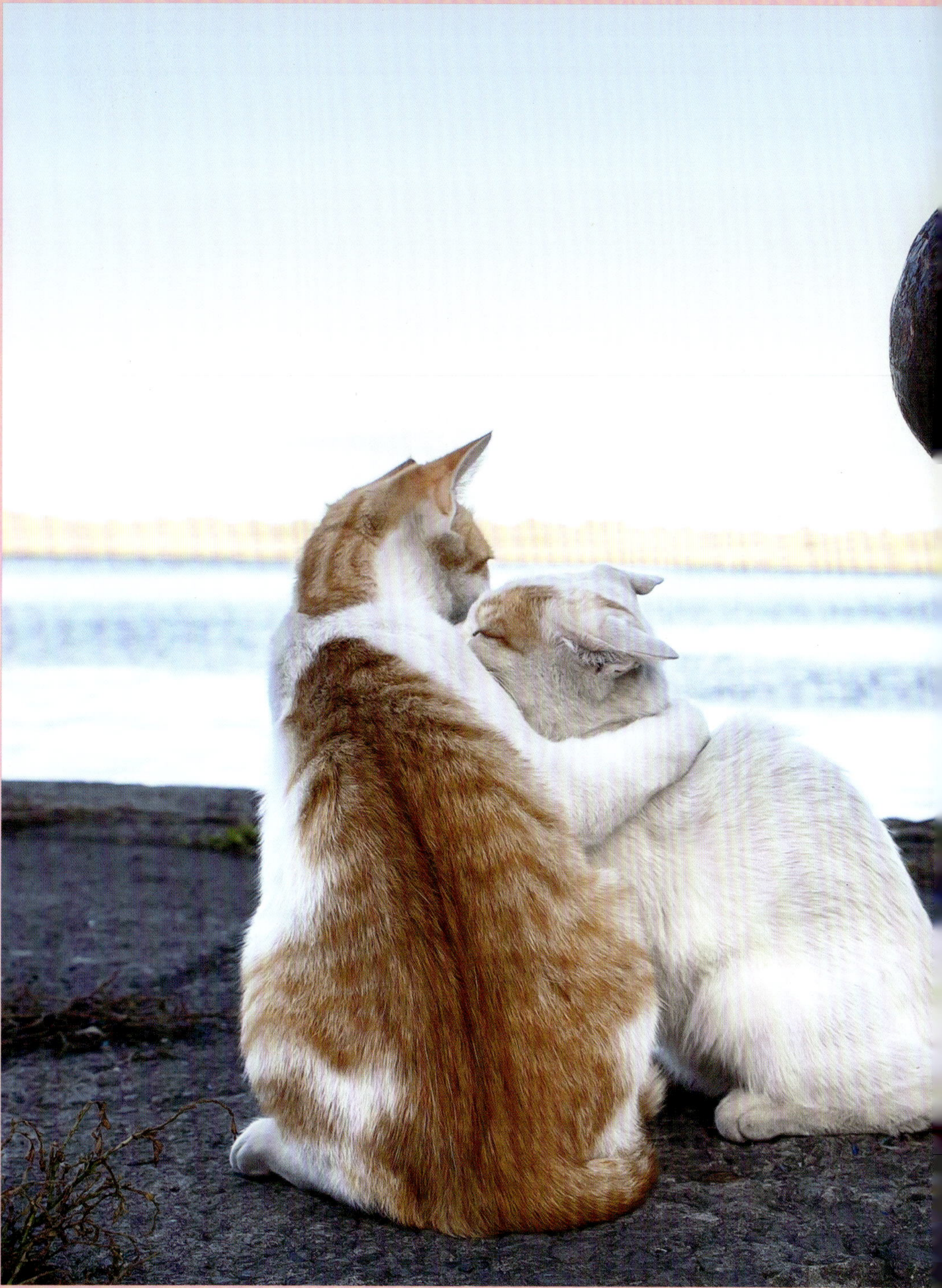

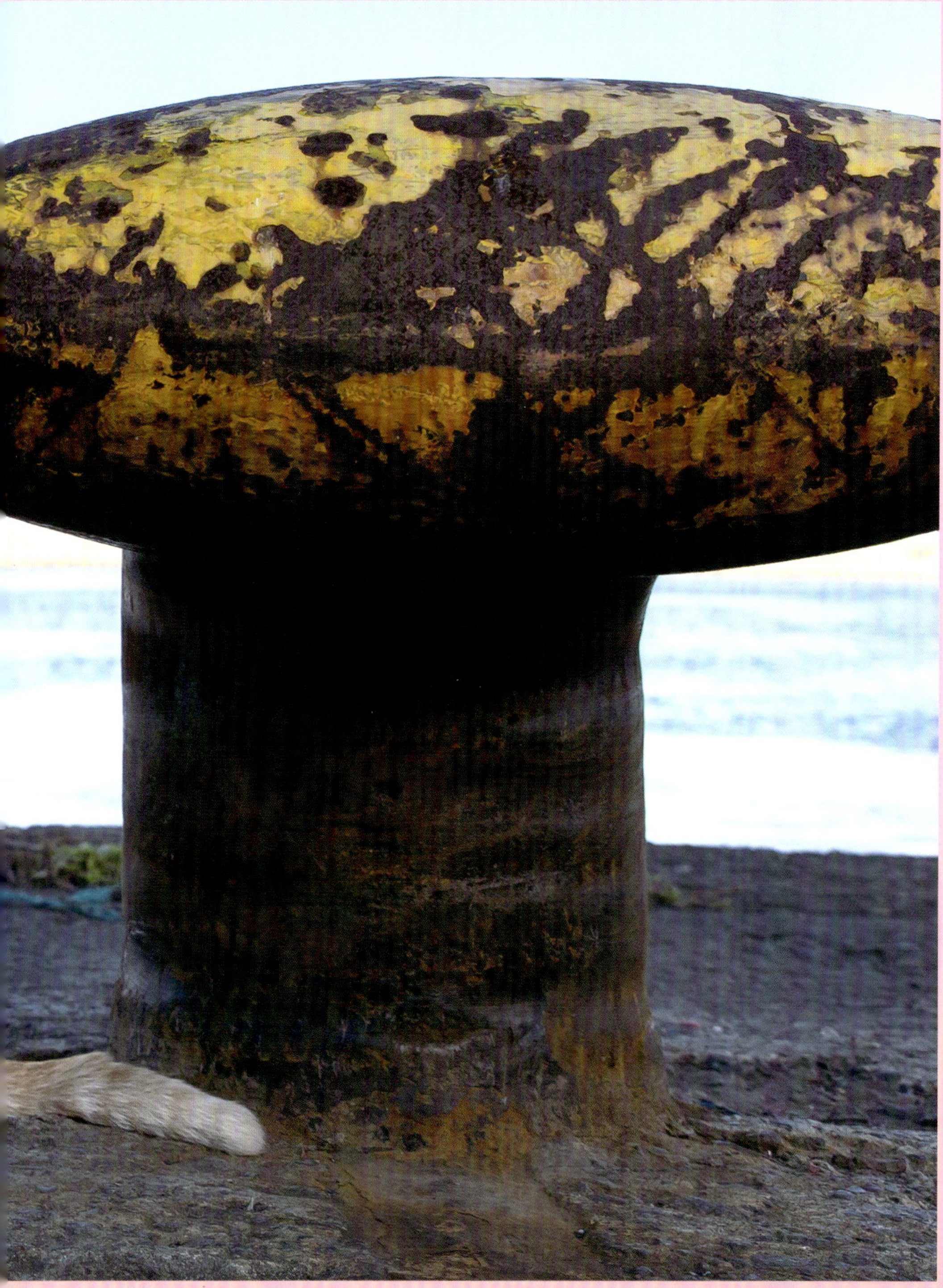

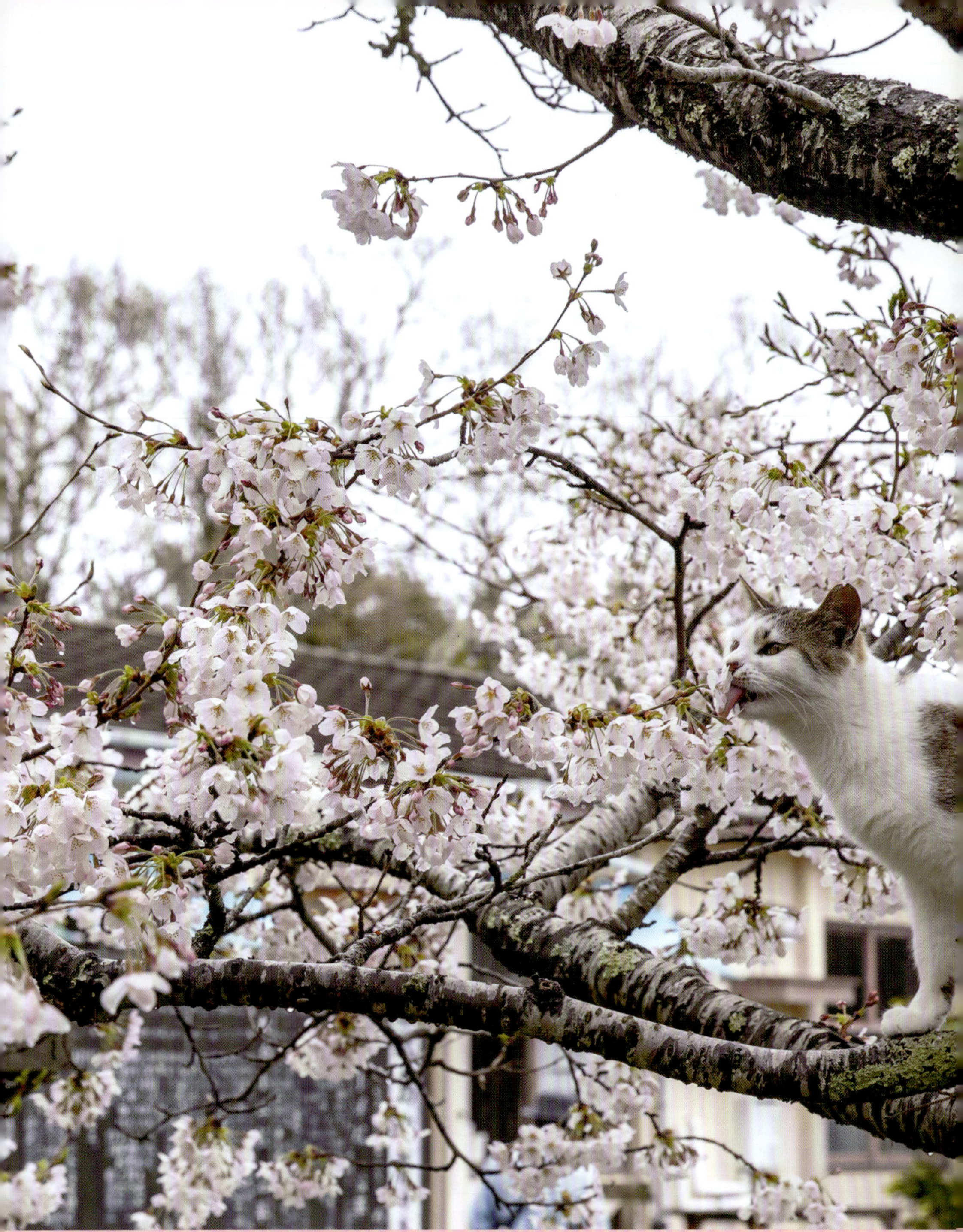

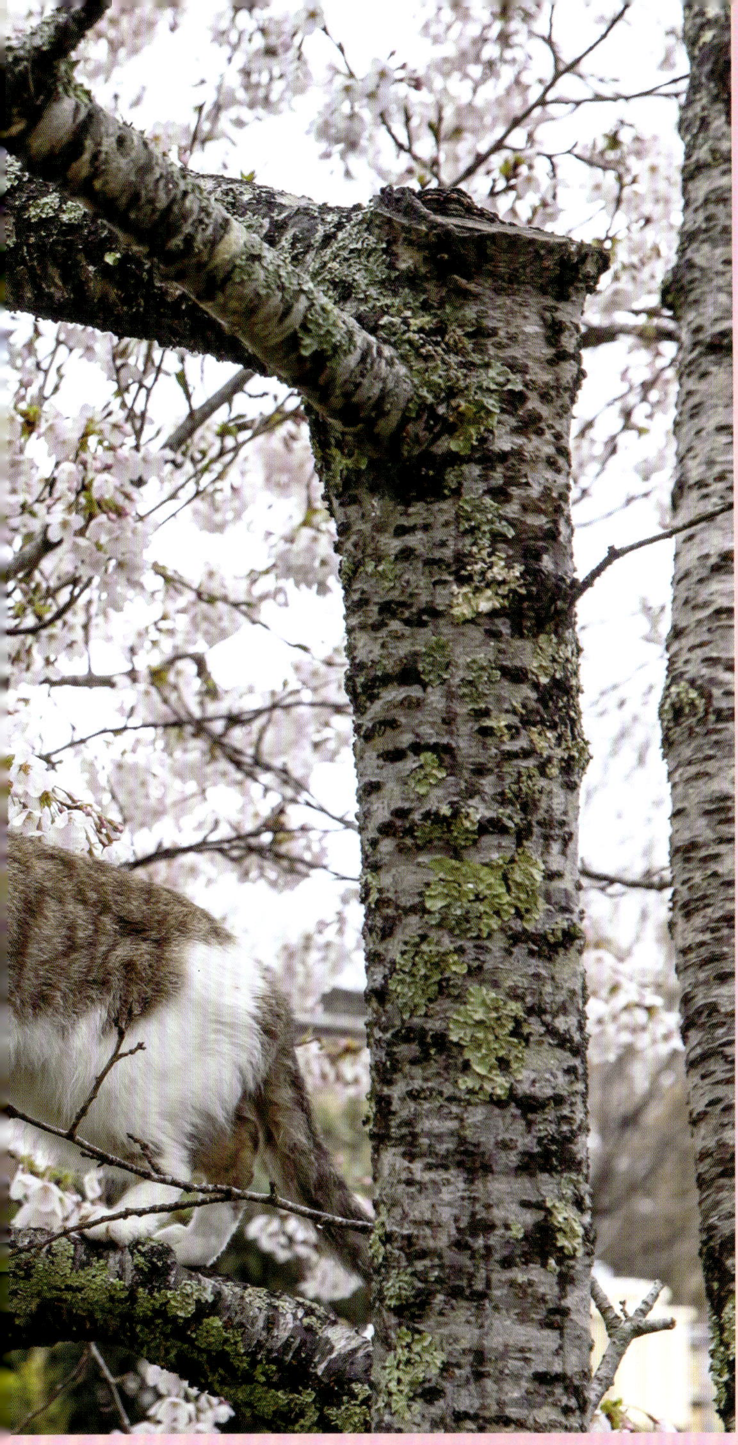

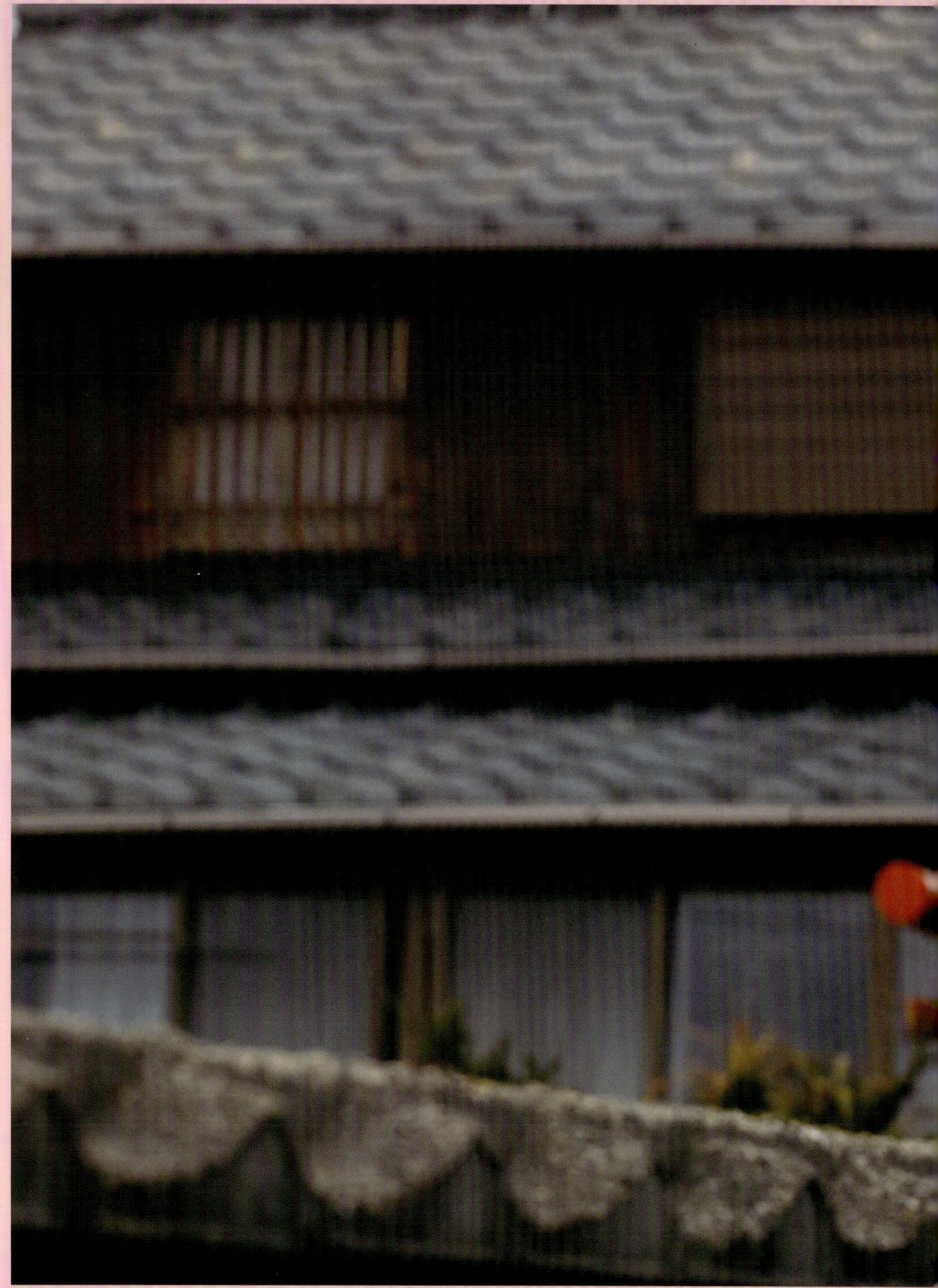

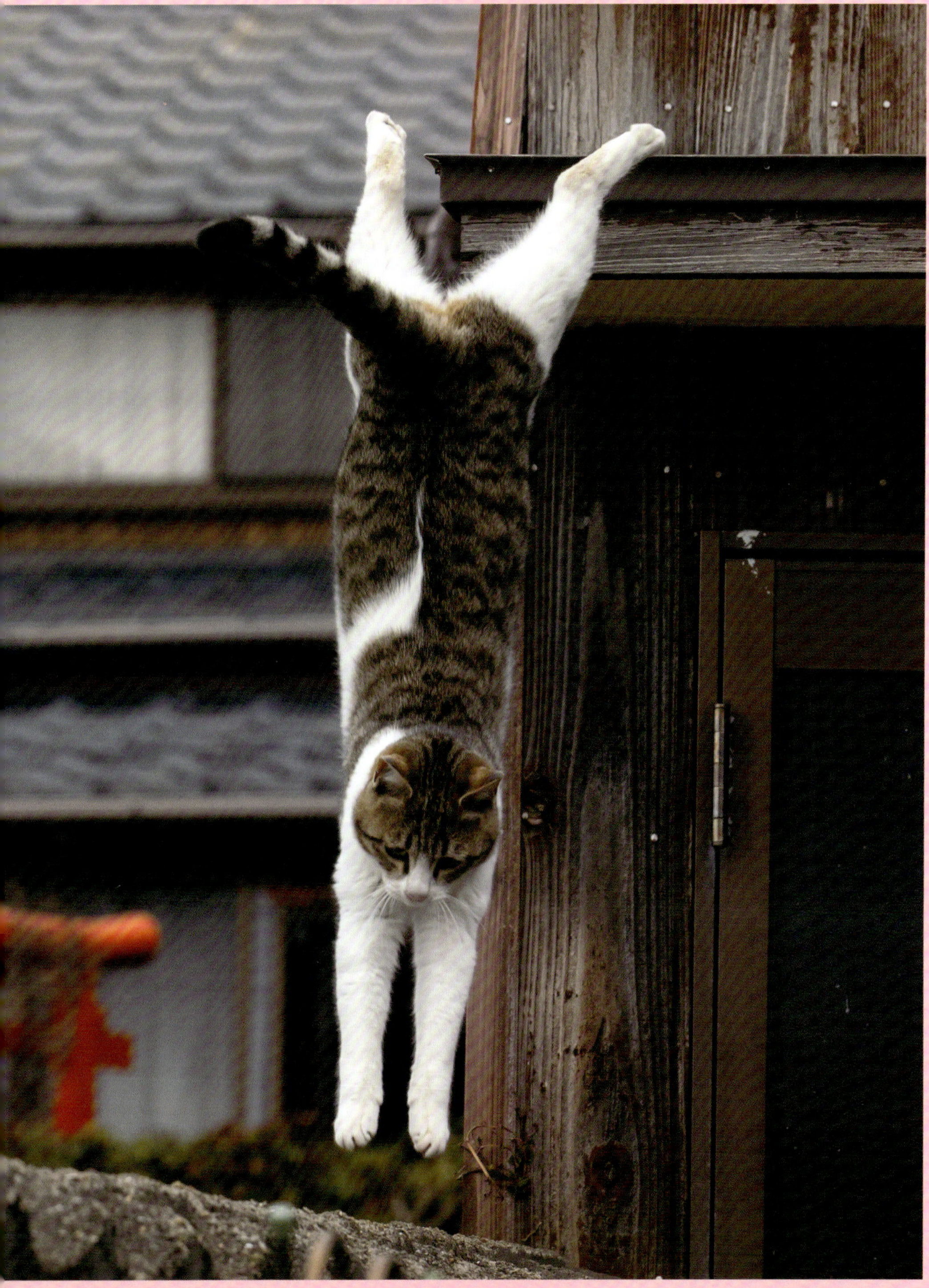

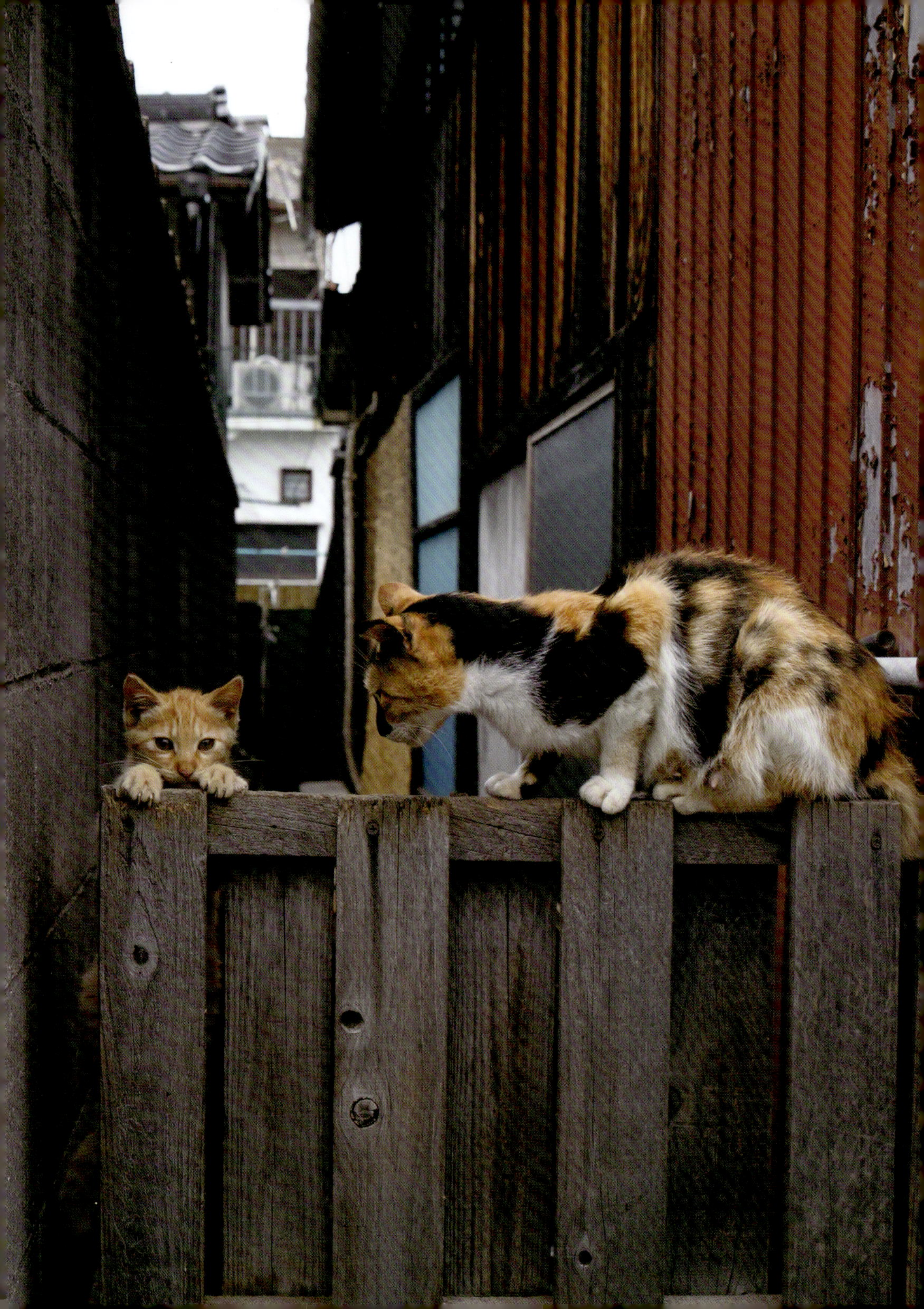

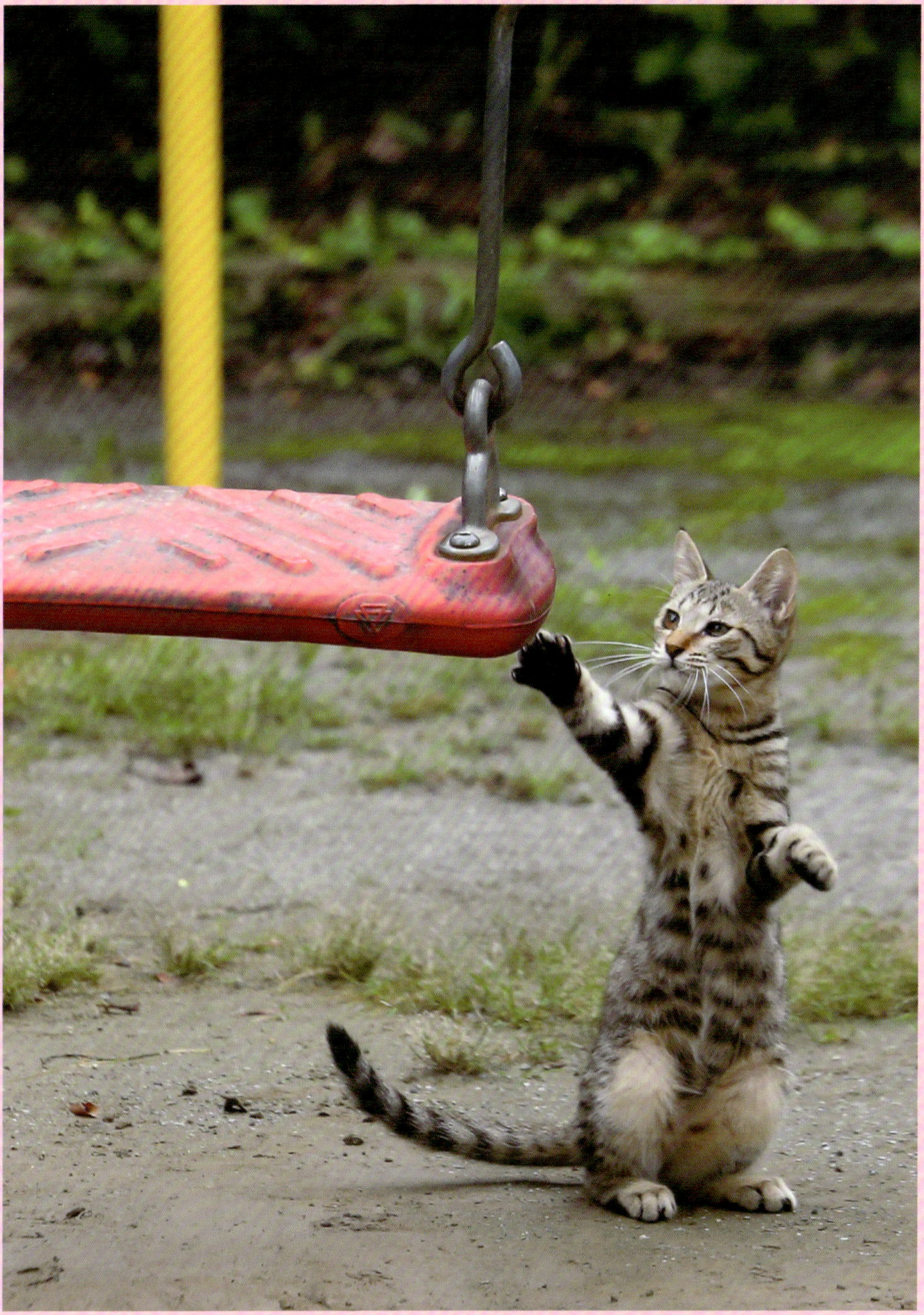

猫・ネコ

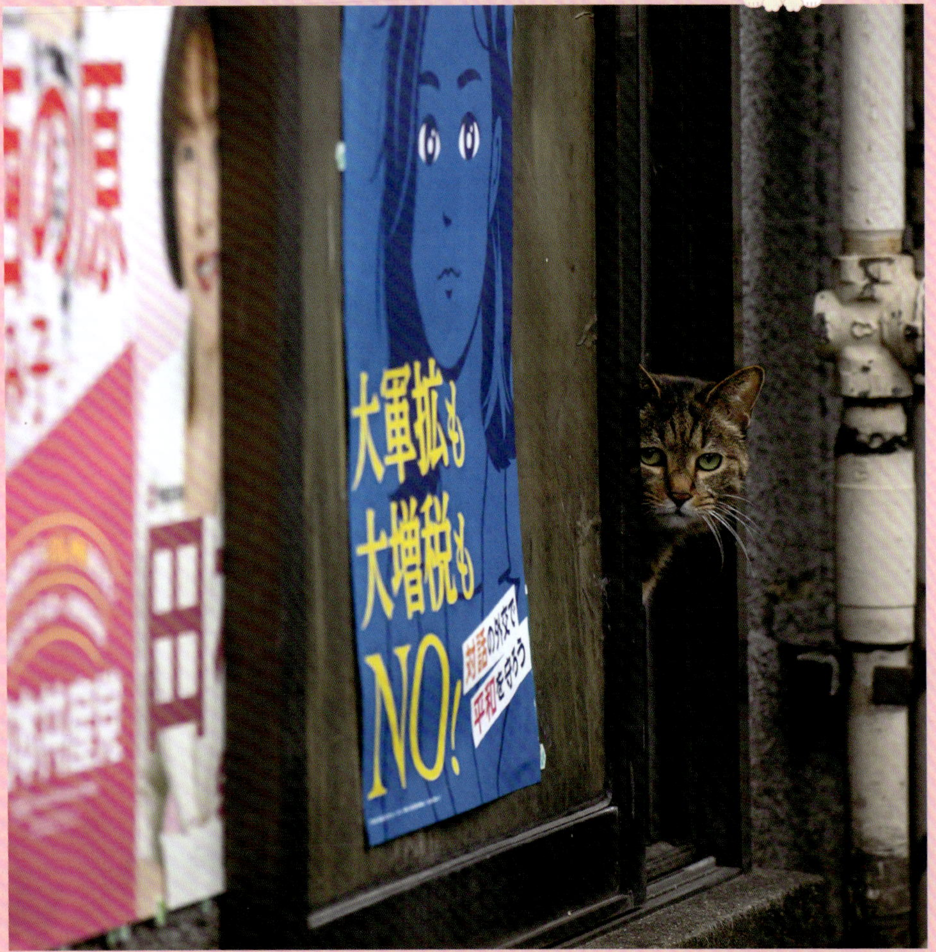
大軍拡も
大増税も
NO!
対話の外交で
平和を守ろう

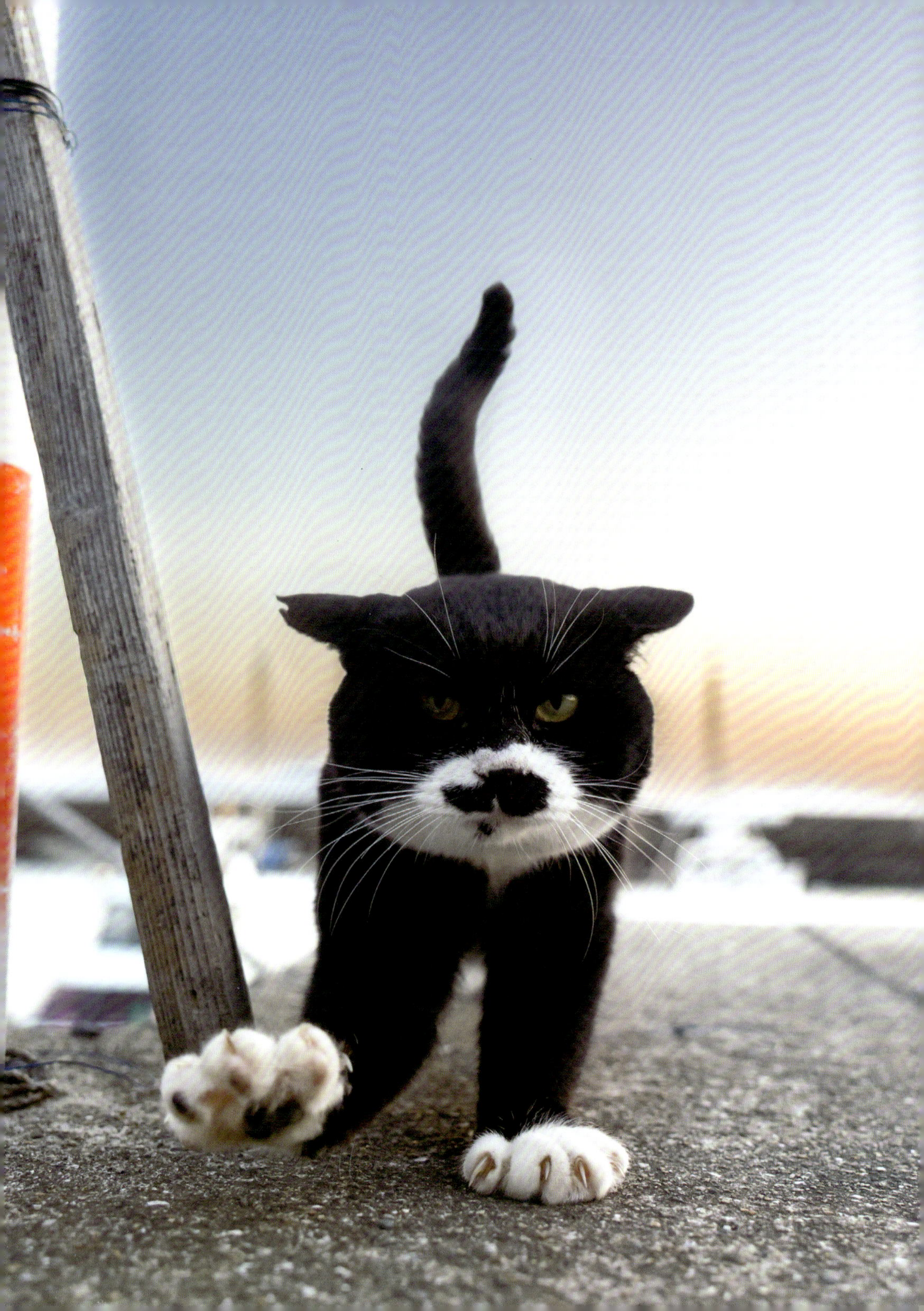

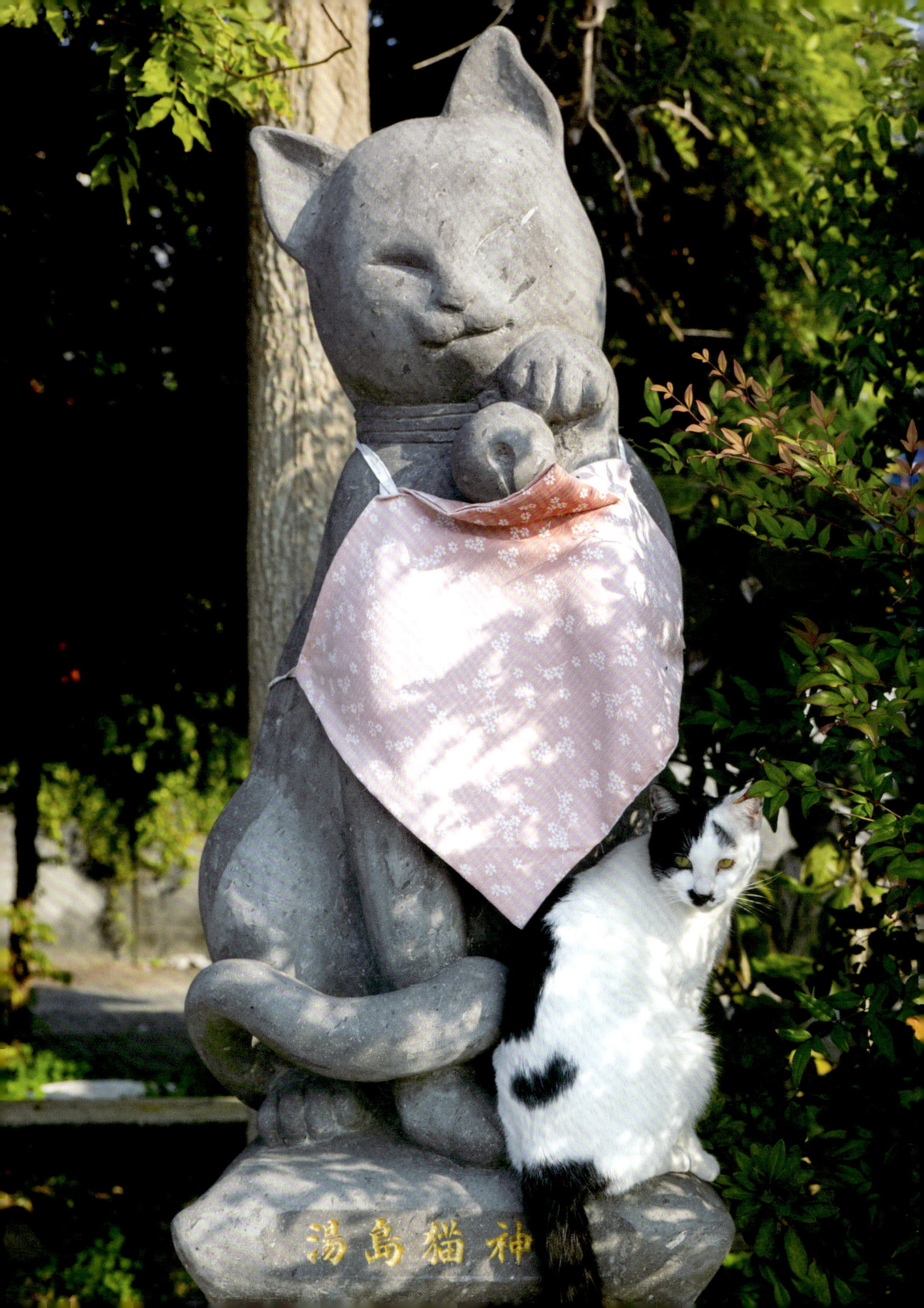
湯島猫神

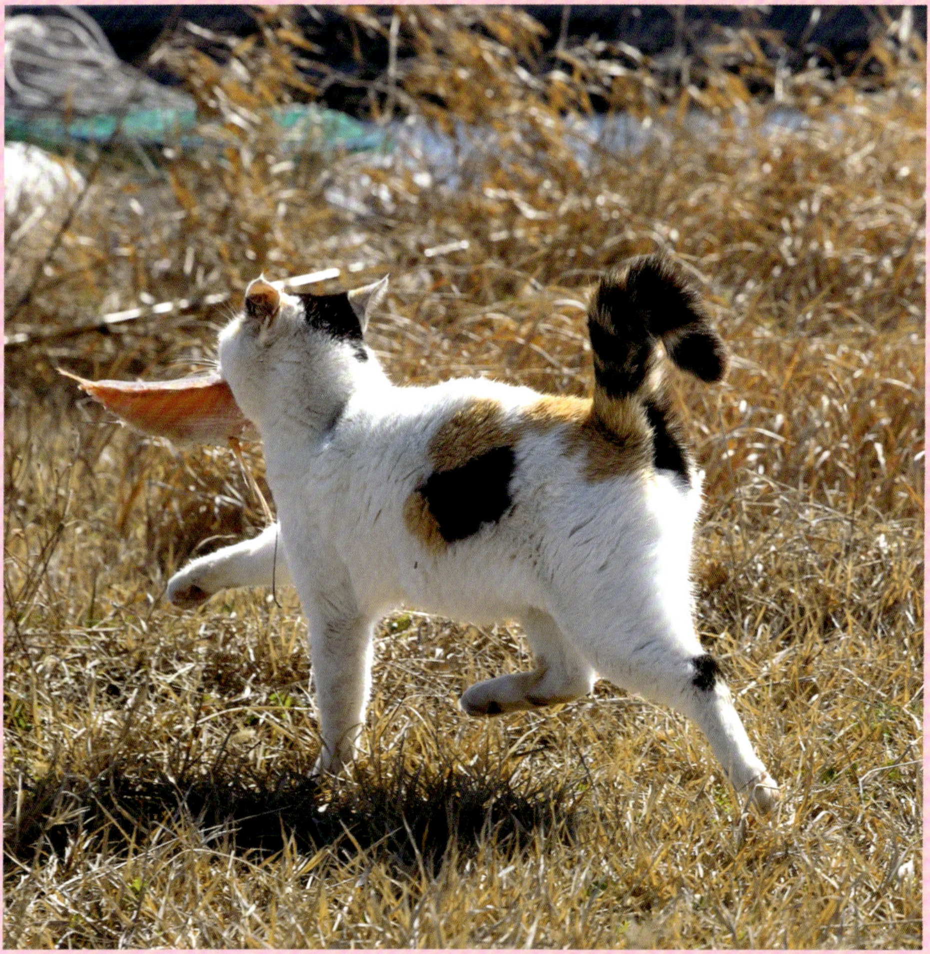

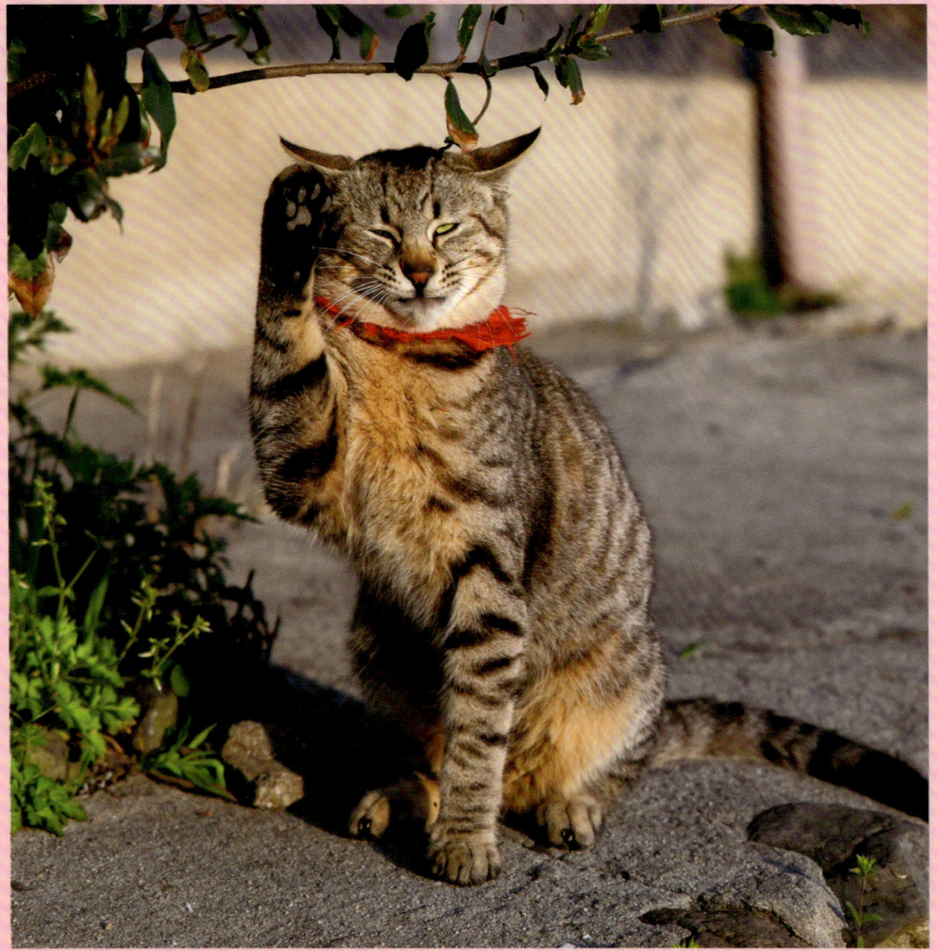

猫・ネコ

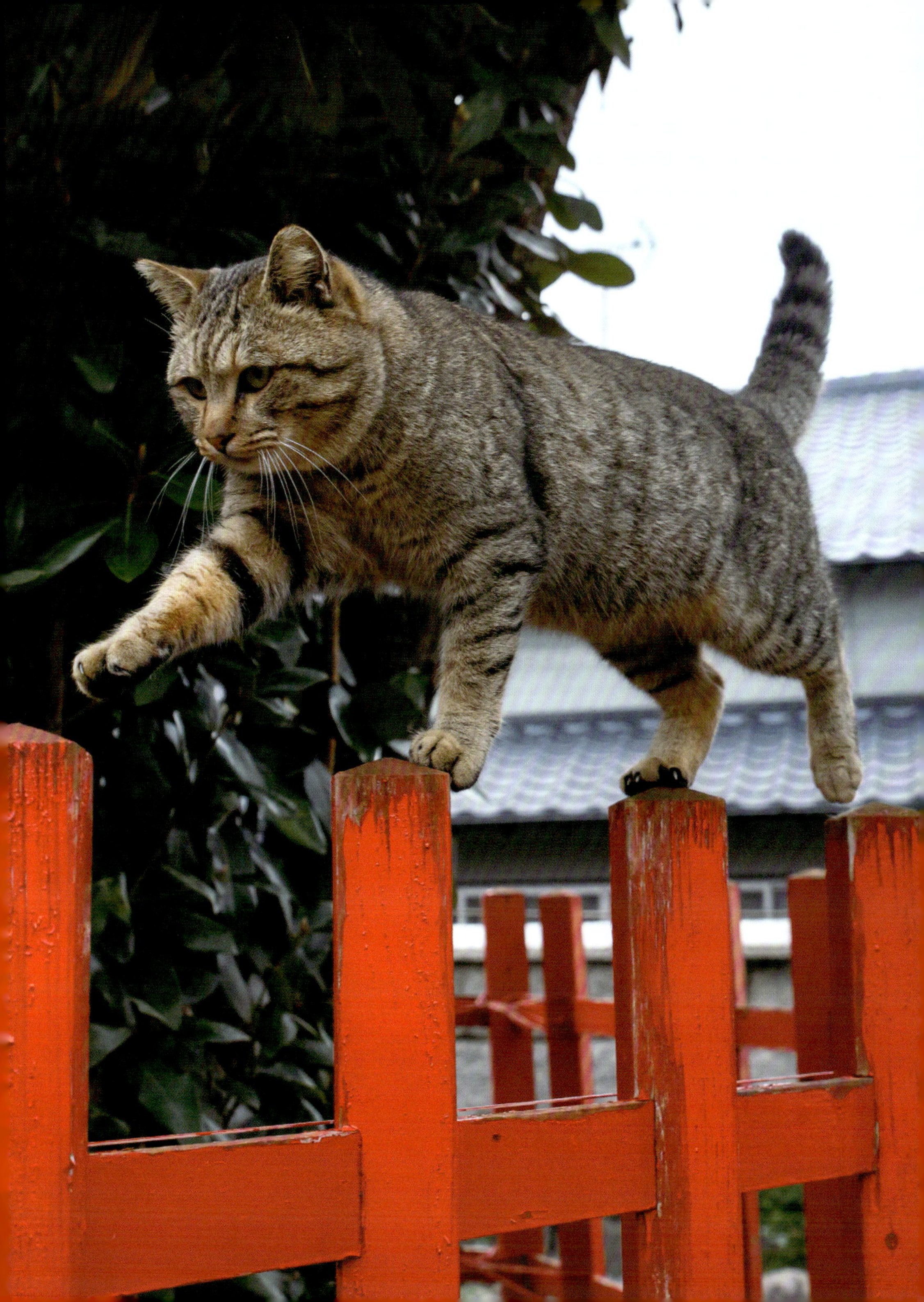

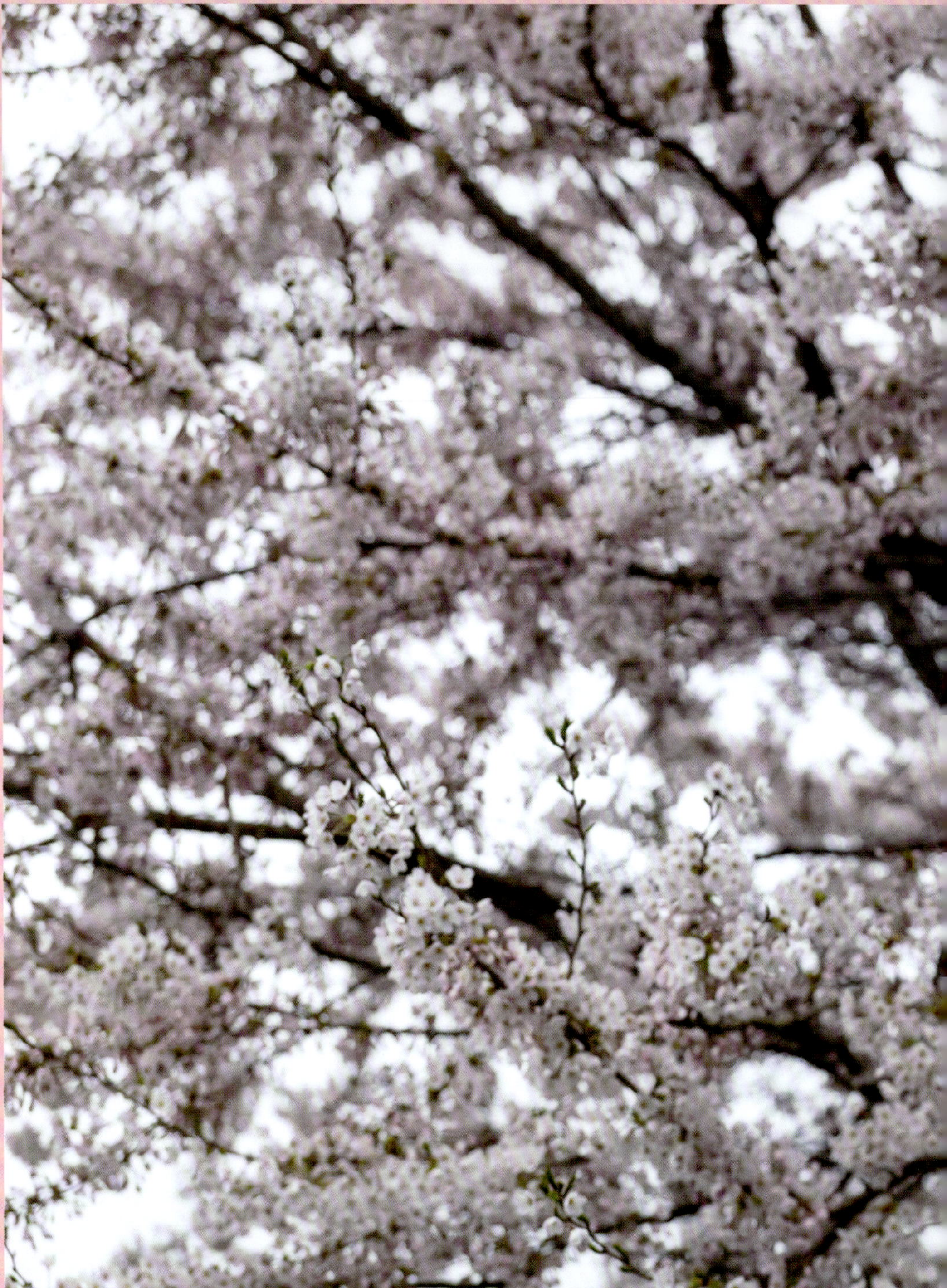

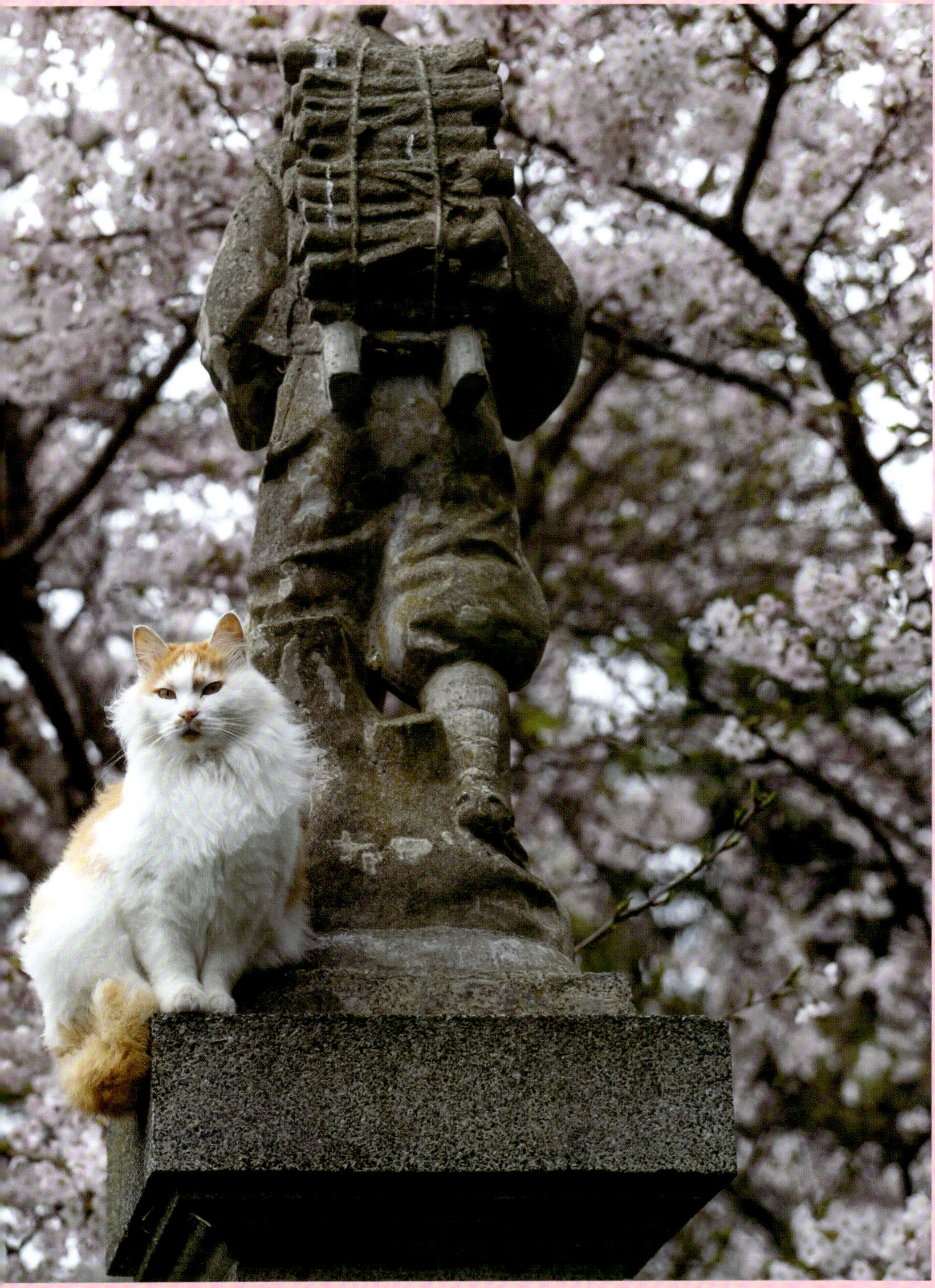

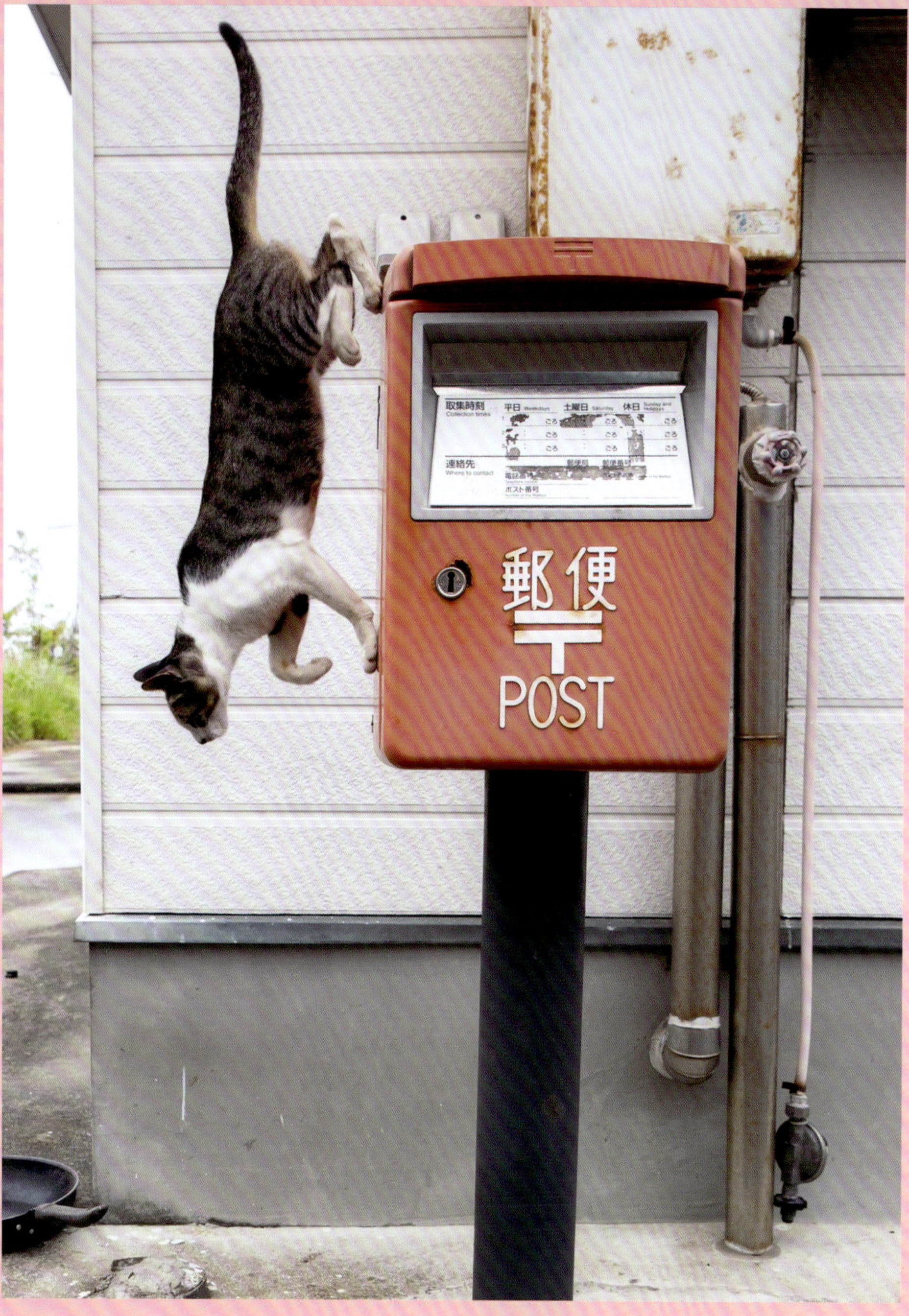
郵便
POST

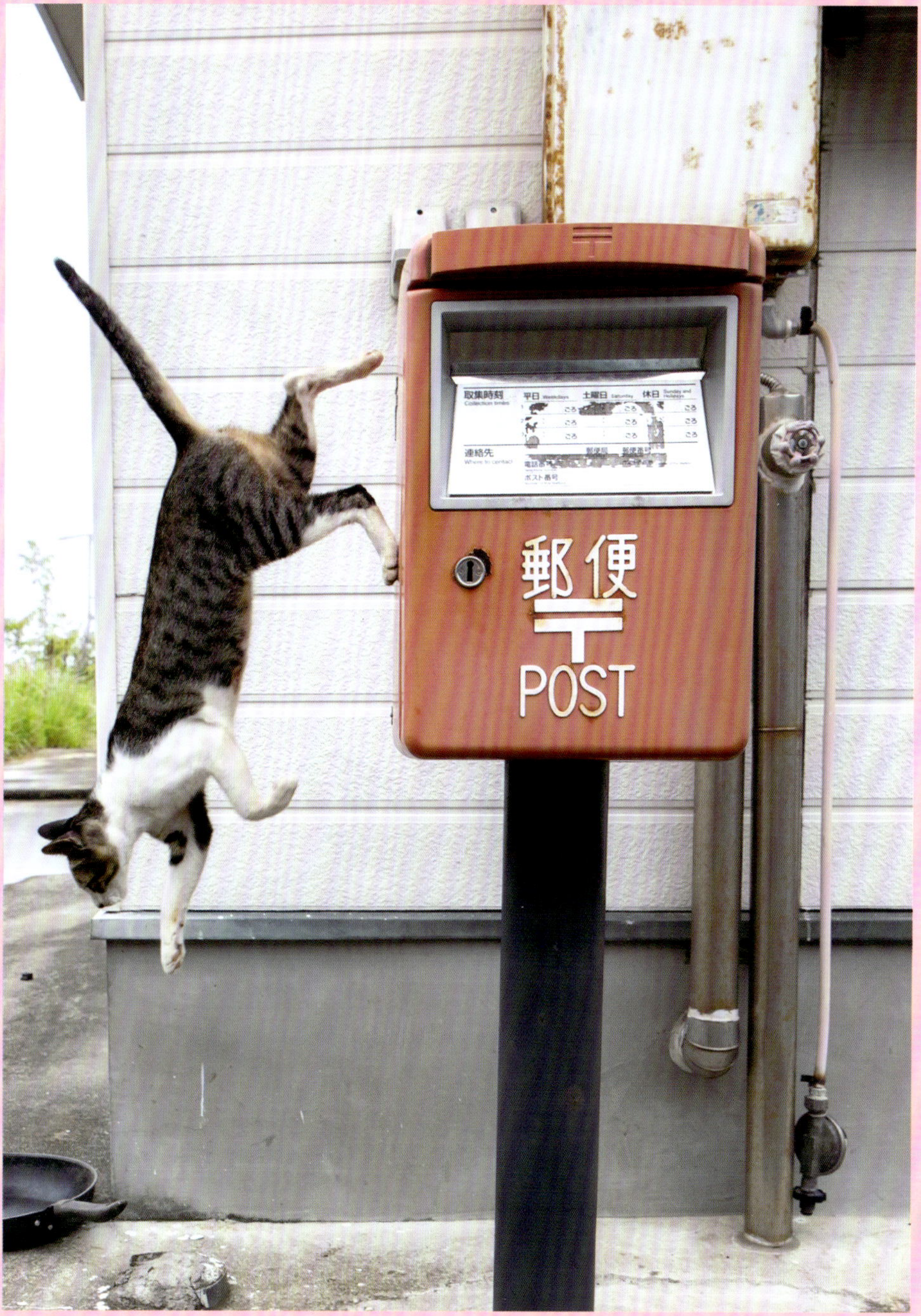

猫・ネコ

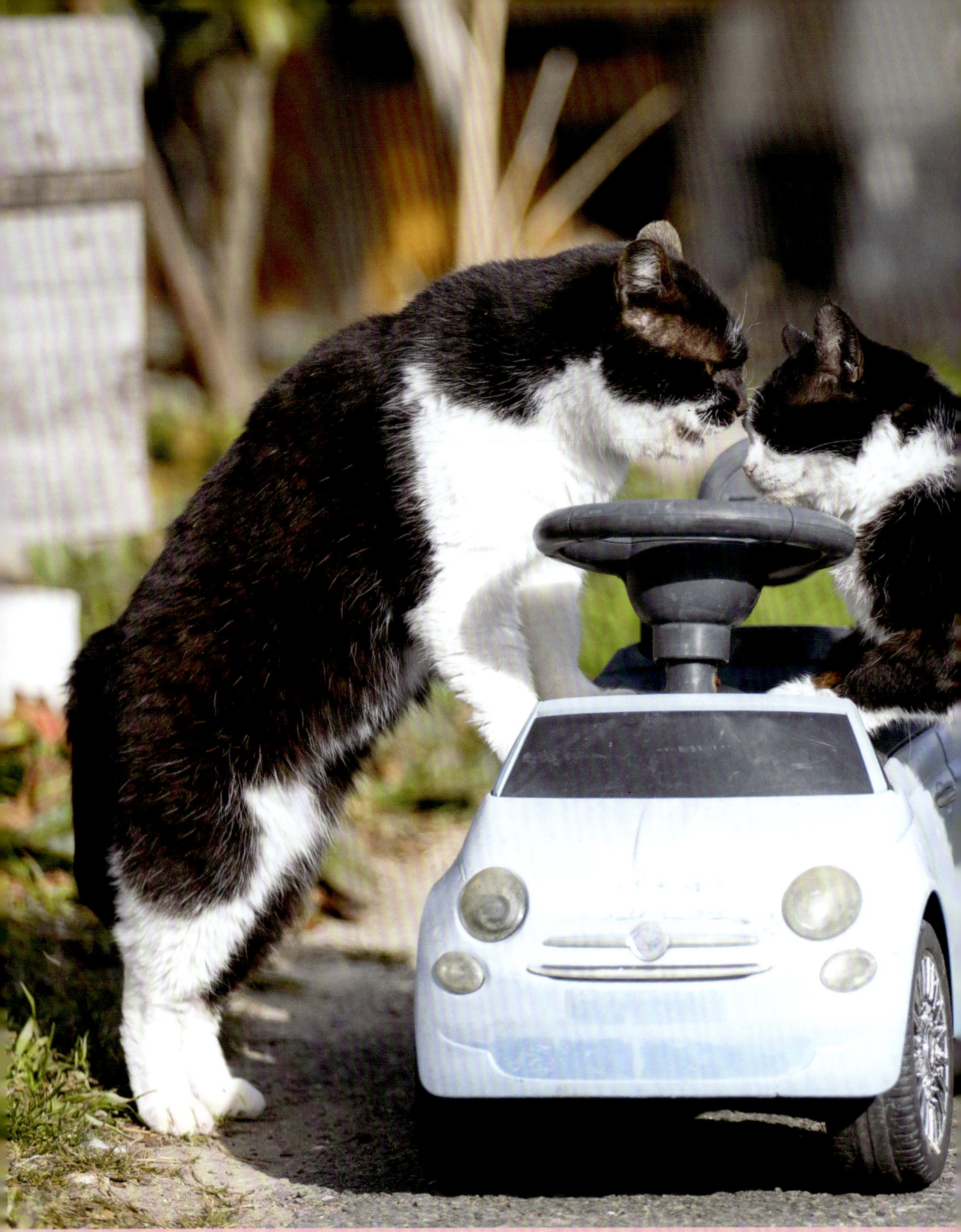

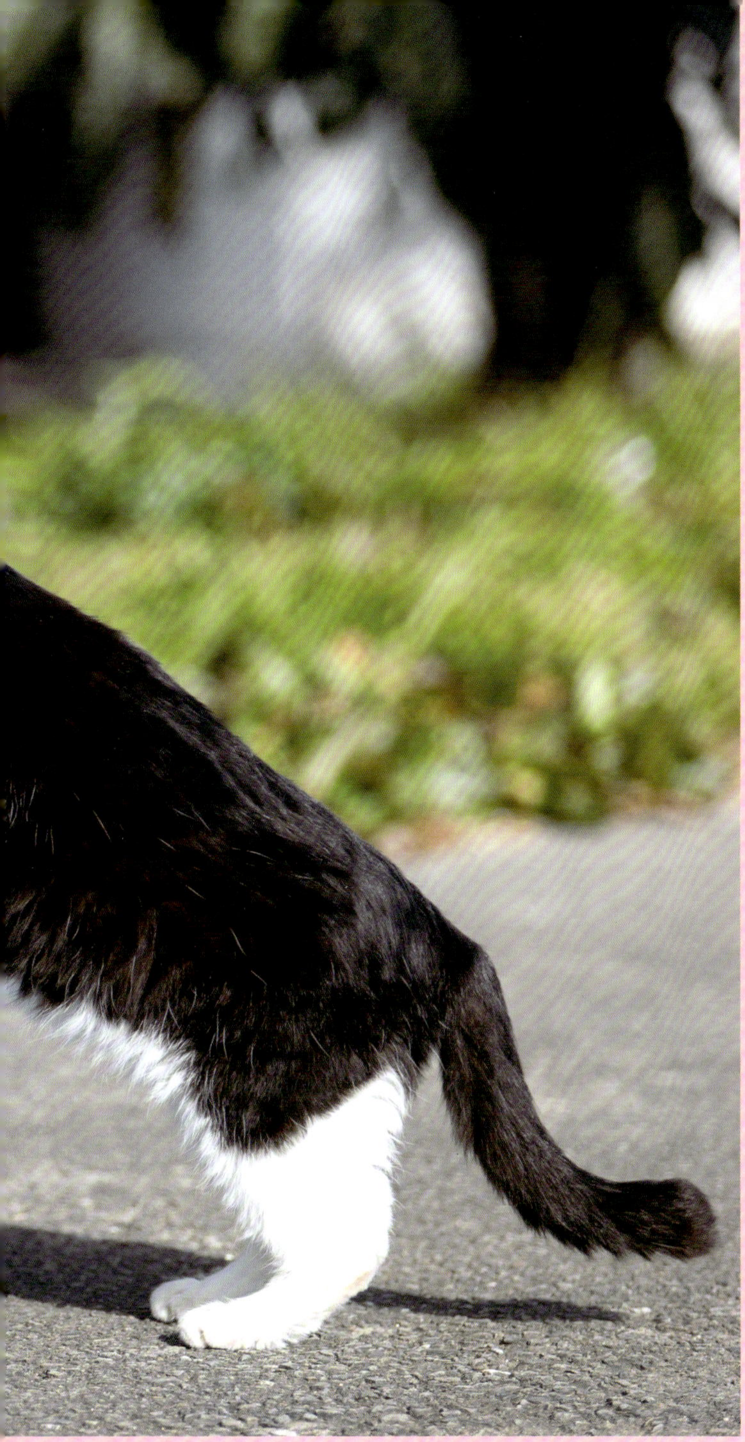

猫・ネコ

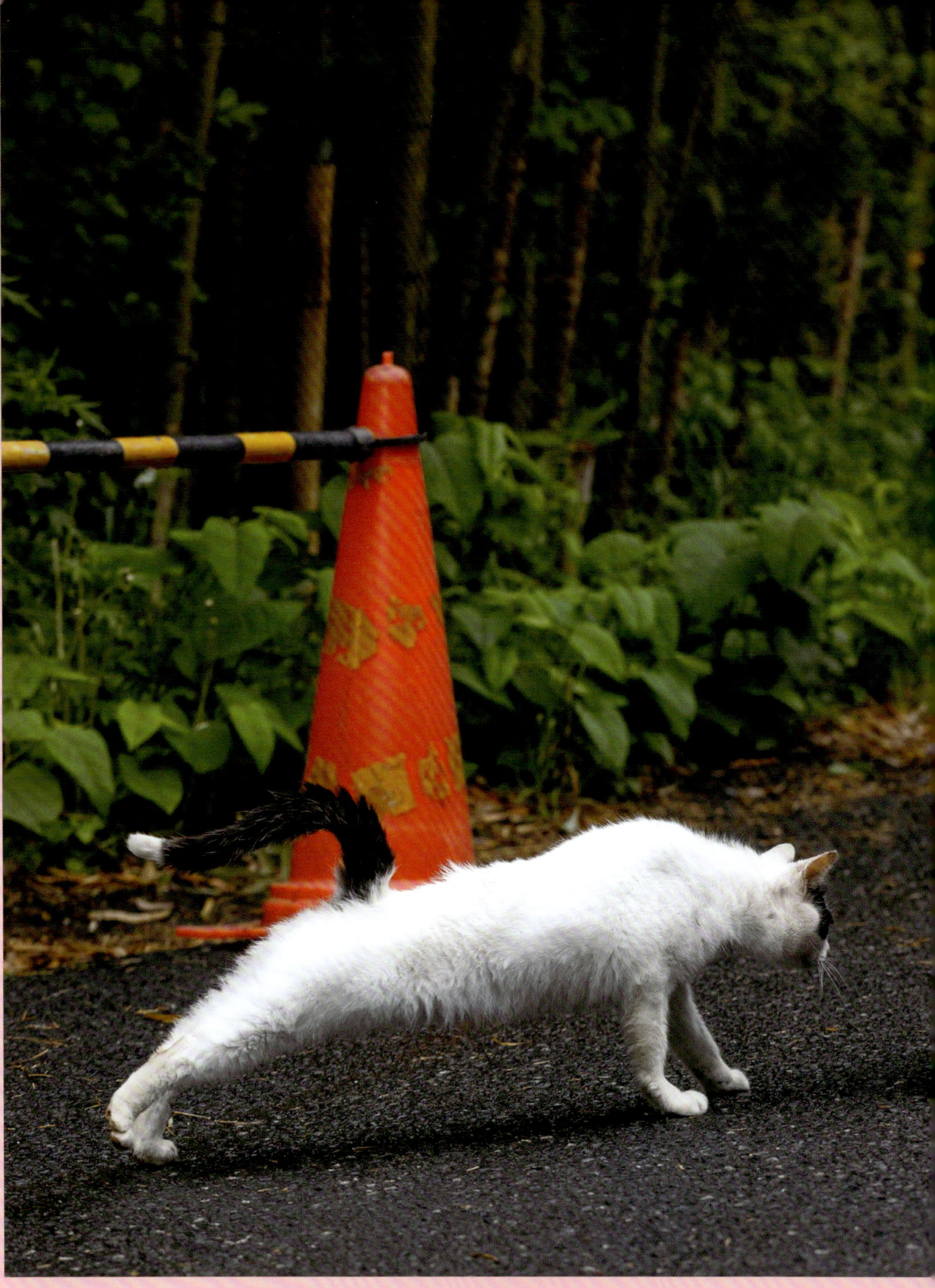

猫・ネコ

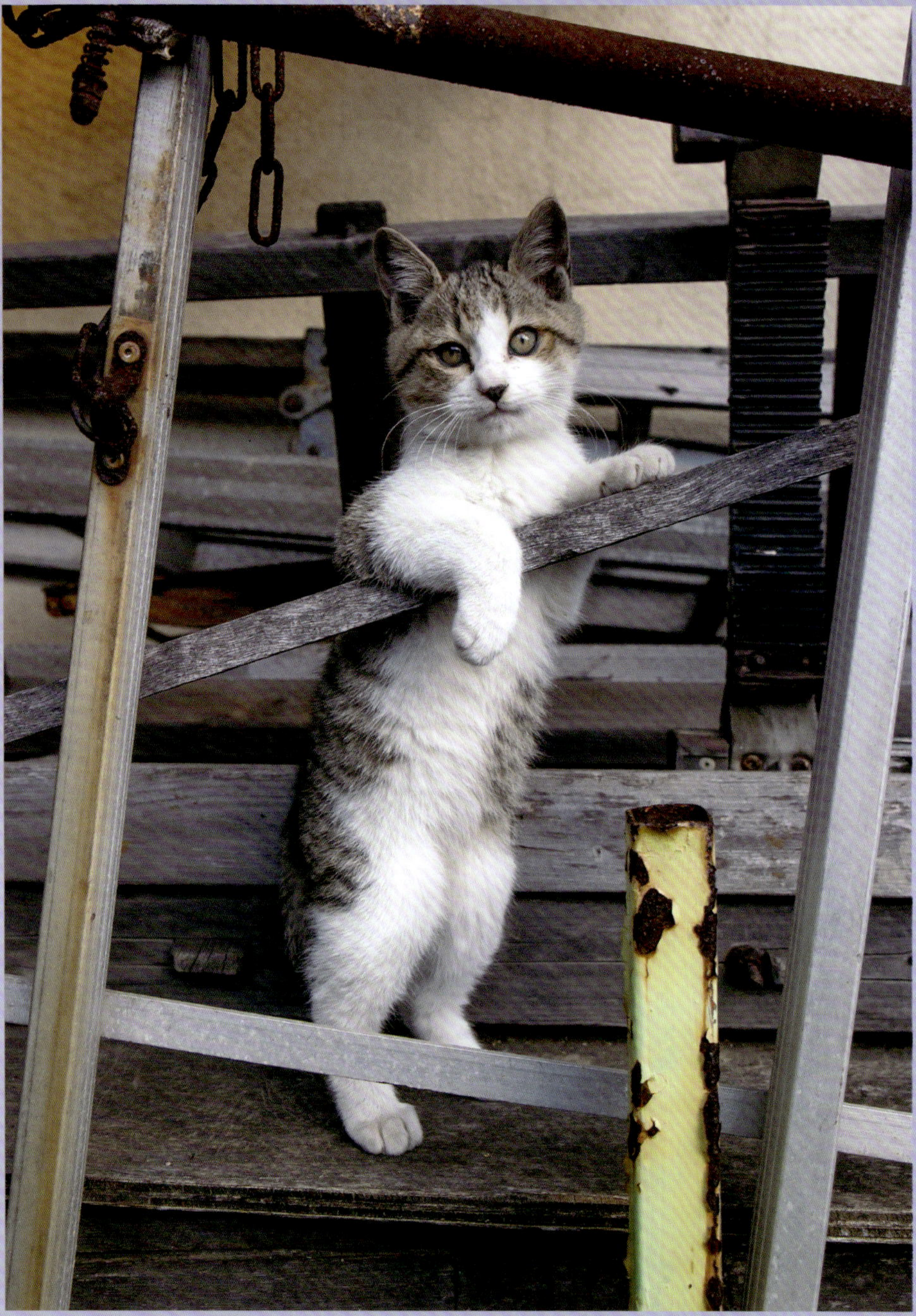

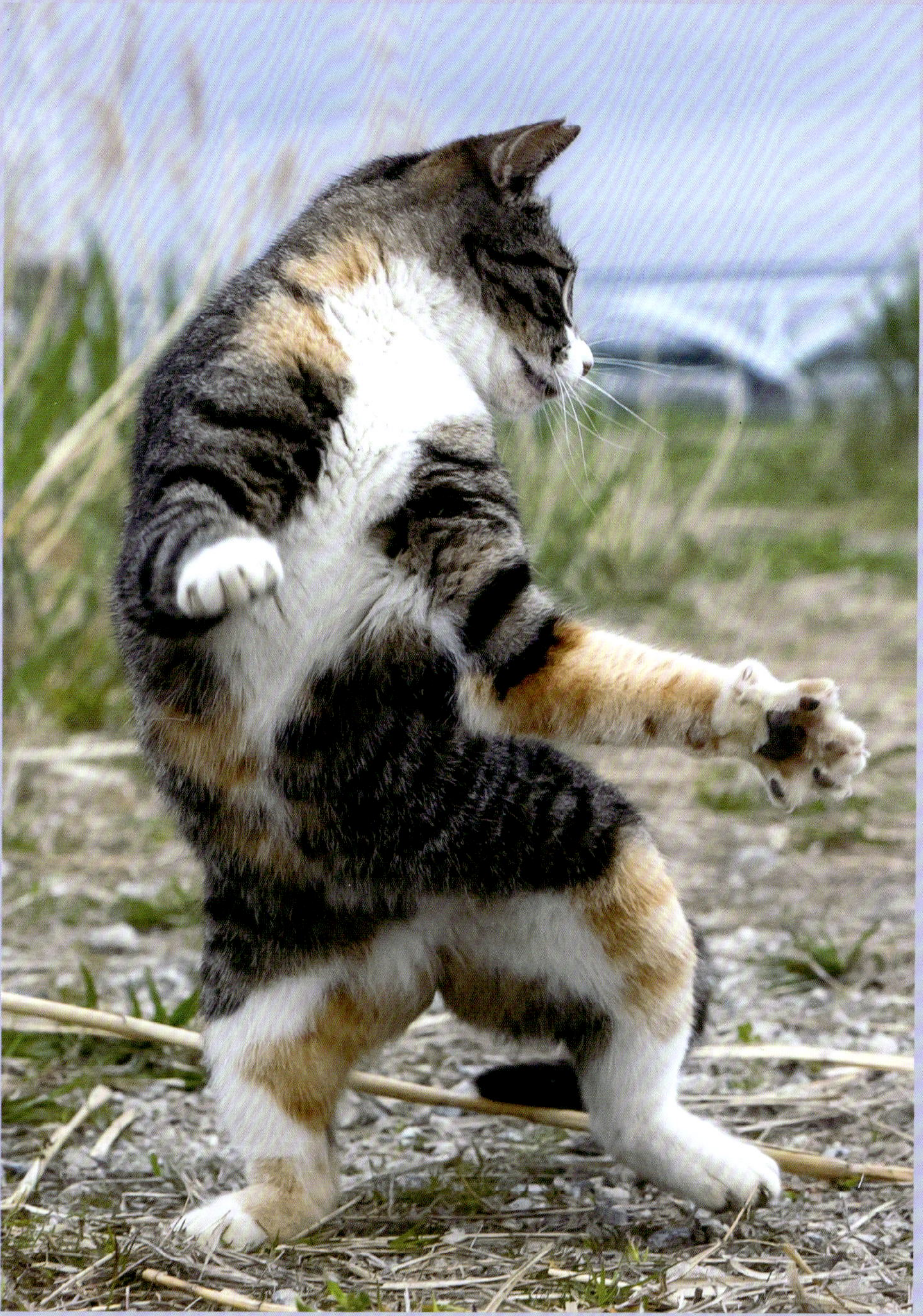

猫・ネコ

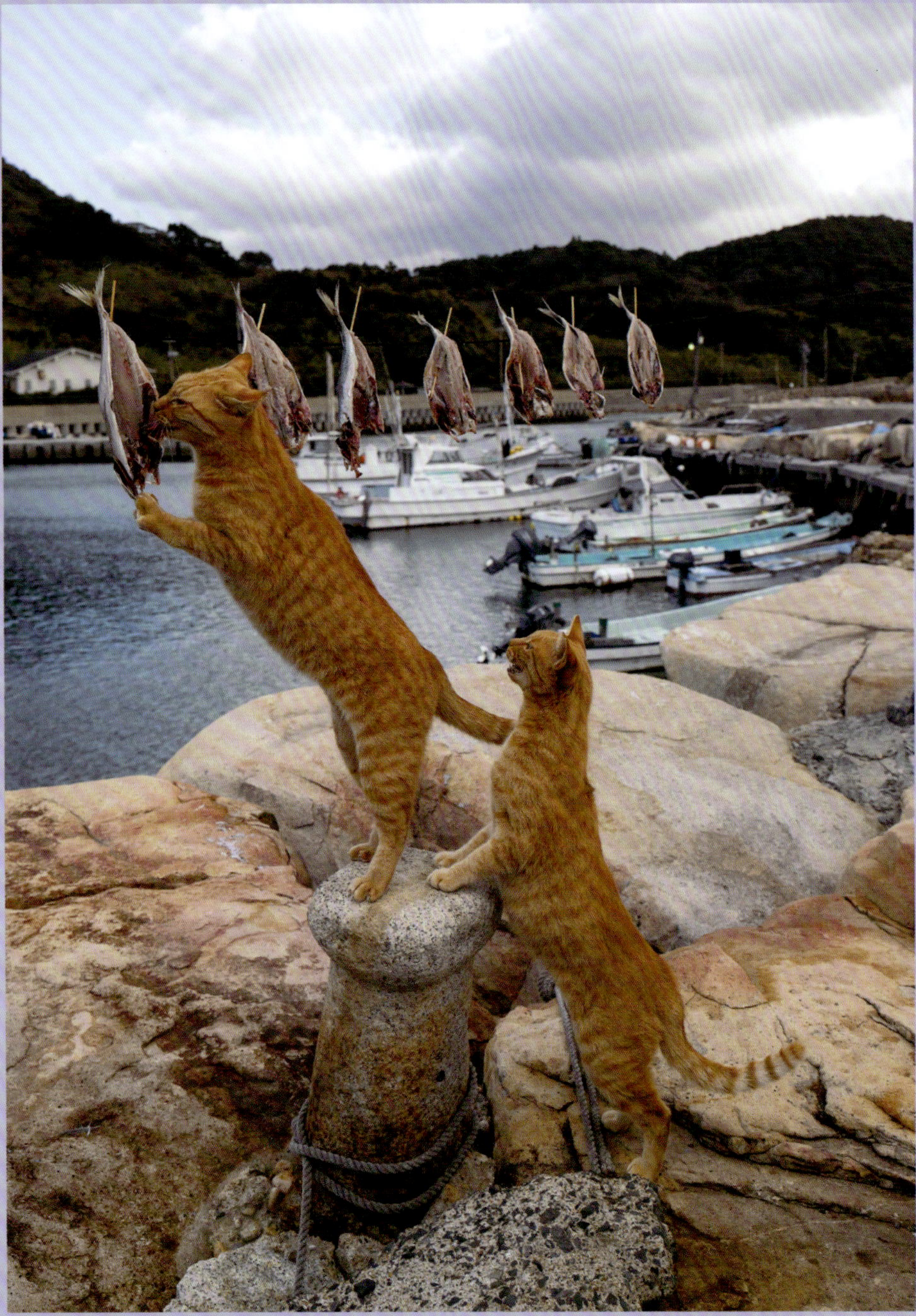

猫・ネコ

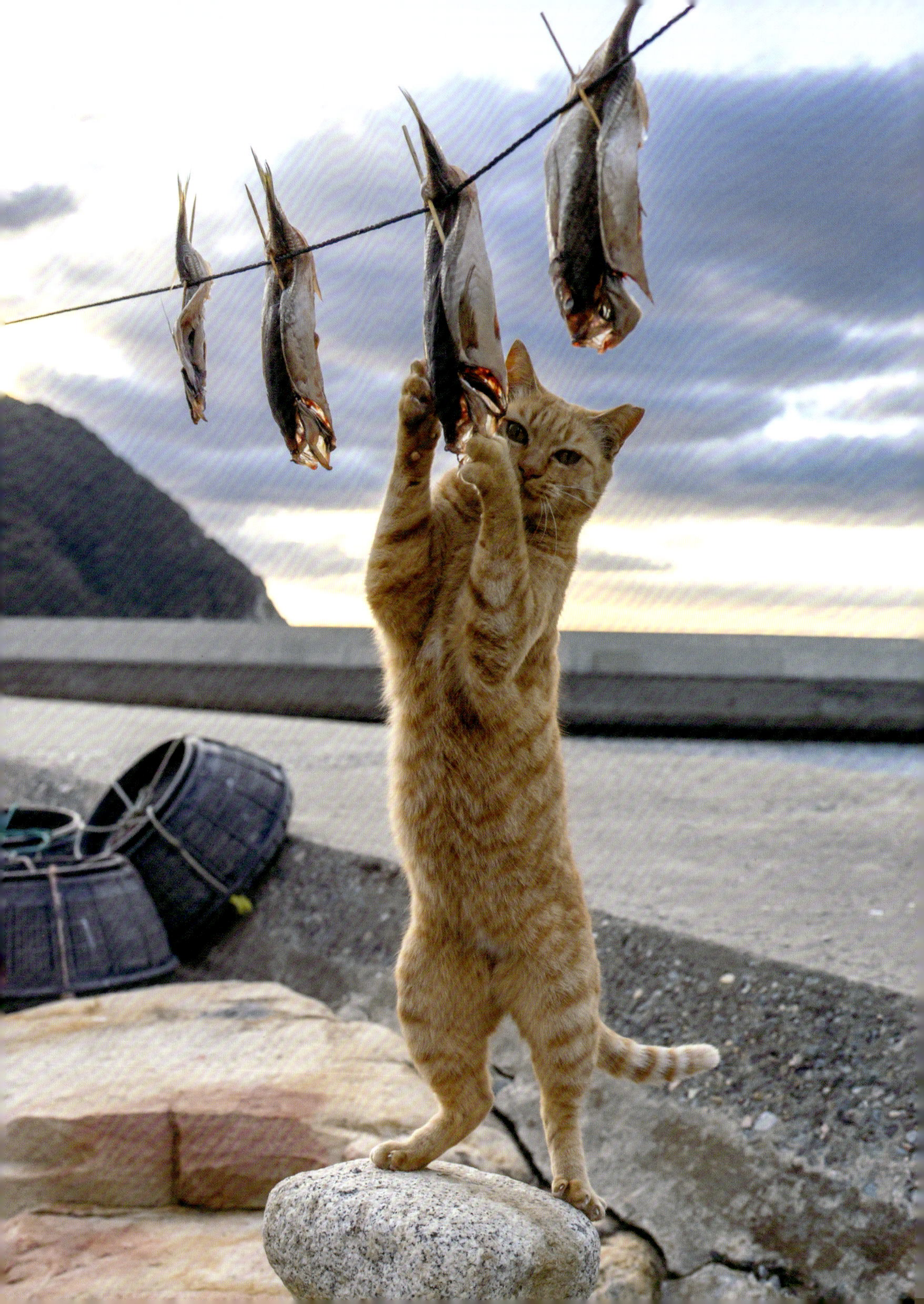

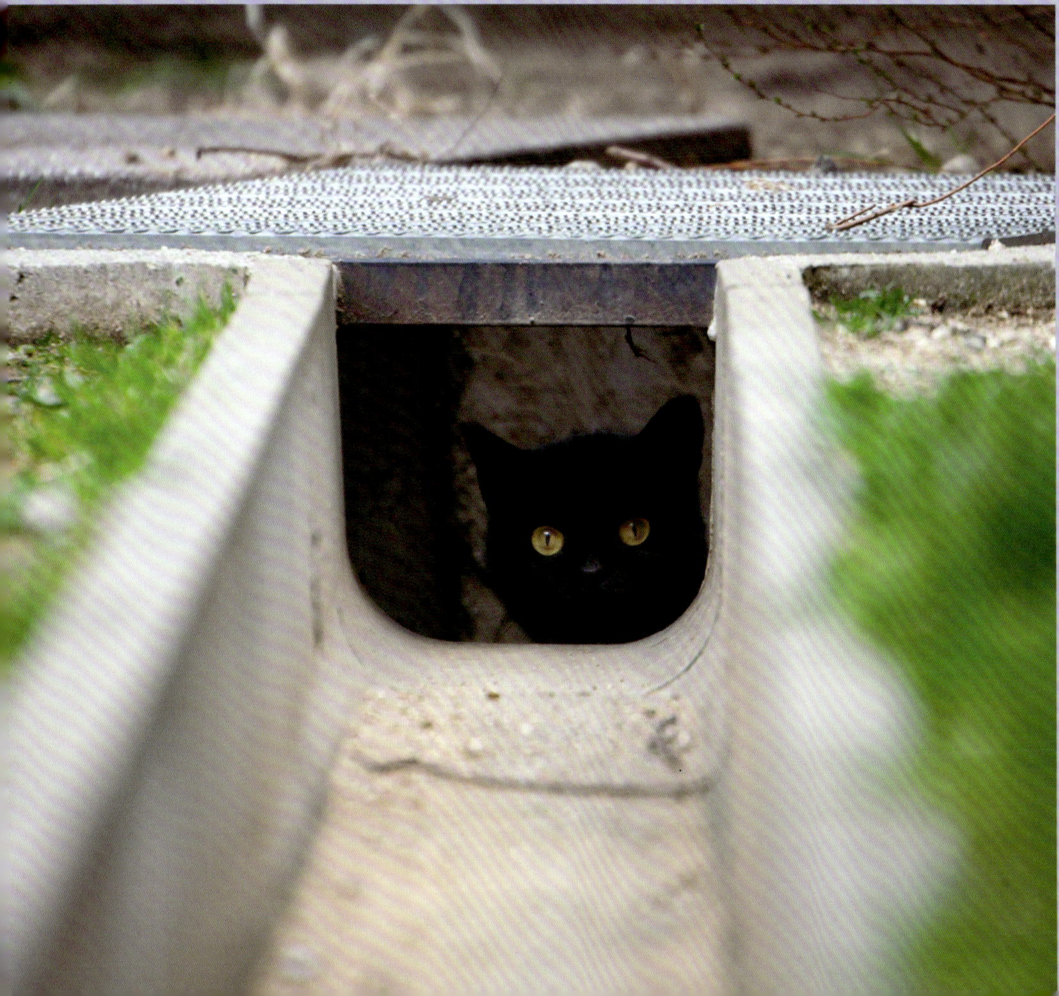

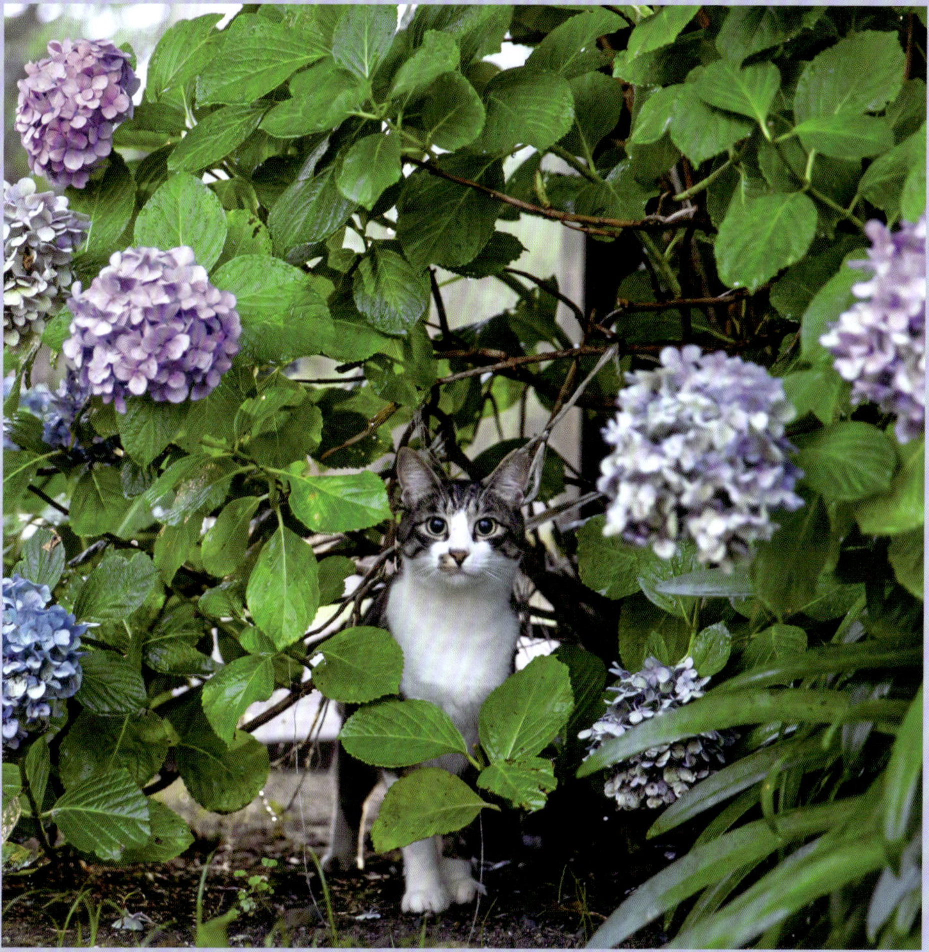

猫・ネコ

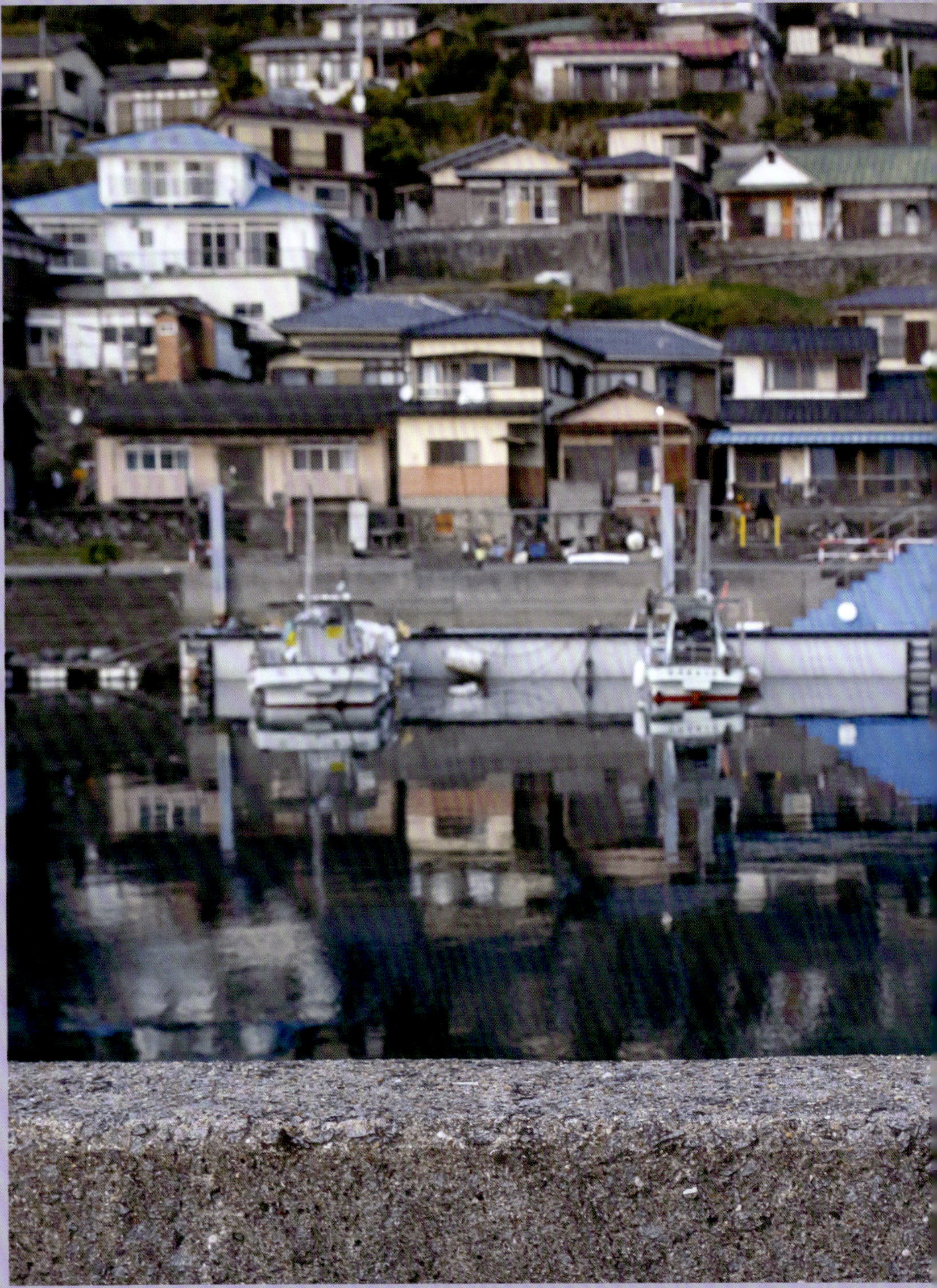

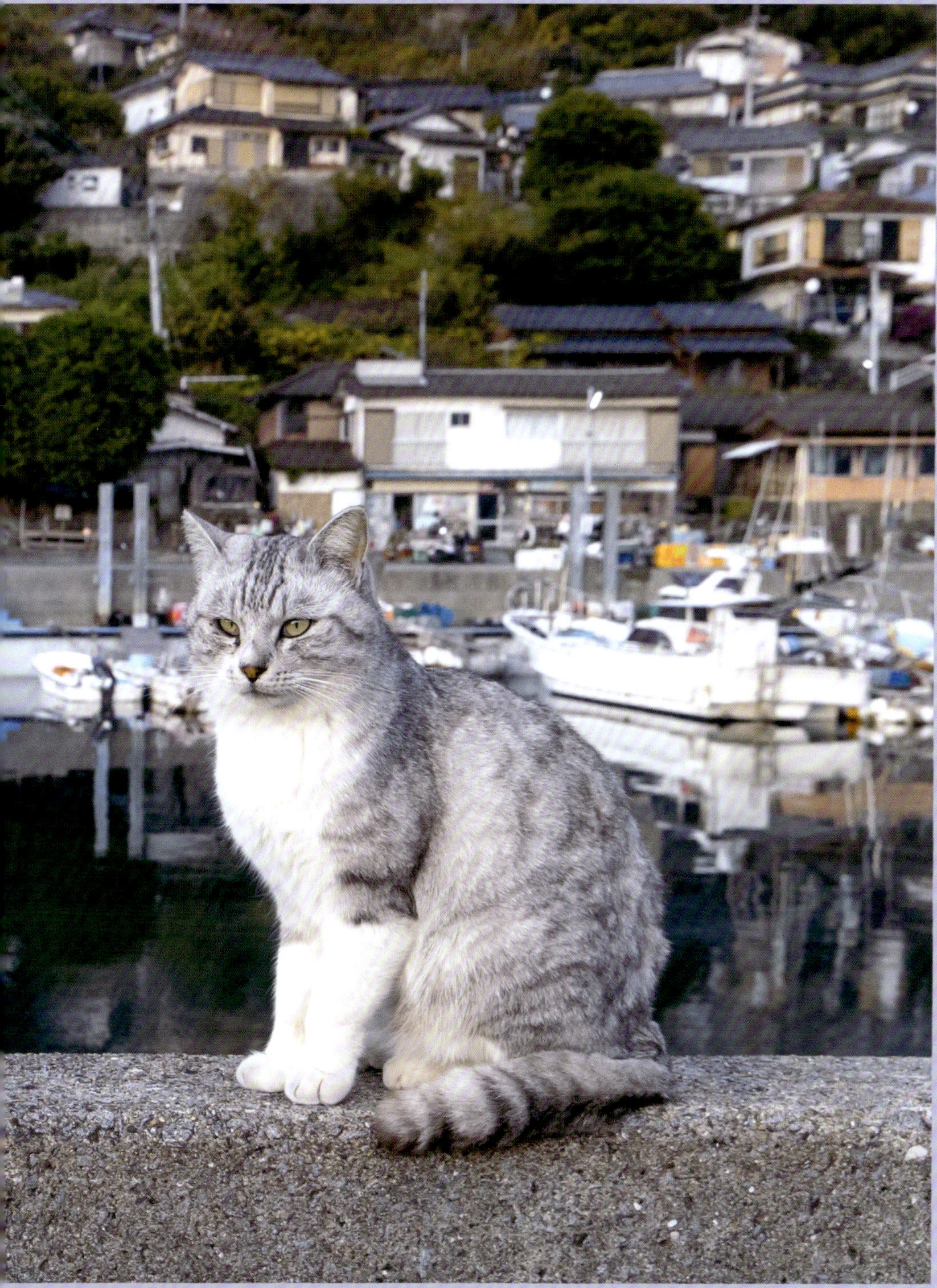

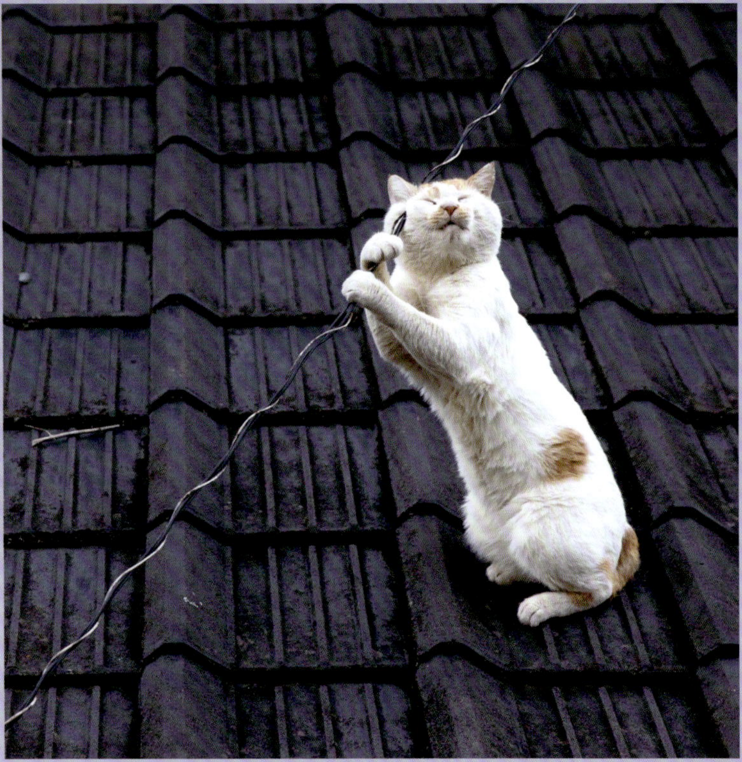

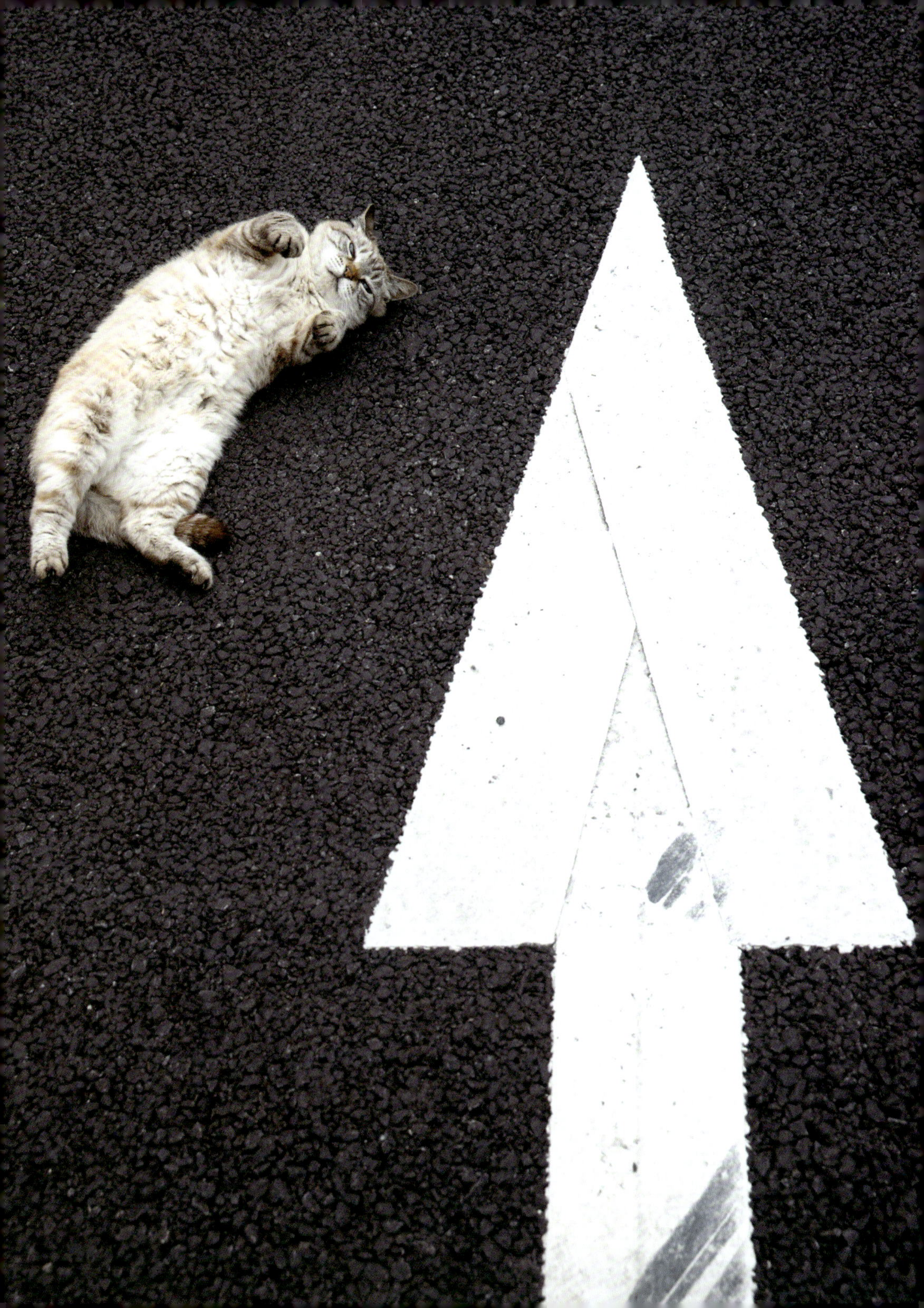

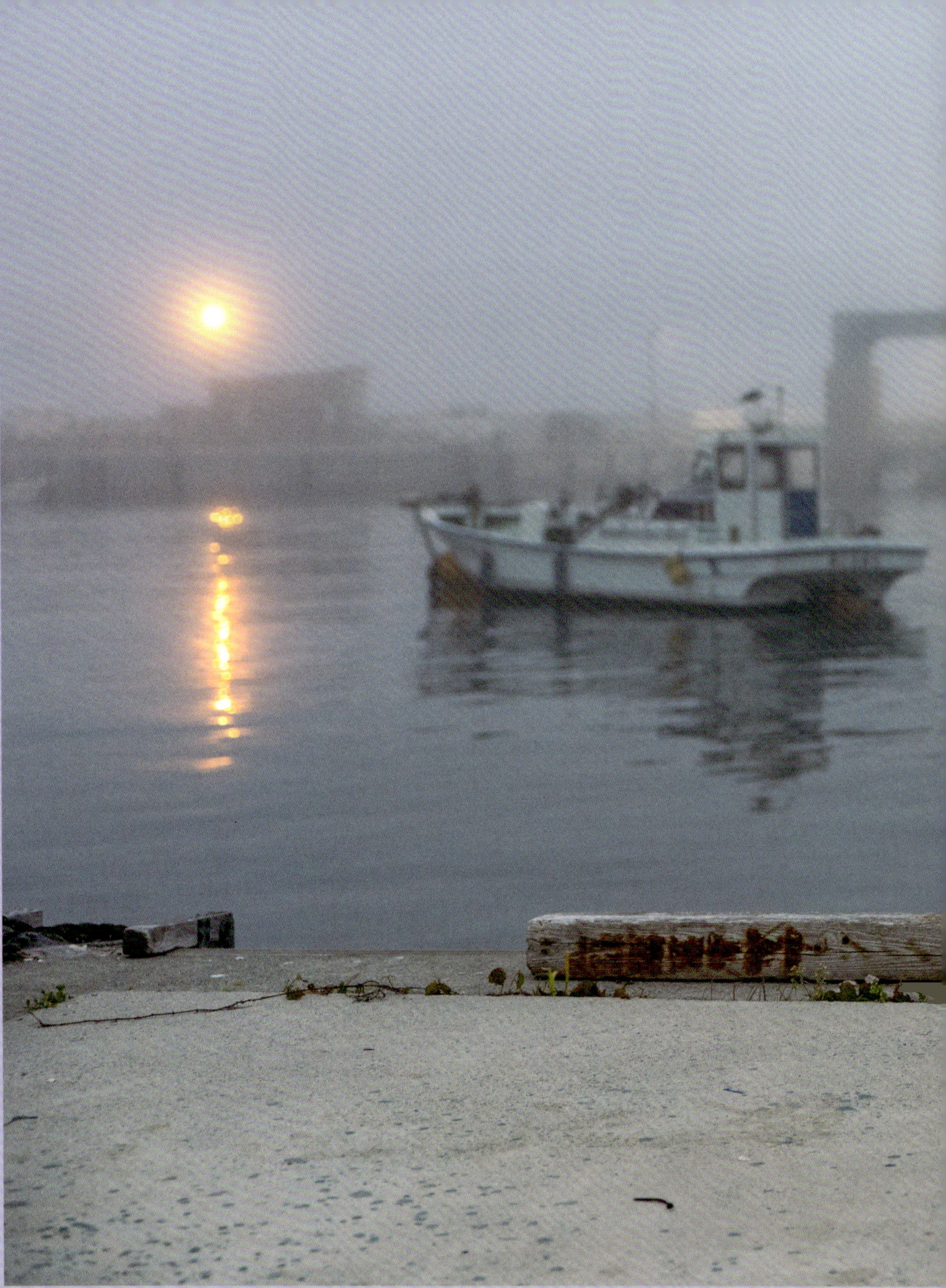

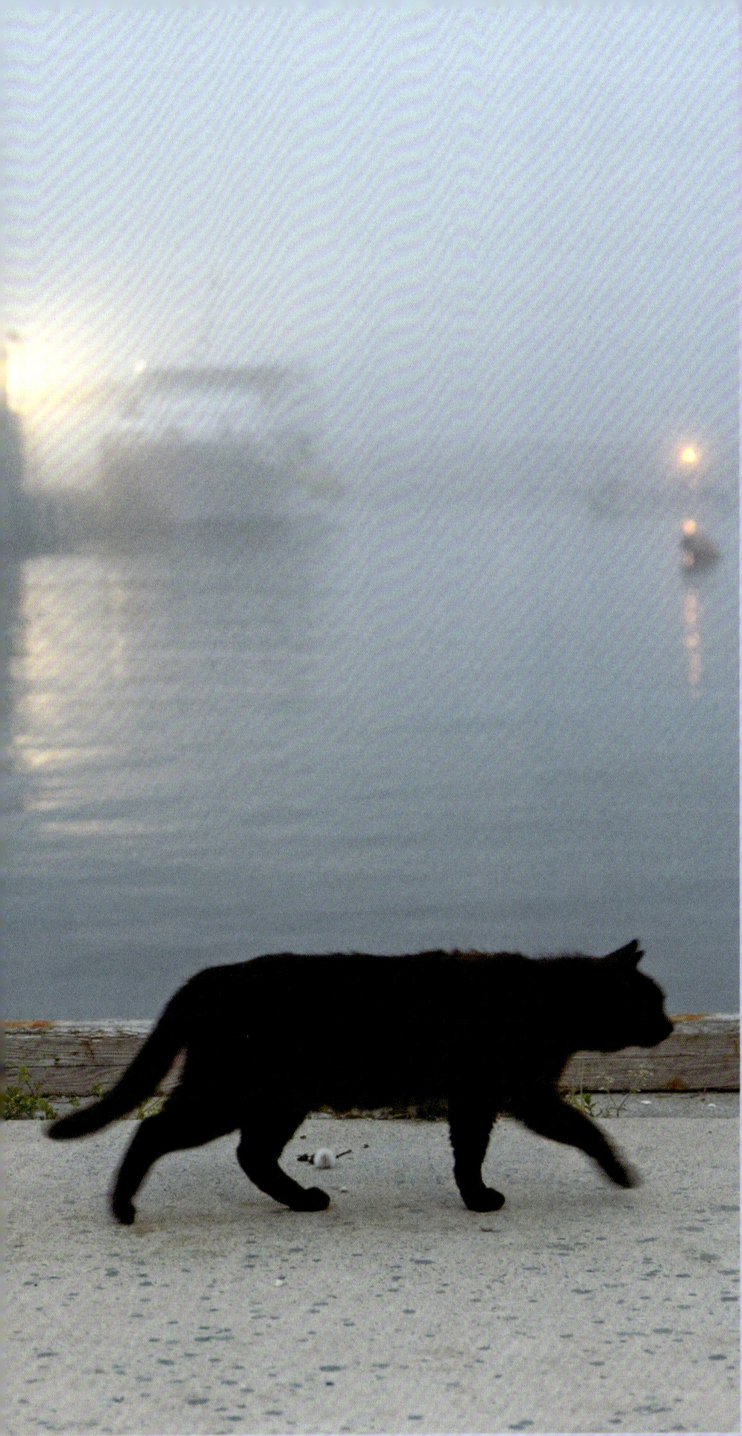

猫・ネコ

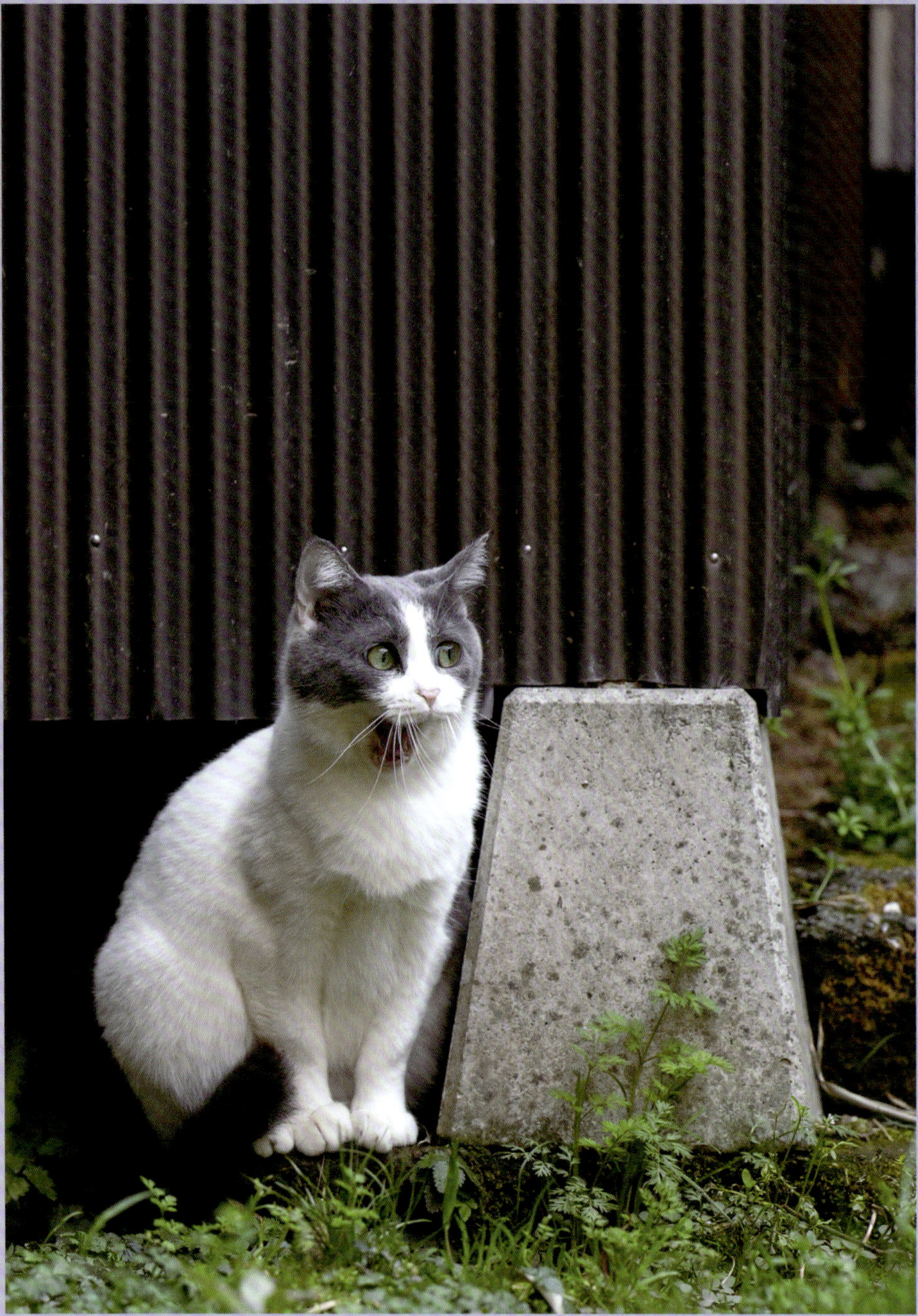

猫・ネコ

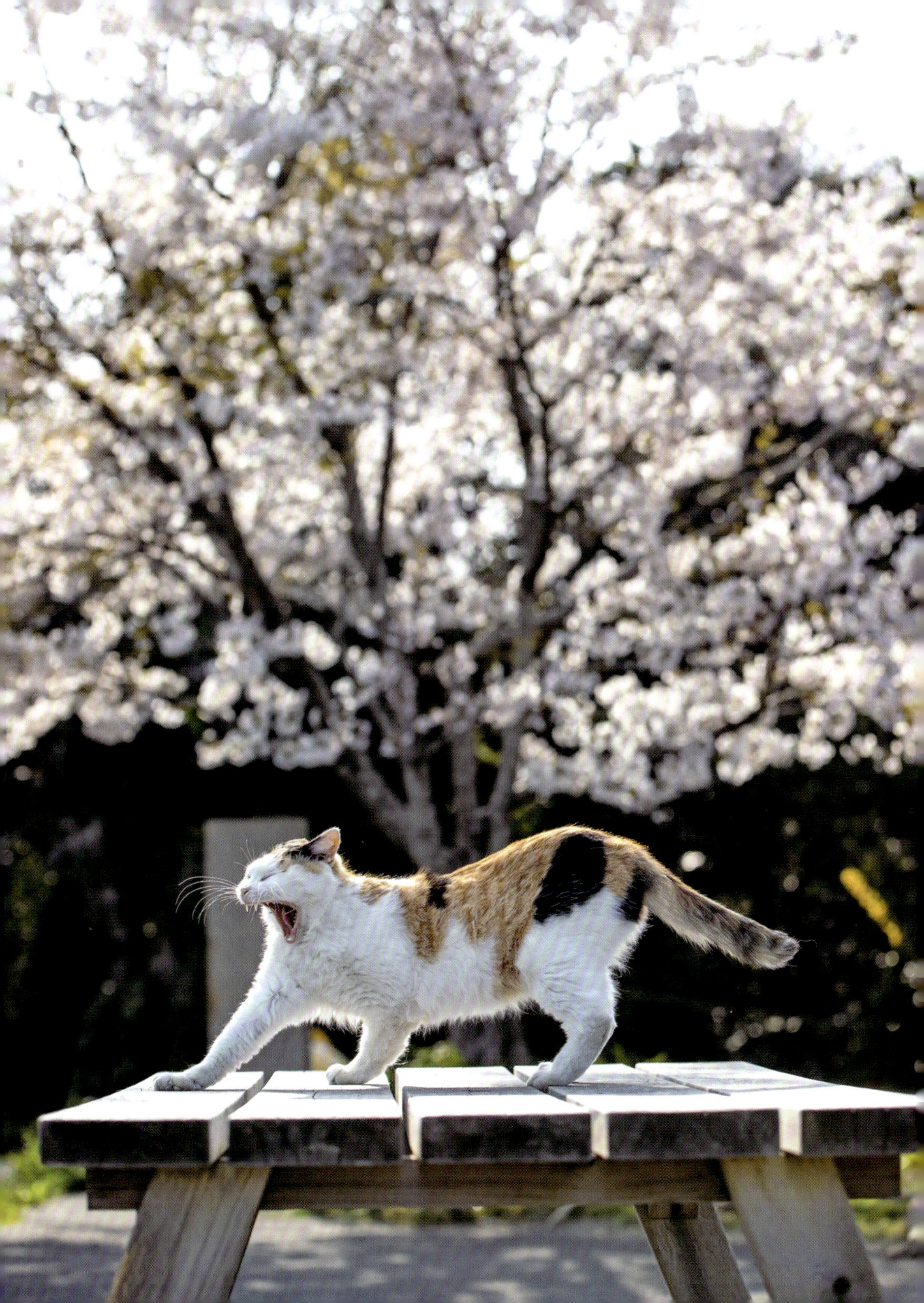

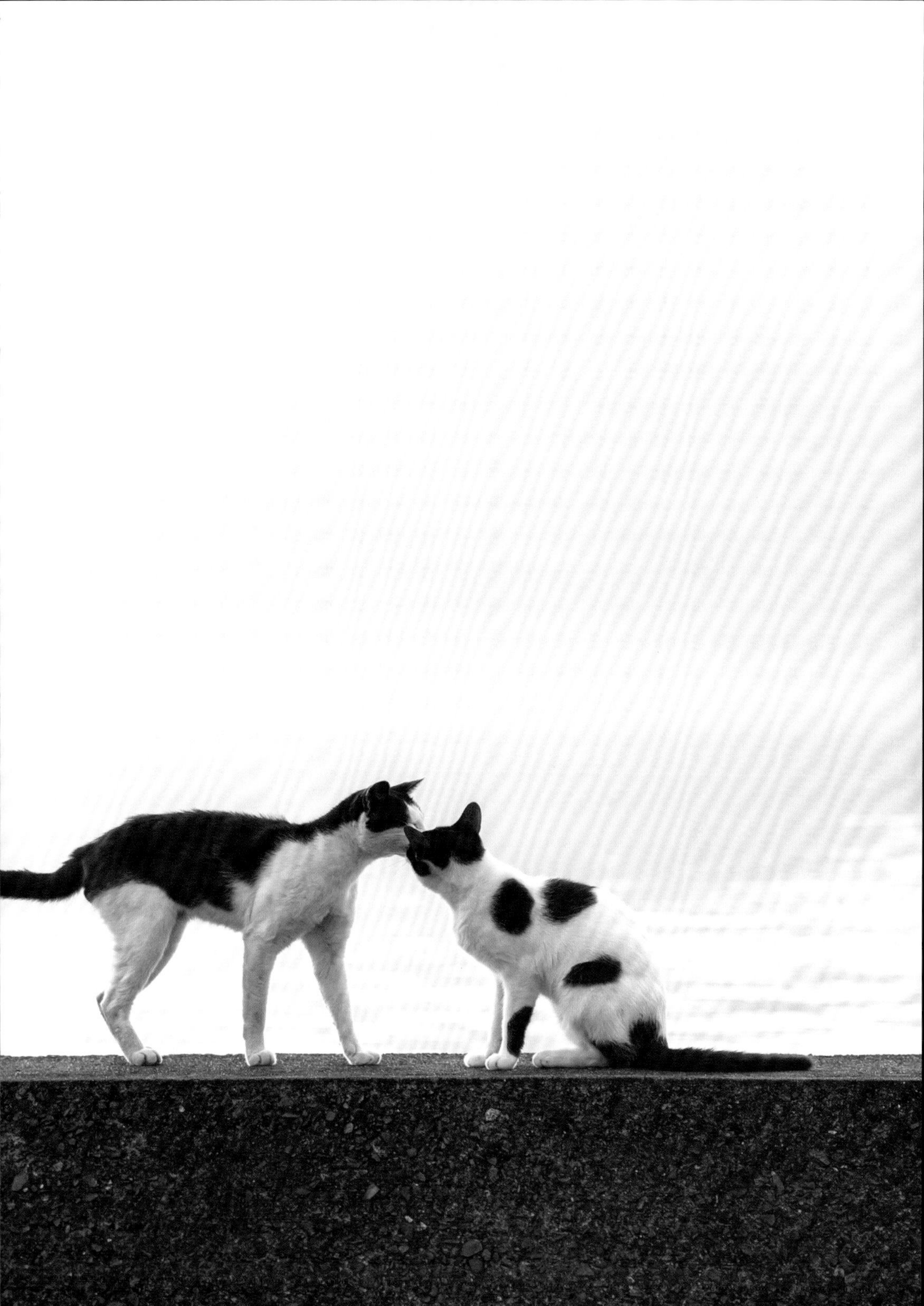

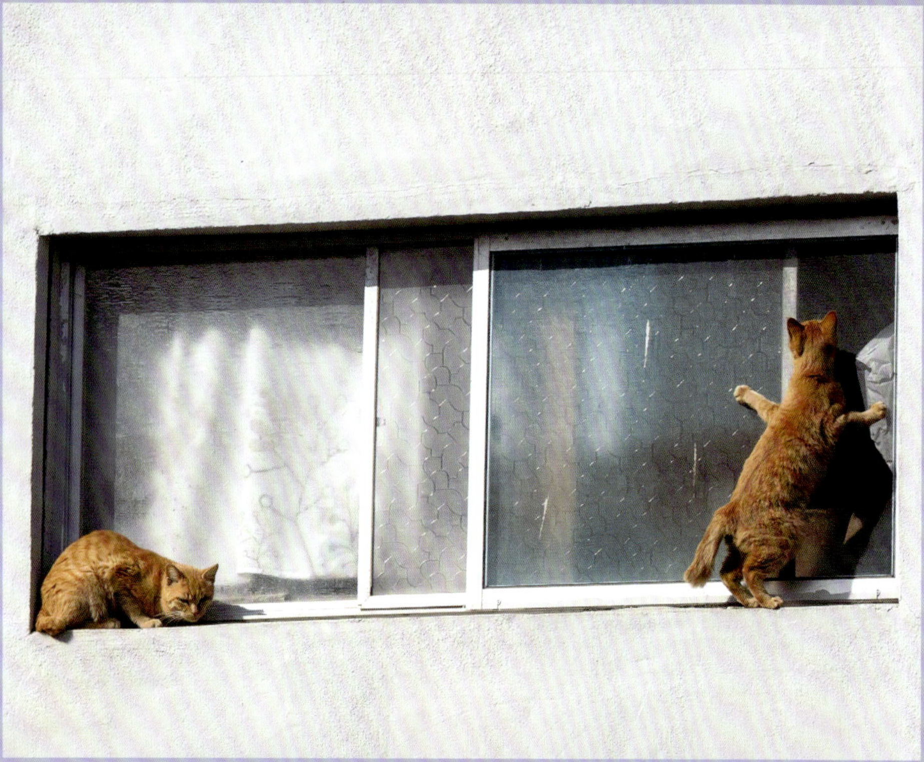

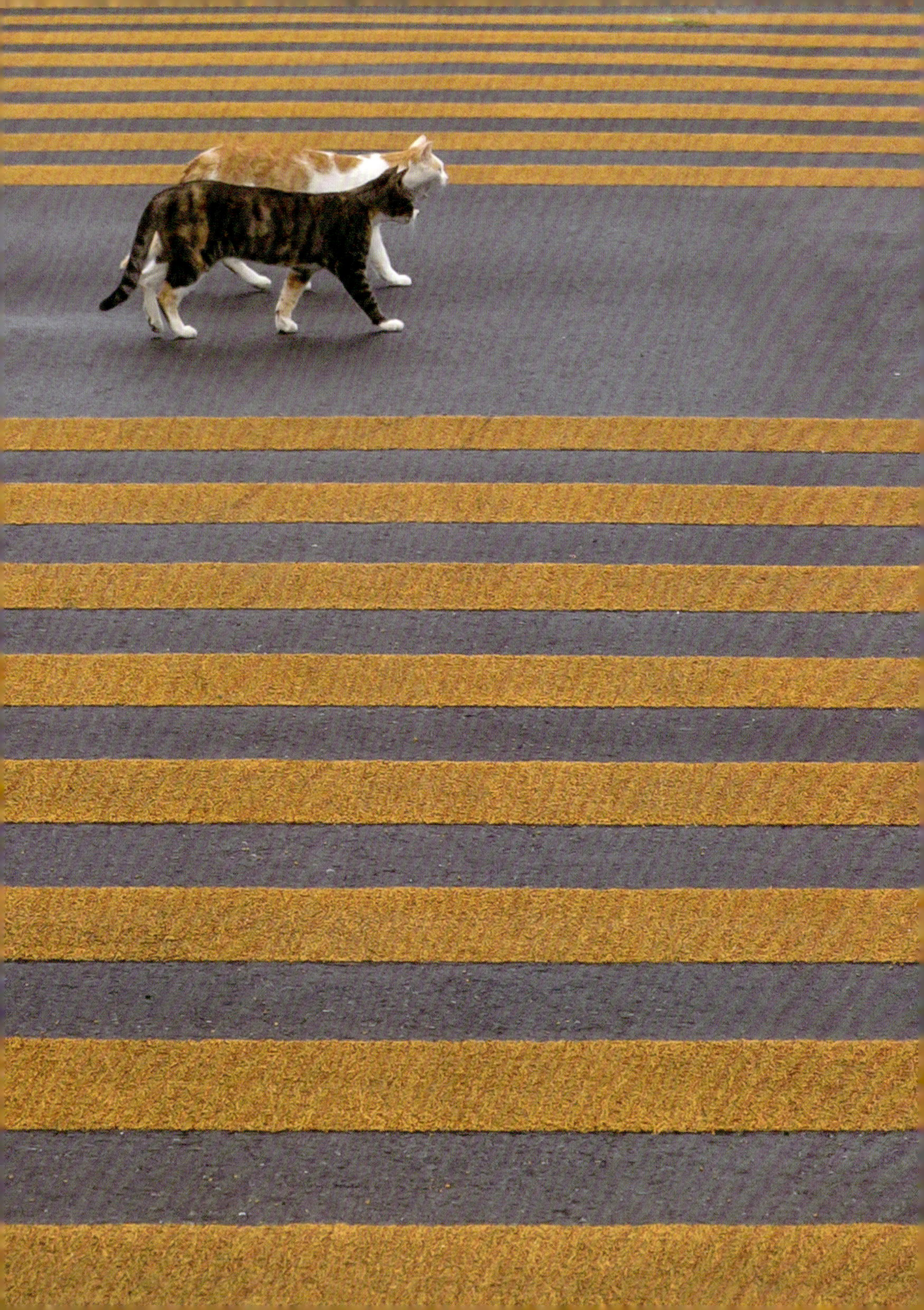

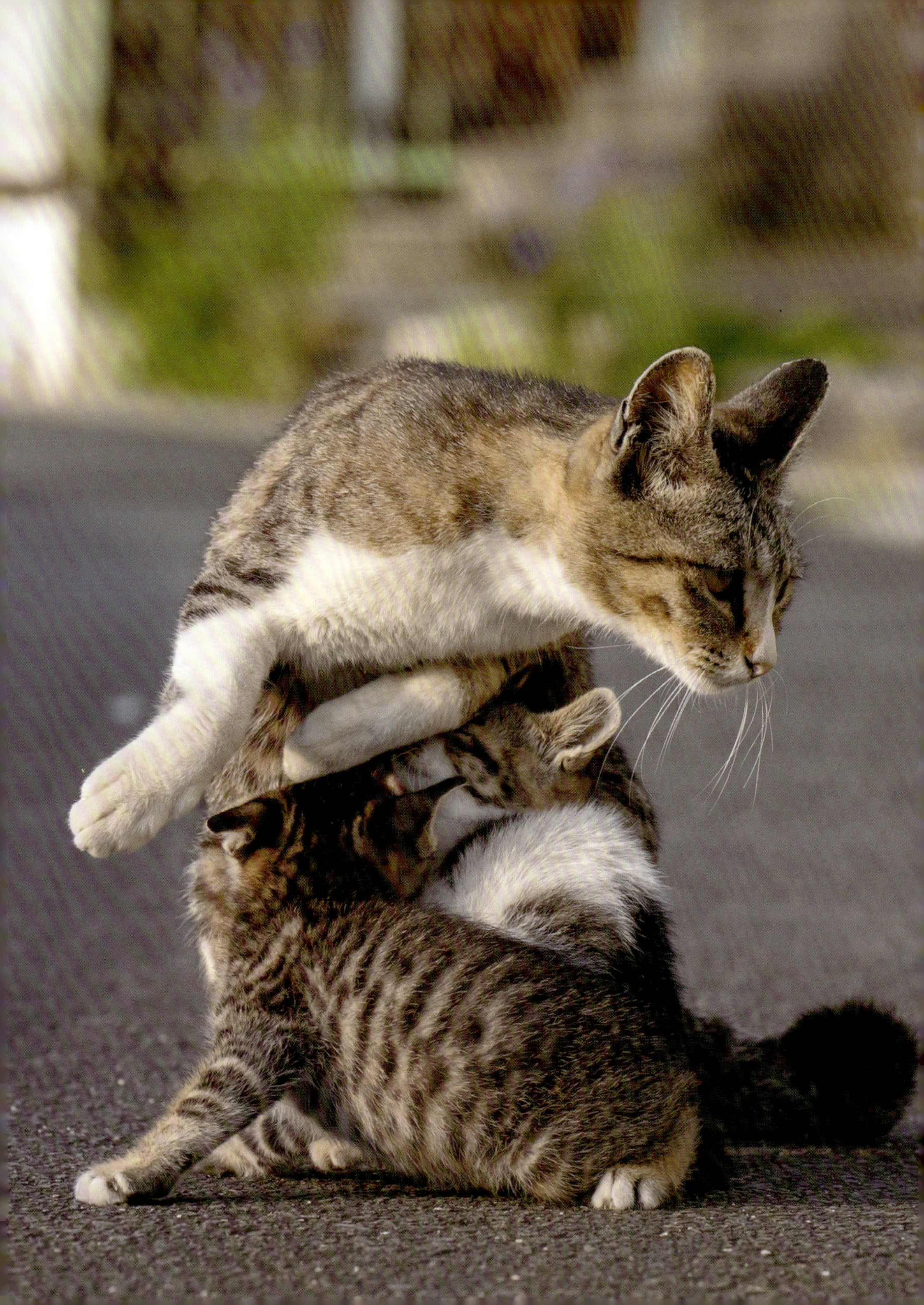

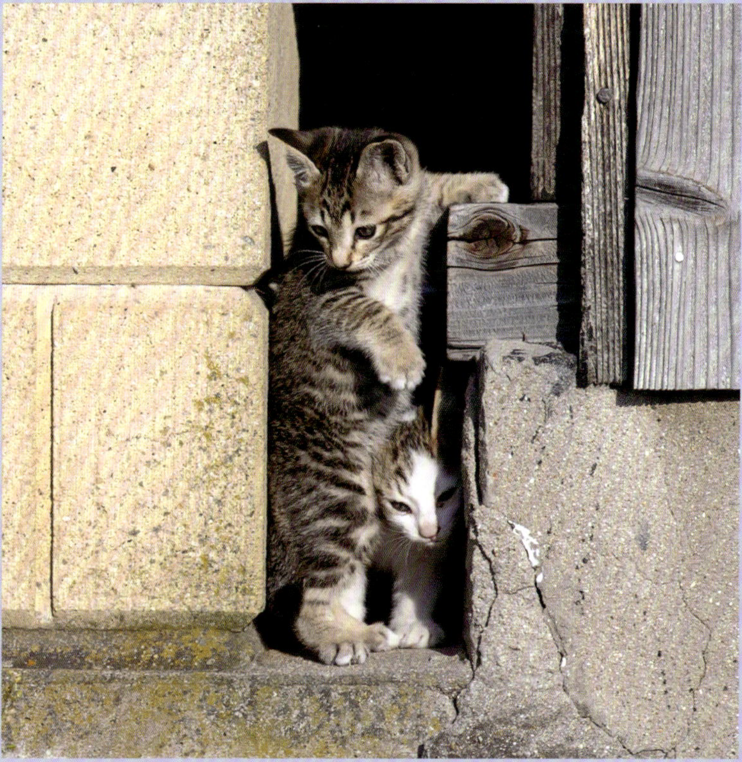

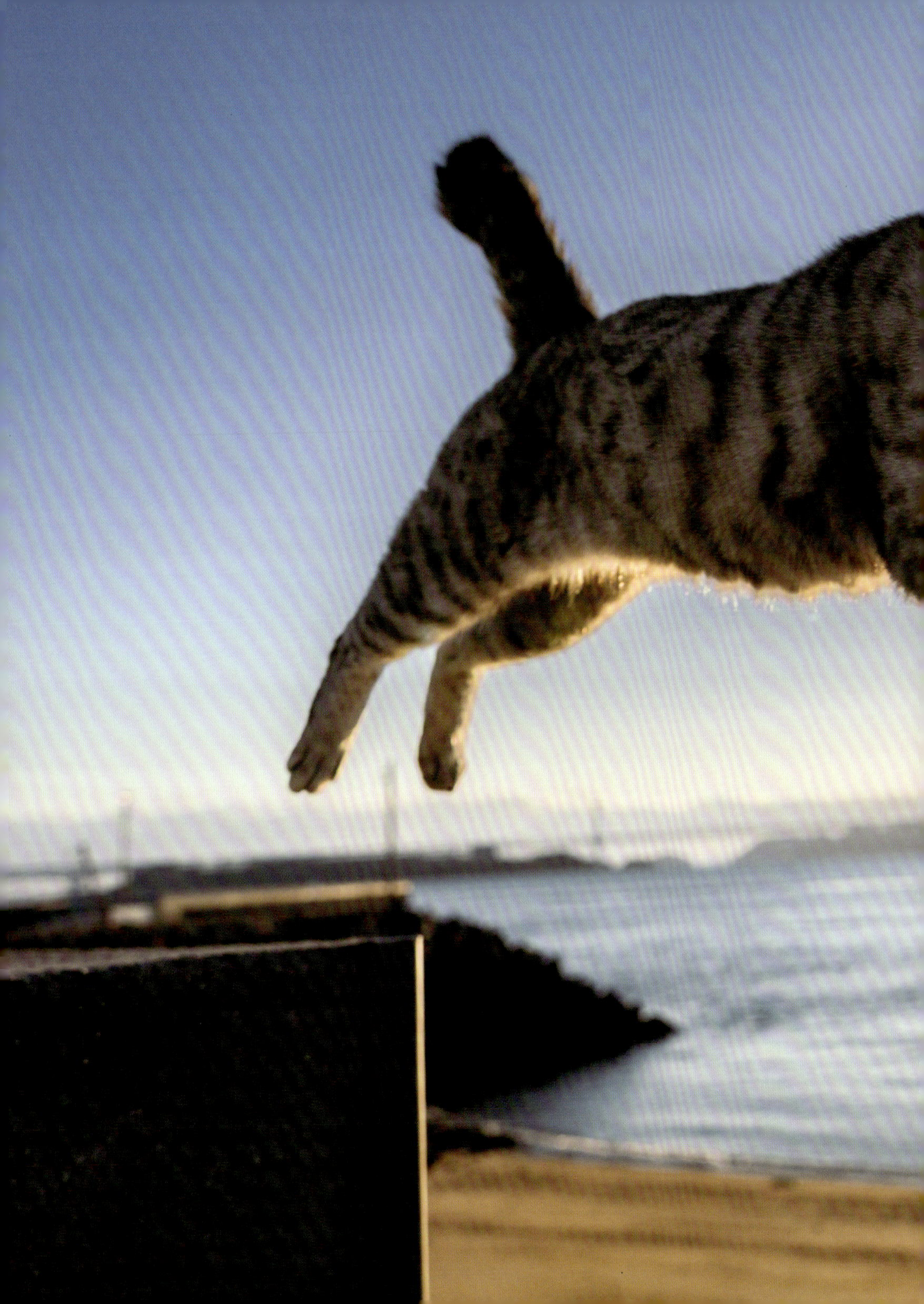

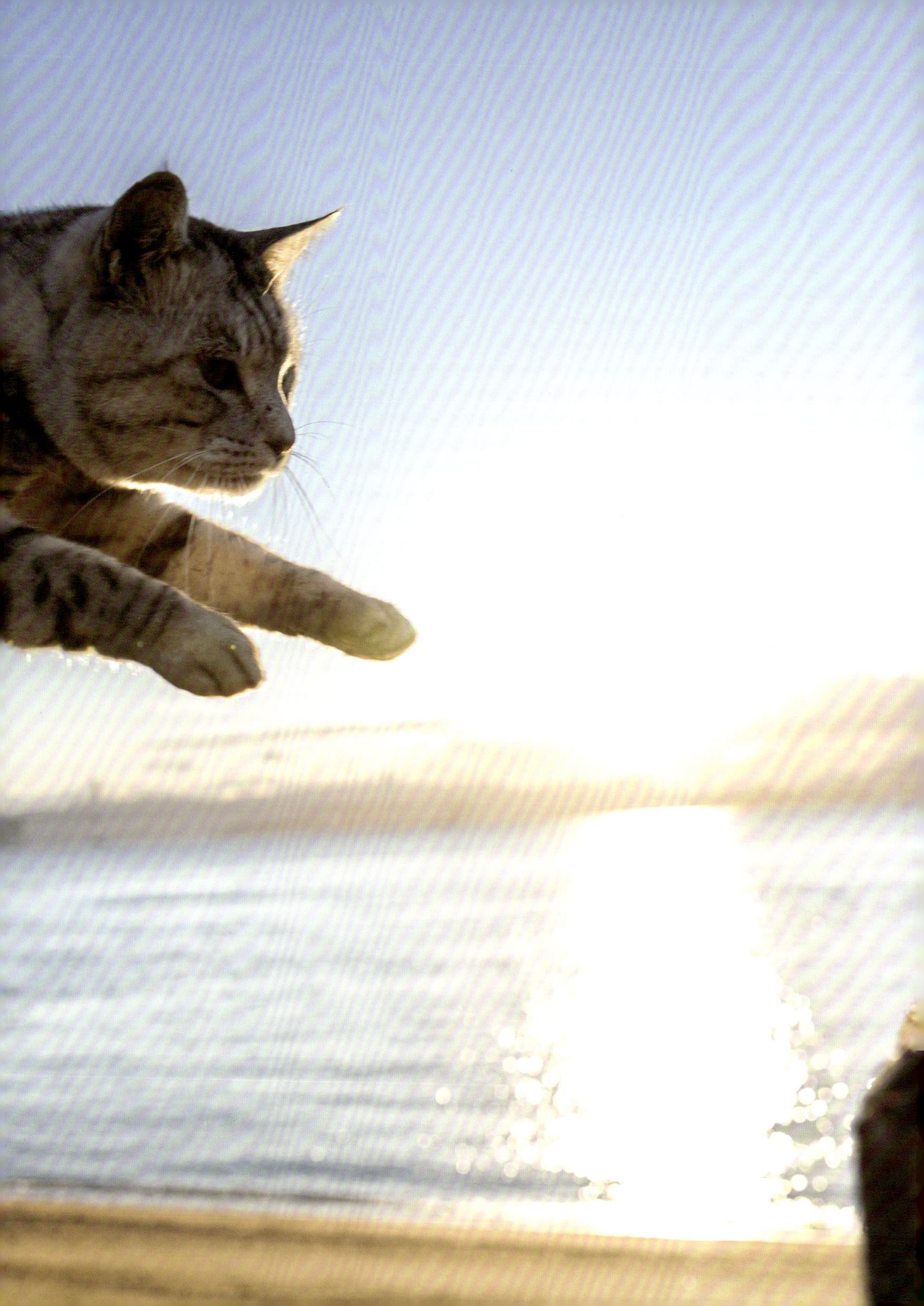

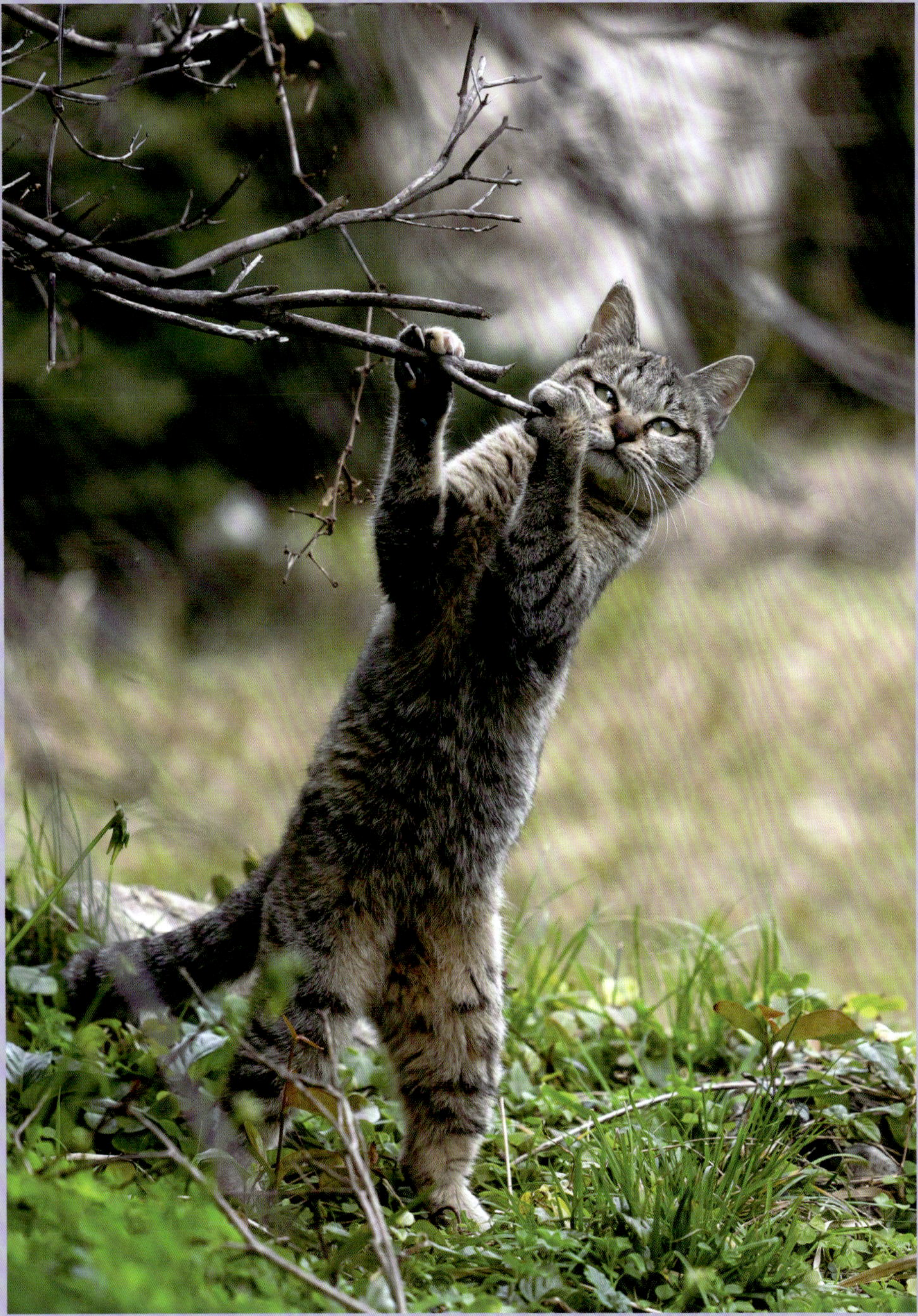

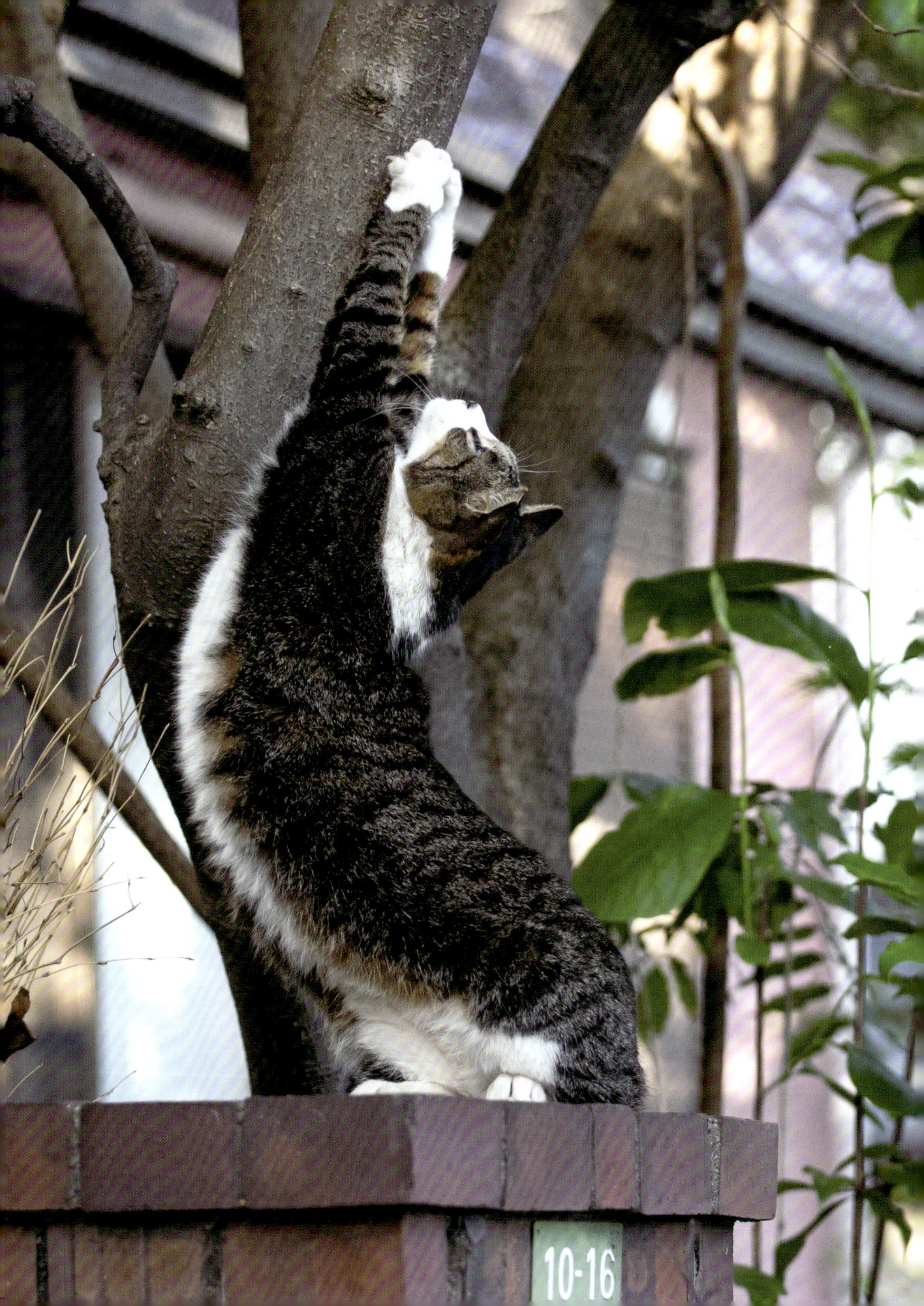
10-16

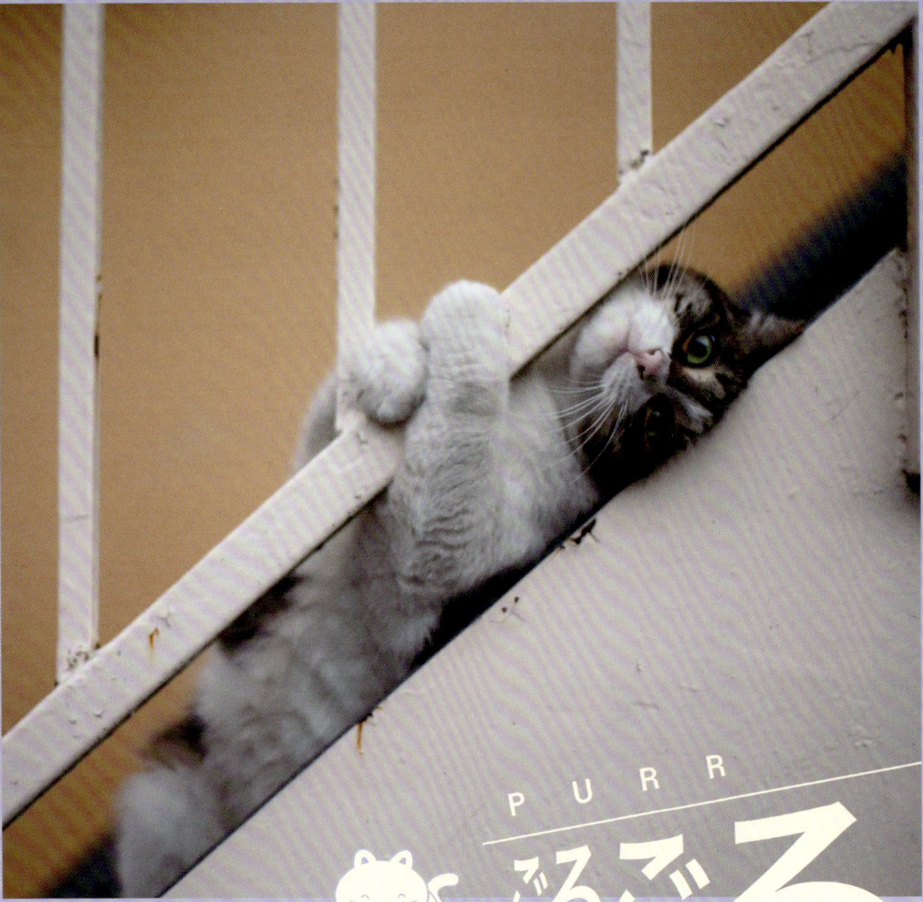

PURR

ごろごろ

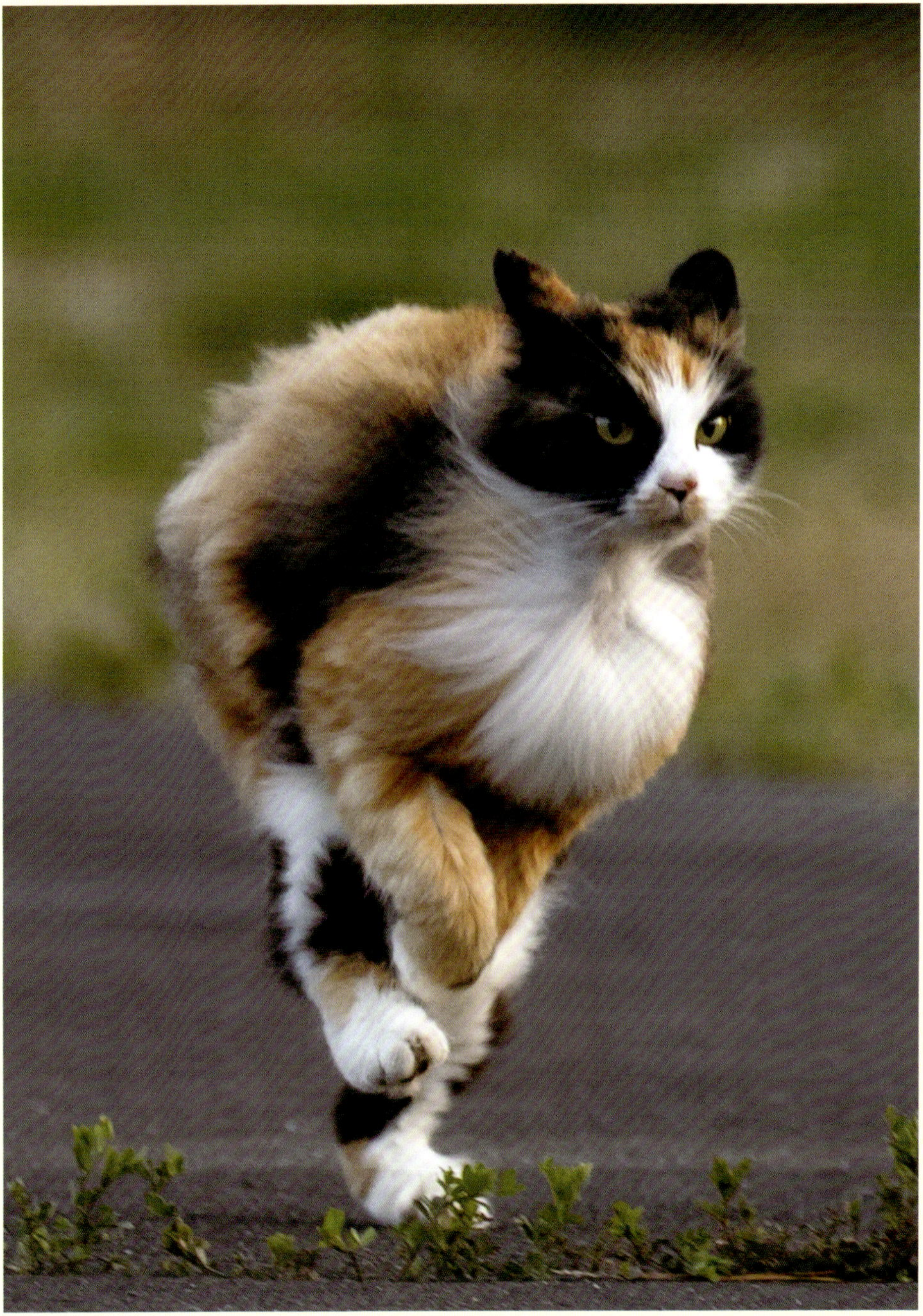

猫・ネコ

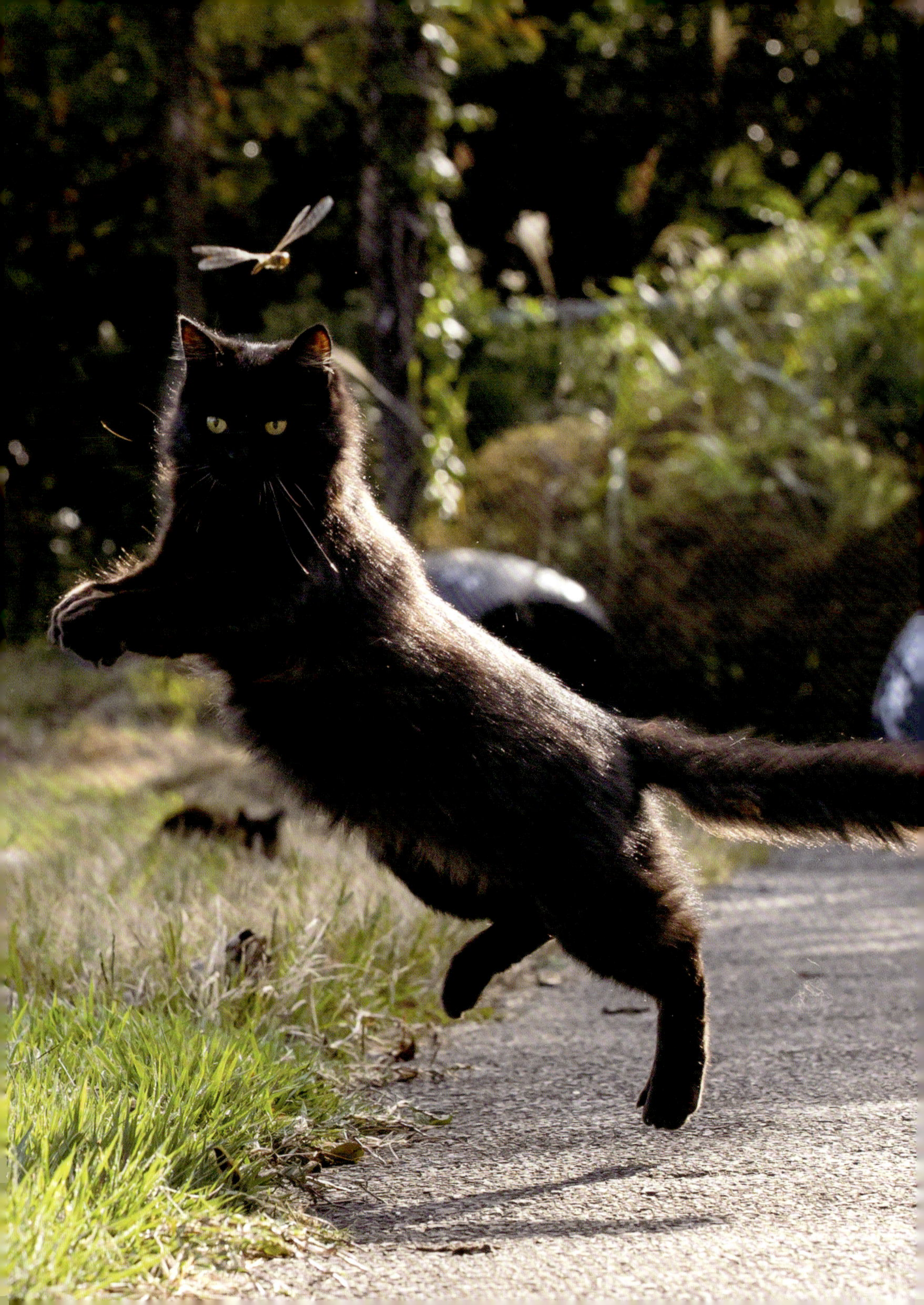

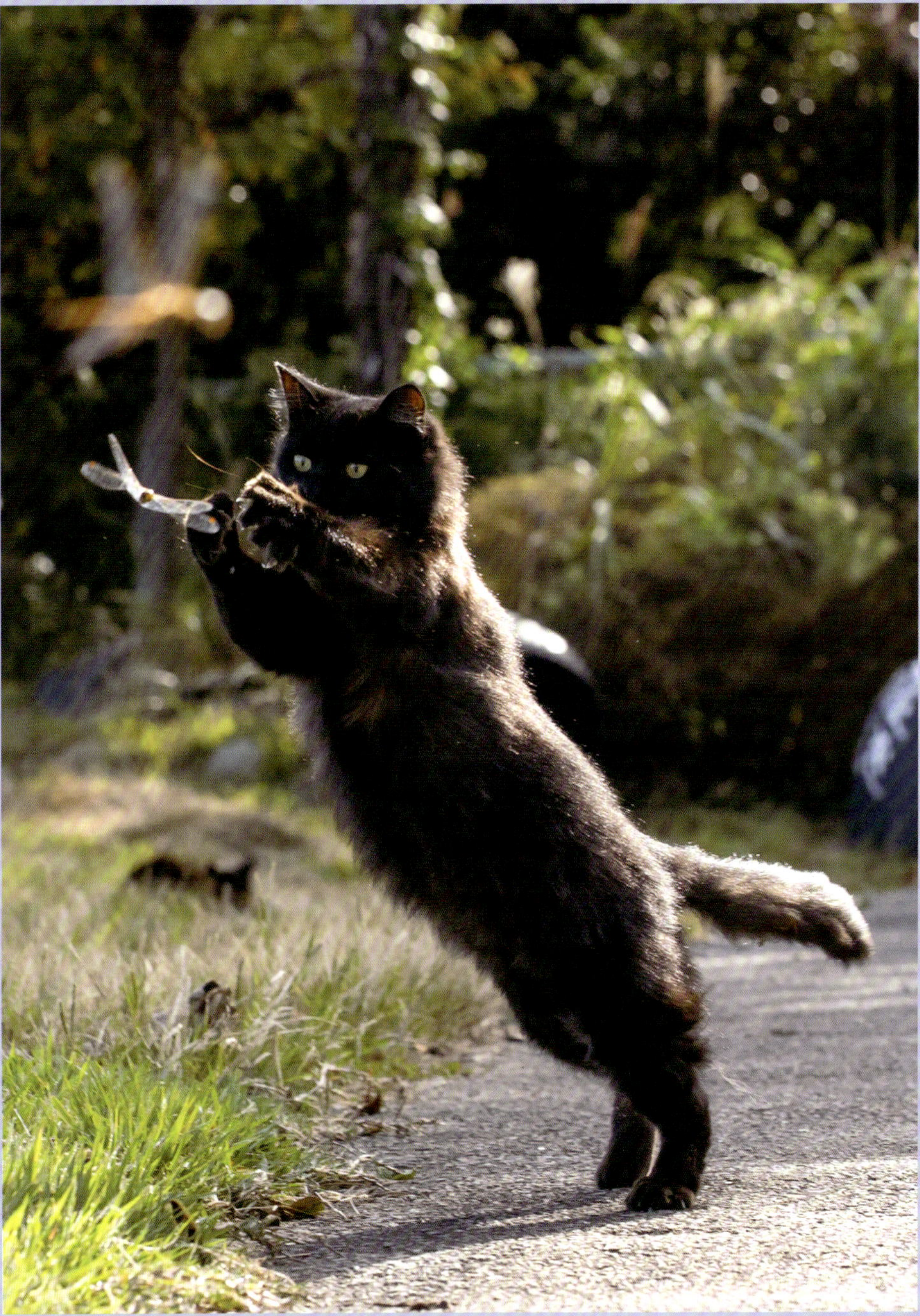

猫・ネコ

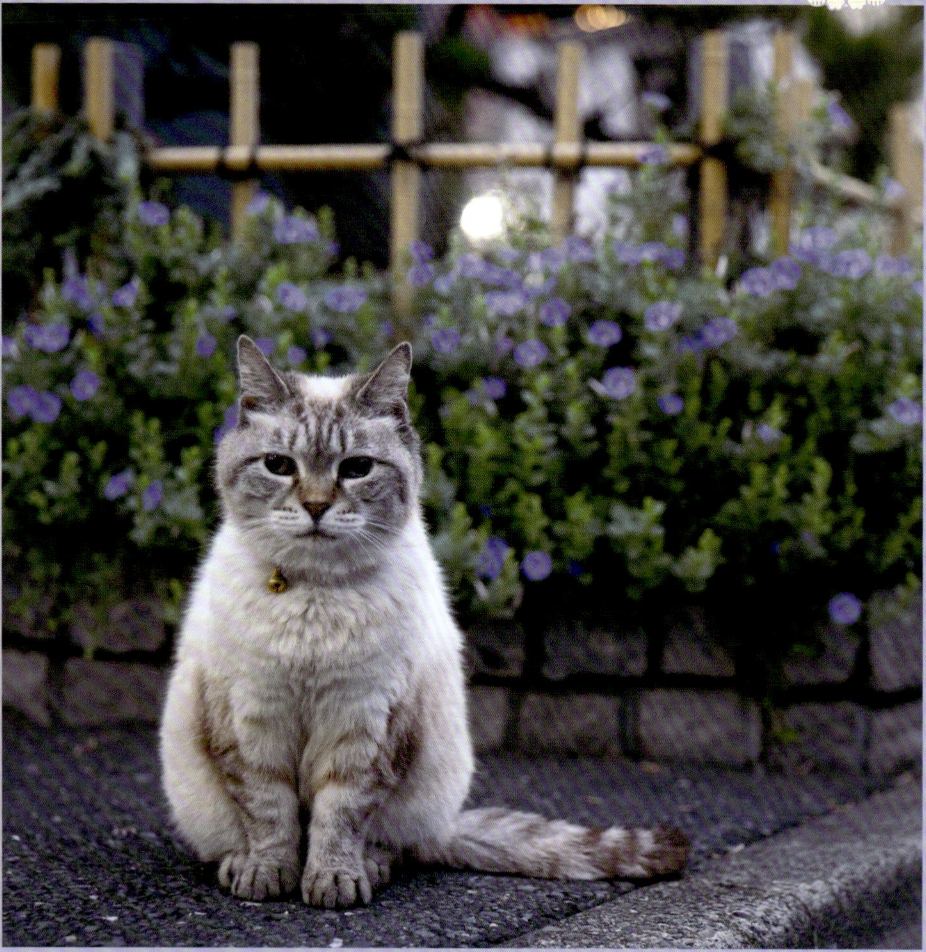

猫・ネコ

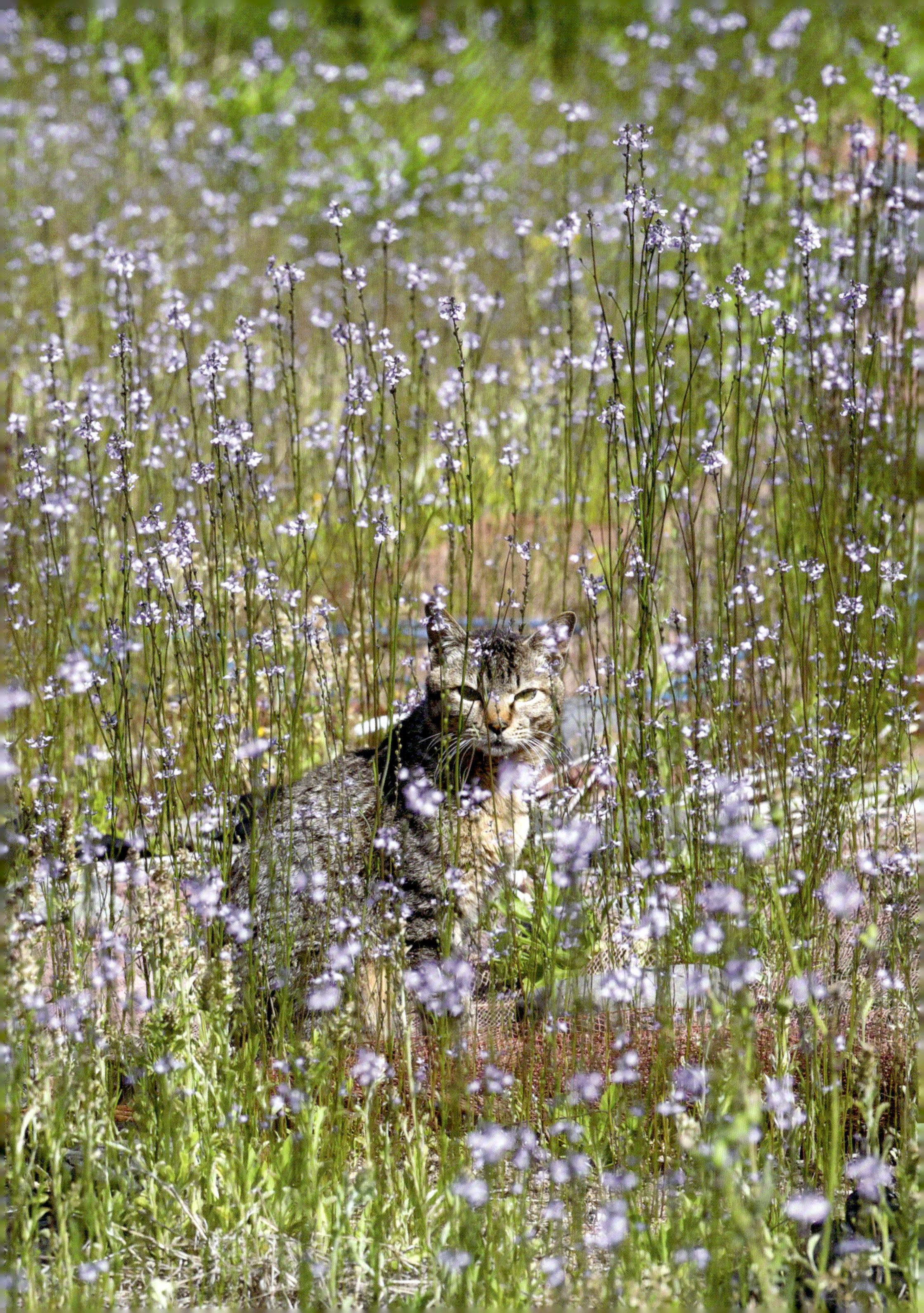

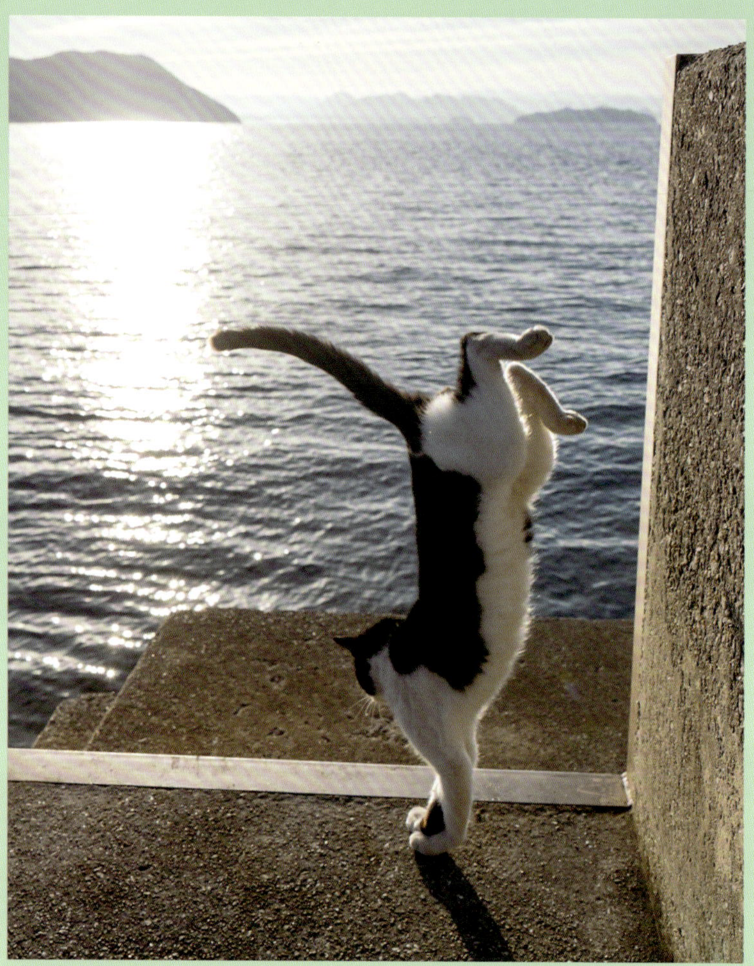

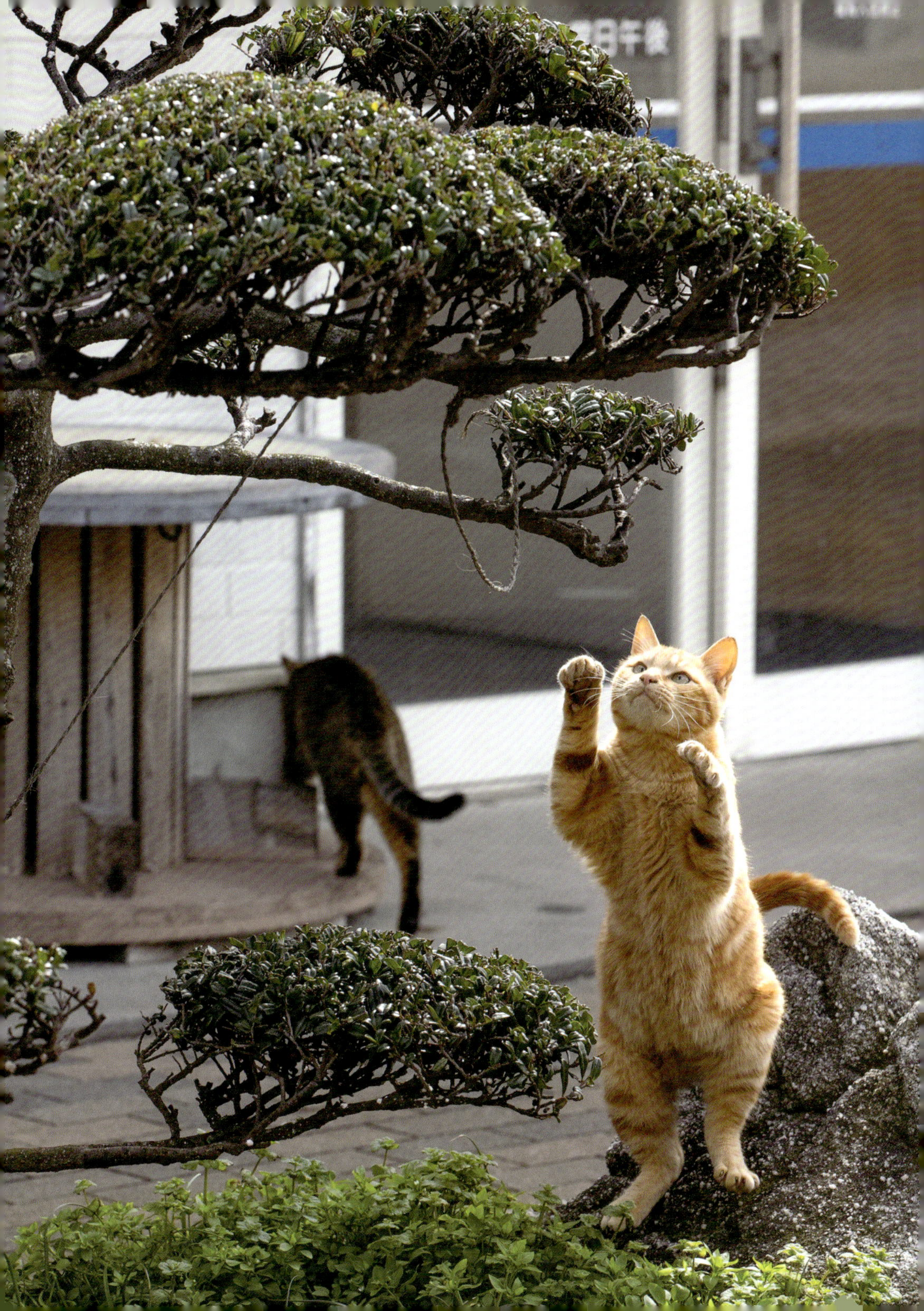

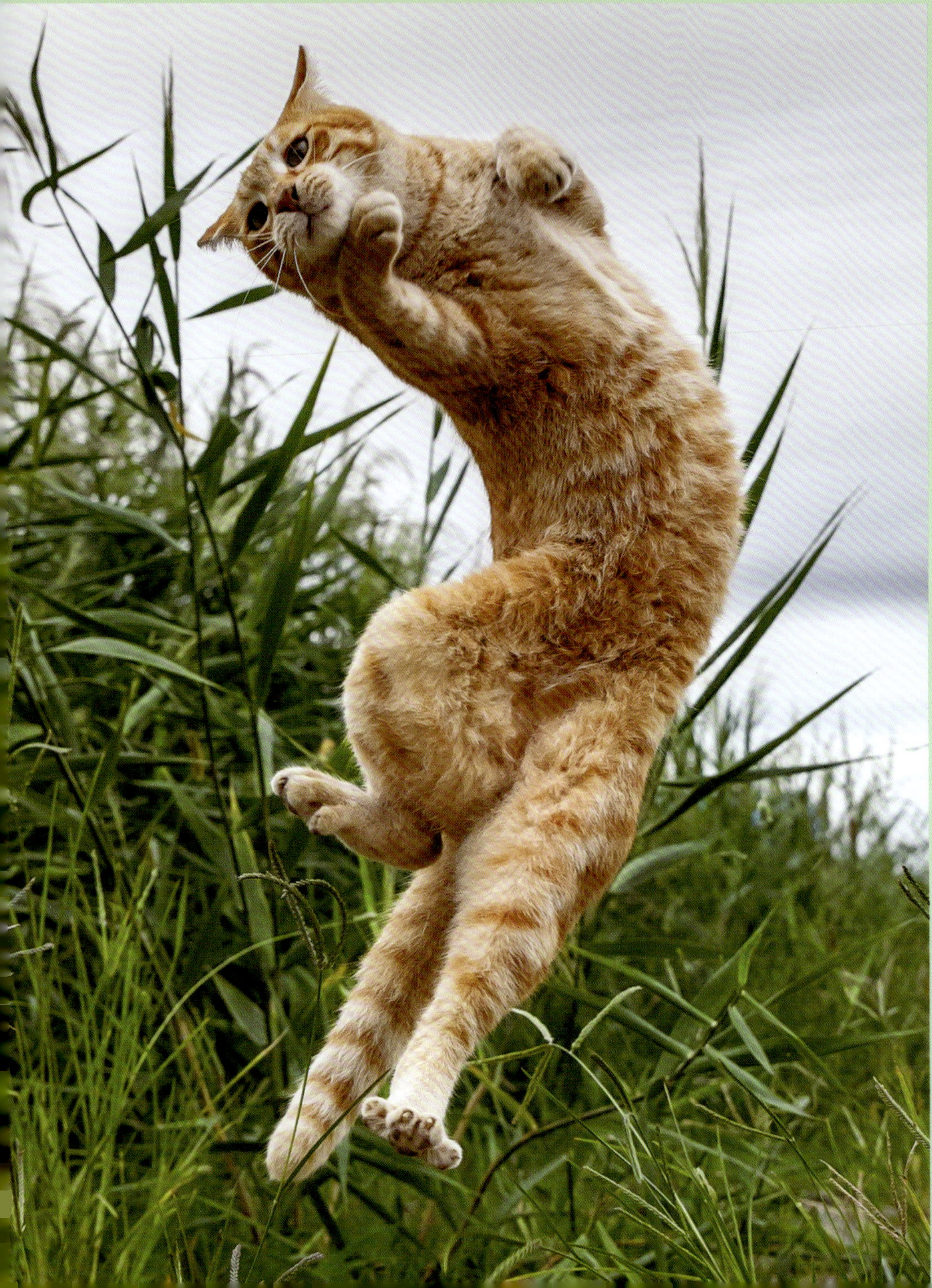

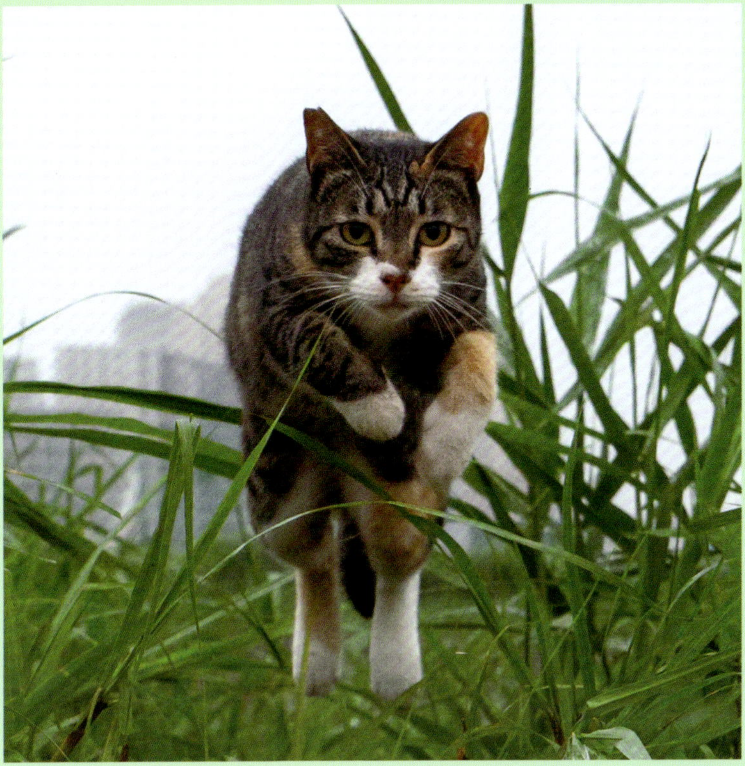

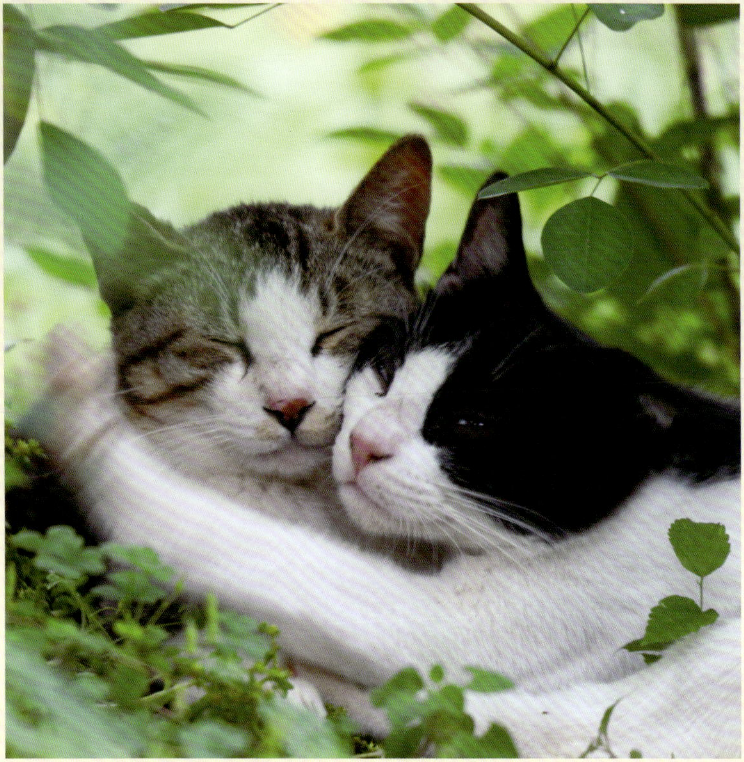

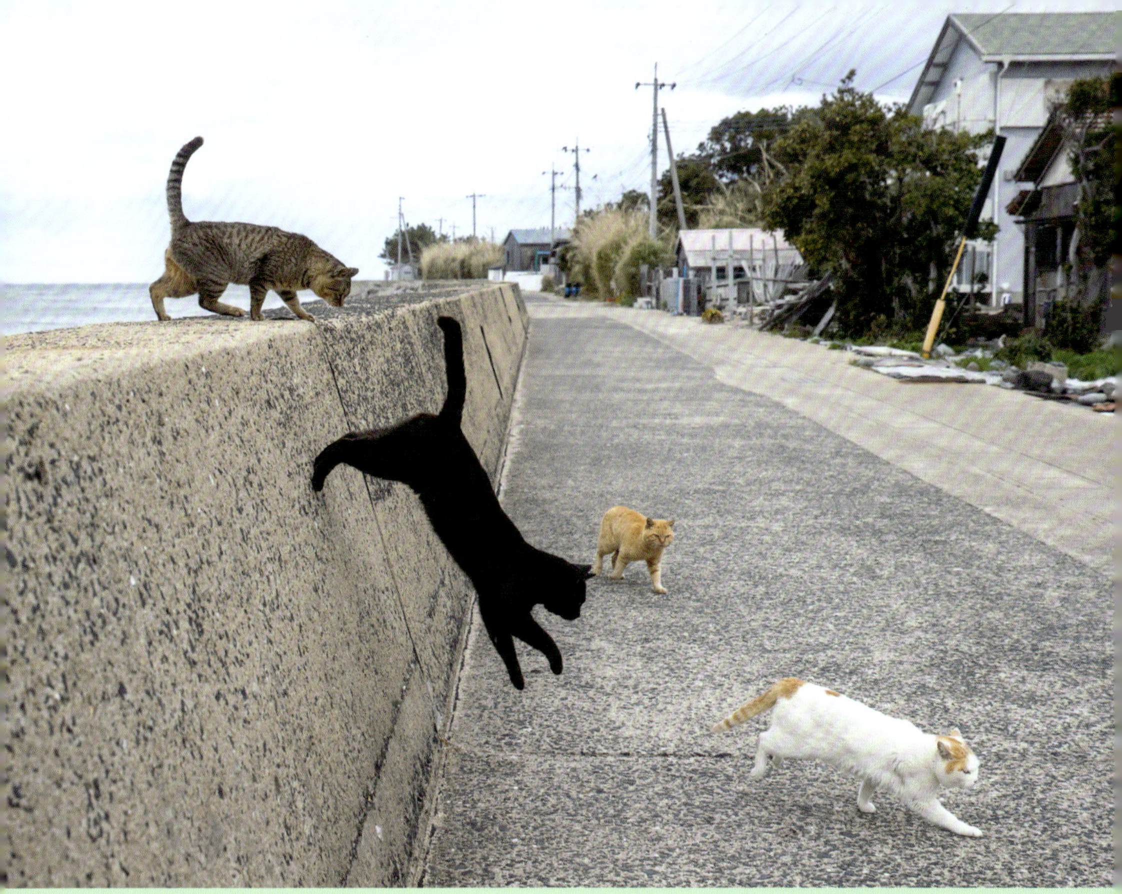

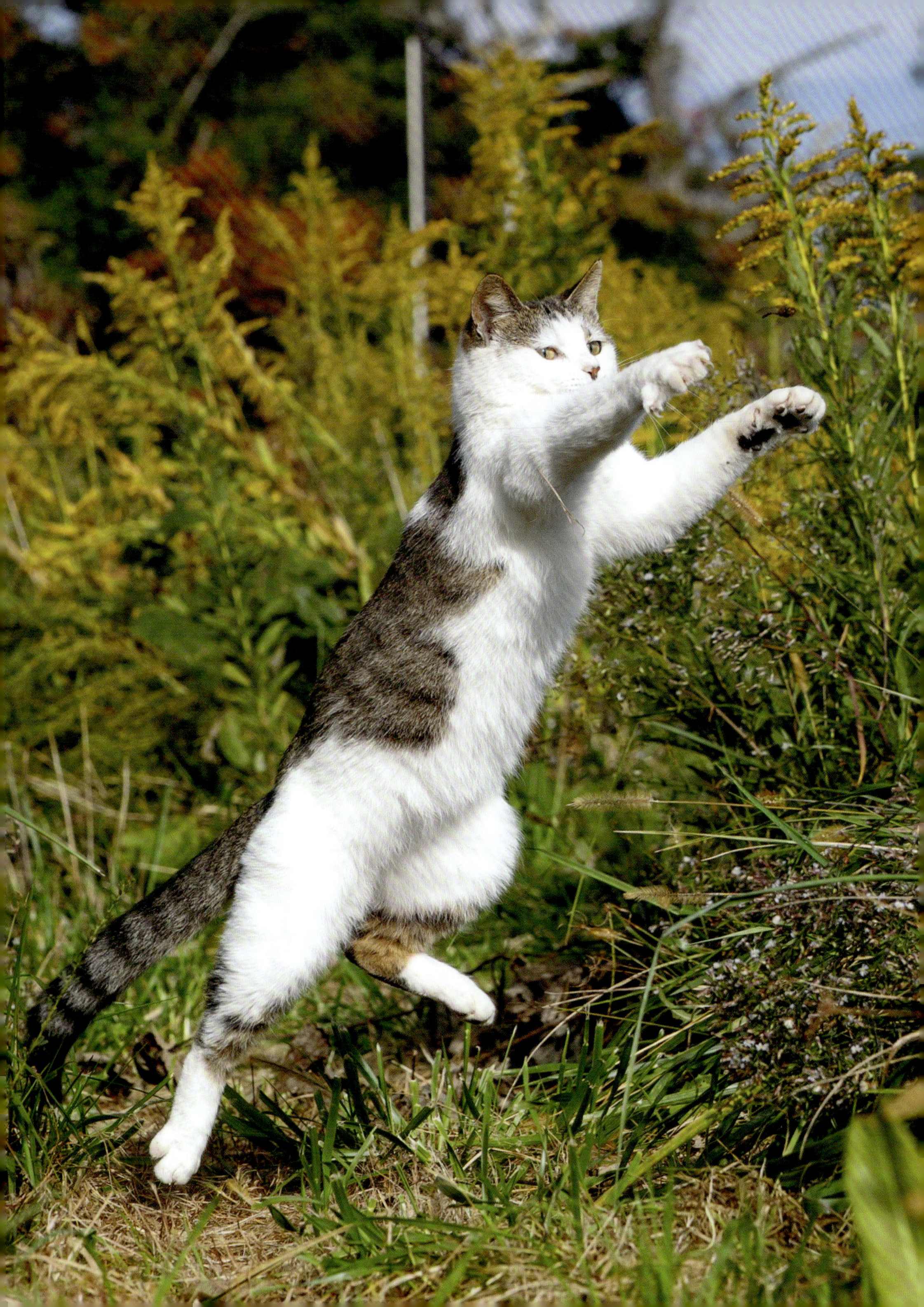

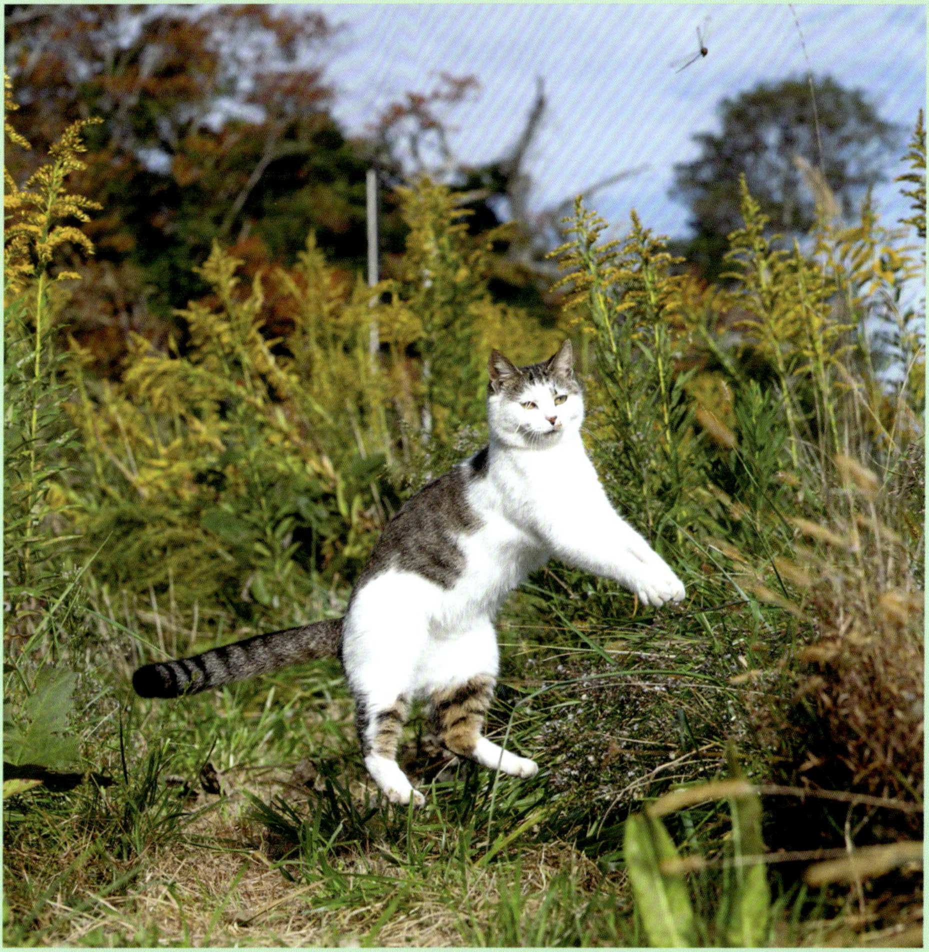

猫・ネコ

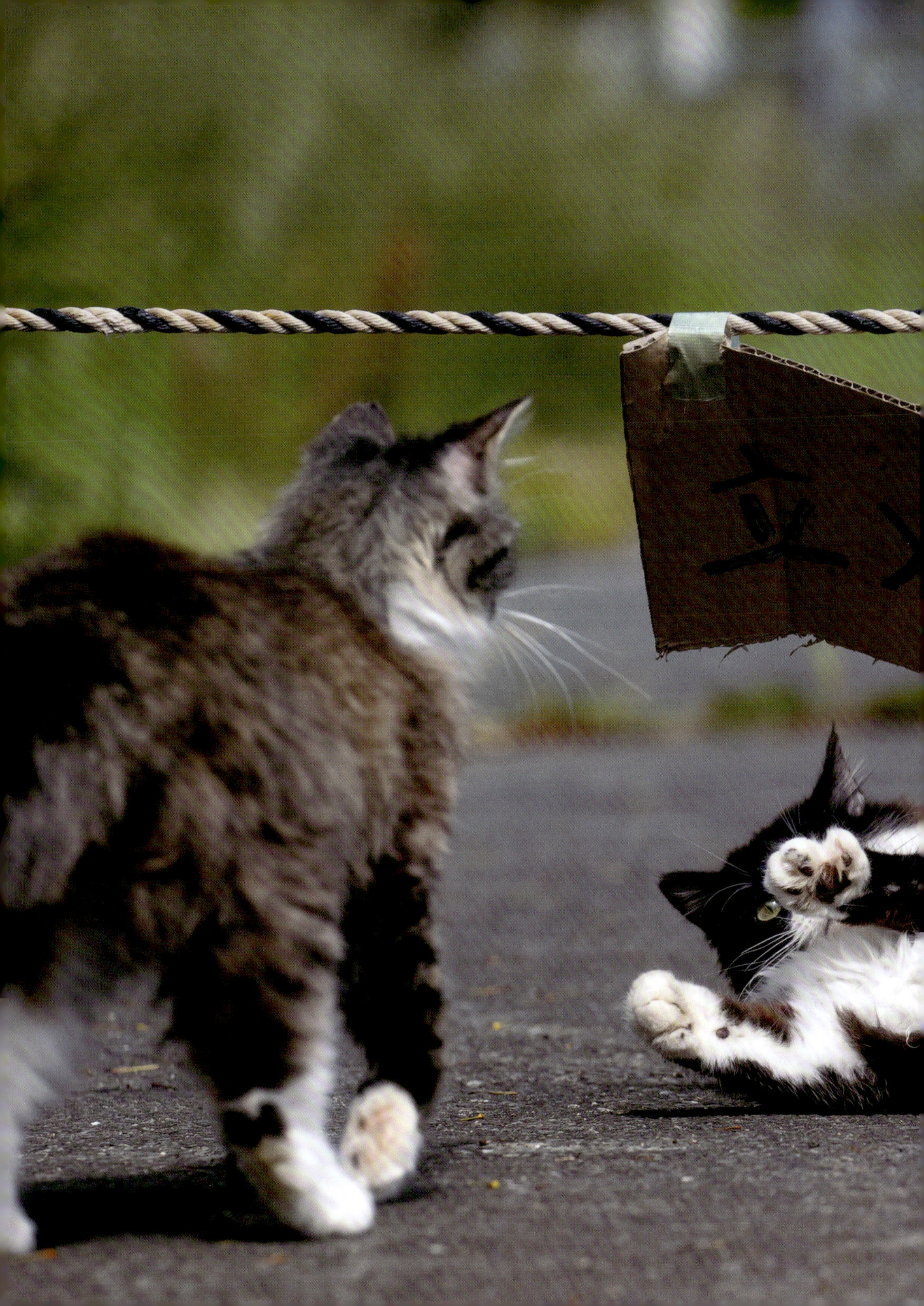

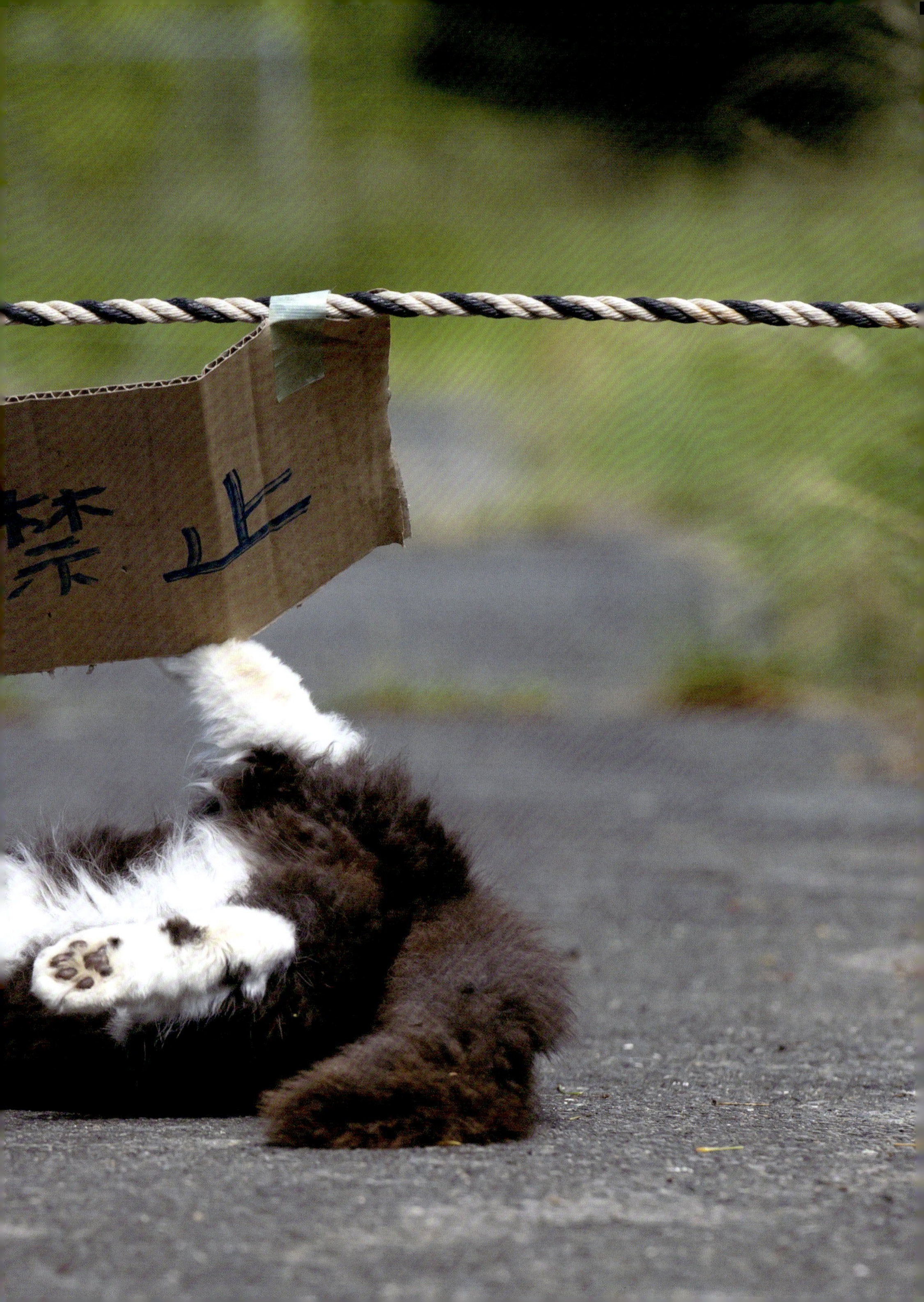
禁止

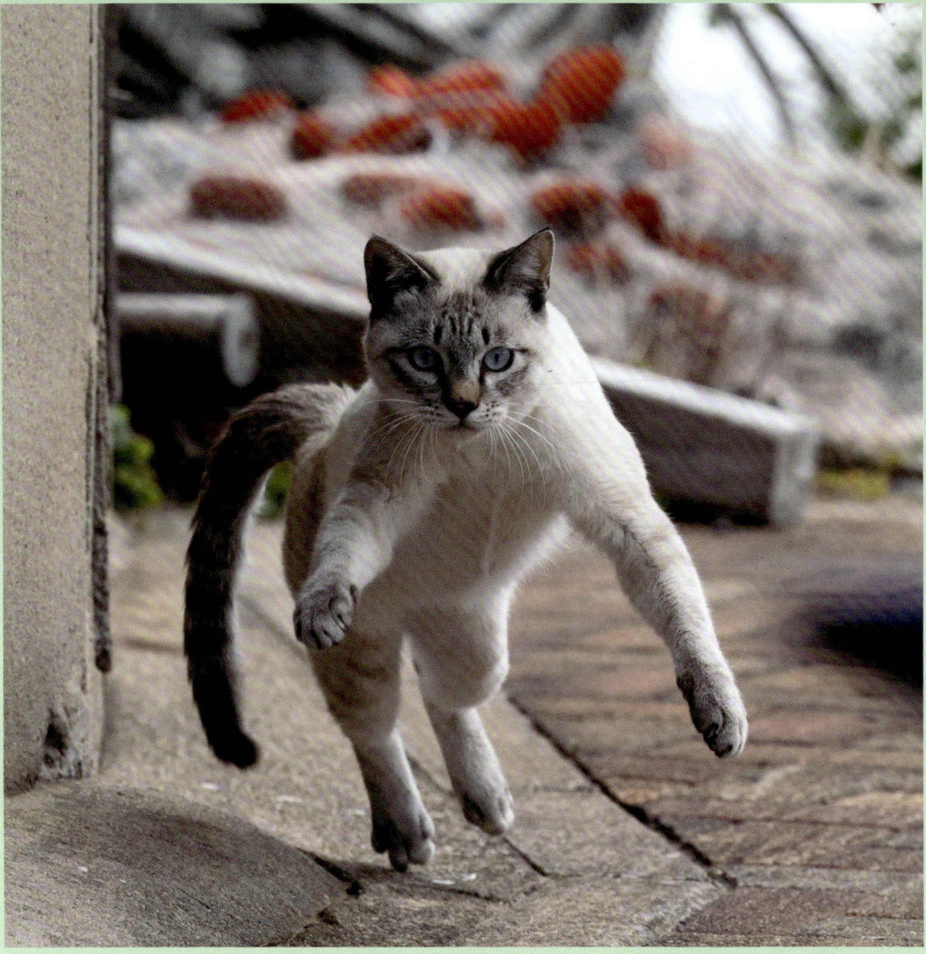

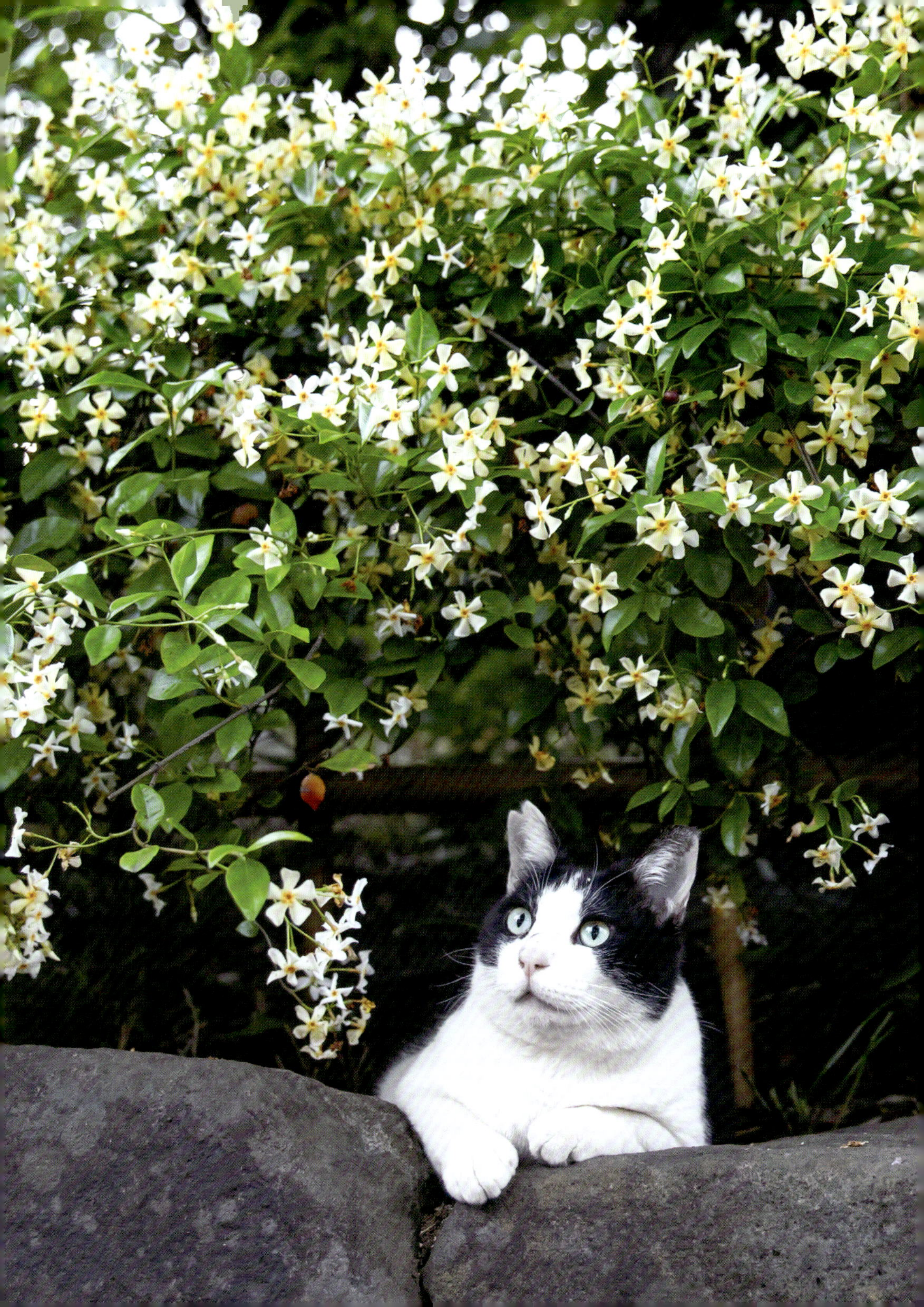

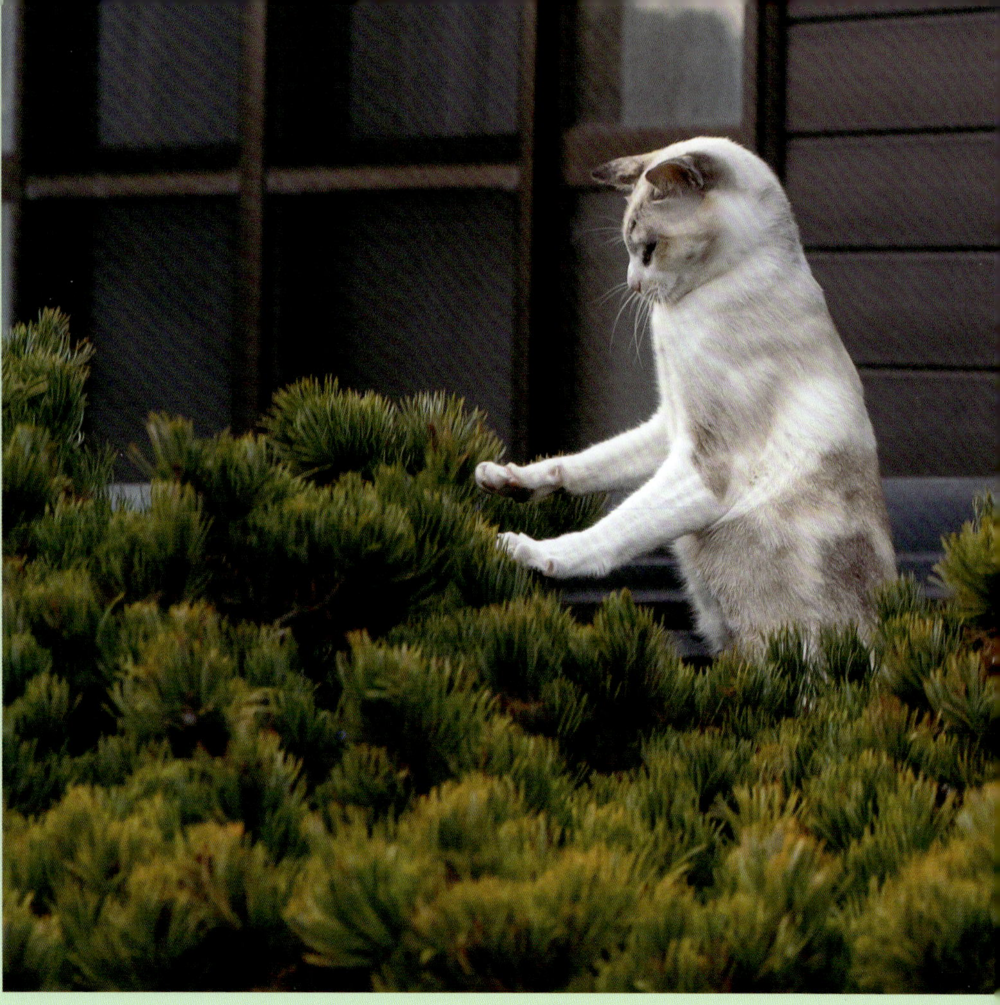

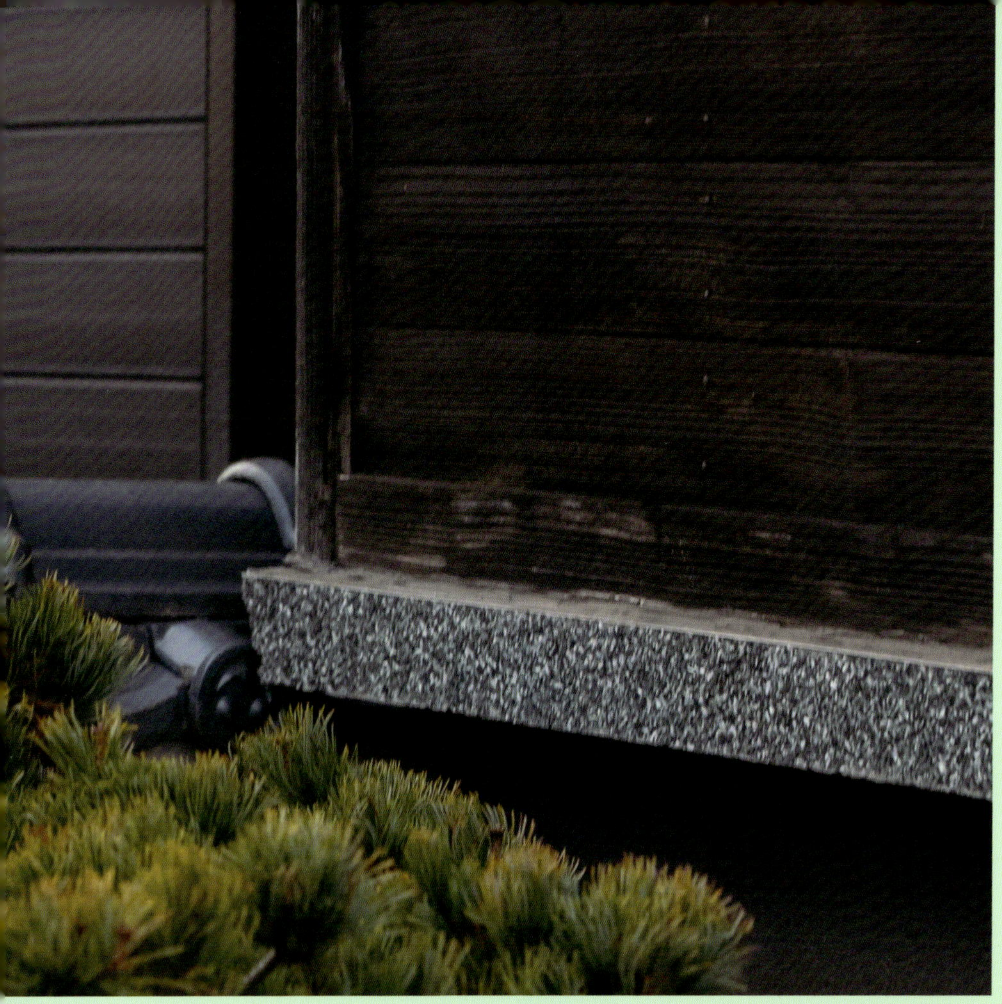

猫・ネコ

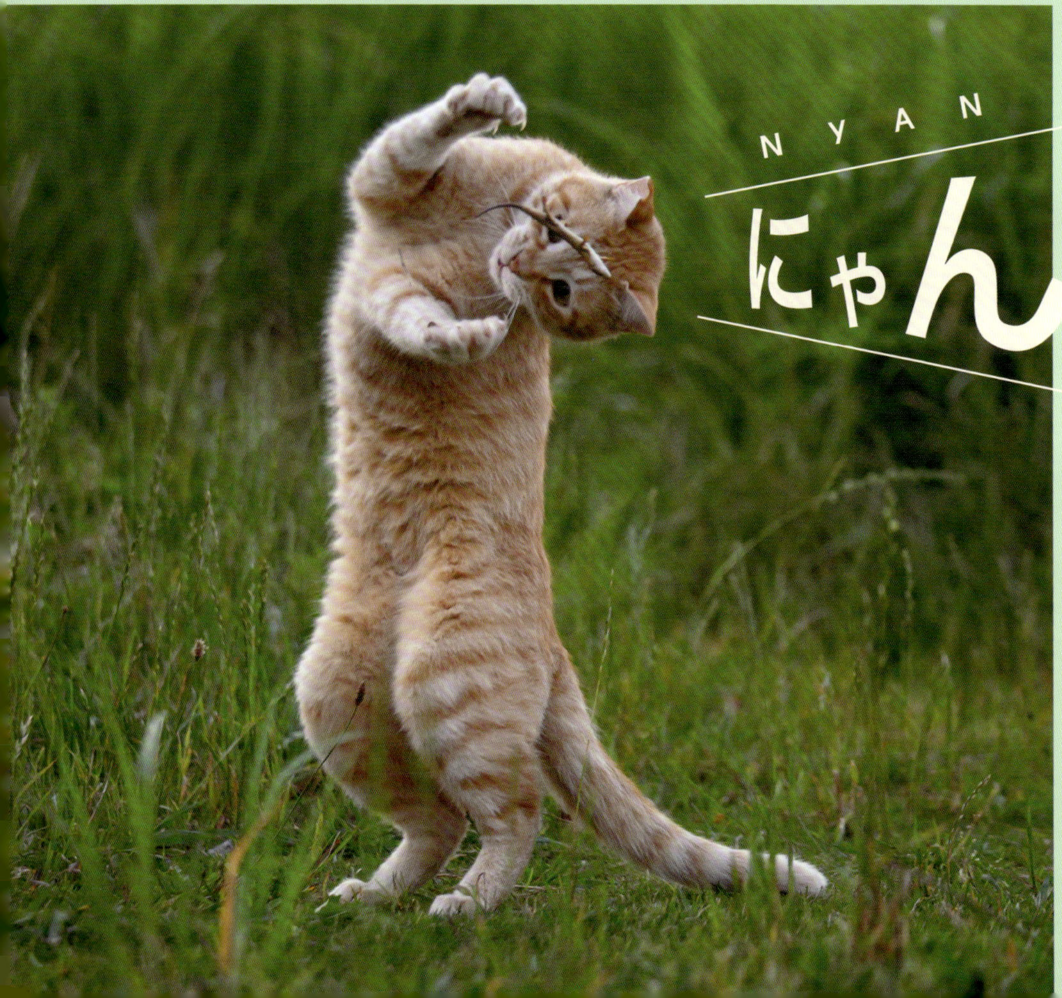
NYAN
にゃん

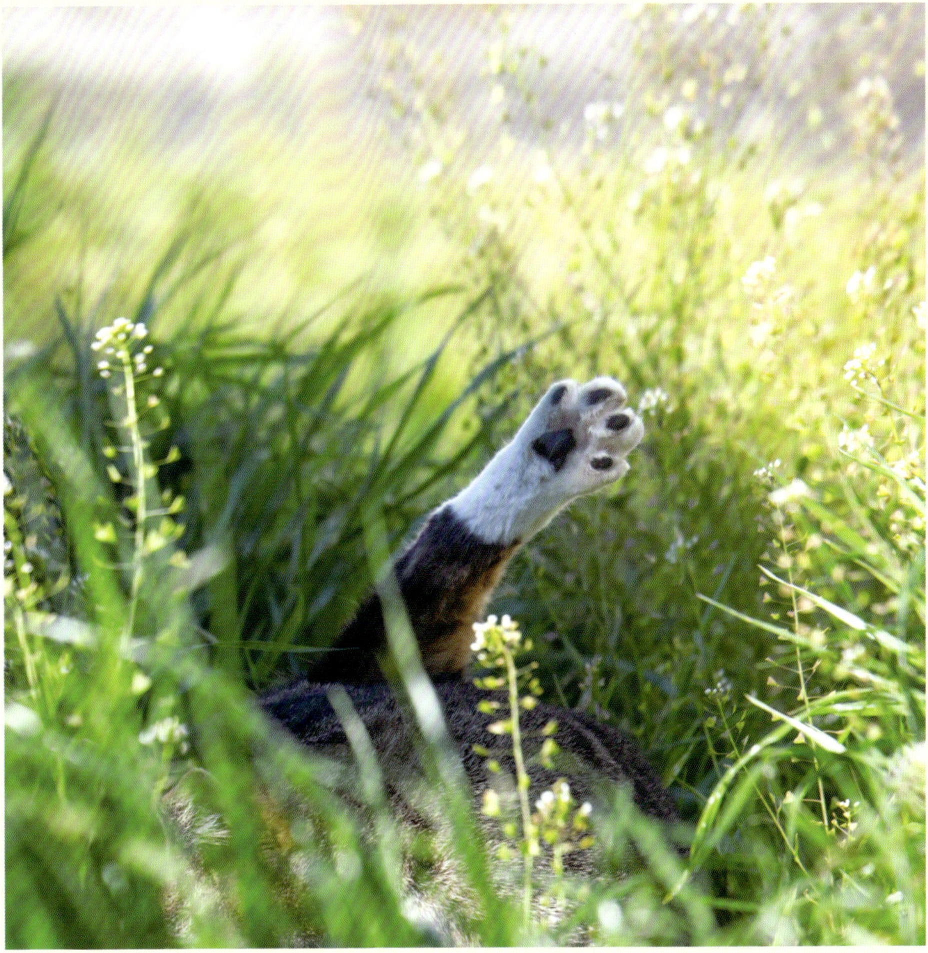

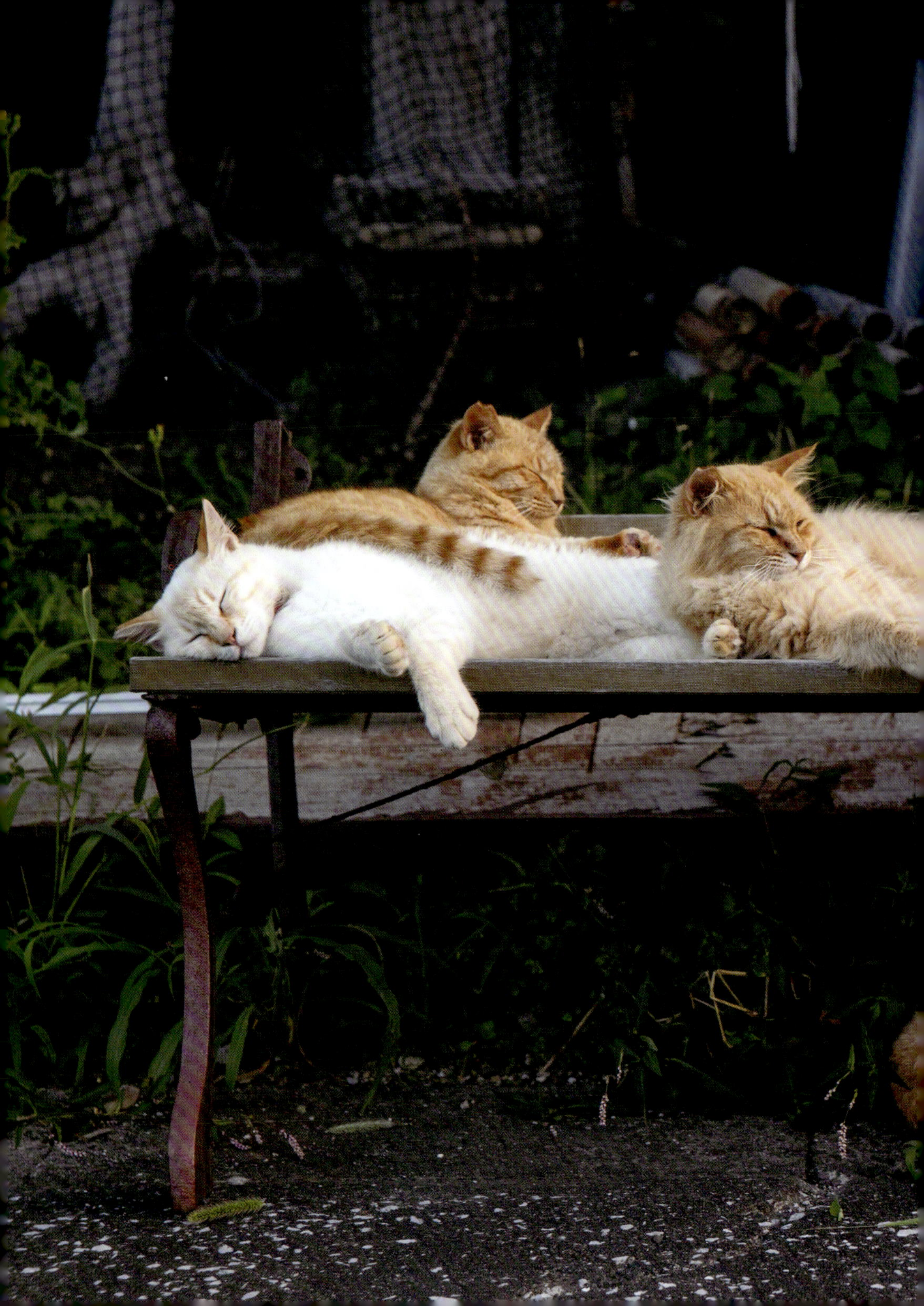

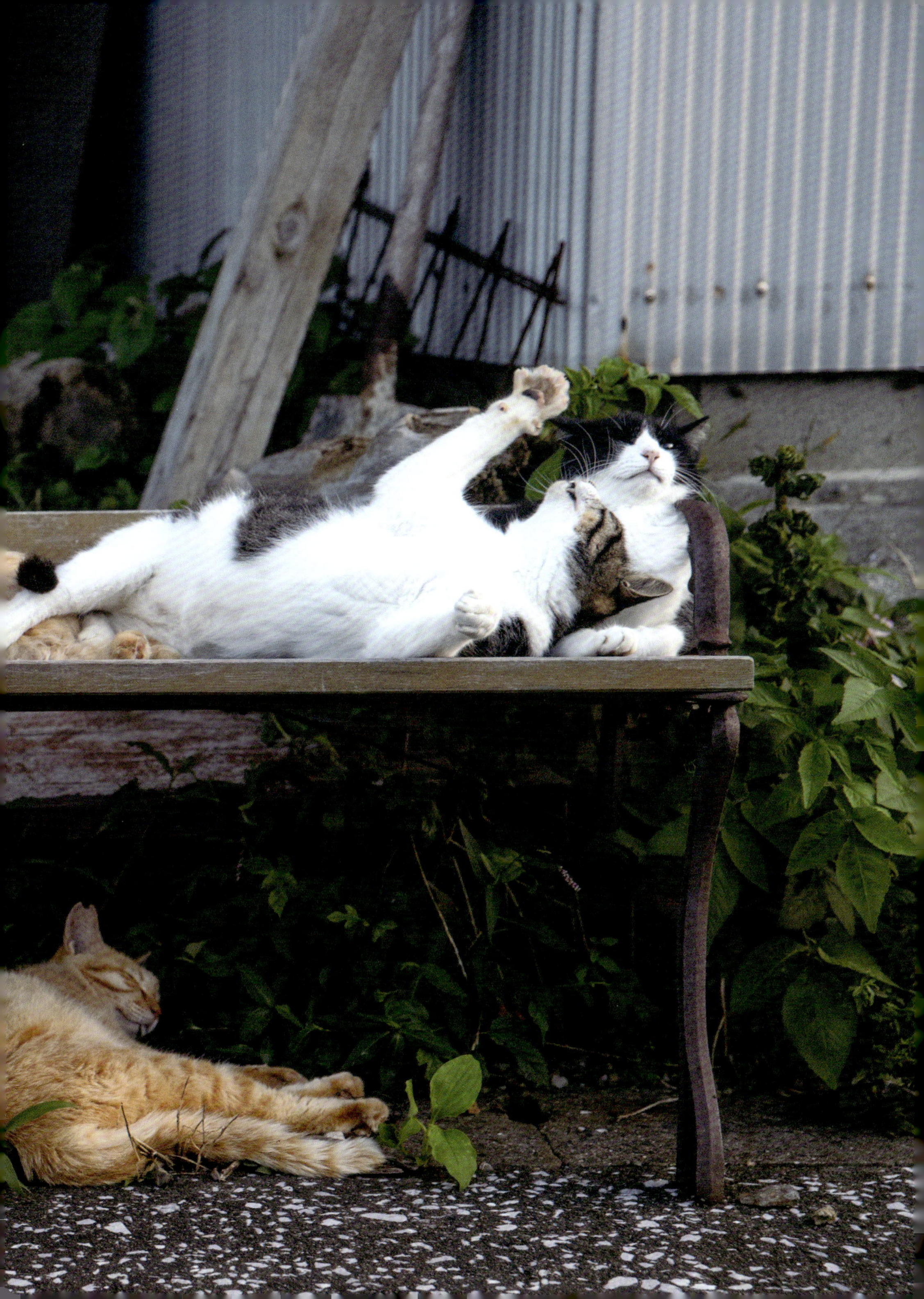

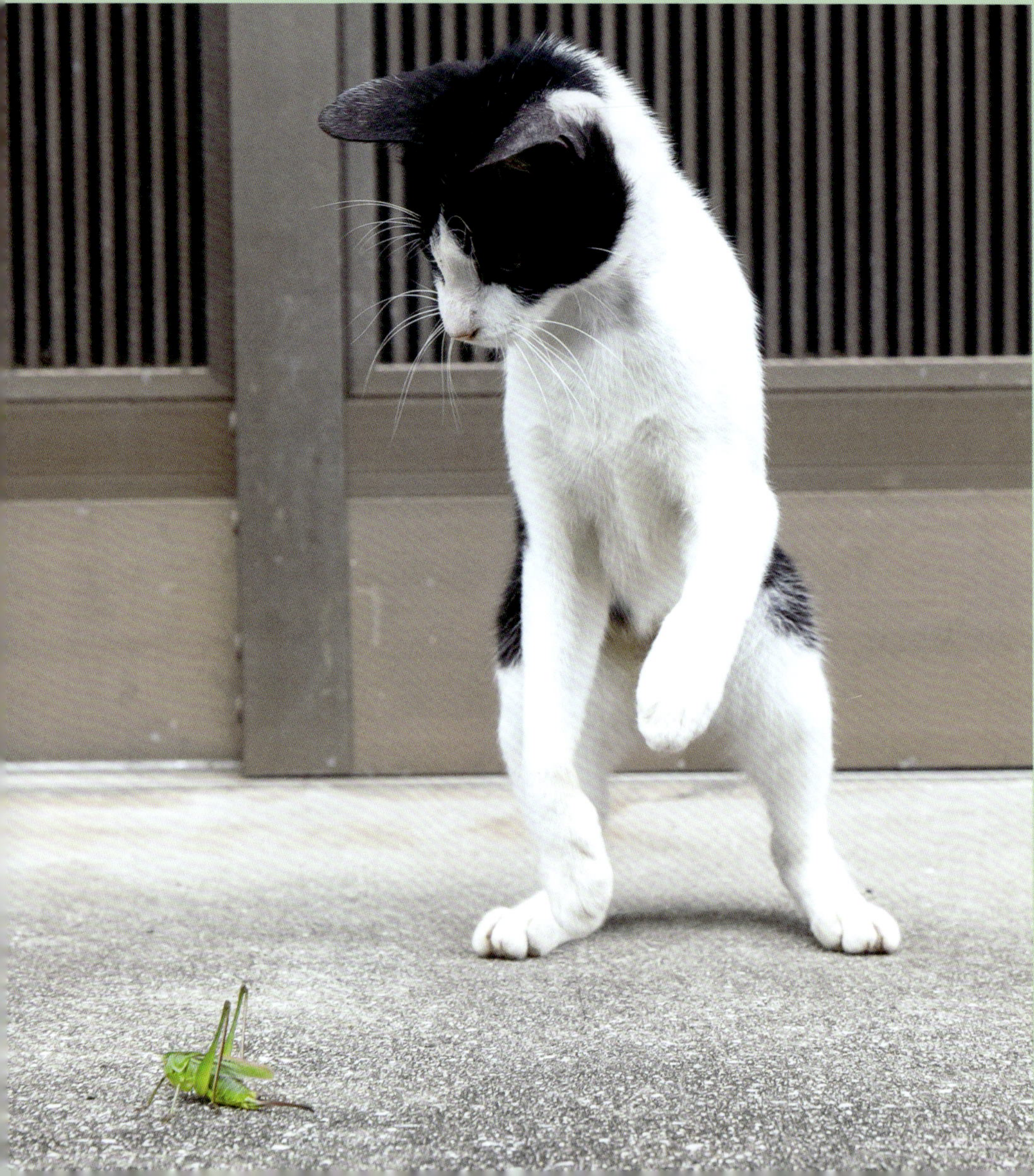

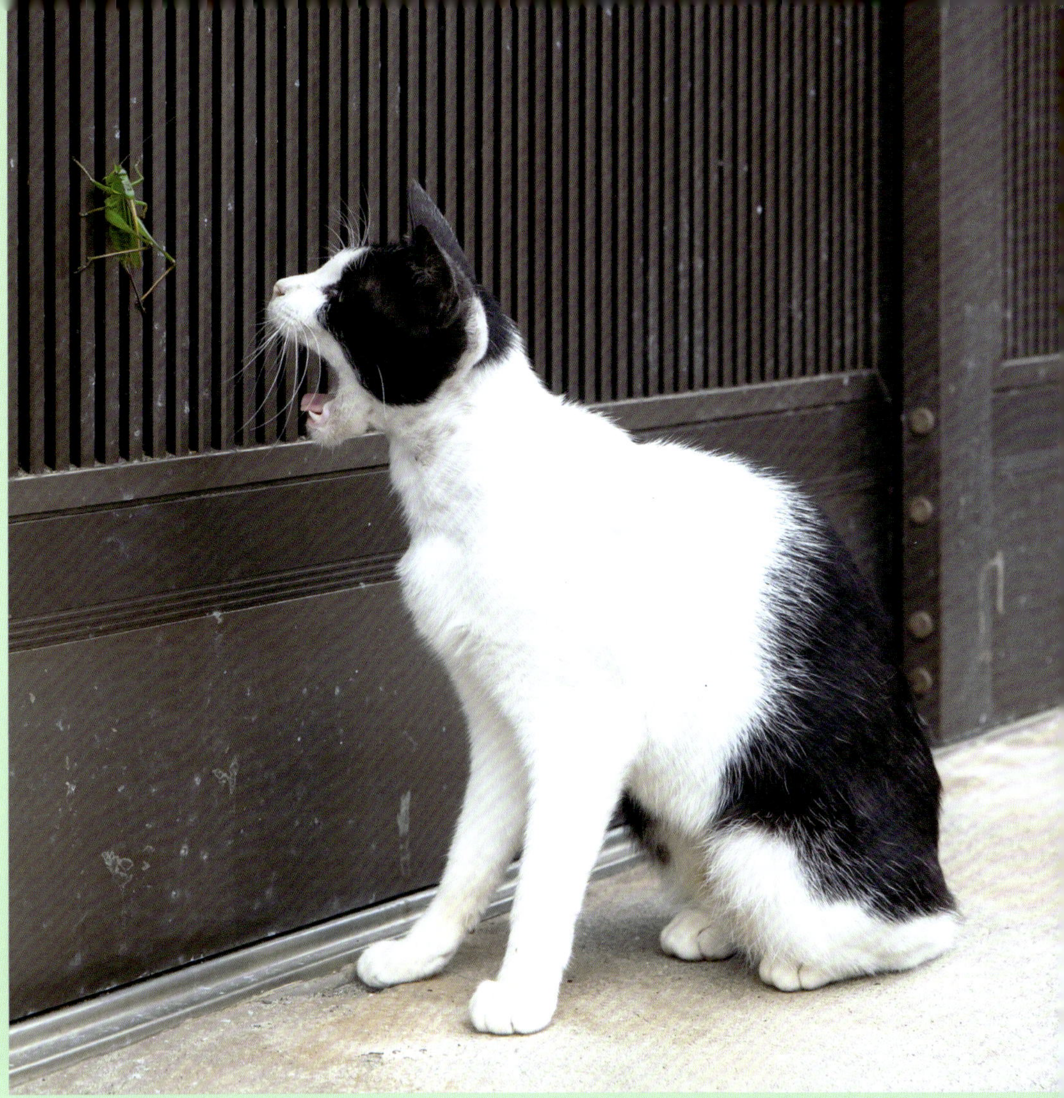

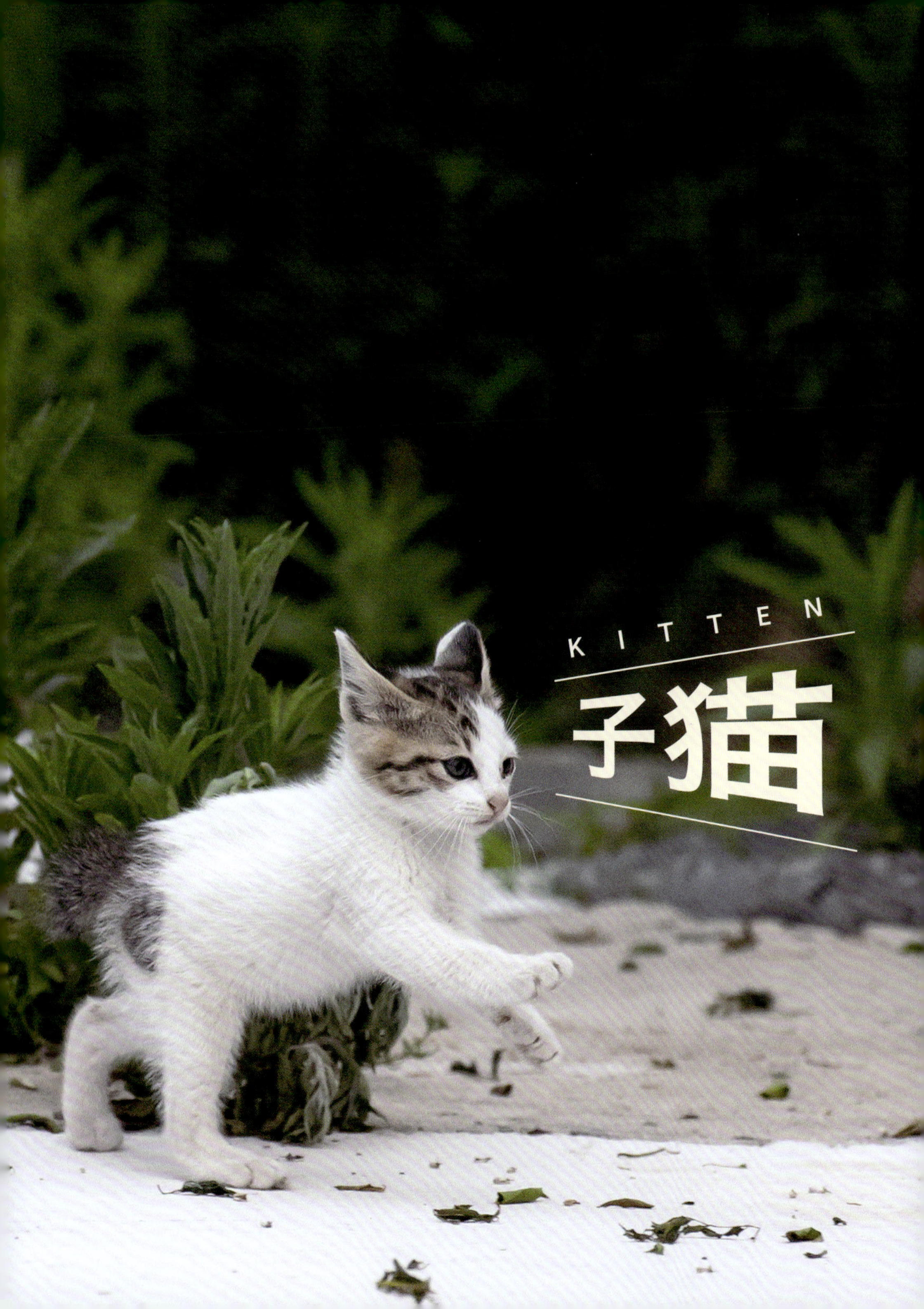
KITTEN
子猫

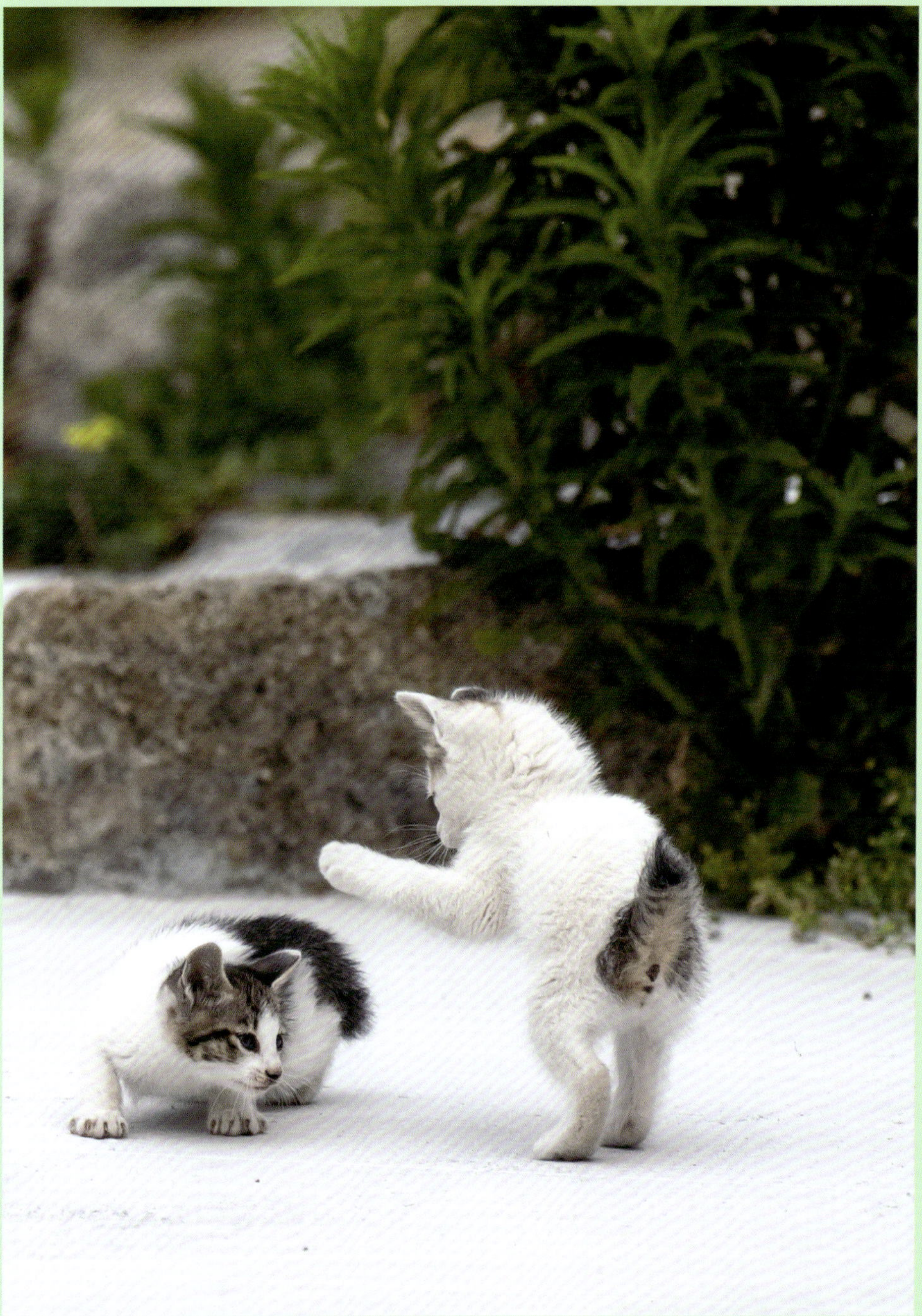

猫・ネコ

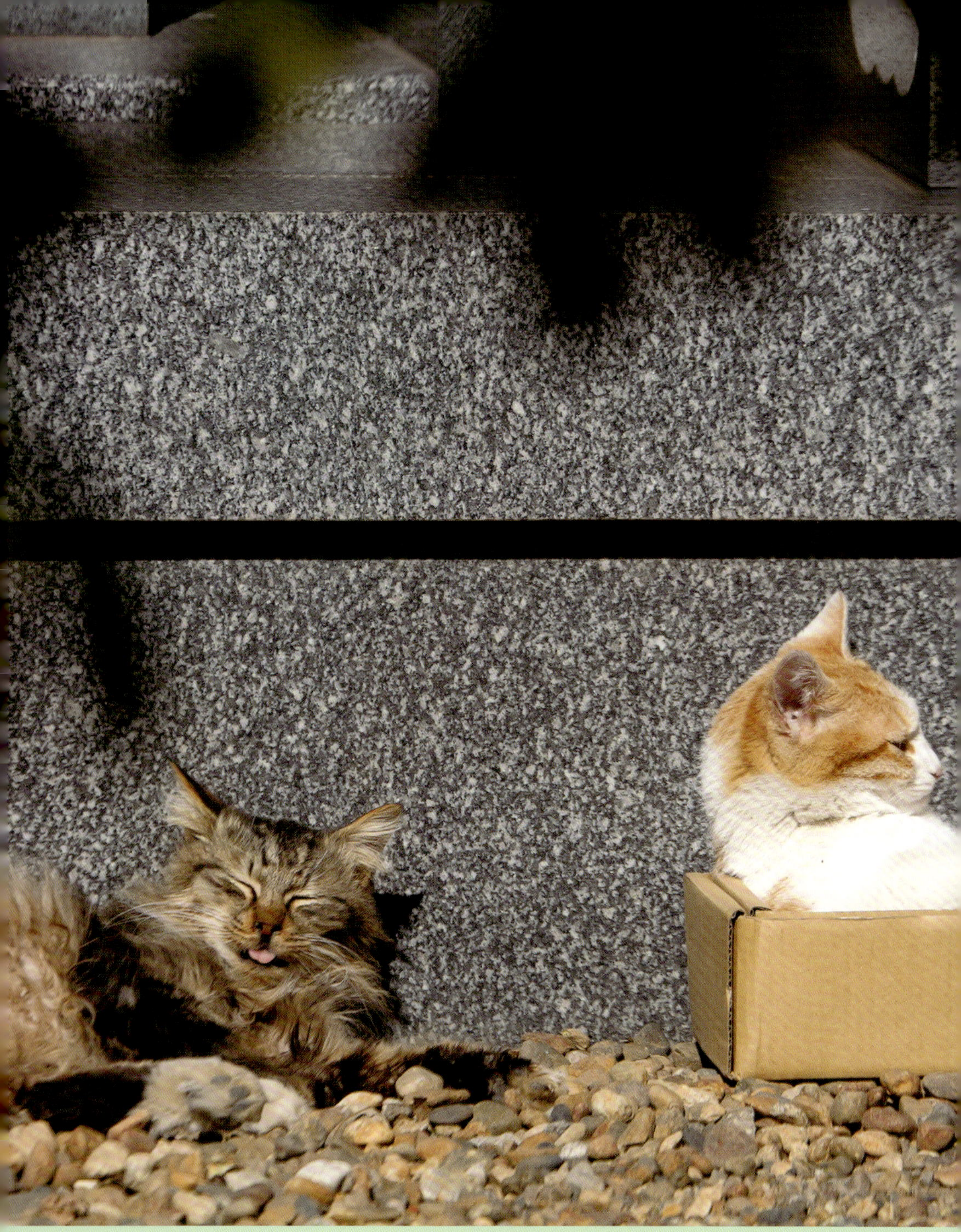

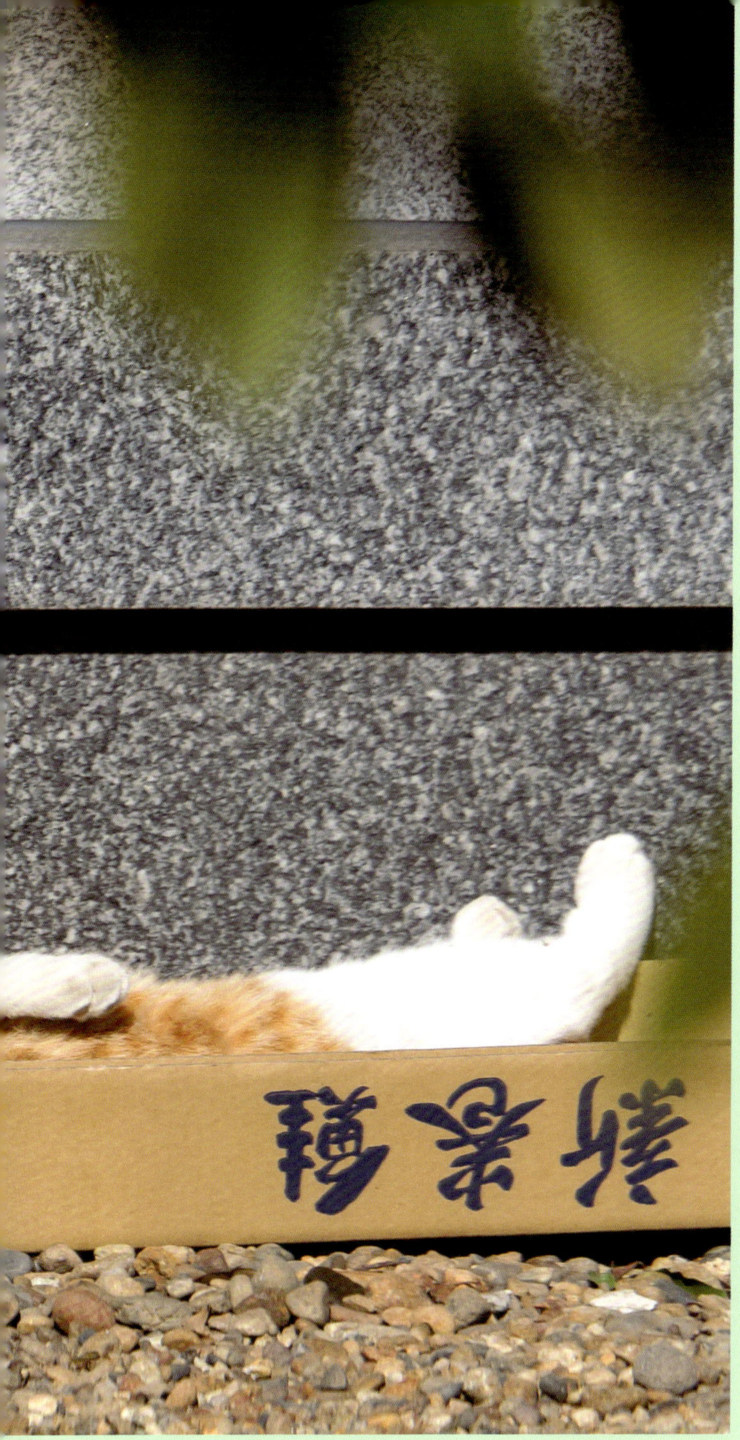

猫・ネコ

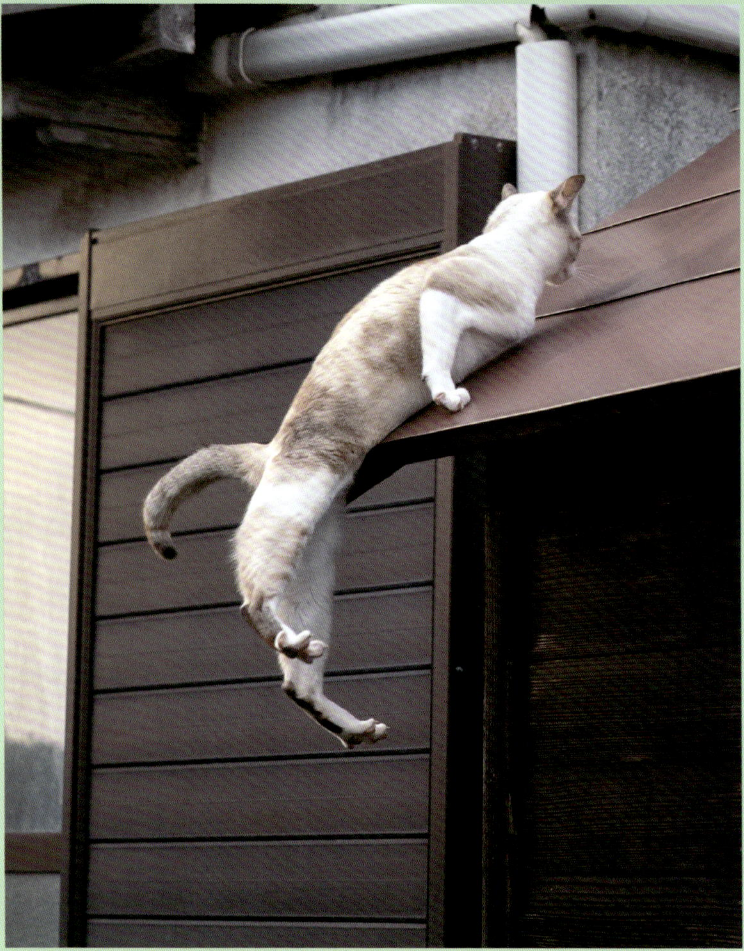

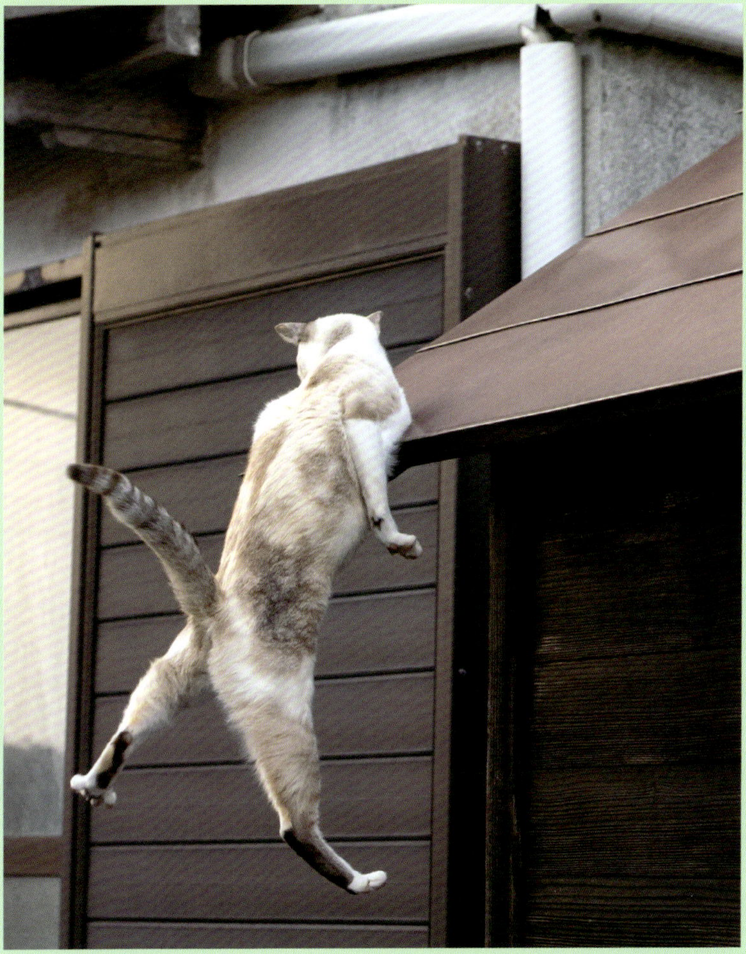

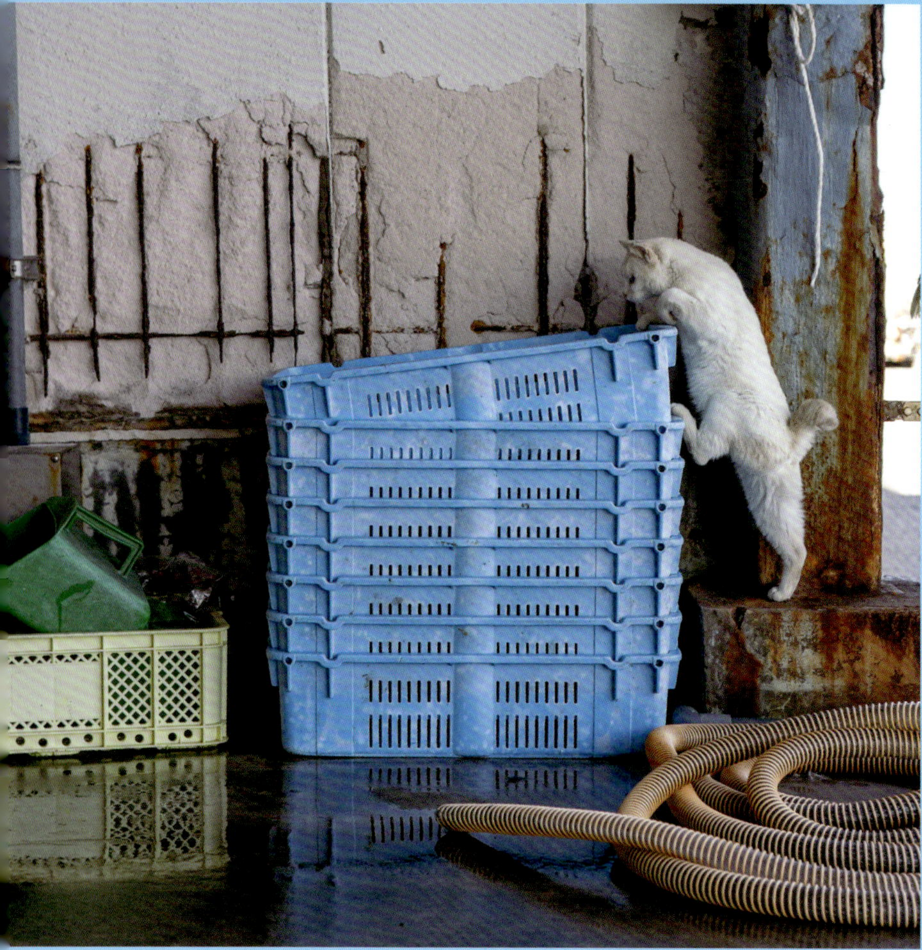

猫・ネコ

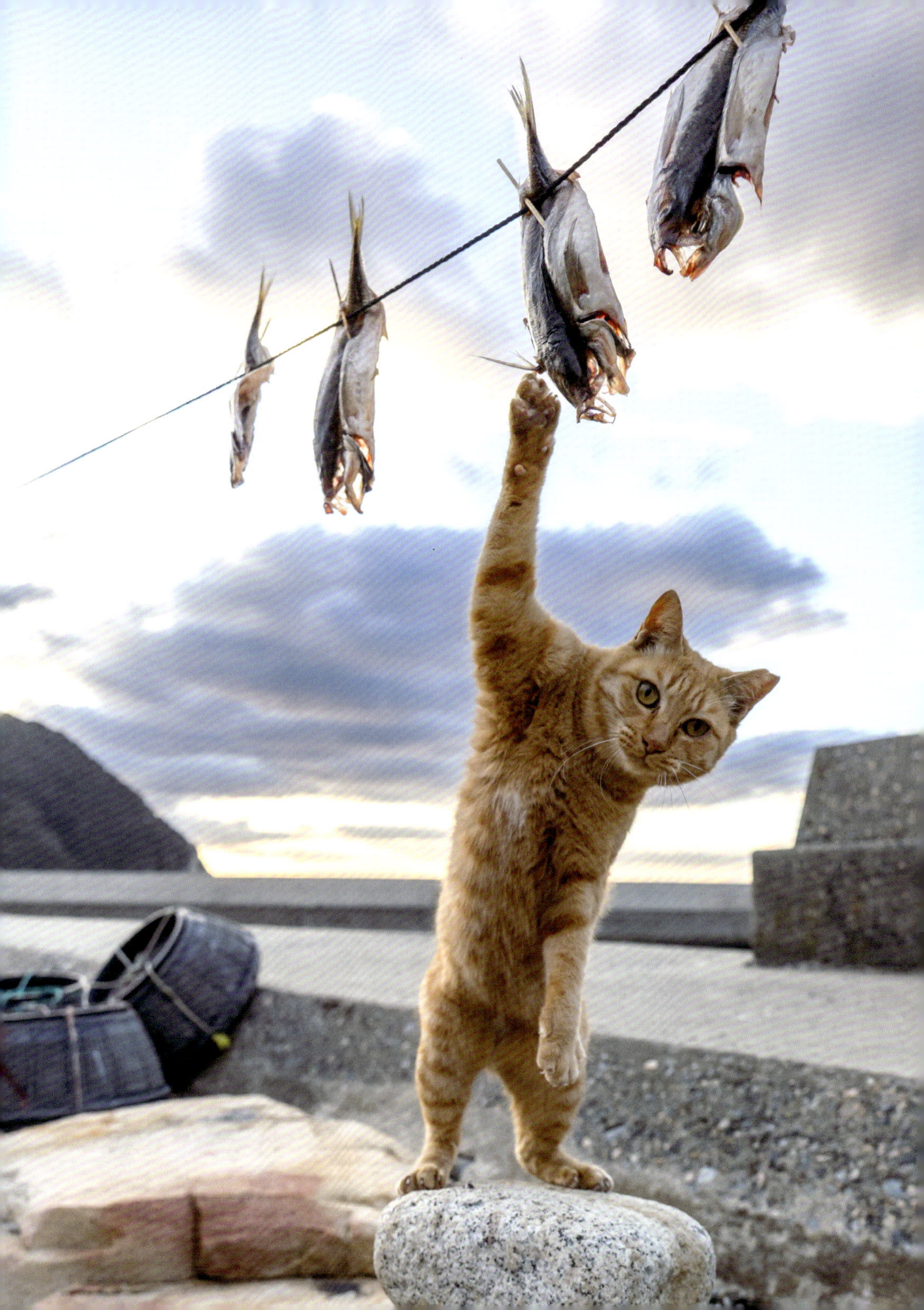

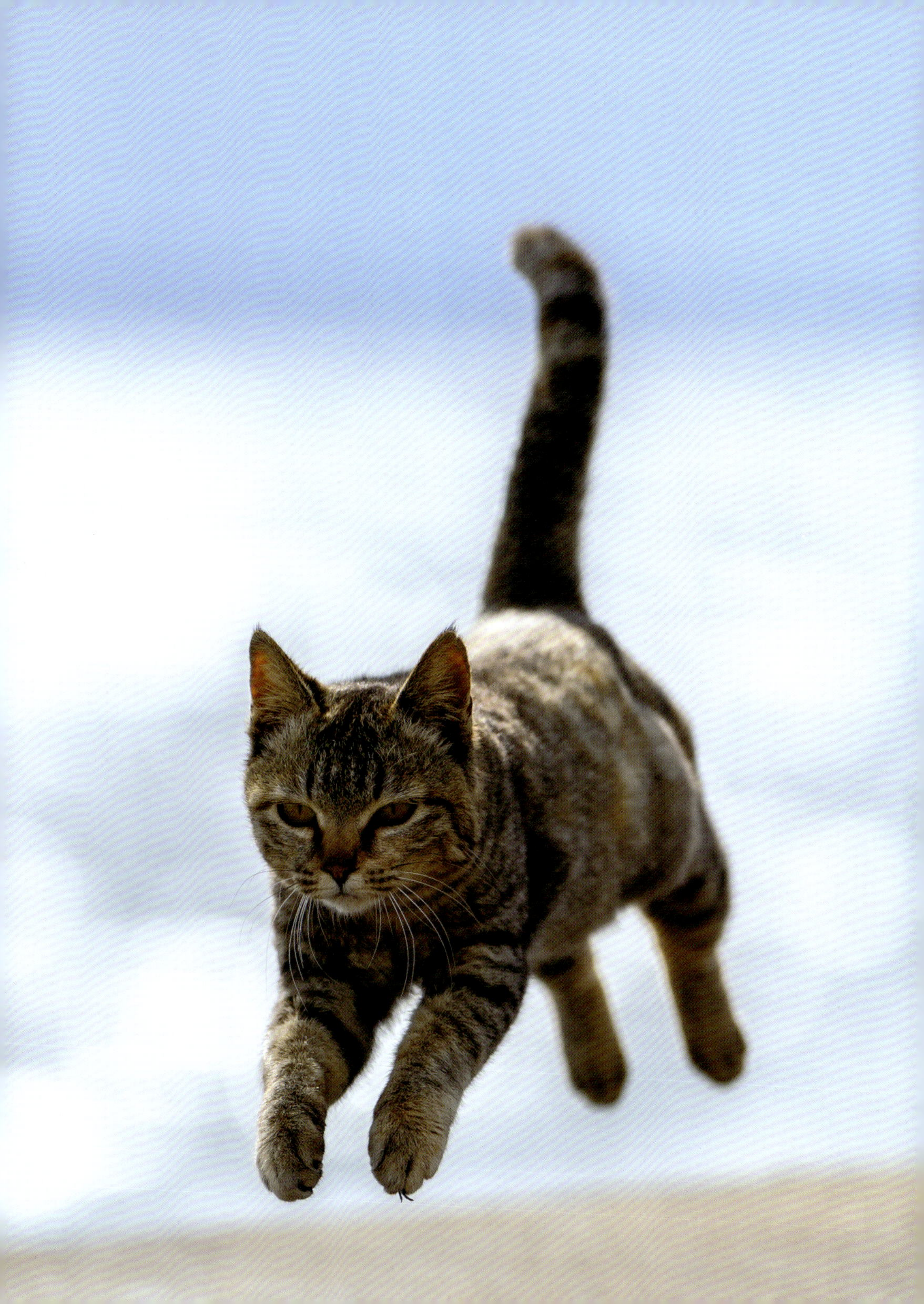

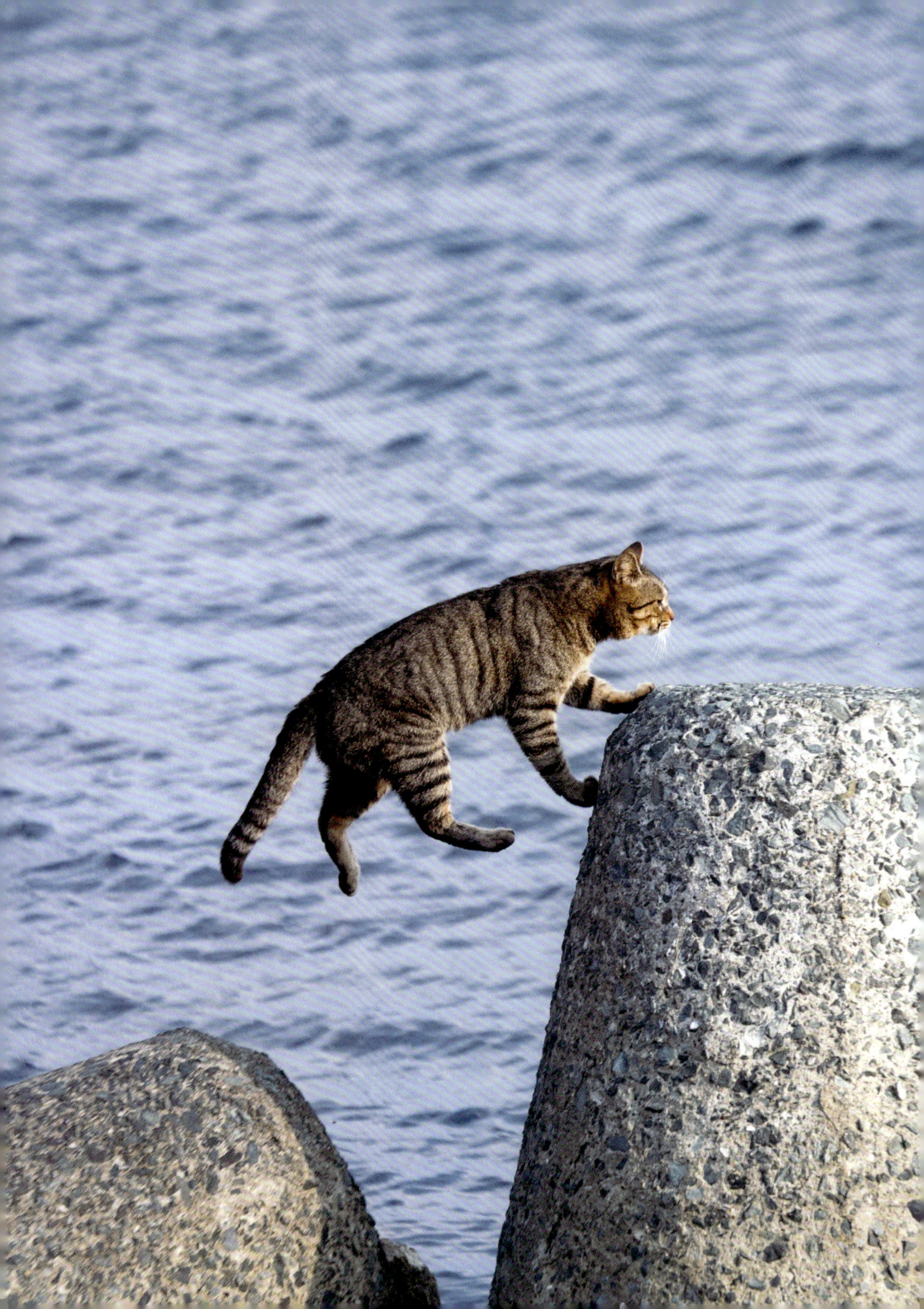

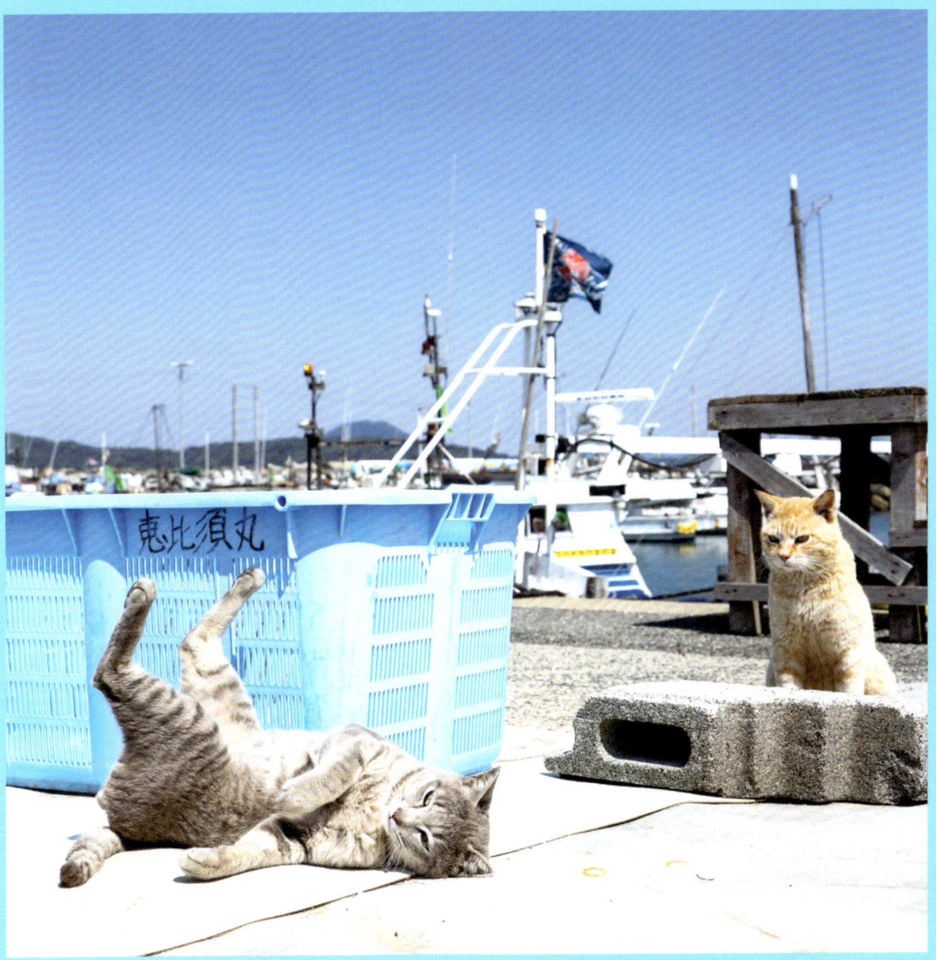
恵比須丸

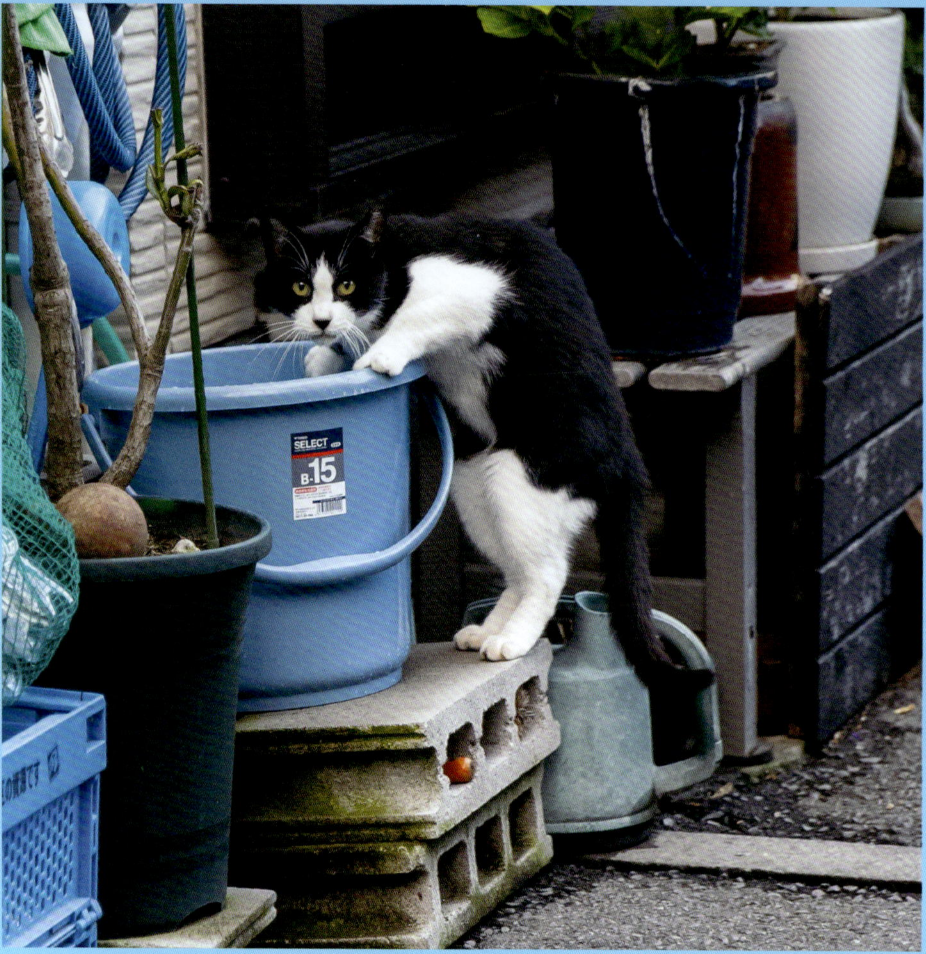
SELECT
B-15

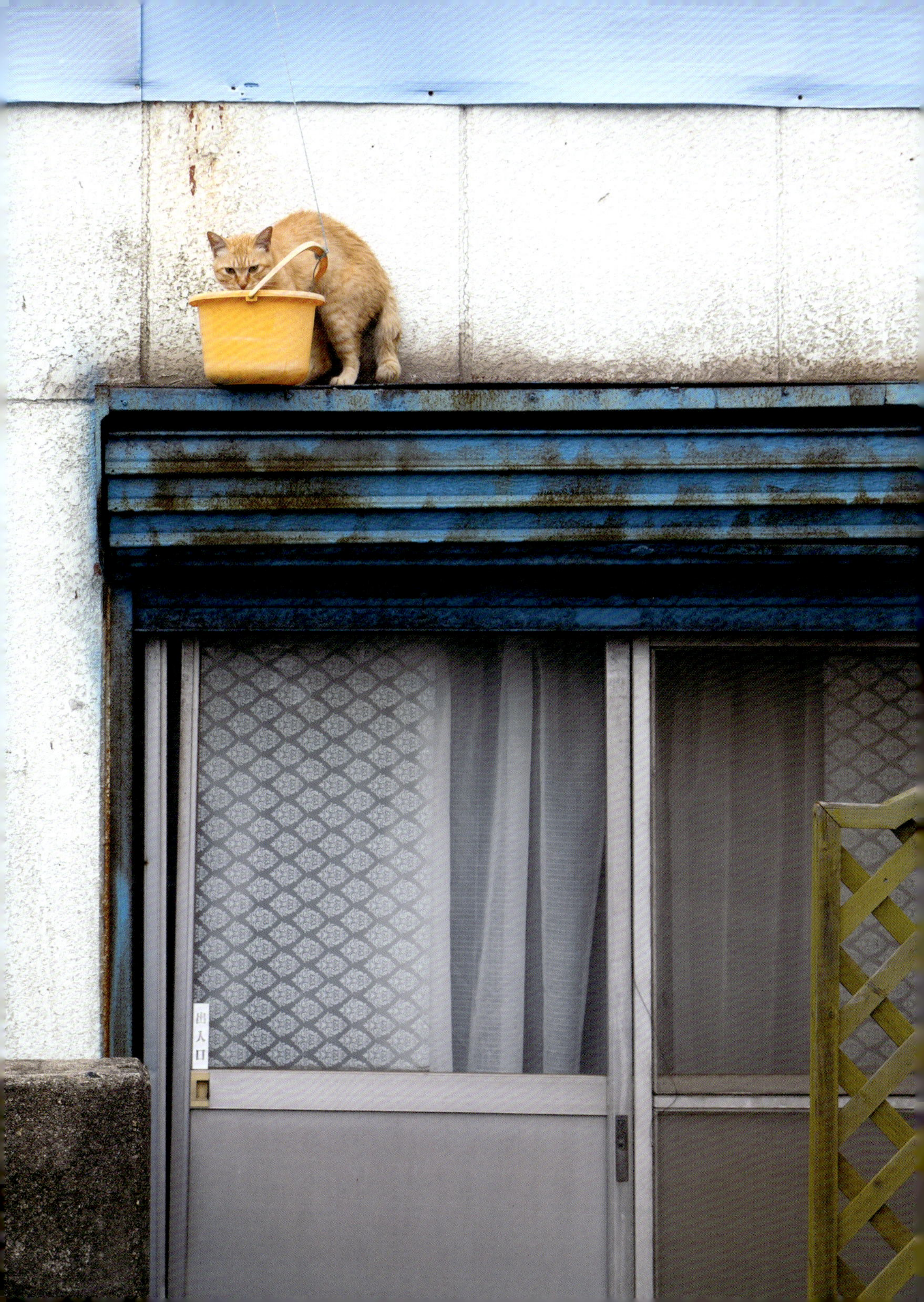
出入口

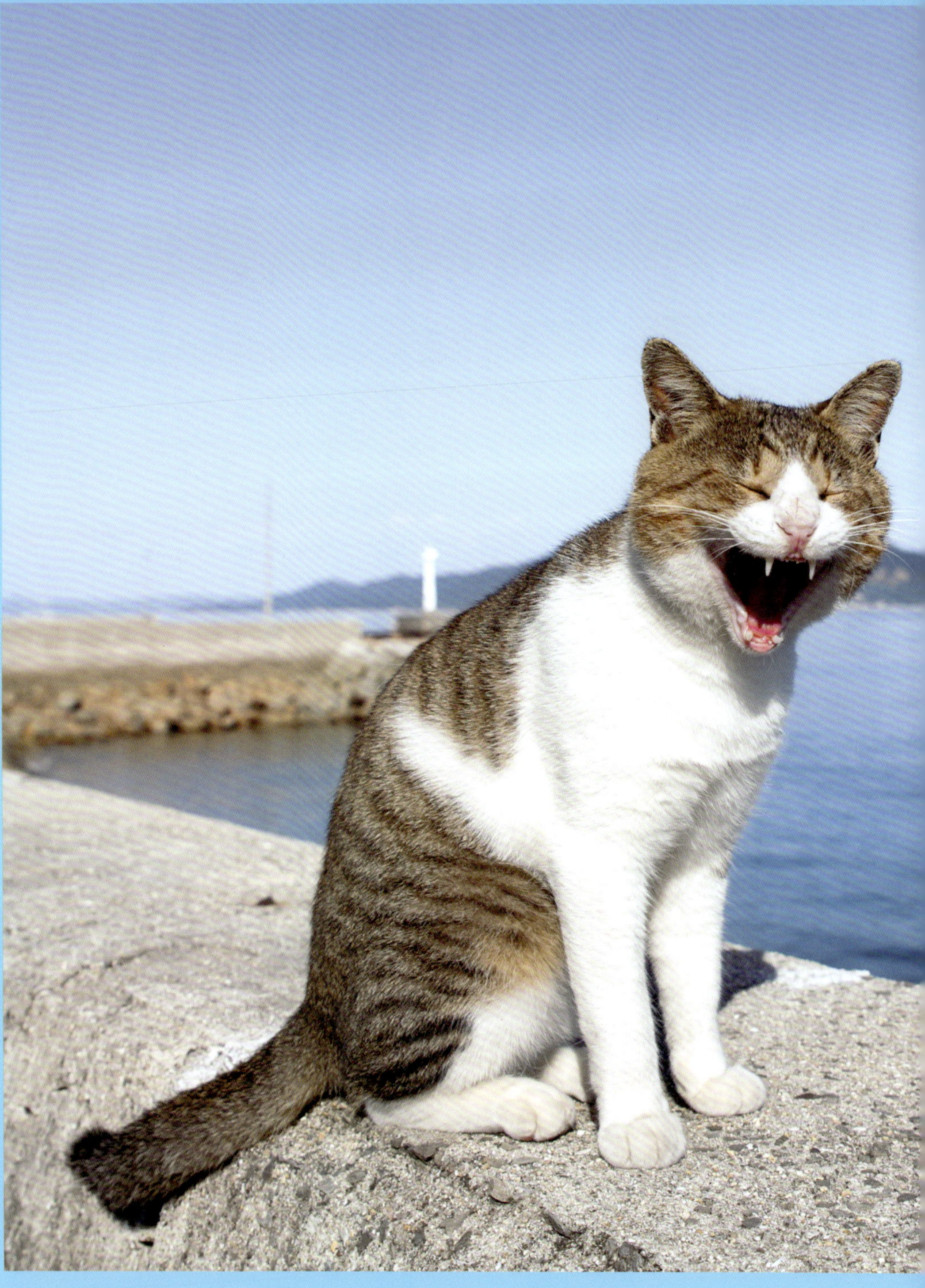

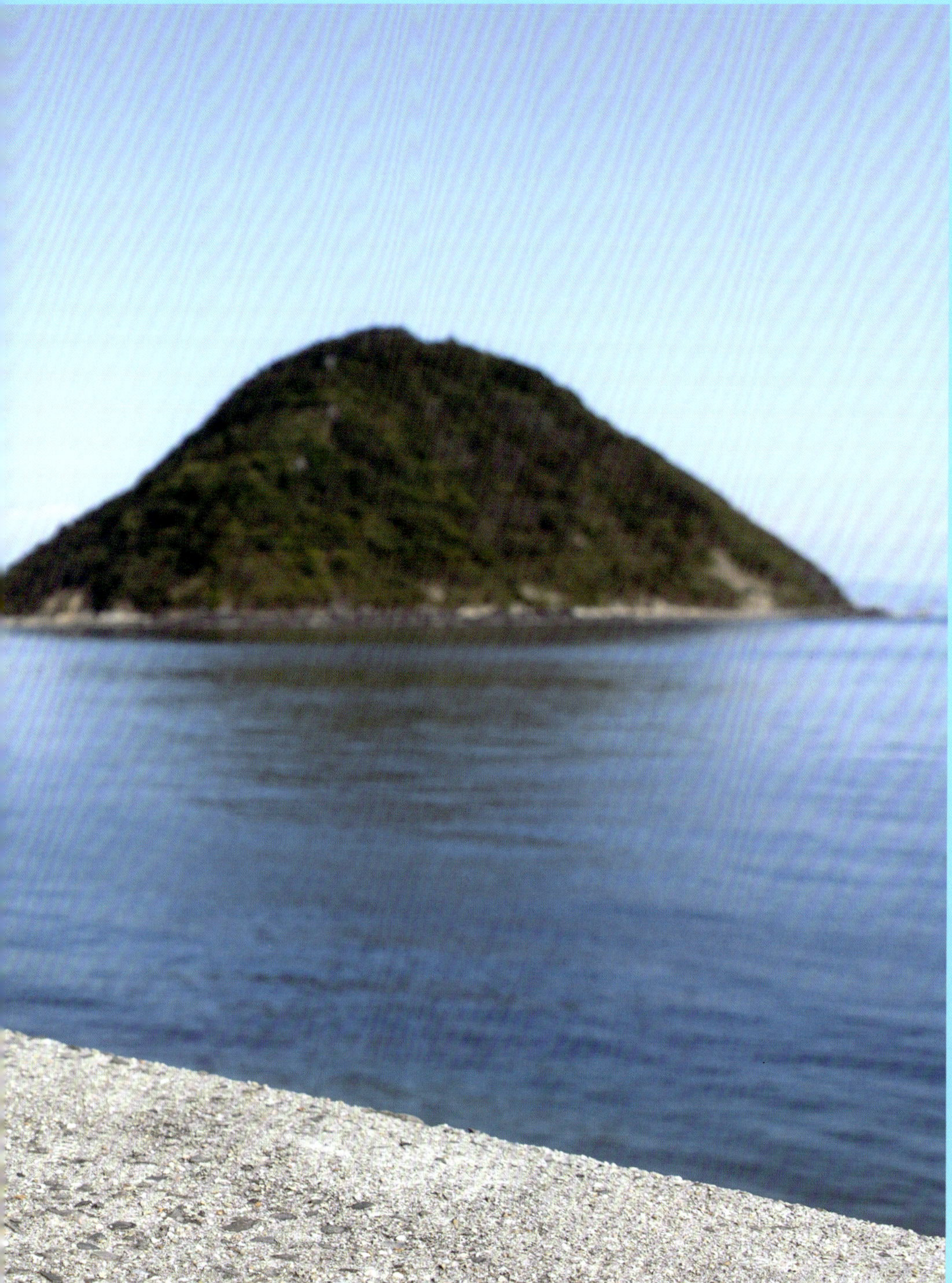

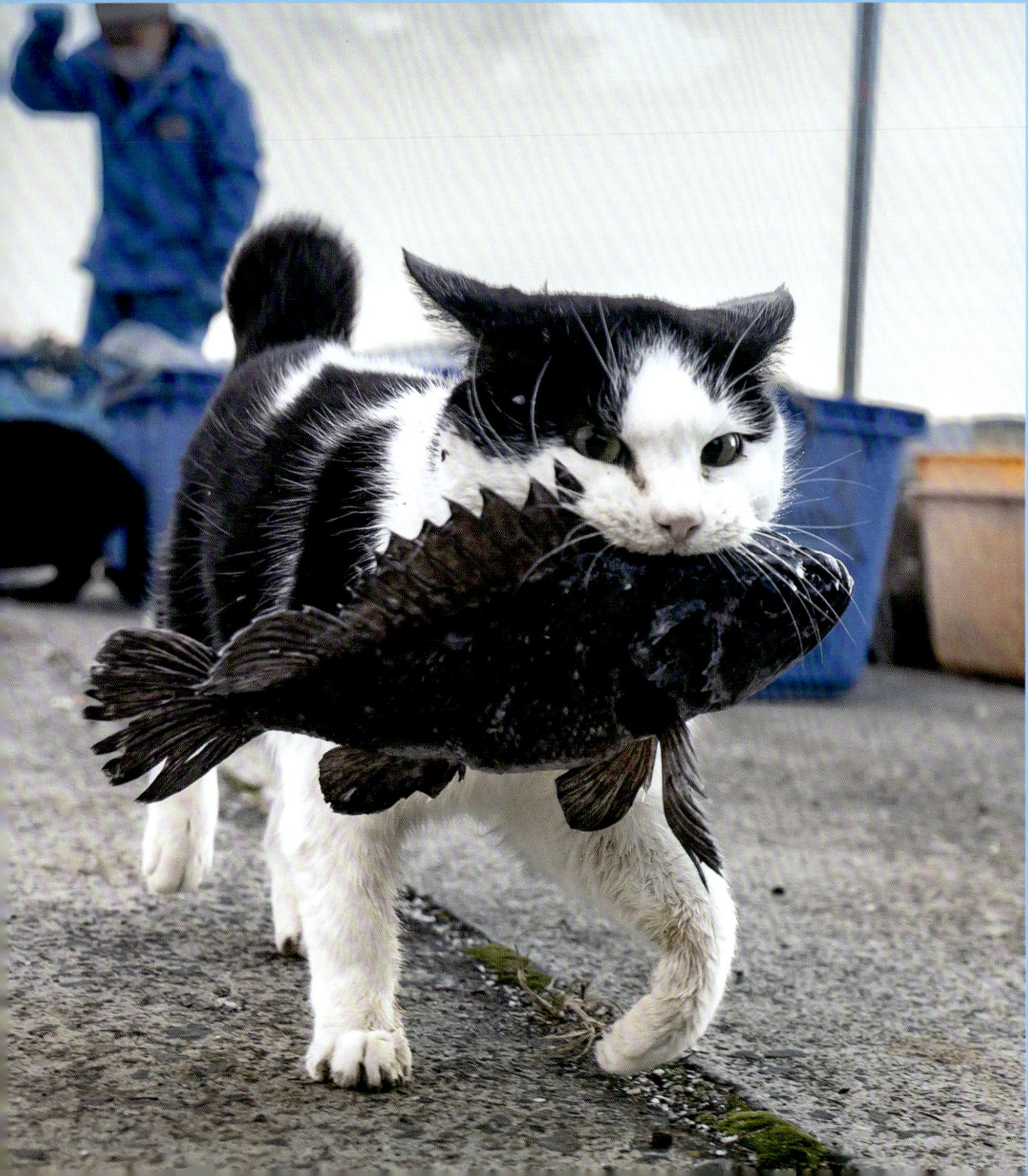

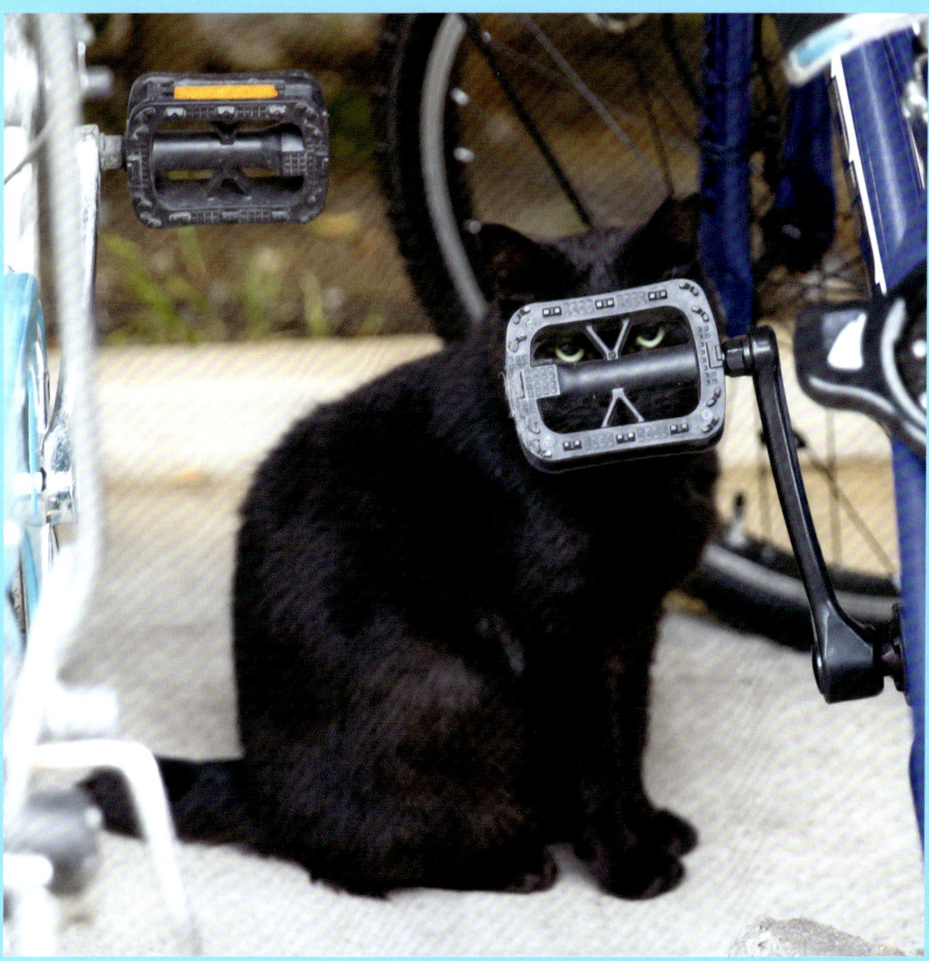

猫・ネコ

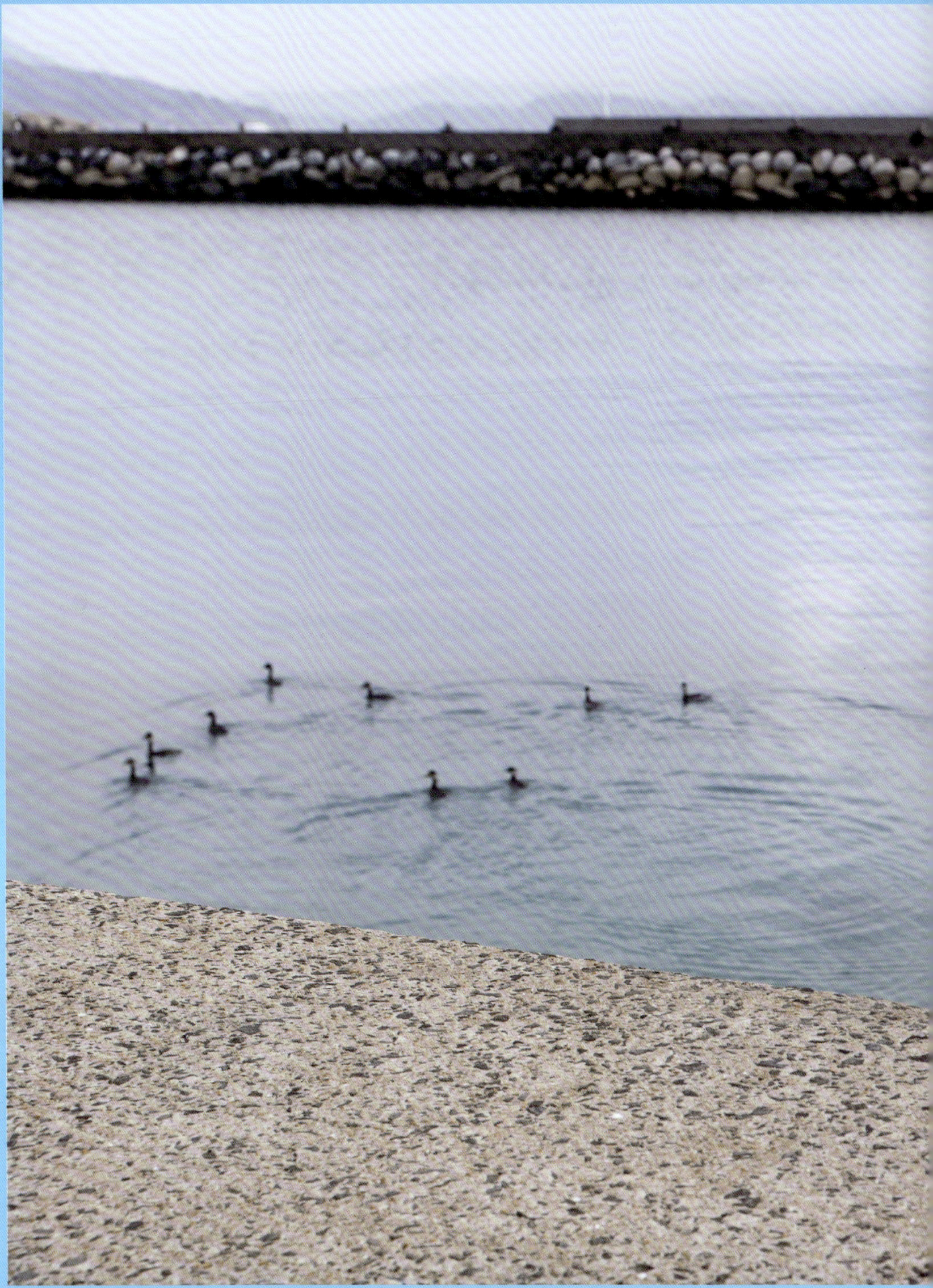

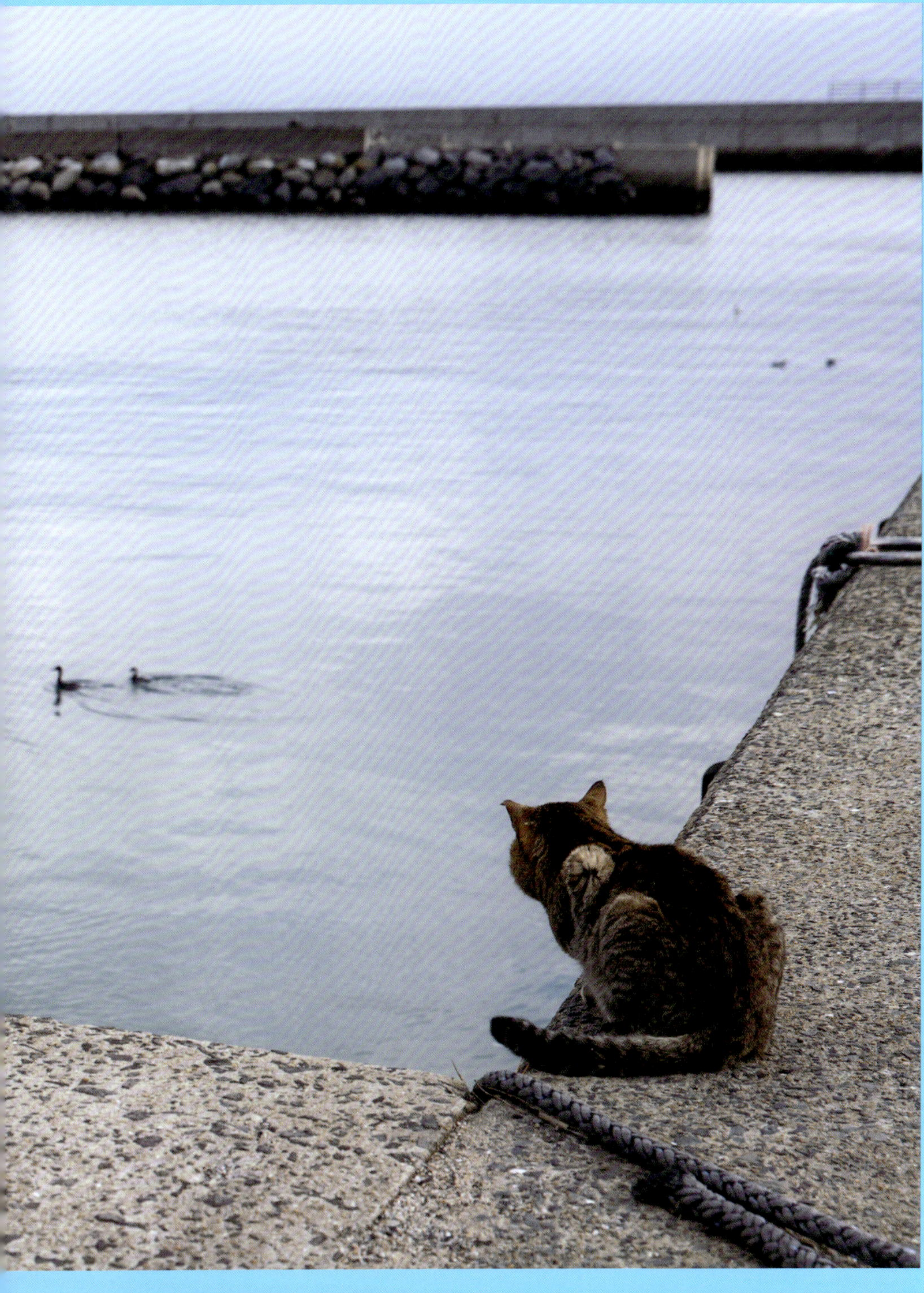

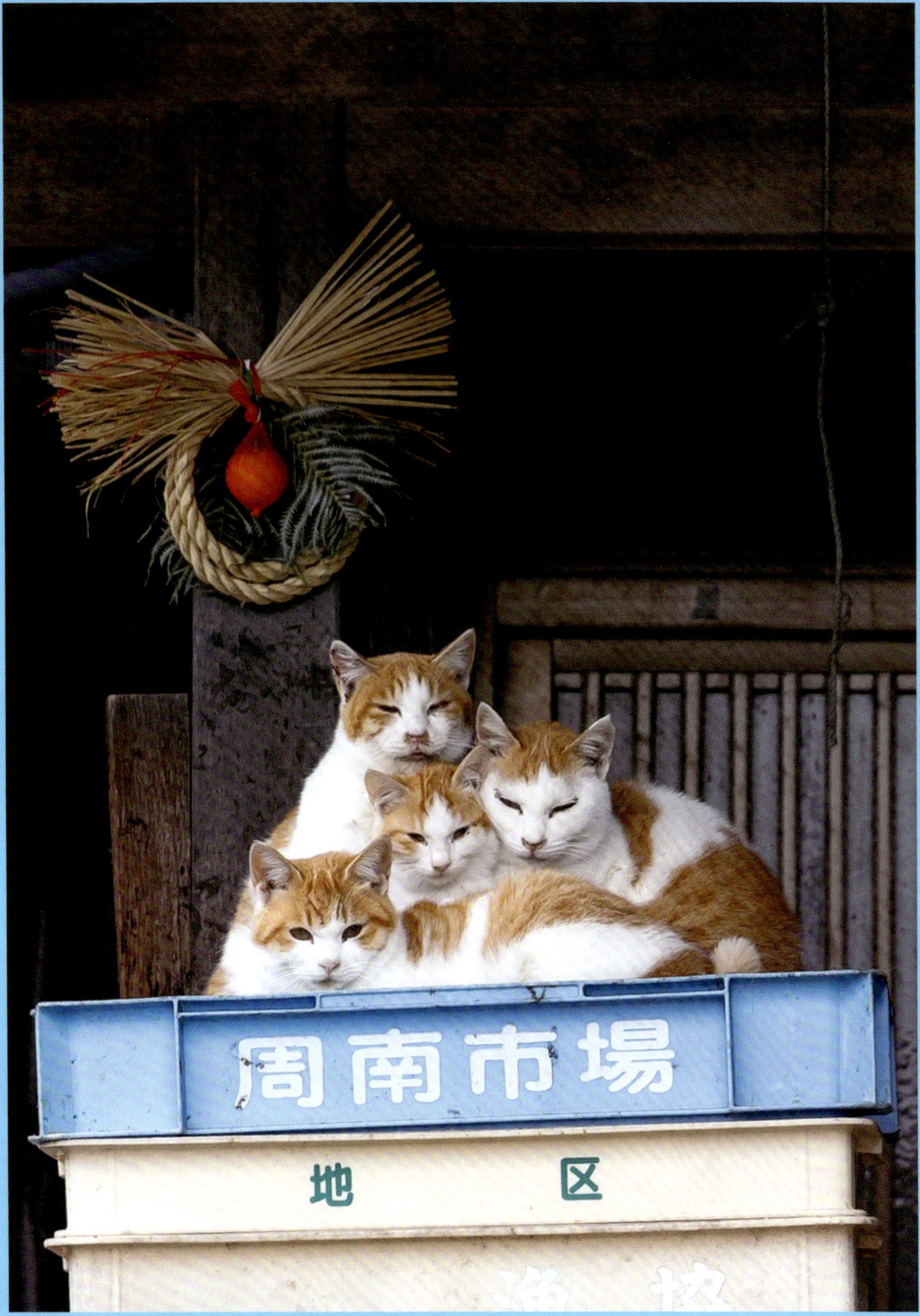
周南市場
地区

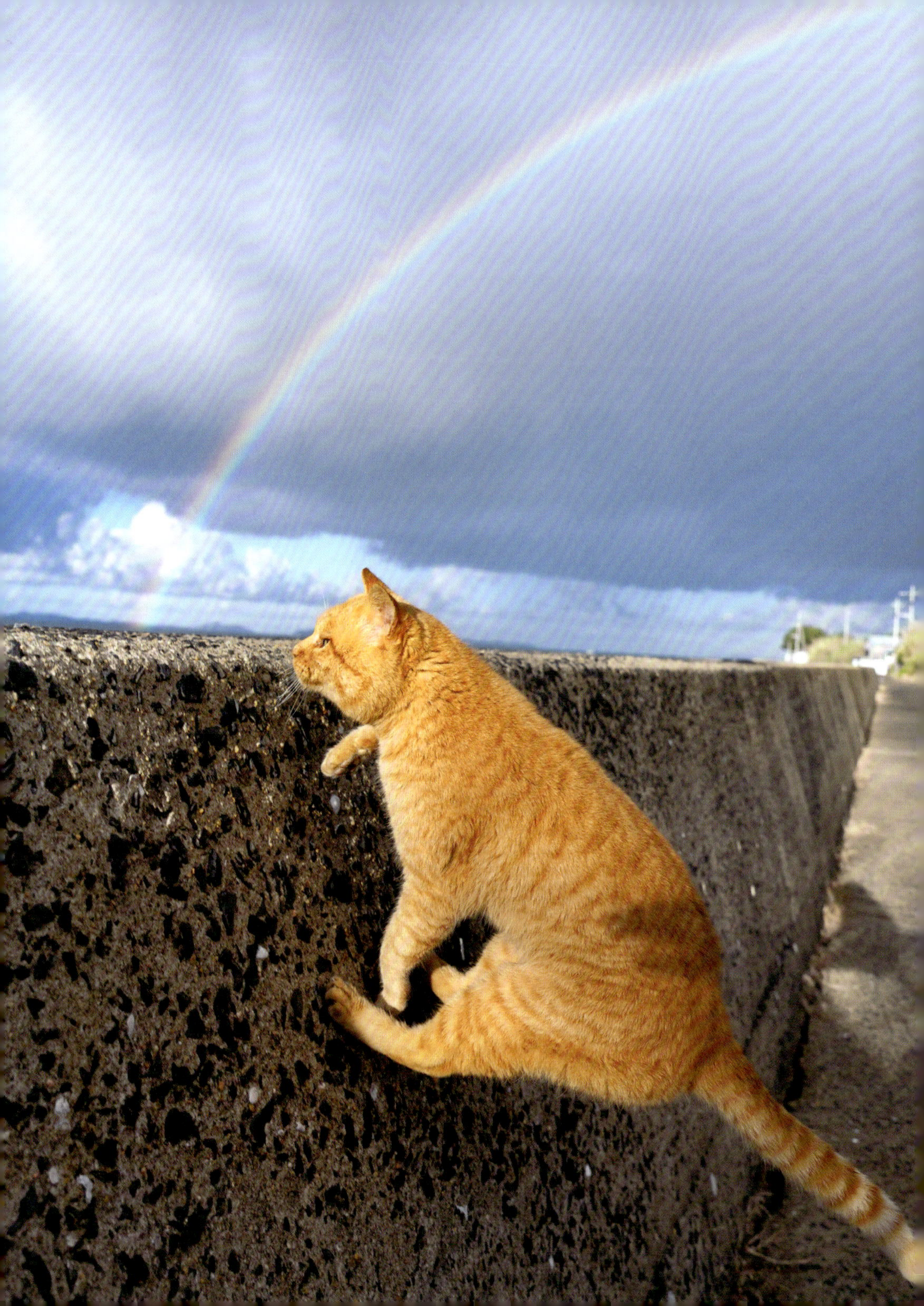

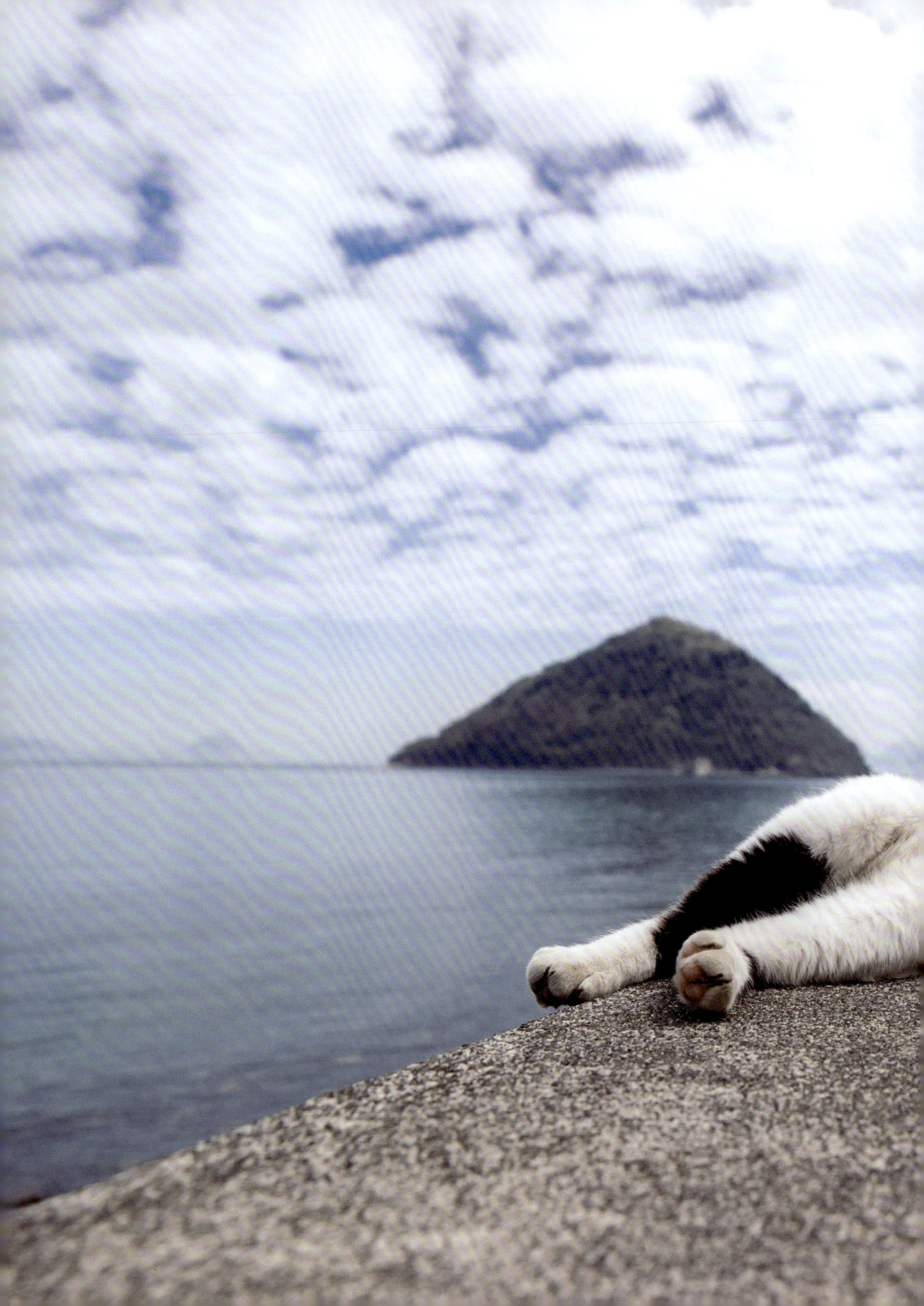

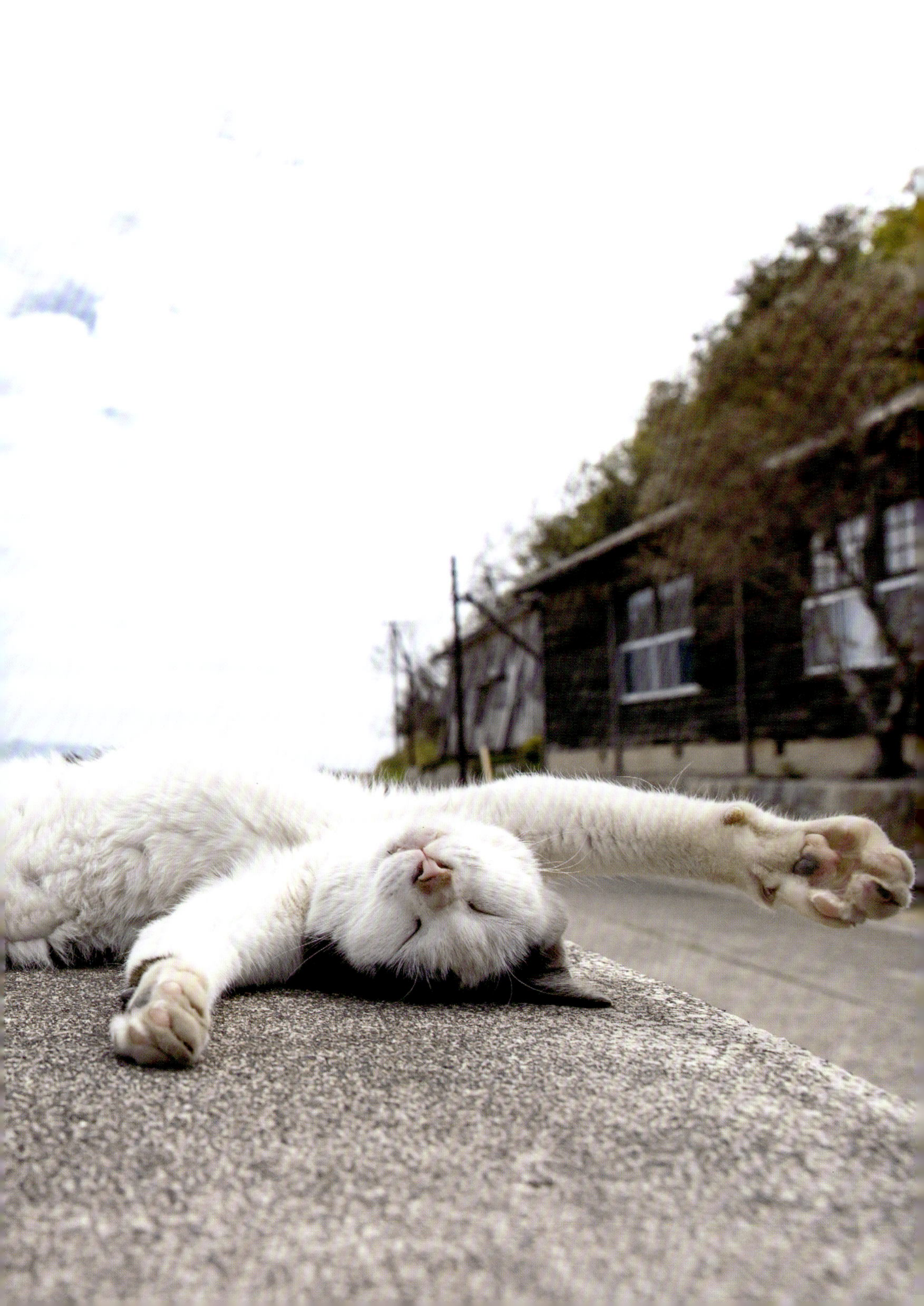

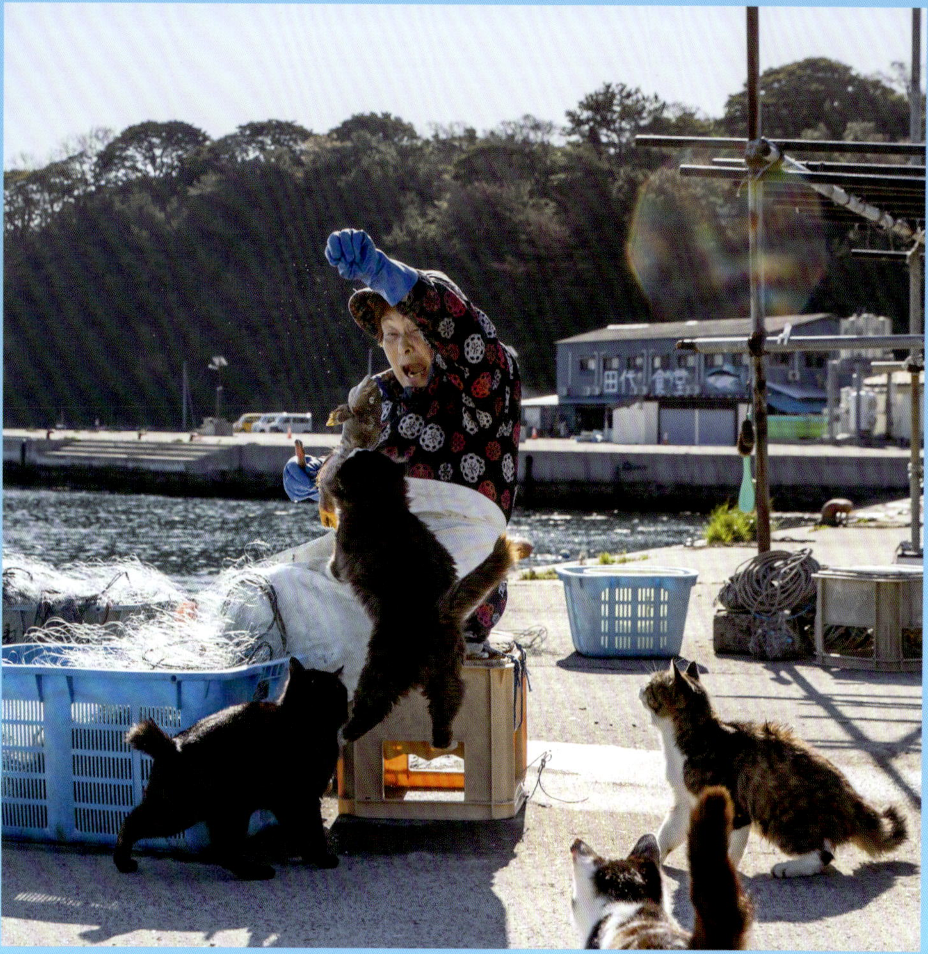
田代

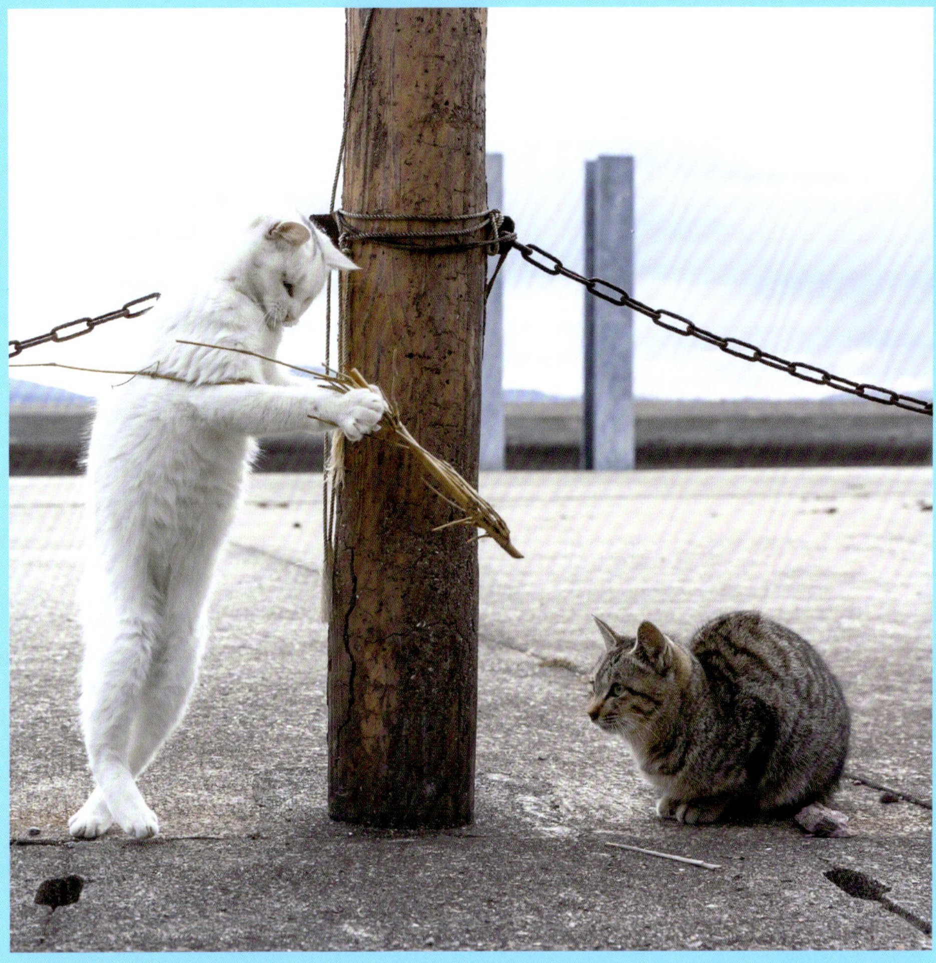

猫・ネコ

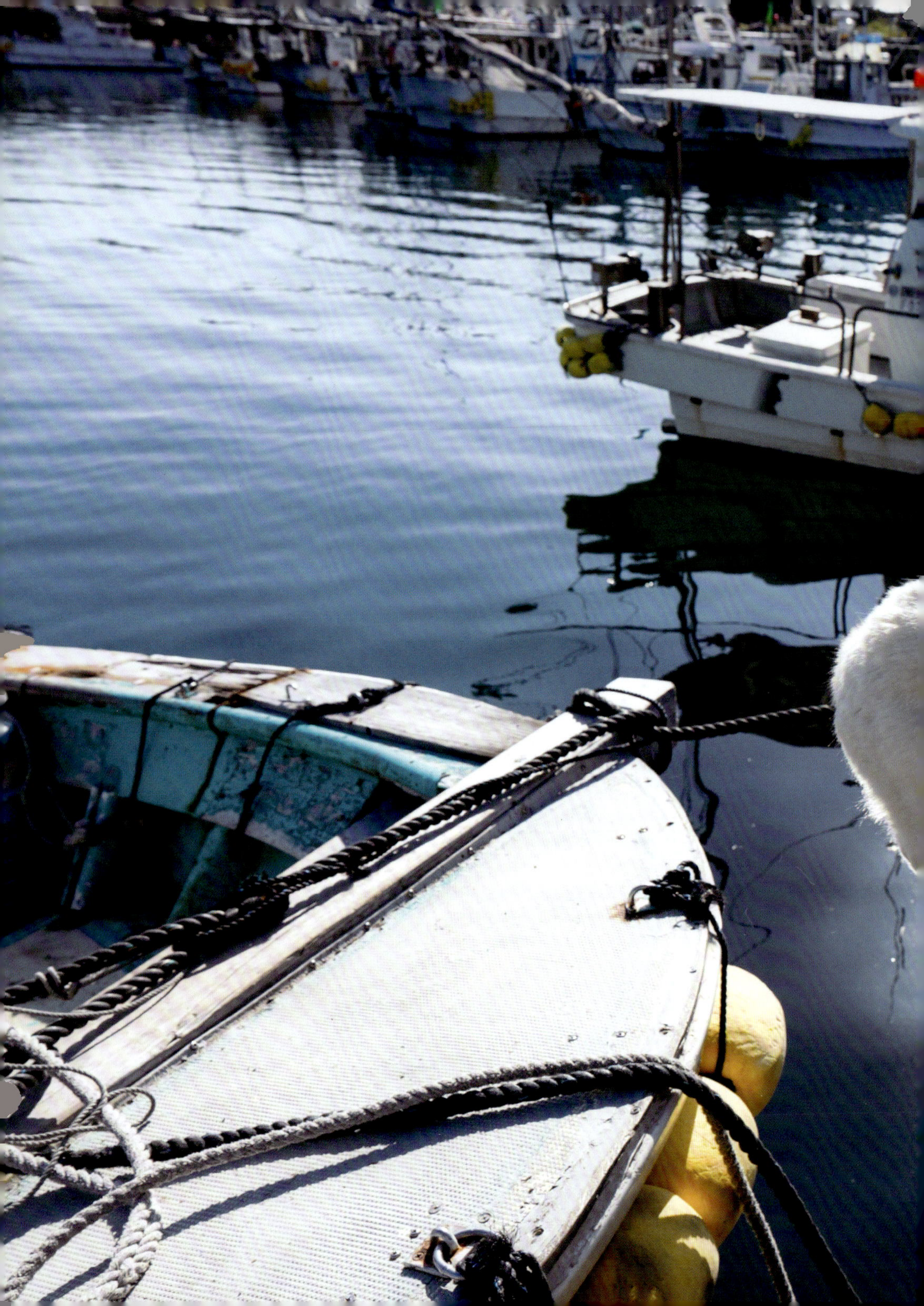

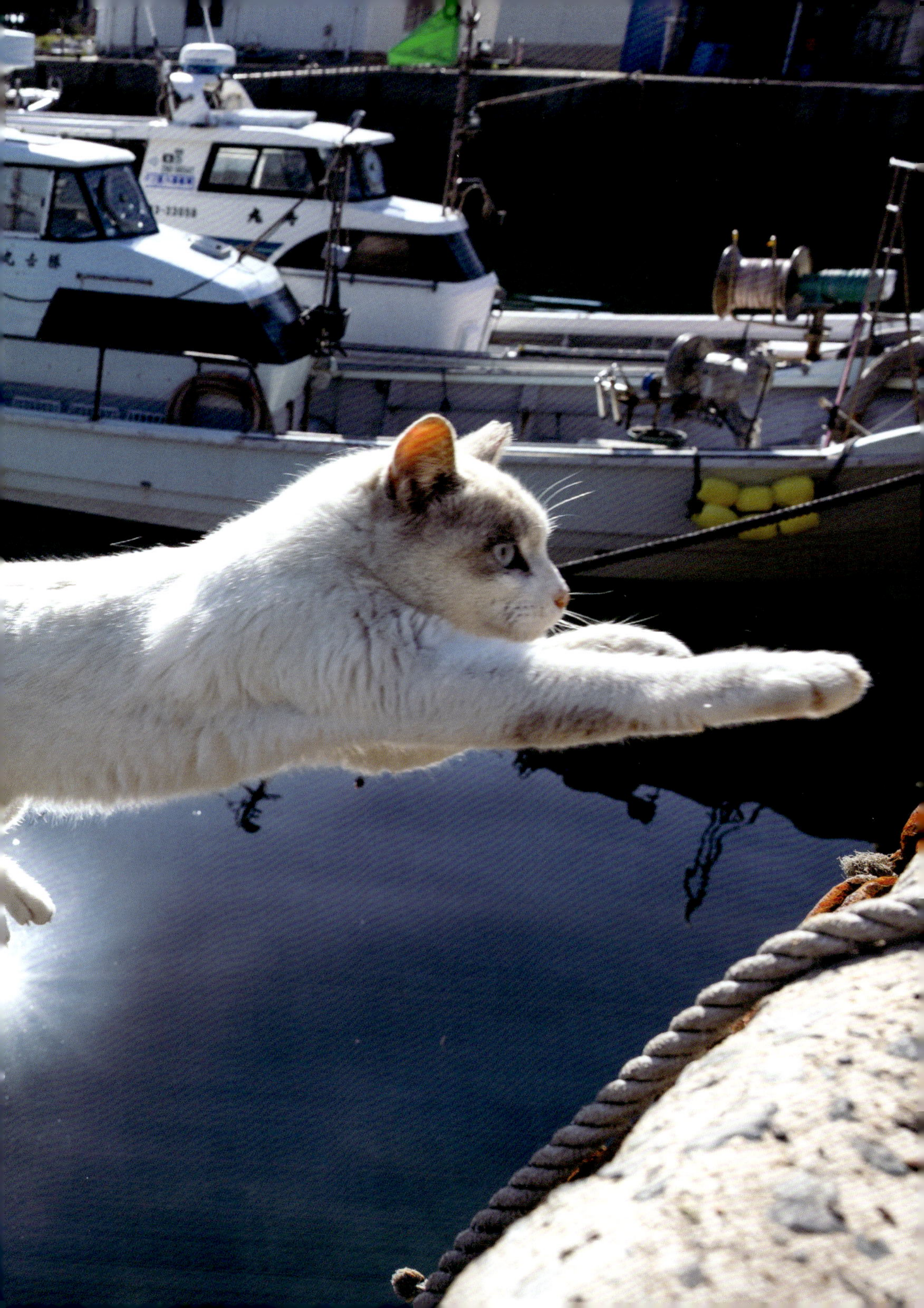

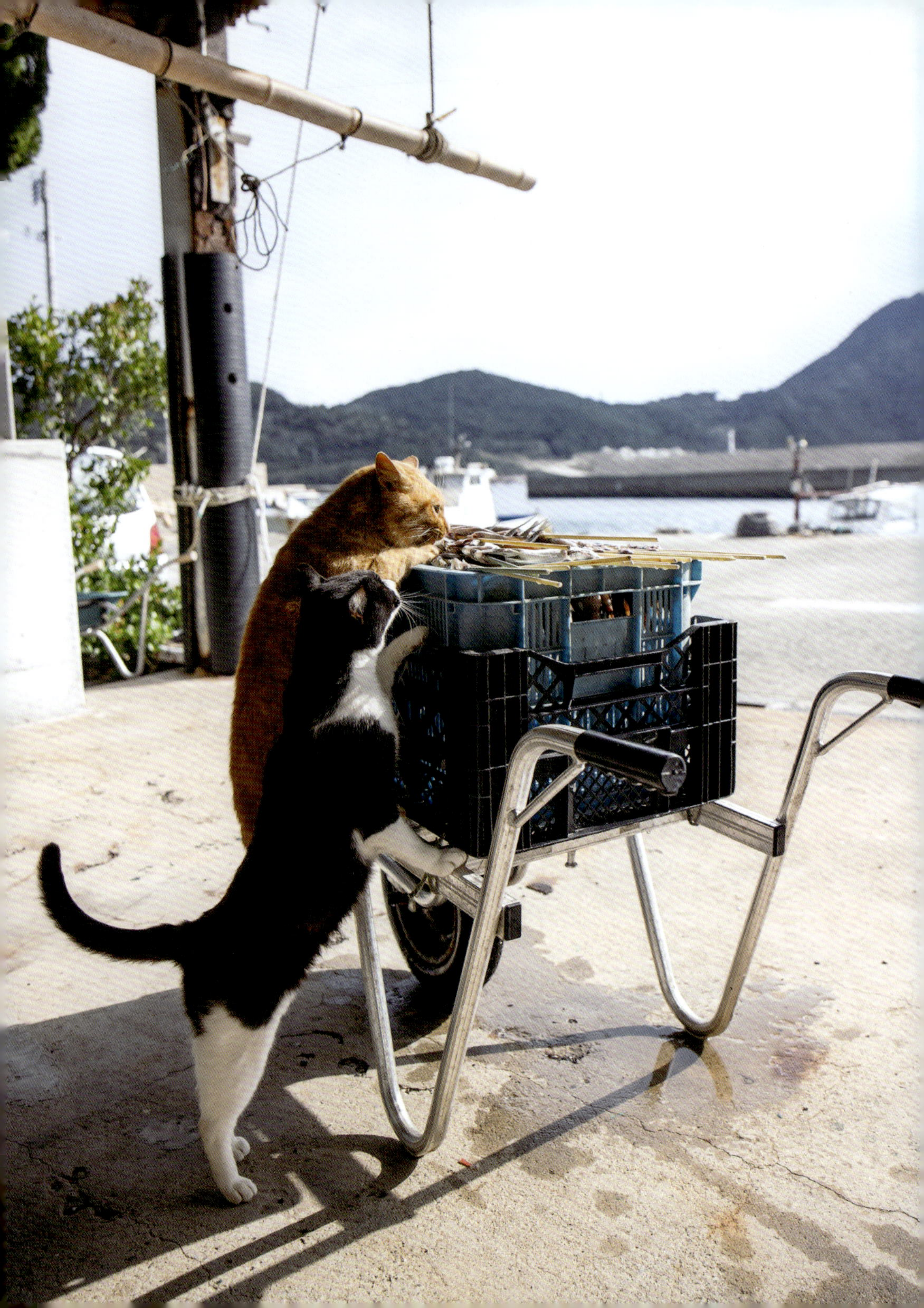

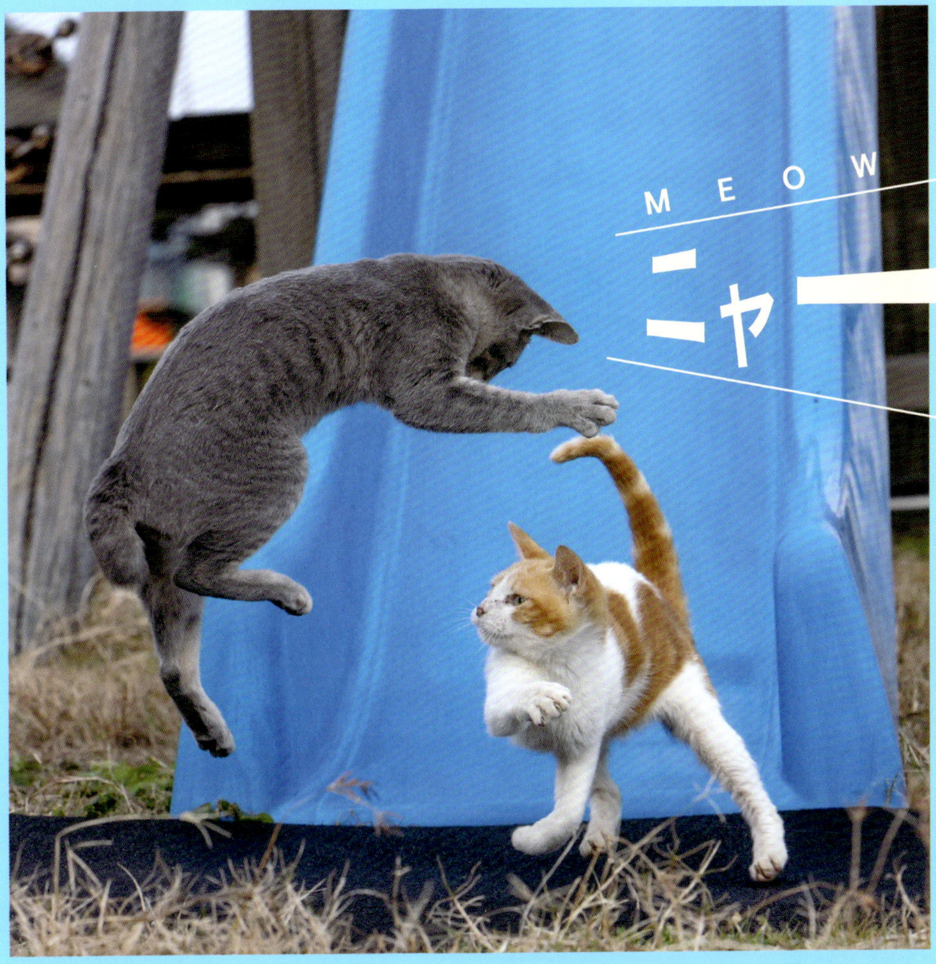
MEOW
ニャー

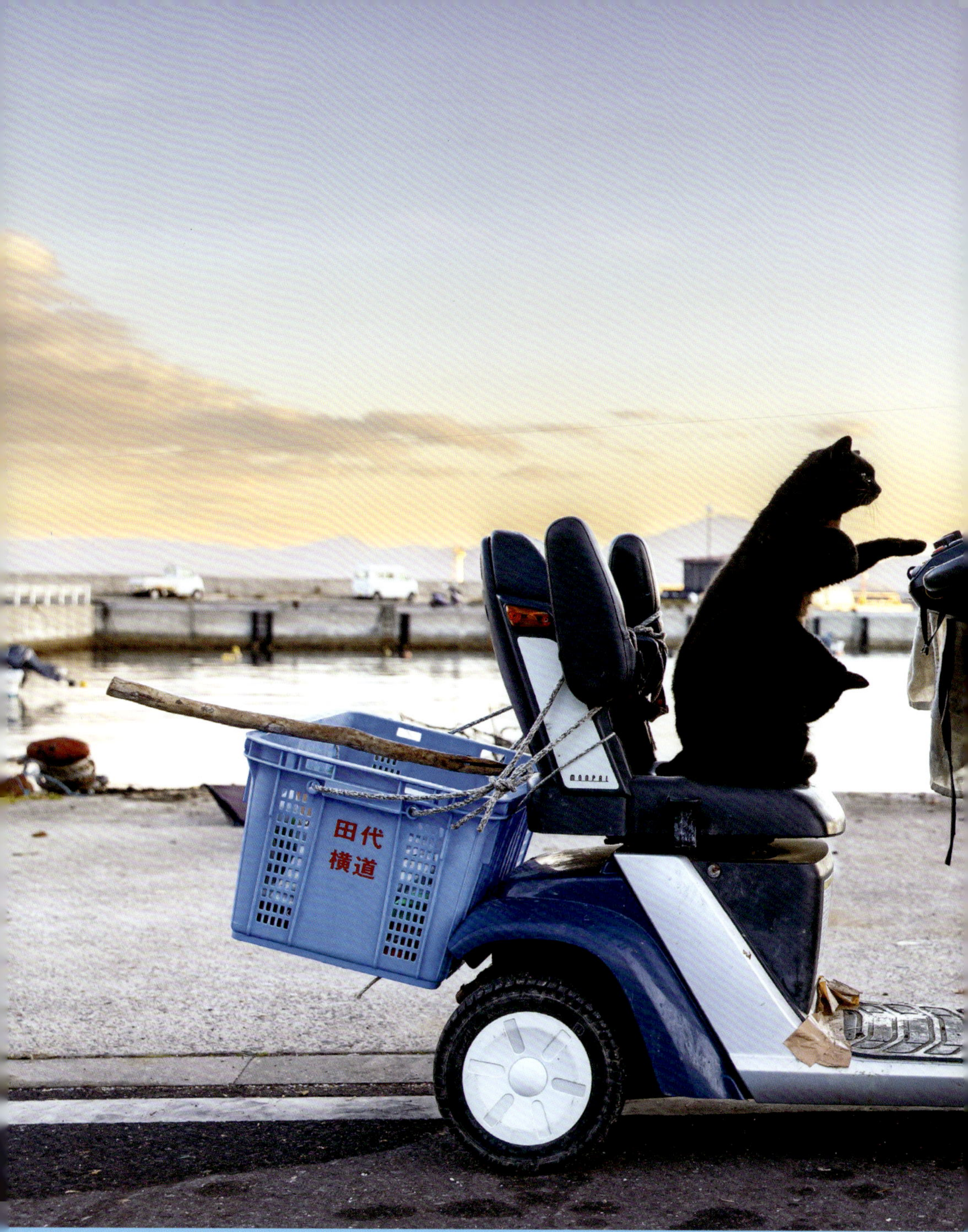
田代
横道

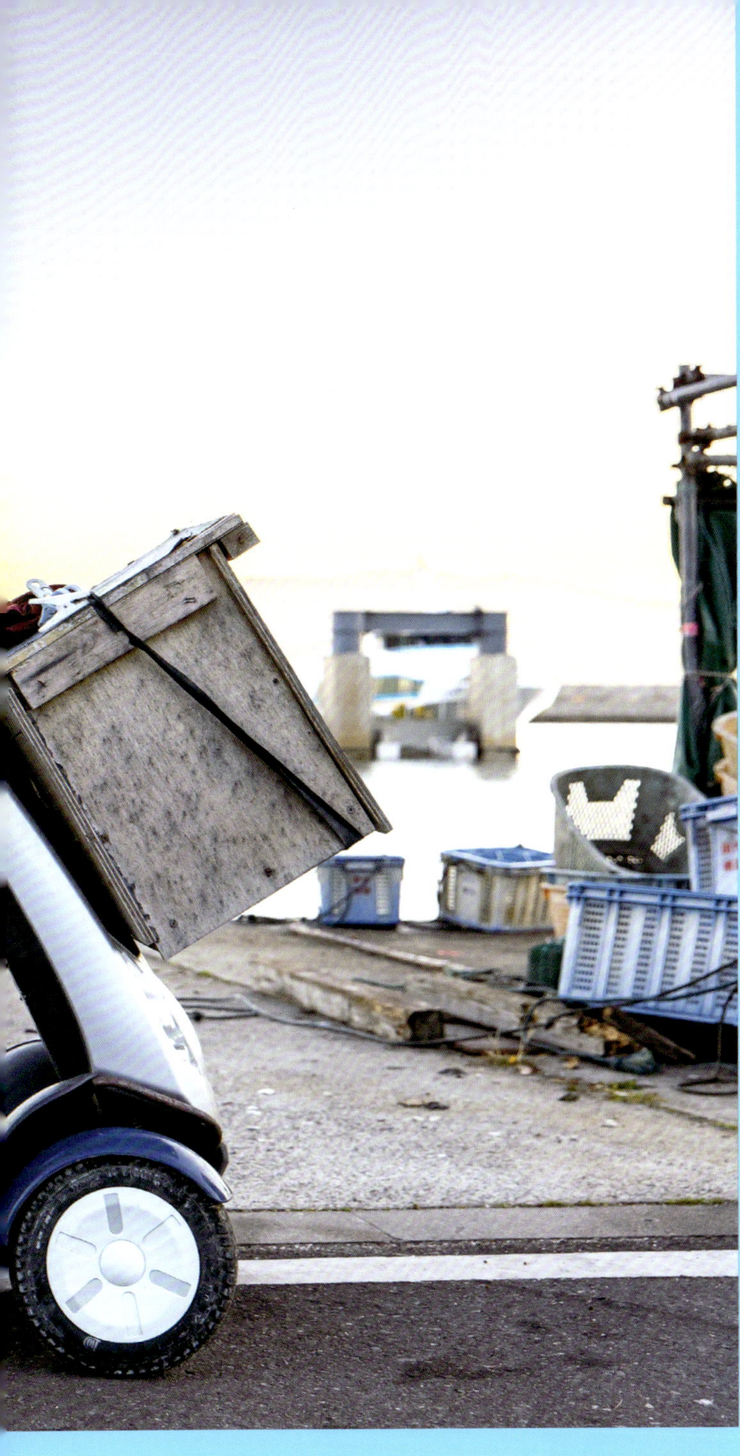

猫・ネコ

Smith Street Books

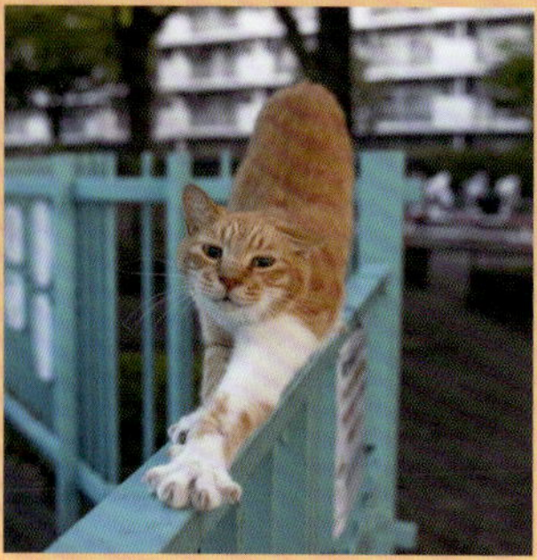

Published in 2026 by Smith Street Books
Naarm (Melbourne) | Australia
smithstreetbooks.com

Distributed outside of ANZ, North & Latin America
by Thames & Hudson Ltd., 6–24 Britannia Street,
London, WC1X 9JD
thamesandhudson.com

EU Authorised Representative: Interart S.A.R.L.
19 Rue Charles Auray, 93500 Pantin, Paris, France
productsafety@thameshudson.co.uk; www.interart.fr

ISBN: 978-1-9232-3976-0

Smith Street Books respectfully acknowledges the Wurundjeri People of the Kulin Nation, who are the Traditional Owners of the land on which we work, and we pay our respects to their Elders past and present.

Publisher: Lucy Heaver
Design and layout: Michelle Mackintosh
Production manager: Aisling Coughlan

Printed & bound in China by C&C Offset Printing Co., Ltd.

Book 434

10 9 8 7 6 5 4 3 2 1

MIX
Paper | Supporting responsible forestry
FSC® C008047
FSC
www.fsc.org